Also by Justin Kaplan

Mr. Clemens and Mark Twain: A Biography

Walt Whitman: A Life

Mark Twain and His World

Bartlett's Familiar Quotations
(general editor)

Back Then: Two Lives in 1950s New York
(with Anne Bernays)

The Language of Names: What We Call Ourselves and Why It Matters
(with Anne Bernays)

LINCOLN STEFFENS

Portrait of a Great American Journalist

JUSTIN KAPLAN

SIMON & SCHUSTER PAPERBACKS
NEW YORK   LONDON   TORONTO   SYDNEY   NEW DELHI

Simon & Schuster Paperbacks
A Division of Simon & Schuster, Inc.
1230 Avenue of the Americas
New York, NY 10020

This Simon & Schuster trade paperback edition November 2013

SIMON & SCHUSTER PAPERBACKS and colophon are registered trademarks of Simon & Schuster, Inc.

For information about special discounts for bulk purchases, please contact Simon & Schuster Special Sales at 1-866-506-1949 or business@simonandschuster.com.

The Simon & Schuster Speakers Bureau can bring authors to your live event. For more information or to book an event, contact the Simon & Schuster Speakers Bureau at 1-866-248-3049 or visit our website at www.simonspeakers.com.

Interior design by Eve Metz

Manufactured in the United States of America

10 9 8 7 6 5 4 3 2

The Library of Congress has cataloged the Touchstone edition as follows:
Kaplan, Justin.
Lincoln Steffens : portrait of a great American journalist.
  (A Touchstone Book)
  Includes index.
  1. Steffens, Lincoln, 1866–1936. 2. Journalists—United States—Biography. I. Title.
PN4874.S68K3   1988   070'.92'4 [B] 88–6457

ISBN 978-1-4767-6638-6

Foreword

By 1974, when this biography of Lincoln Steffens was first published, Americans had been rocked by successive exposés of gross misconduct in government and civil society. Defying Justice Department injunctions, *The New York Times* published the Pentagon Papers and laid bare blunders, arrogance, and deception in official accounts of the war in Southeast Asia. Sparked by reporters Carl Bernstein and Bob Woodward, the *Washington Post*'s relentless probing of the Watergate break-in eventually forced President Richard Nixon out of office. Some years earlier, Rachel Carson's *Silent Spring* examined the damage done by common insecticides, and Jessica Mitford's *The American Way of Death* showed how the funeral industry preyed on grief and gullibility. Ralph Nader's *Unsafe at Any Speed* indicted the auto industry for its flagrant disregard of safety standards. Michael Harrington's *The Other America* revealed the extent of poverty in a supposedly prosperous and compassionate nation. Recently, the *Boston Globe*'s "Spotlight Team" exposed a pattern of sexual abuse and suppressed evidence involving clergy on the highest level of the American Catholic Church. These and other instances of investigative reporting that made a difference are squarely in the muckraking tradition of Lincoln Steffens, whose classic study of municipal corruption and malfeasance, *The Shame of the Cities,* came out a century ago. Today, shaky justifications of the war in Iraq, big business primacy in U.S. domestic and foreign policy, and corporate and financial scandals would have demanded and received

Steffens' attention. He scorned an obedient press, as it is sometimes accused of being, that accepts official information at face value and transmits it to the American public.

The Shame of the Cities was not the first major event in the history of what became known in Steffens' time as muckraking and, in our time, investigative journalism. But its publication was nonetheless a defining event, and Steffens remains one of the heroes and exemplary figures of his profession. A career journalist, Steffens (1866–1936) pulled together in his book a series of articles he had written for *McClure's,* a large-circulation monthly magazine. His assignment had been to study the governments of New York, Chicago, Philadelphia, and three other major American cities. Relying on interviews, documents, insider sources, and legwork, he showed the extent to which organized misconduct—graft, fraud, bribery, embezzlement, chicanery, the buying of votes and the selling of offices—was rampant in city halls and, by extension, in any activity, business or political, driven by gain. His duty as a reporter, as he saw it, was to get to the bottom of things to uncover the "unofficial, unresponsible, invisible, actual governments back of the legal, constitutional 'fronts.'"

In the practice of exposure and either overt or implicit excoriation, Steffens' distant predecessors were the Hebrew prophets Isaiah and Jeremiah, and Jesus as he cast out the money changers. Among immediate predecessors were the historian Henry Adams, who raked over politics and high finance in the Gilded Age, and the reformer Henry Demarest Lloyd, whose subject was monopoly, stigmatized in the title of his book as *Wealth Against Commonwealth.* Among Steffens' leading contemporaries in the literature of exposure were Ida Tarbell, historian of the Standard Oil Company; Jacob Riis, author of *How the Other Half Lives,* a report on New York's slums and their inhabitants; Ray Stannard Baker, author of *Following the Color Line,* a pioneering study of racism in the United States; and Upton Sinclair, whose novel *The Jungle* described in gruesome detail the inner workings of the meat-packing industry. These writers had no collective name until 1907, when Theodore Roosevelt, borrowing an image from John Bunyan's *The Pilgrim's Progress,* referred to them as "the men with the muckrakes," blind to the positive aspects of American life and able to see only the filth at their feet.

Instead of retreating in the face of this attack from the heights of Roosevelt's bully pulpit, Steffens and the other muckrakers co-opted his dismissive label, wore it proudly, turned its negative into a positive, and went about their work of exposure and implicit protest. Eventually the reading public, having passed through one of its periodic phases of purging and self-flagellation (another was Prohibition), grew tired of a heavy diet of articles (an estimated two thousand of them by 1912) that revealed misconduct on almost every level of American life. Taken together, the work of the muckrakers seemed to depict a world that, according to Finley Peter Dunne's comic philosopher, Mr. Dooley, was a "wicked, wicked, horrible, place," little better than "a convict's camp."

In time some of Steffens and his cohort may have begun to suspect that exposure itself might be a form of provocative testing that only alerted a corrupt system to its vulnerabilities and in the end made it even stronger. But the work of the muckrakers nevertheless continues to suggest that informed skepticism, disciplined probing, dispassionate reporting, heroic persistence, and innate mistrust of authority are among the imperatives of investigative journalism. In Steffens' view, the journalist was to be bloodhound and hunter as well as watchdog. The job of reporting today may be tougher than it used to be: a firewall of spin, denial, censorship, and legally mandated withholding on grounds of security, the public interest, and confidentiality surrounds information vouchsafed by governmental, military, and corporate institutions. But such protective strategies had been at least anticipated and often frustrated by Lincoln Steffens in *The Shame of the Cities* and the several sequels he went on to write.

Like Henry Adams, Steffens cast his *Autobiography* in the form of an education, a story both of learning and, as he said, "unlearning," the result of putting assumptions to the test of experience and discarding those that failed to hold up. To great and lasting acclaim, *The Autobiography of Lincoln Steffens* came out in 1931 as the United States began its slide from an era of good hope, prosperity, and "normalcy" to a depression that lasted into the years of the Second World War. At sixty-five, with his muckraking years behind him, Steffens had begun to think of himself as a forgotten man. To his surprise, his *Autobiography* was both a critical and commercial success, gave him a second public life, and quickly established itself as an essential book in the American canon. Rich in anecdote, portraits of famous contemporaries (Gertrude Stein, Benito Mussolini, and Ernest Hemingway, among others), and a skeptical, hard-won, and compassionate wisdom, *The Autobiography of Lincoln Steffens* is the story of how a great reporter learned and practiced his craft. It is also the story of America's reformist and radical experiments in the early decades of the twentieth century.

The son of a Sacramento businessman, banker, and civic leader, Steffens grew up in a Victorian showplace that was emblematic of conservative middle-class values. (The family homestead later served as the California governor's mansion.) He enjoyed the assurance, hopeful outlook, and leisurely education of a child of privilege. After attending the University of California at Berkeley, he enjoyed two heady and inconclusive years of European travel and study before his father summoned him home to settle down and choose a career. Steffens chose newspaper journalism in New York and proved himself as reporter and editor before becoming one of the stars of *McClure's*. He had moved meanwhile from acceptance of business values to a critical position and eventually to the radical position to which he remained faithful for the rest of his life. He became a guru of the Left. In 1919, already reputed to be a Bolshevik sympathizer and publicist, he had returned from a visit to Soviet Russia to report (in one of several versions), "I have seen the future, and it works." This mantra was to ring in Western ears for decades before the collapse of Soviet Russia in 1989. That Steffens in the end was proven wrong by history is another episode, this one posthumous, in his life of instructive "unlearning."

Contents

CONTENTS

PART ONE

CHAPTER ONE

Angel and Savage

I

FROM THE AGE OF ABOUT EIGHT ON, Lincoln Steffens chose to remember, he was a boy on horseback roaming at will, and he rode out of Sacramento each day he could. He rode along the levees to the bridge over the Sacramento River at the western edge of the city or north to the railroad trestle over the American River, where he stopped to swim. The bridge tender warned him the current there was strong enough to sweep him clear to San Francisco, a hundred miles away. Sometimes he raced out of the city to play tag and hide-and-seek with other boys lucky enough to own horses. When he grew older, he rode far into the red-and-yellow Sacramento Valley. The peaks of the Sierra Nevada rose beyond the valley's farms and cattle ranches, fruit orchards, and fields of wheat and barley. During the 1870s, when he rode into the valley, the railroad quickened its pace of encroachment and enclosure. Coolie gangs were cutting into the wilderness, but a boy still could feed off the country on birds, catfish and rabbits, on melons and peanuts, on the openhandedness of ranchers and farmers.

Within a year after gold was found thirty miles up the American River, at Sutter's Mill, Sacramento had grown from a crossroads settlement of four houses to a speculative hive of ten thousand people, and the frontier receded into history. In 1860, six years before Lincoln Steffens was born, the city became the overland terminus of the Pony Express, glorious but short-lived, and the first courier, clad in buckskins and equipped with a Colt six-shooter and an 18-inch knife, galloped eastward. The following year three wise businessmen of Sacramento filed papers to incorporate the Central Pacific Railroad of California. By the end of the decade the valley's farmers and ranchers groaned under the economic domination of Leland Stanford, Collis Huntington, and Mark Hopkins. "Why," the farmers asked, "must it cost more to carry barley a hundred miles coastward by rail than to carry it halfway around the world by ship?" (Looking ahead to the imminent completion of a transcontinental railroad system, the economist Henry George in 1868 had predicted an era in which a few people would become rich and most would become poorer than before.) For Steffens as a boy on horseback the city stood for duty, not adventure; work, not play. On his rides out of Sacramento, he was to recall many years later, "my pony carried me not only from business but from the herd also and the herding habits of mind."

II

FOR LINCOLN STEFFENS' PARENTS, the push to move on had been just as forceful as his, but westward. His father, Joseph Steffens, was born in Canada, of German and Irish stock, and was brought up on a farm in Carroll County in northwestern Illinois. Too small and frail for a life behind the plow, a "scrub" among his father's seventeen children, he was sent off to school, first to a seminary in Rock Island, then to a commercial college in Chicago. He was a schoolteacher for a while, and for three years clerk to a paint and oil company in Freeport, Illinois. Joseph Steffens was trained to the desk, the high stool and the ledger, but even so, like many a Western boy, as his son recalled, he had grown up determined to go farther west. He accumulated a small stake, and his employers provided a letter of reference, which characterized him as "Engaging, persevering, and perfectly honest," "a good faithful business man." Early in the summer of 1862, when he was twenty-five years old, he left Freeport and set out for California.

He traveled across the country as a mounted scout with a wagon train. (For him, and for his children, the perils of that overland trip and its Indian skirmishes were symbolized by the bloodstained arrow he kept on a shelf.) After weeks at oxen's pace over plains, desert and mountain passes, the wagon train passed into a sea of sunshine, the Valley of the Sacramento River, and disbanded. Leaving that sort of adventure behind him once and for all, Joseph Steffens went on to San Francisco. By the end of September he was working as a book-keeper, at a salary of $50 a month, for a firm dealing in paints, oils and glass.

Shortly after, in the San Francisco boardinghouse where they were both staying, he met another westward emigrant, Elisabeth Louisa Symes. She had been born in England and transported as a child to Hoboken, New Jersey, where, applying her shrewd intelligence to the trade of seamstress and the problem of survival, she decided that the East was too crowded for a girl of her small prospects. By way of the Isthmus crossing she sailed for San Francisco, in the hope of finding a husband and a more ample life. She and Joseph Steffens were married in January 1865.

Their first child and only son, named Joseph for his father and Lincoln for the murdered president (but called "Len" or "Lennie"), was born in the Mission District of San Francisco on April 6, 1866. "We were waiting for an opportunity to write you about a little occurrence belonging to my family," Joseph Steffens wrote home to Illinois. "On the morning of the 6th last Louisa presented me with a splendid boy that weighed 9½ pounds, one of those lively kicking fellows that you have heard people wish they could find. The boy is just the boy of these United States, being a little ahead of anything of this city—and as we have all nations represented here we can easily infer as to how he will appear abroad."

Louisa subsequently bore three girls. By 1874, when Laura, the youngest, was born, Joseph Steffens was well up on the economic and social ladder. In Sacramento, where they had moved in 1870, they fitted easily into the solid middle class and were second in rank only to the possessors of historic railroad and mercantile fortunes. Steffens had advanced quickly from bookkeeper to manager of his firm's Sacramento branch and then to full partner, and over the next thirty years he became a director and vice-president of the California National Bank of Sacramento, president of the Board of Trade, a 32nd-Degree Mason, and president of a winery known for its clarets and sauternes. "I am, politically, an organization man," he said—he was the Republican candidate for mayor in 1884 (missing election by only 31 votes out of 4,000) and a state delegate to the Republican national convention in Chicago in 1904. He was also president of the state museum association, a director of Sacramento's principal benevolent association, and an accomplished speaker at public events. In the spring of 1881 he went East with his friend Albert Gallatin, a business associate of Collis Huntington and Mark Hopkins and therefore one of the leading citizens of the city and state, and contributed a series of travel letters to the Sacramento *Record-Union*. All in all, in a mercantile society he represented success, and when the muckraker Lincoln Steffens in time came to pass judgment on "the typical business man" as "the chief source of corruption" in politics, his own father could not have been too far from his mind.

Not having had all the education he wanted, Joseph Steffens used what he had to the full, and his wife, having had none, believed in it even more passionately. Together they planned for their son and, unusual at the time, for their three daughters as well, a life prepared and shaped by education at every turn. The girls attended the University of California at Berkeley and Leland Stanford's new university at Palo Alto, and then went on to further study. Louise, the oldest girl, trained as a nurse at Johns Hopkins. The middle daughter, Dot, was the first woman to earn a degree in psychology at the University of Göttingen. After college and graduate study at Leipzig, Laura became one of the organizers, as well as historian and chief defender, of the county free-library system in California.

"They were always talking about school," Steffens said about his parents. They agreed that "their children's gifts should have all the schooling there was." The boy was forced to take music and drawing lessons long after it was clear that he had lost all interest. Inevitably he reacted against this pursuit of every mustard seed of educable talent. He discovered early the chasm between school and "real life," and also the fact that school could be another way of never leaving home. He moved from one extreme to another. In elementary school he was a failing student, in secondary school a rebellious one, and in college an indifferent one. Then, shifting abruptly, he threatened to become a perpetual student who moved from one European university to another in pursuit of changing goals in ethics, psychology, the history of art. And, much later: "I wish I had had an education, so that I could have really started with what was known, and so go on to the news," he said. "Damn these universities, all of them. They have made my life one of unlearning, literally."

Standing as outward signs of Joseph Steffens' success were his houses, progressively larger and more ornate: first a small house near the Sacramento River and the old Pony Express office; then, during the 1870s, what his son remembered as "a little larger house" near the railroad yards and a slough where he hunted mudhens with his slingshot; then a "big" house, which Joseph Steffens built "uptown" near the new grammar school that his children attended. The boy had his own room now for the first time, and behind the house was a stable with stalls for four horses. Finally, in 1888 Steffens bought from Albert Gallatin a ten-year-old Victorian showplace on the corner of 16th and H Streets. The house had a steep mansard roof, six Italian-marble fireplaces in the ground-floor rooms, fanciful carpentered dormers, and a tall gingerbread tower topped with a spire. Various outbuildings, including a big stable and a spired gazebo, stood on the ample, well-tended grounds. The Steffens family now lived in a "palatial residence," a county historian wrote in 1890, "one of the most noble structures in the city," a building which natives pointed out to strangers "with pride." This residence, with all its real and symbolic connotations of wealth and status, was what the university student, reporter, and muckraker Lincoln Steffens thought of as home, and it was there that two of his sisters were married. In 1903, his children grown up and gone away, Joseph Steffens sold the house for $32,588.53 to the State of California, and it became the Governor's Mansion, a circumstance that in later years, when he came to the mansion to plead unpopular causes, provided the son with a certain amusement.*

The boy dug in his gardens of radishes and grapevines, raised chickens, sold flowers from a sidewalk stand, and sometimes handed out apples and cookies to people passing by—it was his way of saying that his parents, for all their rise in the world and their generosity to him, still lived too frugally, were too close-fisted with strangers. Indoors he played at railroad engineer, steamboat captain, vaquero, and

---

* In 1917 a high-explosive bomb destroyed part of the house and occasioned a statewide roundup of members of the Industrial Workers of the World, the revolutionary labor group with whose aims and leaders Lincoln Steffens was substantially in sympathy. Nominally, if not in actual use, the house remains the "Governor's Mansion," even though described in recent years as an eyesore and a firetrap, and bounded by interstate truck routes.

wagon-train driver; and as he grew older he dreamed of becoming a jockey or a military leader like Napoleon. All the while Louisa Steffens was occupied with her son, whom she idolized and to whom she imparted an enormous self-confidence. Only son, beloved of his mother, he felt like a conqueror, as Freud said, a prince. Yet she wanted to keep this son at her side as long as she could, and for her sake he wore his hair in blond curls until neighborhood boys one day went beyond calling him sissy and stuffed horse droppings in his mouth. His mother was gay, talkative and quick, an enthusiastic visitor and whist player, squirrellike in the way she accumulated odds and ends, especially medicines and remedies of all kinds. Her punishments were impulsive, rarely considered—a slap or a rap with a thimbled finger, and then it was all over. It was she, the boy remembered, who gave him his first spanking—spanked him herself, she said, because she was afraid his father would spank him too hard. For Joseph Steffens was ruminative, slower to anger, more deliberate and frightening: the boy spent nights lying awake, waiting for the punishment promised for morning. "Each of my parents thought the other did not understand me," Steffens recalled, "and I agreed with both of them."

"All I want is a pony," the boy said to his father one year as Christmas approached. "If I can't have a pony, give me nothing." Christmas morning came, his stocking was empty, there were no presents of any kind for him, and there was no pony. He sobbed and ached all over with the strongest feeling of injustice he had ever felt, was rude and angry with his sisters. The parents quarreled. Later that morning the pony arrived. What the boy saw through his tears was splendid. The Indian pony had a black mane and one white foot and a white star on its forehead, and on its back was a brand-new saddle, all carved and adorned with silver and fringe. Suddenly, the boy had everything he wanted, and so, he wondered much later, was that Christmas the most beautiful or the most miserable morning of his life? He knew only that he had moved from misery to happiness so fast that a grownup could hardly have stood it without his heart breaking.

When Steffens came to write about this episode in 1927 his feelings were almost as intense as if it had all happened the day before: for fifty years he had carried the scars of that morning on his heart, had been depressed every Christmas. Partly out of teasing, more out of a sense of hurt at his son's quick loss of faith, the father refused to tell him that in all likelihood the pony had been delayed by some mishap, in fact had been ordered well in time and had been promised for delivery on Christmas morning. The boy himself, dealing with his own tears and disappointment as well as his sudden joy, only suppressed the rage and resentment that were surely there but which, in the way that children have, manifested themselves as increased affection and gratitude. Such ambivalence underlay his feelings toward his father and toward respectable citizens, people one depends on, and authority in general.

Bearded, clothed in his banker's black coat, Joseph Steffens embodied stern community values; he demanded unquestioning obedience and backed up his finalities and assertions with a wave of the hand that meant that it was futile to argue with him. His son grew up to believe that it was futile to argue with anyone. It came as a surprise to the boy to discover that his father was not always right and sometimes knew less than he did—about horse races, for example. The adolescent Steffens, for a while an exercise boy and apprentice jockey at the track in the state fair grounds, learned how races were fixed and horses pulled in order "to catch the 'suckers' and give the racing men and jockeys a chance to make some money." By one of the paradoxes that Steffens later applied to reform politics, the villain here was not the jockey who held the horse in when the horse was fighting for the bit. The villain was the sucker: the sucker was the "cause" of fixed races just as the businessman was the "cause" of the conditions which allowed bosses, machines, and graft to flourish.

"I blamed and I hated the suckers who spoiled everything," Steffens wrote about his experiences at the track. His father, who sat in the grandstand with other businessmen, talked about breeding and form, and bet the favorite to win, was no different from any other sucker. The boy got his information from insiders and knew better. Joseph Steffens was no longer a "household god." "Nothing was what it was supposed to be," his son recalled, except for the politicians he saw in action in the state legislature at Sacramento. They were at least consistent. Leland Stanford was in turn governor and senator, but his railroad was king, and politics in the State House meant railroad politics: bribery, stripping of public lands, an artificially depressed labor market.

Still, it was Joseph Steffens who nurtured his son's independence and gave him the pony to widen his freedom. This was something left from the frontier. There were other traits that Joseph Steffens inherited from his own pioneer father. He liked to play practical jokes, some of a peculiar, unacknowledged cruelty in the way they violated a child's trust. Once he invited Lennie to sit on a stool near him, kicked the stool out from under as the boy lowered himself, and laughed. (Sixty years later Lincoln Steffens' recollections of such instructive steps in his life of unlearning remained undimmed, and when he found marbles in his bed he knew that in his own son his father had come to life again.) As sudden and dismaying as Joseph Steffens' pranks were his spells of wordless brooding and withdrawal. From adolescence on, his son was subject to the same depressions and silences, the same life-poisoning sense of futility. Respecting, loving, and also at times dreading and resenting this inscrutable father, the boy grew up mother-bound. Mainly he remembered her "not as a girl, not as a woman, but just my mother, unchanging, unchangeable, mine as my hand was mine." She was an extension of him, and the world was an extension of her.

His three sisters deferred to him as first-born, only son, elder brother, family hope. And he, in turn, took them for granted and could hardly recall incidents in which they exerted a force on him, although their influence, he knew, was surely there. "Perhaps," he told Laura, the youngest and most wholly adoring of his sisters, when he was already sixty, "the influence was not explicit, but only general and subtle." That influence, combined with their mother's superabundant love, must sometimes have been as stifling as the Sacramento summers, which he was afraid might turn him into another of the valley's commoners, "the lazy Mexicans" and "demoralized Italians." "We must get away from that hot place," he told his sisters when he was twenty-five and a student in Leipzig, "and revive our lost energy, quit moping around, and awake to the movement of life. I think what saved me was the circumstance I left the town young."

Late in his life Steffens said that the dominant and, by implication, even maiming force in his childhood was too much love, given too freely, too early, accepted too confidently. ("Half her love is mine," he could say of his sister Louise.) This was the "general and subtle influence" of his mothers and sisters. "One of the wrongs suffered by boys is that of being loved before loving," he wrote, and generalizing too conveniently from his own, only partially explored instance, he said that boys never learn to love, never have to. In his own "angelic stage" he was so certain of his grace and centricity, of his power to attract the love and trust of others that this remained a life skill which, along with a shrewd, artistic curiosity about the world, helped make him such a superb reporter and interviewer. Politicians, bosses and boodlers, dynamiters and corporation lawyers were to open up to him in a way that was candid, confessional, even self-incriminating. But the delicate balance of mutuality by which children test out their world had betrayed him early. Indulgence made him less able to tolerate deprivation, and all his life he invited unequal relationships in which, as pupil or mentor, as lover of women older or younger than he was, he received more love than he gave. He was to say that "the best rectification" of that one-way traffic in love was his feeling for his infant son, born when Steffens was nearly sixty.

He recalled that when he was six or seven and playing alone in a hut he had built for himself in a fig tree, a strange boy, a little older, had climbed up into that secret place among the branches and told him about, showed him, sex. "It was perverse, impotent, exciting, dirty—it was horrible," he wrote in his *Autobiography*. He was not able to write about sex "usefully or clairvoyantly or even beautifully," he told his sisters, but still he had to write about sex if his self-account was to have any wholeness. And so he recounted how he had been both fascinated and shamed by what he learned in the tree house. For a while he could not bear to have any member of his family touch him, he felt so dirty. His confusions grew when a servant girl in the house made advances to him. He remembered her hungry eyes and how her hands explored him. Later, after he found and pocketed some money his parents dropped on the stairs, he remained silent when they accused her of stealing it and then dismissed her. A liar and a thief, as he saw himself, he had passed from his "angelic" to his "savage" stage the victim of a mother-bound, puritan split of love from sexuality. "As I grew up," he told a friend many years later, "I discovered, somehow, that men and big boys disassociated the romance and the animal sensuality of love. . . . I was started off in this direction by that first experience of mine which coupled dirt and disgust, a sort of horror of fascination, with my image or sense of love."

Other rifts appeared. The Steffenses were conventional Christians; they went to church out of social habit and they sent their children to Sunday school. Lennie had begun to feel the perplexities of adolescence, he was afraid that he would never be capable of love, and he spent hours weeping over his soul and praying. He went to church not out of duty but for salvation—in church "the music was wet even if the sermons were dry"—and he talked of becoming a preacher when he grew up and of preaching the word to others, just like his grandfather Steffens, a rigid Catholic in his youth, later a convert to the Methodist church militant.* This religious purpose reflected also the influence of a country woman, Martha Neely, who lived with her husband and brother-in-law on a fruit farm in Florin, seven miles out of town. The boy had come riding there on his pony one day and after she fed him dinner she asked him to come back whenever he could. She needed him. She was an Easterner, like Louisa Steffens, but more cultivated and worldly—she missed theaters and music and the life of the cities, but most of all she missed having a son. She kissed and fondled the boy, fed him cake, jam and pickles, even bathed and dressed him and put him to bed. Hoping to displace the sexual torments that she could only have aggravated, she prayed with the boy and they read the Bible together; she convinced him that he should become a preacher of the word when he grew up. She did not mind that for the most part he used her as a stopping-off place, for food, shelter and love, and it was only from a distance in time that he realized that here was another one-way relationship. Twenty years later, after she was dead. Steffens still

* Steffens' career as reformer, Christian evangelist, and advocate of Christian solutions to social problems bears in part the impress of his grandfather's example. (The religious impulse appears to have skipped a generation.) On his death in 1881, a church newspaper in Illinois described the Reverend Joseph Steffens as "a bold defender of the 'faith once delivered to the saints,' a forcible expounder of the doctrines of the Bible, and a fearless, persistent, and zealous advocate of evangelical religion. He was often heard to speak in class meeting concerning himself, as 'a brand snatched from the burning,' and of his marvellous and miraculous conversion and salvation. Paul-like, he was stricken down in his wickedness and persecution, but arose to the dignity of a child of God and an ambassador for Christ—'a light in the world.'" (Steffens-Wheelwright Papers, University of California, Berkeley.)

felt the need to apologize to her husband. "I suppose I was selfish as a child, as children are wont to be. Perhaps I did not give affection for your kindness."

Steffens' parents followed his conversion patiently, but eventually religion, along with his sense of vocation, abruptly went underground, not renounced, but repressed, to reappear years later when Steffens preached the Golden Rule, planned to write a life of Jesus, and declared himself something more dangerous than an anarchist— "a Christian." So the influence of Mrs. Neely and her convictions had persisted even though during Steffens' adolescence it was succeeded by displacements more distressing to his parents. Smaller than boys of his age, afraid sometimes that people were laughing at him, he became a dandy, studied the Eastern fashion plates and tried to dress beyond them. Then he experimented with drinking. From "the broad road to the pulpit" he turned onto "the narrow road to hell"; imitating grownups and heroes, he learned how to cock his foot on the bar rail and his elbow on the polished wood, order up his rum, and give the impression that at the age of fifteen he was already headed straight for perdition. Sometimes, in the bravado of this negative identity, he pretended to be drunker than he was; at other times he could not help himself and fell into bed. He watched himself becoming selfish, destructive and hostile, vain and domineering, a side of him that his schoolmates, who never accepted him as one of them, recognized and labeled "damn stinker." The freedom of the boy on horseback had turned into the lawlessness of a boy propelled into an adult world without model or direction; and, in turn, the mature Steffens looked back on this period with shame, dismay and the uneasy recognition that his "off" side still showed itself from time to time in curt dismissals, flashes of arrogance and cruelty, depressions.

He had gone through grammar school near the foot of his class and had not done well enough to graduate with it. At fifteen he had had to repeat a year in order to go on to high school, to say nothing of the career of education and distinction his parents still expected for him. Their patience had finally come to an end; they admitted that their policy of freedom had proved a failure. "They shared my guilt," Steffens said. In the fall of 1881 they sent him away from home to board at St. Matthew's Hall, a private school in San Mateo.

It was a military academy, and Steffens guessed he was going to learn soldiering there and maybe go on to West Point.

III

DURING THE EIGHT YEARS BETWEEN 1881, when he left home in some disgrace, and 1889, when he was graduated from the University of California at the age of twenty-three, Steffens groped his way through alternations between his "savage stage" and a new sort of dispensation. Rebellions and conversions were all mixed together. He saw himself as a ruffian, lawless and destructive, but at the same time the world of critical intellect was being opened to him, and by the end of the cycle he became, by his own definition and for a long time, a student.

At St. Matthew's Hall he was thrown in with the sons of other well-to-do parents who believed there was nothing like a military school to encourage sobriety and application and were therefore bound to be disappointed, as Joseph Steffens was. The smart gray uniforms had a kind of snob value in San Mateo and back home during vacations, but the boys hated everything else that had to do with drill and discipline, were bored and restless and complained that the only off-campus recreation they were allowed was going down to the depot to watch the trains.

Homesick for his horse and his freedom, Steffens found consolation in the exercise of ego and power. He studied up on tactics and the manual of arms and became captain of cadets. He also studied up on *Tom Brown's School Days* (an assigned text for the Berkeley entrance examination) and learned enough from Thomas Hughes's account of English public-school life to introduce a fagging system; this derived its authority from Steffens' discovery, through the "soft disturbance" he heard at night in the dormitories, of "an ancient, highly organized system of prostitution." He claimed to have presided, through blackmail, over "a sort of reign of terror." It lasted until the system came to the attention of the headmaster, who whipped the underlings but not Steffens himself. "My first essay into muckraking cost me nothing," he recalled. The next time he was not so lucky. He had arranged to have a barrel of beer brought from the town, and as a result some of the boys got moderately frisky and were caught. Steffens was sentenced to twenty-two days in the St. Matthew's guardhouse. In disgust, and perhaps acting out of some sense of accountability as well, Joseph Steffens sold off the colt the boy had raised and trained himself. This, the more bitter punishment of the two, put an end to Steffens' boyhood on horseback.

During this time in the guardhouse Steffens experienced one of his several conversions. He was fed up with his Napoleonic posturings and savageries, with that entire negative and self-hating identity that, though he could not shake it altogether, he still recognized for what it was, an ugly, painful, but unavoidable stage of growth. During his stay in the guardhouse—an experience to which he gave some of the overtones of Saint Ignatius of Loyola's convalescence and illumination—he turned to reading "histories and solid things," Herbert Spencer, Darwin, and a book whose title he could not remember but which he used as his text for a graduation-day oration on the futility of war, one way of saying goodbye to a military academy. By the time he escaped from St. Matthew's, Steffens had demonstrated a literary bent: his best academic work was in composition and elocution, he was editor of the school literary journal, and he did some miscellaneous writing on his own, including verse published in the Sacramento *Record-Union*.

His guardhouse conversion, much as it meant to him, had come too late to prepare him for college. He applied for admission to Berkeley in May 1884 and again in August, when he decided to change from a classical course to one in letters and politics, but he was refused. His father, as Steffens recalled, blamed himself for having chosen the wrong kind of preparatory school for his son. He had indeed chosen the wrong school, Steffens reflected many years later, "but the right school for me and my kind did not exist."

Having learned from the failure of St. Matthew's, Joseph Steffens gave his son freedom once again. As a special student in a private school in San Francisco, with private tutoring on the side, Steffens had a room of his own and was free to come and go as he pleased. He explored the city, developed an appetite for the theater, went for walks along the ocean beach to the Cliff House. He had had another "conversion," which he attributed this time to the influence of his classics tutor, Evelyn Nixon, an Englishman. Saturday evenings, after their tutorial hour, Steffens stayed on as Nixon's friends—"all

Englishmen, all Oxford and Cambridge men, all exiles"—arrived to drink wine and argue religion, ethics, politics and literature late into the night. One of them made an effort to turn Steffens into a philosophic anarchist. Sunday mornings the boy sat on the rocks near the Cliff House and with the sounds of waves and harbor seals in the background puzzled over the evening's talk. In contrast to the rote-school world, he was sharing in a discourse of ideas and intellect, in which he heard, surprising and new to him, "the free, passionate, witty exchanges of polished minds." Instead of answers, he heard questions. The closed world of his childhood, in which nothing remained to be done except for a kind of caretaking activity on the part of successive generations, was replaced by an open, challenging world. "Everything remains to be done," Nixon told him, "everything." "He woke me up and set me right," Steffens told the tutor's daughter nearly fifty years later.

But it took longer than Steffens remembered for Nixon to have this effect on him. When he finally entered Berkeley, in the fall of 1885, he was nineteen and a half, a year or two older than most of his classmates, and certainly more experienced and toughened. He was restless and angry, in the grip of a compulsion to move, along with most of the undergraduates and at times the university itself, against rather than toward his tutor's values. "I was mean, as a horse is mean," he wrote, "because I was unhappy myself." That spring, even before he was enrolled, he had taken part in an expedition designed "to teach the president a lesson"—the president being a Harvard graduate named William T. Reid, a former San Francisco high-school principal, who was thought to have treated his Berkeley undergraduates like high-school boys. Steffens joined a band of students who got drunk one evening and wrecked the contents of Reid's ground floor by swinging a ladder back and forth and up and down through a front window. Reid resigned soon afterward and was succeeded, during Steffens' time in college, by four other presidents, a turnover which suggests that the uproar of Berkeley, never a settled or a settling place, was inherent in the administration as well as among the students. Even the most affectionate pictures of Berkeley life in the 1880s and 1890s emphasize a spirit of restiveness and violence which, as on other campuses then, took the ritual forms of hazing, rushing, rowdyism, riots, vandalism, stealing, book burnings, a general discomfiting of the faculty, and, in the special sense in which most of the students were ever to understand the term, class warfare. "If the boys in our universities want to fight, let them fight, and consider it a thing to be thankful for," wrote the future muckraking novelist Frank Norris in defense of student life at Berkeley:

> They are only true to the instincts of their race. We Anglo-Saxons are a fighting race; have fought our way from the swamps of Holland to the shores of the Pacific Coast at the expense of worse things than smashed faces and twisted knees. One good fight will do more for a boy than a year of schooling.

Steffens said that once he and some others stole chickens from a professor's coop, wrung their necks, and stuffed them in a sack. They dropped the sack and ran when the professor's lights went on. The faculty member, a professor of legal ethics as well as a theologian, understood guilt and punishment; he invited the boys over to eat the chickens at a Sunday dinner.

The chicken-stealing episode sounds harmless enough when abstracted from the *Autobiography*, but Steffens fits it into a gray pattern of wrongdoing. To the list of self-accusations, which included stealing, drunkenness and occasional violence, he added cheating, which he said he learned from a professional gambler in San Francisco. "We liked to steal," Steffens wrote, and even when he had quite enough extra money at college to pay for theaters and operas and girls, he and his roommate "went on playing and cheating at cards for the excitement of it, we said, but really it was for the money."

Steffens' passion for military science was as strong at Berkeley as it had been before; during his last two years in college he even held an outside job as drill instructor in a school. Known as a martinet ("damn stinker"), he became commandant of the cadet corps, wore a blue uniform and a plug hat and carried a cane, and drilled the undergraduates two hours a week. To be commandant, as Steffens implied in his *Autobiography*, was to assume a prickly and swaggering arrogance. "I led my class in the most unpopular and meaningless of undergraduate activities. I despised it myself, prizing it only for the chance it gave me to swank and, once a week, to lord it over my fellow students." He had grown a mustache, which he curled and waxed, and he wore his hair short and brushed back from his forehead in a vaguely Prussian style. He had an air of command, which compensated for the fact that he was not quite five feet seven inches tall and felt that he was wanting in looks and stature.

He found a replacement for his admiring sisters in a Berkeley girl, Etta Augusta Burgess, whom he called Gussie and was to know, on and off, over the next forty years. She had grown up in the town with a stern, obsessively neat New England mother, from whom she had rebelled but who imprinted upon her nonetheless a feeling of incompetence, a volatile mixture of aggressiveness and vulnerability that was to trouble her long relationship with Steffens. When she met him, she was a special student at the university, taking courses in German, English and music, torn between the urgings of what he recognized years later as her "free soul" and her "Puritan mind."

Together he and Gussie went riding and quail shooting. Evenings he called at her house near the campus. He liked being with her. She was "a beautiful nature," he said, even though she was not the kind of companion he hoped to find some day. She had little depth or maturity; she was, in fact, a "baby girl," as his sisters also seemed to him; and she was younger than he was, by two years. But he thrived on her love and found himself posturing for her, using her to feed his vanities and conceits. At the beginning, he hardly realized what their relationship meant to her. Gussie cared about two things: her ambition to be an opera singer, and Steffens, whom she wanted to marry. When he realized this he was alarmed and guilty. He did not really love her, he admitted to himself, but he had at least a passive accountability for the fact that she loved him; and, moreover, his feelings might change. The way to solve the problem was not altogether satisfactory to him, but at least it seemed honorable. Soon after he left college they agreed to become secretly engaged.

Steffens' involvement with Gussie may have removed him somewhat from undergraduate politics, social fashions and athletics, but still he remained a representative collegian of his time, a rich boy at home in the standard décor of briar pipes, banners, crossed rackets, guitars, bullpups, and Indian clubs. He enjoyed the standard activities of beer drinking, midnight pranks and serenades. He played baseball, football and tennis, was an officer of his class in his sophomore year and president the next, and he was caught up in that fraternity mania mixed with violence that was sweeping American colleges. At Lafayette College Stephen Crane, threatened by upperclassmen with the usual hazing business, drew a pistol; he was never bothered again.

At Berkeley in his second year, Steffens and two other fraternity pledges took part in a Theta Nu Epsilon initiation ceremony in which one student, an editor of the literary magazine, was badly injured; the administration considered expelling them all or seeking the kind of legal action indicated in any other case of aggravated assault. The president referred the problem of punishment to a faculty investigating committee, and there it died, but only after a general denunciation of the fraternity system and the extraction from Steffens of a promise that he would have nothing to do with any future mystic rites.

Despite his later claim that he had shunned the fraternities as all bunk and pretension, Steffens was glad to belong to Zeta Psi, the oldest of Berkeley's Greek-letter societies. And it was on his urging that Frederick Willis, his closest friend in college, also joined. Willis was interested in theosophy, the survival of the soul after death, "sacred occultism," and parapsychology, and considered himself an expert mesmerist. Like many other students he had given himself over to the passion that motivated William James, in 1884, to establish an American Society for Psychical Research with its various committees on Thought Transference, Hypnotism, and Apparitions and Haunted Houses. In the Zeta Psi fraternity house near Bancroft Way, Steffens took instruction from Willis and began his own experiments with mesmerism, clairvoyance and thought transference. From time to time he used Gussie as a subject and put her in a trance, from which she would awaken with a headache and a glimpse of the future—*their* future—gloomy and menacing. Willis, who was to follow these pursuits to their paravocational end (he practiced in Brooklyn as a doctor of "mechano-therapy" and "mental therapeutics"), credited these talks and experiments with opening Steffens' mind and removing the sharp edges from his "materialistic tendency." At any rate, when Steffens was in Germany a few months after graduation, he tried to communicate with Gussie by thought transference, remembered the fraternity house as "a second home," and told Willis he was homesick for it.

During Steffens' time at Berkeley, the undergraduate college, which in 1873 had opened its two buildings to an enrollment of about two hundred students, was still new, small and rural. The quail he shot with Gussie had been flushed from under the oaks on the edge of the college grounds. But the coyotes were gone. Now, the students said, one heard instead the Berkeley Choral Society. In more significant ways, too, Berkeley was being transformed into a great university. As an intellectual community, as a breeding place for philosophers, William James had said in 1883, "it's a poor place"; and some of his disciples who had been invited to teach there came with a sense of going into exile. Yet it was at Berkeley, fifteen years later, that James, reading his paper "Philosophical Conceptions and Practical Results," first announced pragmatism as a theory of truth and formulated his subsequent creed. As far as its faculty was concerned, during a mere decade and a half Berkeley had become a center of American science and philosophy. It had been stirred to this growth by two of James's disciples, the philosophers Josiah Royce (who had been an undergraduate there) and George Holmes Howison, and by the geologist Joseph Le Conte and his brother John, physicist and generalist. Looking back in 1900 over a lifetime of teaching, Joseph Le Conte marveled at the speed with which this Western outpost had sprung up from provincial insignificance to a place alongside the four or five oldest and richest American universities. After some dalliance with the name "Peralta," the town and campus had been named for Bishop George Berkeley, the Irish idealist-philosopher. Now, at least as far as the university's faculty was concerned, the democratic intellect seemed to vindicate Berkeley's belief that "Westward the course of empire takes its way."

Relatively little of this ferment, in Steffens' experience, was communicated to the undergraduates. There was "a significant uniformity of opinion and spirit among us," he wrote. "The American is molded to type early. And so are our college ways." Among those ways was an emphasis on answers rather than questions, obedient classroom recitation, and meaningless examinations. The students became expert in meeting administrative requirements or in developing a kind of jail-house lawyering to circumvent them. Having decided to follow his own line of interest and let the rest go Steffens soon found himself involved in a running dispute with the authorities over credits, hours, and his intermittent attempts to escape from mathematics and the physical sciences into literature, political science and history, in all of which he excelled. In a series of labored petitions he fought his way over the obstacle course, but even by the spring of his senior year it was not at all certain that he was going to meet the requirements for a degree. A poor student by administration standards, he graduated at the bottom of his class.

Ultimately, Steffens said, "the relation of knowledge to life, even to student life, was ignored," and the undergraduates passed from college into the world sapped of curiosity. Twenty years out of Berkeley, but with this experience in mind, he was to encourage his Harvard protégé, Walter Lippmann, to conduct a discussion group designed to expose students to the problems they would encounter after college. And Steffens continued to regret that there had been nothing of the sort during his time. "It might have saved me years of fumbling," he wrote to President Robert G. Sproul in 1933; he was referring to the left-wing Social Problems Club, which the Berkeley adminstration had just outlawed. "It would have provided something that was missing there when I was a young student."

At the end of four undergraduate years he rejected Berkeley as having been insufficiently pure and at the same time insufficiently applied. He escaped part of his education, he was to say, and he managed to get over the rest. But at least by default college had forced him to choose his own direction. His "conversions" had coalesced with his developing needs. Out of an unacknowledged rejection of his father's values, out of resentment against authority, out of impatience with the university's mindless (as he saw it) discipline, and out of scorn for the university's emphasis on careers instead of knowledge, Steffens became, at least by his own standards, an *intellectual*, a European term about to pass into American usage.

He was to stay aloof from the direct pursuit of wealth and power, to see himself as critic, interpreter and analyst of a society for which these seemed to be the chief goals. Was there, he had begun to ask, pondering his own reading and what he knew of democratic society, a reasonable basis for political and social behavior, a scientific basis for ethics? "They did not understand me very well," he wrote about his fellow students, most of whom were preparing to be lawyers and engineers and businessmen, "nor I them, because I preferred those very subjects which they called useless, highbrow, cultural. I did not tell them so; I did not realize it myself definitely; but I think now that I had as a boy an exhausting experience of *being* something great. I did not want now to be but rather to know things." And, corroborating this, his fellow students noted that Steffens was mov-

31

ing in a direction alien to theirs—in the class yearbook they described his "college occupation" as "would-be aristocrat."

In college Steffens had written a novel, which only his mother admired, and a scattering of verse. "The Viking's Boat Song," by J. L. Steffens, U.C., '89, appeared in the June 1887 issue of *The Berkleyan*, the university literary magazine:

> *On to the strife, row!*
> *Ours be the first blow.*
> *Speed let our strength yield,*
> *Soon it shall swords wield.*
>
> *Our victory long in our land will be sung.*
> *Dire vengeance for death from our foes will be wrung;*
> *And death is the predestined fate of us all.*
> *The slain feast tonight in fierce Odin's great hall.*

As he pushed off from Berkeley's safe shore, Steffens was planning to be a scientist or a philosopher, or possibly a writer. The "would-be aristocrat" already displayed an antipathy to business, politics and the "system" itself with its web of conventional promises, incentives and deliveries. Implicit in his stance were the enmities that were to find expression, for example, in the Progressive historian Charles A. Beard's interpretations of the Constitution and Jeffersonian democracy as the results of economic conspiracy. "I hunted far enough," Steffens said about his independent reading in history at Berkeley, "to suspect that the Fathers of the Republic who wrote our Sacred Constitution of the United States not only did not, but did not want to, establish a democratic government." This is Steffens the autobiographer writing in long retrospect, but it was clear that as a student Steffens had already absorbed large doses of economic determinism, a heady notion however flatly he articulated it at the time. "Whatever may be the sentiments and ideas which are conspicuous at any period in English history," he argued in a senior paper on "The Relation of Political Theory to Political Practice in England," "they are merely coverings and excuses for the self-assertion of class interests. The higher the class, of course, the more aggressive it is."

In a short story Steffens wrote when he was only two or three years out of college, he summed up his career choices as he saw them that June. His protagonist undergoes an intellectual conversion comparable to his own, becomes engaged to a girl much like Gussie, and enters the world of "practicalism" and "expediency." After a while he mutters bitterly about the price he has paid for success: "I *have* committed suicide." By the time he wrote this, Steffens had taken the opposite road. He declined his father's invitation to take over the family interests. "Whatever I might do," he said, "I would never go into business." And he declined his father's offer to buy for him, as a combined graduation present and family investment, a share in a San Francisco daily newspaper. Instead, moving obliquely in the direction of his ultimate competence, he announced that he was going abroad, to Germany, as a student.

CHAPTER TWO

The University of Europe

I

LIKE OTHER AMERICANS WHO HAD GONE AS STUDENTS TO GERMANY, the Berkeley philosopher George Holmes Howison came back eager to spread the word of a new freedom and scholarship which, he believed, only the Germans possessed. The University of Berlin, where earlier in the century Hegel had taught, was, second to the army and the fleet, Kaiser Wilhelm II's pride, a world center for the study of science, philosophy and letters, the model that the older universities of Göttingen and Heidelberg now sought to emulate. Berlin represented the spirit of national purpose and greatness that had invigorated imperial Germany ever since the great victory over the French in 1870–71. "We seemed to have passed from the inorganic to the organic realm of life," Howison wrote about his arrival in Germany, "to have escaped from an unstable sea of human society, and landed on its *terra firma*." Howison's persuasive memoir, "At a German University," was published in the June 1887 *Berkleyan* along with Steffens' "Boat Song."

At a time when, back home, "university" had mainly come to mean just a college putting on airs with a couple of vocational schools, the German university had become something quite different. Its purpose was the "ardent, methodical, independent search after truth in any and all of its forms, but wholly irrespective of utilitarian applications," as Steffens read in James Morgan Hart's

34

standard account for Americans aspiring to study abroad. "A German university," Hart said, speaking directly to Steffens' disenchantment at Berkeley, "is the one institution in the world that has for its motto, 'Time is *not* money.'" This divorce from the acquisitive life was to be seen even in the behavior of the ordinary German who on Sundays, a time of gloom and deprivation back in America, went with his family to the band concert and the beer garden. "The people of Hamburg know how to live," Steffens had decided after only a few days in Germany. "They work for the means of living happily, not to make money." Soon, in his letters home, he was contrasting the German businessman with his own banker-father in Sacramento, who was compelled by "the competitive spirit" to devote himself to business day and night, while his imagination and taste withered away.

Once landed on this *terra firma* of human society, an American student needed hardly more than his passport and the equivalent of about $25 to be inscribed on the rolls of the University of Berlin and from then on to be flattered by his landlady, who greeted him deferentially as Herr Doktor. Even the smallest remittance from home went a long way toward the enjoyment of the good life, three fixtures of which, as George Santayana remembered from his time at Göttingen and Berlin, were the uniforms, the music and the beer. Like the *pfannkuchen*, hot and crisp at the edges and served on a pewter platter, the living was cheap and good.

A student's bedroom and study, heated by a ceiling-high porcelain stove, were likely to be in a private house a few minutes' walk from the university. He breakfasted in his rooms on coffee and rolls, strolled in the botanical gardens or in the grove of giant horse-chestnut trees that filled the square behind the university, attended his first lecture of the day. Later he might go to the museum, the Tiergarten or the Royal Library, or sit at a café reading the English papers and drinking coffee with whipped cream. He took his midday dinner at a family restaurant, where for about half a dollar he had soup, fish, a roast with vegetables, compote, salad, dessert, coffee and wine. At a students' restaurant more or less the same meal, with beer, cost about a quarter. Afternoons he attended other lectures, if he chose—there were few formal obligations at the university, no required attendance.

Evenings, after his landlady had served his supper of bread, cheese and beer, he went off to concerts and the opera with the discount tickets that were part of his university privileges. Afterward there were the cafés with card games in the back rooms, wine, dancing, and often brawling that spilled out into the streets. Berlin for a student was freedom, and this included a sexual freedom unknown in middle-class America: aside from conventional transactions with prostitutes, liaisons with servants and working girls, casual or partly regularized, were so common that they attracted hardly any notice.

For an American it was even cheaper to travel than to live in Berlin. Between terms he visited Switzerland and Italy by train or went on long walking tours. Years later Steffens still remembered these trips—a summer's walk through the Black Forest, Beethoven's Seventh Symphony at the Gewandhaus in Leipzig, country beer halls—as having been so free of care that it was perverse for him to try to repeat them as an older man. All in all, one thing Steffens learned as a student and remembered as an expatriate was that the good life—abundant, unpressured, inexpensive and morally liberated —meant Europe and always would.

He had gone abroad at a time when the cultural traffic between Germany and America was busiest. American authors—in particular, Mark Twain and Bret Harte, General Lew Wallace and Emerson— were in vogue in Germany, and so were American visitors, who flocked to Bayreuth to worship at the shrine of Wagner and then moved on to the watering places to gamble and take the cure. During the 1880s, over two thousand American students, more than in the decades immediately before or after, were enrolled in German universities, and they left with a lifelong gratitude that was to make it impossible for them to be at all whole-minded when America entered World War I against "the Hun." By then two generations of students had come home believing in German solutions to American problems, and for two generations of innovating university presidents, who themselves had studied abroad—Andrew D. White of Cornell, James B. Angell of Michigan, G. Stanley Hall of Clark, Nicholas Murray Butler of Columbia—the German university was the supreme model. When he was seventy-six, Butler still held that the University of Berlin had "reached a height of intellectual distinction that no other institution of higher learning has ever attained." Carrying new standards of independence and thoroughness, American scholars went home and founded graduate schools, psychological laboratories, faculties of political science, economics and sociology.

And there was something else they learned that left its mark on Steffens' generation of reforming scholars and intellectuals. For all their scorn of the utilitarian and the merely vocational, the German social scientists, heirs of Bismarck, believed that the state had a mission as a social agency and that the scholar had an obligation to promote the welfare of the community by addressing himself to practical problems.

Every student was familiar with the underlying concepts of the German system, *Lehrfreiheit* and *Lernfreiheit*. The first referred to the atmosphere of consent in which the university professor worked, freely followed his line of inquiry and research, and communicated his findings when he was ready. The second referred to the student's freedom from coercion and rigid requirements. Following his own growth, he was free to choose his own curriculum. He was also free, even encouraged, to move from one university to another, his transcript and certificate of honorable dismissal from one being honored for credit at the next with no suggestion that he was a dilettante. Steffens had this understanding of *Lernfreiheit* when he landed at Hamburg in August 1889 and went on to study ethics and philosophy at the University of Berlin, art history at Heidelberg, and psychology at Leipzig. Before he yielded to pressure from home and sailed for New York in October 1892, he was also a student at the Sorbonne and a reader at the British Museum. All Europe was one university.

II

IN MID-AUGUST 1889 STEFFENS RENTED ROOMS ON THE FIFTH FLOOR of a house located a few minutes' walk from the University of Berlin and settled down to learning a new language. He also felt that he had to put himself through a course of self-purification and discipline. For the first time he was far away from home, yet he scarcely felt liberated. Instead, he was grappling once again with that sense of wrongdoing that had dogged him ever since the day in the tree house when he discovered sex. Now he saw himself as a neutral ground on which good and bad impulses battled for control, and when, despite everything he could do, he felt depressed and listless, he took this as a sign that his lower nature had won out. He was concerned with ideality and the occult, notions of the true and the beautiful, all of

37

which figured in a kind of dreamy, mawkish striving—"I have got to work in the intellectual, while I more and more order the bodily . . ." He translated personal conflicts into an objective problem, the search for a science or system of ethics. He admitted that the conclusions he was to draw from his reading and thinking were "somewhat theoretical," but he claimed to be reasonably satisfied; and, mindful that his father loved him more than all his other children, he said he hoped he would be "worth the coat of many colors which my father is making for his Joseph," that coat being the luxury of an apparently endless European education.

Meanwhile, Steffens looked at German art, mainly through the eyes of Ruskin, and he listened to German music as if he had never heard music of any sort before. "Classical music is a bore," he told one of his sisters, "but if you hear it here where it is played by those who render it as it was conceived, you will no longer find it so." He was intense, and he was naïve; his priggishness was almost the measure of his parochialism; and what his discoveries also suggested was the relative poverty of the arts as he had known them in California.

Other contrasts struck him hard. German civil servants were honest and dedicated; German cities, as every American noted at once, were clean and orderly, free from violence. Back home municipal services were meager at best. The American abroad who now, without fear of assault, walked along sidewalks and paved streets freshly watered and swept had been accustomed at home to picking his way through the mud or along a disagreeable surface of garbage, rubble, and sometimes dead animals. "They say New Yorkers never know how filthy their streets are until they get back from a tour through Europe," Steffens wrote, "and I suppose that applies to most of our cities. I guess it will to Sacramento." Filthy streets were merely signs of a larger failure. Americans came home believing, along with James Bryce, author of *The American Commonwealth*, that "the government of cities is the one conspicuous failure of the United States," and some of these Americans spent their lives trying to remedy the failure.

As news of political campaigns reached Steffens from home, stories about business failures and "the criminal neglect" of California's timberlands—left at the mercy of fire, ax and the railroads—he came to decide that in nearly every respect the public interest in America was neglected. The government back home "is the nastiest and vilest on *earth*," he said. "Italy is the worst-governed country I have seen, but even Italy, I think, is better governed than America." And as for the Germans, "I envy them their official life, their city organizations, their *aristocracy*" (which, by his understanding, included intellectuals and scholars), and he was even willing to predict that despite the Kaiser's "martial spirit," the future direction of Germany was going to be "constitutional, peaceful."

Learning German, he read Heine, Edward Zeller's history of Greek philosophy, the daily newspapers. He was pleased with the progress he was making and with his self-discipline: he forced himself to stay away from English-speaking natives and visitors, and he figured that in two months he had not spoken English more than three hours. Once in a while, feeling twinges of nostalgia for his family and California, he turned to the next-best thing. He celebrated his first Thanksgiving abroad in the company of 450 other Americans who assembled in the garden dining room of the Kaiserhof and to the music of an orchestra concealed behind a bank of flowers enjoyed an un-German banquet of oysters on the half shell, turkey with cranberry sauce, mince pie and pumpkin pie. (The turkey, Steffens noted, tasted as if it had been "seasick coming over.") Afterward there were dancing and singing. During the evening Steffens talked to some other California students and a San Francisco banker who boosted their home state and expansively invited them over to his hotel another day for a square meal.

The meal, at least, promised to be a positive gain, but most of Steffens' encounters with his countrymen, when they did take place, made him uneasy. The Americans seemed, above everything else, breadwinners, day laborers, specialists, who had no intrinsic interest in "culture" or "ideas." And they, in turn, were skeptical of his goals. They could hardly help seeing him as still the "would-be aristocrat," a dilettante, a sensibility without a talent, and a slightly comic, cautionary figure familiar to them from the popular literature of the self-made man. Steffens did have some of the earmarks of a classic type of bookish mooncalf, *ewige Student*; and his somewhat vaporous intellectualism seemed to be the instrument by which he hoped to put off the dark hour when he would have to take his place in his father's world of business and politics. "I am a conundrum to my fellow-students from America," he wrote to Willis. "Since I am not going to become a professor or teacher, they do not understand why

I am studying such a subject as philosophy. They, in fact, cannot see to save them how I can make a cent out of it. The idea that there is any other motive never seems to occur to them." There were exceptions, of course—other Americans who followed a wandering course that led through philosophy, psychology and ethics.

When Steffens was studying art history at Heidelberg in 1890 he met a young German, Johann Krudewolf, who, unlike the Americans, shared and eventually reinforced his sense of estrangement from a pecuniary society. From his father Krudewolf had inherited money enough to permit him to remain a student with designs of one day writing historical novels. At twenty-three, already an advanced tubercular, Krudewolf was lonely, indrawn, and of an indeterminate sexuality, and in the American, who unconsciously exercised upon him a remarkable talent for magnetizing love, he saw himself and his ambitions about to be fulfilled. He and Steffens were inseparable. Together they went on a walking tour through the Black Forest, traveled up the river Neckar from Heidelberg to Heilbronn and down the Rhine to Bonn and Cologne. At the end of the summer of 1890 they went to Leipzig, where for nearly a year they shared connecting rooms. All the while Krudewolf was becoming more deeply attached and shyly sentimental. He was upset when he heard Steffens joke with a streetwalker, and bitterly jealous when Steffens became engaged. One American student, recalling years later Krudewolf's intense relationship, assumed that there had been a homosexual attachment. "It never occurred to me," Steffens told him, "that our affection might look like that to anyone." Once again he could say that he had been maimed in judgment by too much love given to him too easily in childhood.

Encouraged by Krudewolf, Steffens planned, when his time in Europe was up, to follow a brief career in moneymaking and then retire to devote himself to a life of "self-culture" and leisure. Meanwhile, he was a university student in Germany, listening with limited comprehension to lectures on art by the historian Ernst Curtius, lectures on the history of philosophy by Zeller, lectures on the problems of philosophy by the Neo-Kantian Friedrich Paulsen, whose face was "beautiful, spiritual," but—"I take no notes because I find the hindrance of language too great to allow me to get his ideas clearly enough. I follow him only vaguely."

Steffens had a more congenial time when he visited the American art colony in Munich. The Americans there had settled in during a historic low point in German painting; some of them were well enough supported by local patrons to have given up any intention of ever going home again. In point of style they had become Germans and had given up painting California landscapes from memory in favor of straight Bavarian genre subjects. When Steffens visited his studio, one successful painter from San Francisco was at work on a large canvas which depicted the homecoming of a young sailor from a long voyage in the South Seas. The sailor and his admiring family sit at a table in an unmistakably German kitchen. In between spoon-fuls of hot lentil soup the boy relates his adventures to his mother. A sister, meanwhile, is dreamily listening to the sea roar of a conch shell. It was all "very beautiful and very interesting," Steffens said about this banality in one of two articles that he wrote about the Munich art colony and asked his father to sell to the San Francisco *Chronicle*. "Let the editor read both," Steffens said, "but he can't take the second unless he will take the first." The articles, which the editor never took, give a much more admiring impression than the corresponding chapter in the *Autobiography*, where Steffens, in re-trospect, dismissed the Munich painters as second-raters, too wrapped up in their café life, their mistresses and talk about "art ideals" to do any real work. Yet these painters, and the art students Steffens came to know in Paris, confirmed him in a new way of seeing himself. As soon as he left home he had started to grow a beard, which he even-tually trimmed into a goatee. And this, his trademark almost, along with the soft Byronic collars he wore and his way of brushing his hair forward in bangs, like an antique Roman, was part of a general style, which for the rest of his life, even though he favored London suits and fine linen and a certain Edwardian flair, carried with it a suggestion of the Left Bank or, as some saw it, the mountebank. In Steffens' muckraking days some of his contemporaries were surprised to find that he looked and behaved not like a journalist but like an artist.

He had gone to Europe, he was to say much later, in order to find out whether there was any reasoned objection to cheating, either at cards at the Zeta Psi house and the Café Bauer in Berlin or in the State House in Sacramento. Just as much as that chronically self-absolving ironmaster Andrew Carnegie, Steffens was a child of the era of Herbert Spencer. Spencer hoped to find a "scientific basis" for ethics in the great process of evolution in which the human species supposedly grew upward from "egoistic" to "altruistic" behavior. Obediently Carnegie got rid of theology and the supernatural, and replaced them with the belief that "all is well since all grows better." Steffens in turn had come to believe, as he argued in a philosophic paper that he intended to submit to the *North American Review*, that the notions of "right" and "good" were involved with the survival of individuals and the evolution of species. He planned an American field trip for the purpose of studying specific patterns of conduct in specific occupations; he hoped to "arrive at the actual fundamental motives of all conduct." It was this experimental bent that he followed years later when he muckraked the cities and the states. In October 1890, a year after he started at Berlin, he followed the same bent when he moved to Leipzig, rented some rooms with Krudewolf, and enrolled in the psychological laboratory of Wilhelm Wundt.

During the ten years since he had started this laboratory, the first of its kind in the world, Wundt, son of a Lutheran pastor, had divorced psychology from theological and moral argument. Experimental, or "psychological," psychology, as Wundt defined it, dealt with mind, not soul: it was the science of experience. The phenomena he studied were sensation, perception and reaction, and he studied them by means of experimental devices—electrical, mechanical, optical, chronometric—which measured the duration and intensity and defined the locale of sensory activity. The first wave of American experimentalists—G. Stanley Hall and James McKeen Cattell among them—had already been trained by Wundt and had gone home to launch the new science there. One of Steffens' friends and fellow students at Leipzig was the Jesuit Edward Pace, who earned his doctorate under Wundt and in 1891 established a psychological laboratory at the Catholic University of America. The following year William James invited Wundt's disciple, Hugo Münsterburg, to come to Harvard and take over the laboratory there. Wundt's influence was to become so sweeping that by 1894 James was worrying that experimental psychology had gone too far too fast—"My private impression is that that business is being overstocked in America."

It was this world of precision, quantification, and above all, as Wundt declared, "facts, nothing but facts," that Steffens entered, full of confidence but also admitting that he was "repelled by the method of studying psychology here—that is, going to physiology and cutting up brains." He was enrolled for experimental work as well as lectures and seminars, and by spring, in obedience to the "hard scientific spirit" of the laboratory, "where we sought the facts and measured them by machinery," he would be building and testing his own psychological apparatus. He was testing not only his own purpose, but also his father's patience.

"Wundt's philosophy is not so repugnant to me as I expected," he told Joseph Steffens at the beginning of the term at Leipzig. "It is not, as I said once, materialistic, but it *is* physical and physiological, and not as idealistic as the men I have hitherto studied under." It took only a month for the doubts to crystallize. Wundt, he wrote home, "is only laying a scientific foundation for a new philosophy and is not erecting the structure himself." Steffens had already decided to go back to Berlin in the spring, but now he had to deal with his father's determination that, whatever the beauty of *Lernfreiheit*, once there he would have to settle down and systematically work for a degree. "I rather regret your decision that the degree must be taken," Steffens said unhappily, "since to me it will be of little service outside of satisfying vanity."

Meanwhile his laboratory work with Wundt had become disagreeable. He had a feeling of drudgery, of being "depressed into a German" by the "deadening" and "creeping" work he had to do. The psychological apparatus on which he had spent months in the laboratory was clearly not going to work; it was a botch. He blamed Wundt, who he claimed had been stingy and forced him to tinker and make do with inadequate materials, and it was all to no end. In June Wundt told him to abandon what he had done and build another apparatus, but this would have meant another year at Leipzig, and Steffens now itched to move on. Running parallel with this cycle of failure in the laboratory was a depression that lasted through the spring. He was miserable and ill-tempered, wrote disagreeable letters home, felt sick. He went to Switzerland with Krudewolf, but this failed to break his mood, and by June he had reached bottom, unable to distinguish between Wundt's laboratory and his own inner landscape, both of which had become unbearable. "Out of my life here almost all of the joy has departed," he wrote to Willis. And as for Wundt (or interchangeably, himself): "His logic is untenable, his ethics commonplace, his system absurd or childish."

The account Steffens gave of that miserable year in his *Autobiography* has a misleading simplicity. He was able to find no foundation in experimental psychology for a science of ethics, he said; in fact, as far as "practical ethics" were concerned, he claimed that one of Wundt's star pupils had deliberately falsified data and conclusions in order not to confound one of the master's "most axiomatic premises." And so, disillusioned as well as disappointed, Steffens had decided to go to Paris for a year at the Sorbonne and study morals ("what is done") instead of ethics ("what ought to be done"). But even in this account he acknowledged that something fundamentally uncontrollable was at work. His fragile structure of purpose and identity had collapsed, and at the age of twenty-five he was a man on the run: "I had lost time. I had lost myself."

He had nothing to show for his two years abroad, he was worried about the future, and all the while the pressure mounted for him to deliver and make an accounting. All he had was some makeshift plans: to give up "the degree business" altogether, to travel around Europe with his parents, if he could persuade them to come over, to spend a year of study in France and Italy, to have some suits made in London, to confer with a certain Professor Gardner, who reputedly had learned to understand monkey language and make himself understood to monkeys. Capping this turmoil, in July 1891 Steffens announced his engagement to an American girl whom he had met that winter in Wundt's lecture hall.

Nearly forty years later, when he was writing about this period in his *Autobiography*, his narrative came to a dead stop; rehearsing the mortifying past he had had to face up to his dealings with the Berkeley girl, Gussie Burgess. She had become so exasperated by his evasiveness that in January 1890 she called on his parents and made the bold, proprietary move of telling them that she and their son were engaged to be married. They listened to her in a frosty silence that culminated for Steffens in a letter from home, full of outrage and accusation, and in April, after considerable soul-searching, he asked Gussie to release him from their understanding. "I hope she will succeed," he told Willis about her plans for an operatic career, "for then I shall not be regretted after a while. Hereafter no more alliances for me unless *I* love, too, unless I should decide to marry a woman of fine intellectual culture." Gussie had displayed more strength than he had given her credit for, but considerably less than he sought and found in his new fiancée, Josephine Bontecou.

III

SHE WAS THIRTY-FIVE, TEN YEARS OLDER THAN STEFFENS, a resolute, heavy-set woman with a strong chin, a probing look and outspoken opinions. She was well-traveled, well-read, fluent in French and German, and she planned a career for herself. She had just spent two years in Germany studying medicine and psychology, despite discrimination against women at the universities (at Leipzig, as she reported in a letter to *The Nation*, one professor had circumvented regulations by repeating his public lectures for her in private). Now she was going on to Paris to study anatomy at the Sorbonne and the treatment of chronic nervous diseases at J. M. Charcot's renowned clinic. With this training she expected to make a career as a novelist, as though all along she had been determined to answer Zola's call for the writer of fiction to be scientist, analyst, and anatomist as well. She was also Ibsen's New Woman, militant, logical, and demanding parity with men. Neither she nor Steffens, it was clear from the start, was interested in a conventional romance leading to a conventional marriage. "She is a strong character, and a trained mental worker," Steffens said, "so she will have a life of her own, besides my own."

The ménage they planned had other unconventional aspects as well. In engaging himself to Josephine, Steffens was also engaging himself to her mother, the divorced wife of a New York surgeon. She adored him, called him "Dear Dear Lincoln" and "Darling Lincoln," and he, in turn, addressed her as "*Mütterchen*" and expected that she would live out the rest of her life with them in family intimacy. He recalled Susan Bontecou, in contrast to her daughter, as "a woman I understood—the only one, I think," by which he also meant she understood him and was patient and admiring. She had other qualities the absence of which he might otherwise have minded in Josephine: she was intuitive and sympathetic, he found kindness and merriment in her, and even though she was old she remained shrewd, alert and in some ways more girlish than her daughter. Susan Bontecou could look back over what seemed the vastnesses of history to the day in 1824 when, a little girl curtseying, she gave a bouquet of flowers to General Lafayette.

"I know that you would like my choice and would like the cool, deliberate way in which we proceeded to bind ourselves together," Steffens wrote to his mother from Leipzig in July 1891. He elided the ten-year difference in age between him and his fiancée:

> That Miss Bontecou is pretty, that she is highly cultivated, of high social connections and fine family—all these may not interest you. But you would like her quiet, affectionate nature and her intense interest in me—an interest not merely intellectual but in every way. She is very practical, not at all sentimental nor conventional, and is devoted to my interests and hopeful and eager for my future.
>
> Your remembrance of the sudden breakage of the engagement with Miss Burgess may lead you to think that this is also to be short-lived. And, in fact, it may be. That is, we have arranged so that it can be brief if either finds anything in the character of the other that may indicate future discontent. But I do not anticipate any such turn of affairs. . . . From a purely worldly standpoint it will be a good match for me, and from an intellectual point of view the best I could possibly hope for, and as for love—we both love more and more every day, and she is as affectionate as ever I could long for. Our engagement is not to be announced for some time.

By October, despite "the cool, deliberate way" in which they had managed their relationship so far, Steffens and Josephine decided to get married. It had to be done secretly, he told her; otherwise his father would order him back from Europe. As dependent as ever on money from home, that October Steffens explained to his father that he had to make a trip to London: to buy books that were unavailable in Paris, to buy a swallow-tail suit and some good English shoes, to consult with a publisher about "arrangements for my work." "I shall use the time well and keep expenses down to the lowest possible figure and hope thereby to be not too heavy on you." He and Josephine took separate lodgings in Queen Square in Bloomsbury, read at the British Museum, sat out the twenty-one-day-residence requirement for a license, and were married on November 4 by the Registrar of the Parish of St. Giles. Then, after a rough channel crossing that made him seasick on his wedding night, they were back in Paris and settled for the winter in a hotel on the Left Bank. No one there except her mother knew that they were married, and so, Steffens recalled, he and Josephine enjoyed both the advantage of the law and the thrill of the illicit.

IV

IN THE LATIN QUARTER, WHICH STEFFENS RECALLED AS A STUDENTS' city—"a simple, idyllic, fresh-water college town"—his life with Josephine followed a quiet routine. Evenings they read together—literature, German and English philosophy, work on criminology by Cesare Lombroso, whom Steffens planned to visit in Turin in the spring. After morning coffee they went off to the Sorbonne. Josephine was studying anatomy and genetics, while Steffens watched the experiments at Alfred Binet's psychological laboratory. Together they attended weekly clinics at the Salpetrière, the public hospital that served him, Charcot said, as an emporium of human miseries. There, striding through the dingy wards on his rounds, he chose the subjects on whom he demonstrated the power of hypnosis to probe and treat hysteria. Like Freud, who five years earlier had been converted by these clinics to the study of psychopathology, Steffens was dazzled by Charcot's dominating personality, his command of his material and his audience. Independently, both Steffens and Josephine remembered a triumphant lecture demonstration during which Charcot, with one tap of his patellar hammer against a table, shocked his subject into a cataleptic trance; as she stood in terror staring over her shoulder at him with her arms flung out, he declared simply, "*La femme de Lot.*" Then, at the height of the laughter and applause, Charcot dismissed his class.

For Steffens' generation, this secular wizardry, which invoked the irrational, pointed forward to the fracturings of the new century, its submission to disorder and upheaval. Among the students who were Steffens' friends in Paris were other harbingers of the new century, the Slavs, "pessimistic people, ambitious, hopeless, bitter, and determined." They were his first exposure to the revolutionary left, to ideology, and to a coming time when all thinking was to become political. These disciples of Marx, Bakunin, Kropotkin, and violence, some of whom talked about killing the Tsar and were dogged by the

French police, were "not afraid," Steffens said, "of the graves they are digging in Siberia."

Delighted to have escaped from the misogyny of Leipzig, Josephine described Paris and the Sorbonne as "the paradise of students," of women students in particular. She had begun a novel that dealt in part with her liberated life with Steffens, and she named her rebellious heroine, Letitia Berkeley, in tribute to his California background. He himself had just finished a story with a Berkeley setting and a novel about Munich and was outlining a novel about American art students in Paris. He said that his work was "psychological," "realistic," and of a sort "which no one has done yet in America and only a few in Europe." He planned a double career, one in business or politics, the other in literature. It was to take him about ten years to discover that he had even less of a gift for fiction than Josephine.

In May 1892, after a trip to Italy, Josephine became sick, and Steffens brought her to Bad Kissingen, a spa in Germany. He attributed her collapse to overwork, but it happened also to coincide with a crisis in their relationship. "We found ourselves drawing apart in a sad and unaccountable way," he recalled three years later. "We ceased to talk together as we had done with so much delight at first; there was missing that peculiar desire for constant mutual confidences, the interchange of thoughts and feelings." The solution was a form of intimate muckraking which reflected their education at the university of Europe:

> We hit upon the simple method of solution known as analysis, diagnosis, and the result was a comprehension of the disease—this, though not a cure, removed the cause of the worst suffering, mutual reproach.
>
> We found by means of the scientific method that something was gone—something which cannot be retained—and, giving it up, we have since learned that that missing link is not an essential to plain, healthy contentment with reasonable bursts of happiness. So far as we could make out we had badly fooled ourselves in our rationalism. The historical method showed that all the while we were thinking we were actuated by intellectual considerations and rational ends, we were driven by the most ordinary impulses of passion, even sensuality. It was disguised by the thoughts which, however, were themselves the product of our natural, but commonplace physical state. That there were ideas of real purport, sentiments of genuine worth and honesty, and some nobility of feeling is, of course, quite

true. Our self-deception was neither weak nor foolish; it was simply inevitable. We drew our form of glamor over our love and made of our ideas our little romance.

Really our emotional bliss was made up of two simple elements, physical curiosity and excitement, and the novelty of the exercise of the privilege of entire confidences between two relatively strange minds.

An "utterly dangerous and untrustworthy emotionalism" had worn off, Steffens said. He and Josephine were relieved, as if this had been what they wanted from the beginning, and they half persuaded each other and themselves that they were now more rationally happy than before. A puritan comedy, for all the scientific method involved, had found a puritan solution: they resigned themselves to a burned-out relationship.

V

IN HIS MARBLE-TRIMMED STUDY AT HOME OR IN HIS OFFICE DOWNTOWN in the Orleans building, Joseph Steffens contemplated his son's stay abroad with mounting distress. Sacramento's eminent businessman, banker and civic leader believed in education but not in education that threatened to continue indefinitely and, along the way, to poison family relationships. The trouble was visible even from abroad. Dot has been saying "some depreciating things about me," Steffens complained to his mother. "Lulu and Laura seem to scorn me altogether." The sisters were now arguing with some bitterness that it was their turn to go abroad and study; Lennie had had his Joseph's coat long enough, they said. And their father had to agree; he had become a little weary of reading letters from Europe which ended on the familiar note, money ("at once—please"), or opened up new avenues of delay.

In the summer of 1892 it was a trip to England to enable the student to finish, before someone else came out with the idea, a "scientific essay"—"An Approximate Theoretical Ethics with its Practical Consequences"—which would "revolutionize Ethics" by turning it into "a real science." "I beg of you to give me the extra time . . ." Joseph Steffens gave him the extra time, and off he went to Oxford, the British Museum, the International Psychological Congress, and various London establishments which furnished him with a new wardrobe of suits, hats and capes. "I was a beautiful thing," he recalled years later, "tailored and educated, dressed outside like an Englishman, and filled up inside with the culture of the American and European universities."

Even when he was finally summoned home in 1892 Steffens insisted on fighting rear-guard actions. "Do you think a short course in a New York business college would be worth the time?" he asked his father. In New York, he said, he was going to spend a few weeks making some literary and publishing acquaintances. He also planned a side trip to Boston and to Harvard, where, with a total expenditure of no more than twenty dollars or so, he intended to learn from instructors and graduate students about "the state of American thought and scientific work." Then, after a stop in Illinois, he would at last be on his way west. As a start up toward business and politics he hoped his father would find him "some humble place at a bank" in San Francisco that would place him only a ferry ride away from the university life of Berkeley. "It would be a bitter thought," he told his father, "if I should have to make Sacramento my permanent home."

Correctly reading all these signs as ominous, Joseph Steffens settled into one of his stubborn silences, and his son, alternately relieved and depressed, began to make the best of what he now knew he had to accept—"I am both eager for and fearful of the start I must make." Entering the life of a business society, he was determined to be solely a businessman and defer to "powers of concentration and unflinching industry."

"I have never been able to swallow Marxian socialism," he was to tell Max Eastman in 1927, and he related this to his European experience. "All I thought I wanted was to understand some simple ethical and social problems, experiment in them and get on to the stage where we could use the results of science to control our environment and our fate—to some extent. I quit Germany and Hegel with a sense of defeat and when I sought light in Marx I recognized an old enemy." His three years abroad as a student, a way of buying time from society, had exposed him to methods of science which were to guide him as a journalist. But now he had come to the end of the theoretical line, just as earlier, and again by his father's decision, he had come to the end of his boyhood on horseback. His father's decision to bring him home forced him to acknowledge his own buried, conflictive practicalism, his impatience with theory, his hunger to explore the unedited realities of American life. "We go to Europe," Emerson had said, "to be Americanized."

Steffens was to come home closer in spirit to the businessmen pragmatists he had rebelled against than to the intellectuals whom he scorned at the end of his life for not being *doers*. He considered his future as a writer with the feeling that he had finally embraced, after three years' apostasy, a twentieth-century creed of realism and utility. "I look to that coming century more than I have to all the others that have been," he wrote from London. "I seldom turn my back on it to peer into the past. My feelings of anxiety, of dread, of impatience, of eagerness to do, would make to a poet a poem, of a strong man a hero, of me ———. I may answer better when I have sung myself in the streets and heard the sound. I say in the streets. A philosophy, a literature, art—they must be able to run a railroad, govern a town, a nation, manage a newspaper and sell goods, or they and what they would conduct are wrong."

To many Americans, as that coming century drew near, the pattern of this conversion was familiar. They were to see it in Theodore Roosevelt's cult of heroic action, his belief in the manifest destiny of men and nations. They were to see it reflected in the literature of success. Ten years after he left Europe and was launched on his career as a muckraker Steffens would have been able to read, with an amused recognition of the parallels to his own experience, a book by the popular editor and author George Horace Lorimer, *Letters from a Self-Made Merchant to His Son*. Lorimer first published the letters in the *Saturday Evening Post*, which under his editorship became the most widely read magazine in America and virtually the official voice of the business community.

In Lorimer's book, a comic version of Steffens' story, John Graham, a rich Chicago pork packer, decides that the time has come to rein in his son Pierrepont (or "Piggy"), who has just spent four years at Harvard smoking Turkish cigarettes and wearing sporty clothes. "Old Gorgon," as the father is known on the floor of the exchange, believes in education. It pays, he says, the same way it pays "to feed in pork trimmings at five cents a pound at the hopper and draw out nice, cunning little 'country' sausages at twenty cents a pound at the other." But there is such a thing as too much education.

After all, he asks Piggy, what use is Latin in a slaughterhouse? "About the only time our products are given Latin names is when the State Board of Health condemns them." And as for a European education, he argues when Piggy proposes to spend some time abroad before putting his nose in the bullring of the family business, why, Old Gorgon's experience is that most boys come back with not much more than a couple of trunks full of fancy clothes. Fortified by Old Gorgon's counsel and his stock of homely anecdotes about the distance between life and theory, Piggy gives up his European plans and begins his climb toward success from the bottom, unloading carcasses at the packing house. He had followed his father's advice "not to play with the spoon before you take the medicine."

Lincoln Steffens recalled that when the Red Star steamer *Noordlant*, westward-bound from Antwerp, arrived at quarantine in New York harbor in October 1892, he was handed an envelope containing $100 and a letter from his father which made him feel as if the ship were sinking under him. The letter, as Steffens reconstructed it from memory, or more likely even composed, when he wrote his *Autobiography*, sounds as if Old Gorgon had written it:

My dear son: When you finished school you wanted to go to college. I sent you to Berkeley. When you got through there, you did not care to go into my business; so I sold out. You preferred to continue your studies in Berlin. I let you. After Berlin it was Heidelberg; after that Leipzig. And after the German universities you wanted to study at the French universities in Paris. I consented, and after a year with the French, you had to have half a year of the British Museum in London. All right. You had that too.

By now you must know about all there is to know of the theory of life, but there's a practical side as well. It's worth knowing. I suggest that you learn it, and the way to study it, I think, is to stay in New York and hustle.

CHAPTER THREE

The City: "Where we had to begin"

I

ABRUPTLY, AND AT THE UNPREPARED LATE AGE OF TWENTY-SIX, Steffens had been thrust into a role directly out of the opening chapters of Horatio Alger's novels *Bound to Rise* and *Strive to Succeed*. "Here I was," he recalled, "a poor but willing young fellow, without parents, friends or money, seeking a start in life" in New York, the biggest of American big cities and the scrambling center of American life. The nature of survival there had a Darwinian purity and challenge, he was to discover. And yet the short story that he managed to sell to *Harper's Monthly* for $50 a few months after his arrival shows a certain wistfulness and regret instead of the Alger spirit. The successful businessman in "Sweet Punch: A Monologue" longs for the "purer, more visionary" life he had planned for himself in college; in a gentle way, while mixing a Christmas drink for his wife, he blames her for his success. It was a peculiarly American situation of a peculiarly American cast, and it mirrored the tensions of Steffens' own marriage.

Josephine was clearly the more practical of the two. From the day they landed she was anxious and gloomy—angry with him for insisting that they keep their marriage secret. He had his own reasons, but she found them unacceptable. "I declared I would never ask my father for another cent, and I didn't," he said in a highly charged passage in his *Autobiography*. "The next money transaction was a

53

loan I made to him." It was unfair, Josephine argued, that because of his hurt pride at having been cast loose so abruptly her mother should have to support them. By January, Steffens owed Mrs. Bontecou over $700 for their living expenses. The underground quality of the marriage—he waited until spring to announce it—colored Josephine's feelings about him and also about his family in California. In one way or another they had all let her down. Later, when she came to be known as a woman of advanced views on marriage and child rearing and the role of women in general, it still colored her feelings about conventional weddings with music and flowers. "Of course, that way you get more presents," Josephine once remarked, with an asperity that seven years of her own marriage had failed to moderate.

She had been impatient with Steffens when, again out of pride, he was reluctant to use letters of introduction his father offered him. It was no time for pride—jobs were scarce, the first pinch of the coming depression could already be felt that autumn of 1892. He tried a couple of business firms, had no luck there or in the brokerage and banking houses, was told to try for some sort of job at the Chicago World's Fair, and at one point worked up a desperate scheme to start a subscription clipping service for authors and politicians. He spent a month trudging from one interview to another, but he was determined, he told his father grimly, "to beat N. Y. and force myself upon the place." He was still thinking of a career in business, not in journalism, when he finally yielded to Josephine's urgings: he used his father's connections and arranged to be seen by Robert Underwood Johnson of the powerful *Century* magazine. Johnson sized up the young man, who made his call in a black suit of impeccable cut and looked older than twenty-six, was impressed by his study and travel, his intelligence and refinement, and recommended him for a trial job as reporter on the New York *Evening Post*. On the strength of this promise of permanence in the city, Steffens and Josephine moved in December from temporary quarters at a hotel and rented a small furnished apartment on 72nd Street near Third Avenue.

Johnson had suggested the *Evening Post*, Steffens wrote home, "on account of my political leanings, and added that I would come into contact with a group of gentlemen, cultivated and refined men." As Steffens discovered, the *Post*, autocratically managed by its editor, Edwin Lawrence Godkin, was above all gentlemanly and observed with distaste a world which appeared to consist chiefly of ignorant mobs and venal politicians. The paper was also conservative, high-principled, chary of party politics, and, in the spirit of *laissez faire*, unalterably opposed to protective tariffs and organized labor. In 1884 the *Post* bolted the Republican party and supported the Democrat Grover Cleveland for President. The paper thereby won from its archenemy, Charles A. Dana of *The Sun*, the derisive labels of Mugwump and later Goo-goo, a jab at the cause of Good Government, which "Larry" (as Dana referred to the *Post*'s editor) always championed. Godkin was dedicated to civil-service reform and unremitting warfare against wickedness in civic life, specifically Tammany Hall, and this dedication had won for his paper a position of spokesmanship out of all proportion to its circulation. Even during the 1890s, when Dana, Pulitzer, and Hearst were each claiming a daily readership figured in the hundreds of thousands, the *Post* rarely sold more than 20,000 copies, but among its readers were politicians and business leaders and editorial writers all over the country. "To my generation," William James said, "Godkin's was certainly the towering influence in all thought concerning public affairs."

Alexander Hamilton had founded the paper in 1801, the New England poet William Cullen Bryant had been its editor in chief for forty-nine years, and since 1883 the *Post* had been dominated by Godkin, a transplanted Anglo-Irish liberal and founding editor of *The Nation*, New England in fervor, continental in influence. In effect, Godkin merged the paper and the magazine. Guardian of the public interest, *The Nation*, which Charles Dudley Warner called "The Weekly Day of Judgment," now seemed to be coming out every evening. As the joke went, the old lady who lived alone and had her copy of the *Post* delivered to the front door had nothing to fear from intruders—"It just lay there and growled all night." It had growled at Blaine when he ran for President, and for about fifteen years it growled at Tammany Hall.

Under Godkin the *Post* was strong on local politics, industry, culture and finance. It was "the Wall Street organ," Steffens said in 1914, and "I was the Wall Street man." The paper shunned crime, scandal, or anything that smacked of yellow journalism. Godkin's aim, as he explained when he became editor, was a paper that "sober-minded people" would turn to when other journals were "hollering and bellering and shouting platitudes like the *Herald* and the *Times*." His determination to run a sober paper only stiffened during the

1890s when the touchstone of successful journalism, according to a Hearst editor, Morrill Goddard, was that the reader took one look at the front page and reeled back exclaiming, "My God! Oh, my God!" In an age of thunder-and-lightning headlines, Godkin hated headlines of any sort.

Even at the cost of demoralizing his reporters, Godkin, like Wundt in Leipzig, demanded absolute factuality: humor, pathos, literary flourish and personality belonged only on the editorial page and in the Saturday supplement ("I do not want literature in a daily paper," he said). Steffens disliked the little that he saw of Godkin and claimed to have been permanently hurt as a writer by the five years of working for him. "What I did not like and still resent somewhat," he told Allan Nevins nearly thirty years later, "is that he objected to individuality in reporting." Steffens recalled that one story he turned in—a simple but charged account, which ran on page one, of the death of a music teacher—so offended the house standard of unemotional reporting that Godkin would have fired him if the city editor and the literary editor had not rushed to his defense. And even though Steffens at first boasted that he worked for "perhaps the finest journal in America"—he said that The Sun, the "best written" of the New York papers, was just as "cynical and shallow" as the Herald— he admitted then that he was depressed by the Post's "analytic spirit," editorial doom-crying, Nestorian loftiness, and disapproval of just about everything that had happened in the United States since the abolition of slavery.

There was, undeniably, a certain coldness about the Post, an unrelieved combativeness, a failure of mercy, a hint of despair—qualities that suggested long isolation from public power and that people were apt to associate with reform in general. After all, one New York lady asked, "What can you expect of a city in which every morning the Sun makes vice attractive, and every night the Post makes virtue odious." And so it seemed to many admirers, including William Dean Howells, who described him as "distinctively the greatest" of the New York editors, that Godkin was simply wearing himself out in furtherance of the creed that corruption must be smashed and the rascals turned out, that the problems of the city lay not in the nature of cities nor in the present social goals nor in the lack of them, but in certain bad men who had taken over the government. Godkin believed he was leading a holy war—but was it only an insurrection?

"With fresh and present outrages to avenge, particular villains to punish, and the mob sense of common anger to excite, it is an emotional gratification to go out with the crowd and 'smash something.' This is nothing but revolt," Steffens was to say in 1904 in *The Shame of the Cities*. "But revolt is not reform, and one revolutionary administration is not good government." For Steffens the job of reporter on Godkin's *Post* had been the start of a long study of the perplexities of reform.

II

STEFFENS HAD RISEN FAST. His first story for the *Post* was about a clergyman who retired and was replaced by another clergyman: that week Steffens earned $1.75 at space rates. After only a month he became the protégé of the city editor, Henry J. Wright, who promoted him past four older men on the staff and gave him assignments which were a little over his head and kept him working in a state of mild anxiety. Now the older men sat smoking in the reporters' room over Park Row while he went out on financial and political stories, some of a "delicate nature" requiring tact and sometimes the shrewd decision just to listen this time and not to print. At space rates Steffens was soon earning about $20 a week instead of $5 or $7, and he was earning extra money from long weekly articles for the Sacramento *Record-Union*.

By February 1893 he was up to a guaranteed minimum of $25 a week at the *Post* and he was getting the most important assignment in a panic time, Wall Street. He expected another promotion any week now and had learned simply to ignore complaints from the other reporters: from their point of view he took his work and himself too seriously; in short, he was too ambitious. In November 1893, toward the end of his first year as a reporter, he was offered another raise and the new *Post* bureau opposite police headquarters on Mulberry Street. He was to have his own office there with a telephone, an assistant to help him cover his beat and a boy to bring his copy down to the paper.

He had been in New York less than two years when Godkin offered him the editorship of a paper in Newport, Rhode Island. Steffens turned it down; he expected that in time he would succeed

Wright as city editor of the *Post*. By 1895 he was recognized by some of his colleagues as the ablest reporter on the staff, one of the best general reporters in the city, a man who could write, on the spot, a professional story on almost anything, from an incident in the streets to embezzlements and catastrophes. One *Post* reporter, Norman Hapgood, recalled with admiration how, after he himself had struggled one afternoon with the facts about the collapse of a downtown office building, Steffens had coolly phoned in a story which even the following day's morning papers, with twelve additional hours before press time, could not improve on for detail, color, and an orderly exploration of the possibilities of faulty construction and bribed inspectors.

In the city, Steffens said, he found "human nature posing nude." He also acquired an education that went beyond the needs of daily journalism—"What reporters know and don't report is news, not from the newspapers' point of view, but from the sociologists' and the novelists'." It seemed that he had finally found his metier and made the jump to maturity. Now, in a short story, he wrote about himself as someone who had been amused "to hear his classmates in college say that they were going West when they graduated. He intended to stay East, and he did." In the East he could apply his laboratory training and his literary ambitions to what was recognized during the 1890s as the prime data of the modern writer: the ferment, the shame and the promise of the cities. "I hope to get facts of scientific value and I may get conclusions," he said. He studied the East Side slums, covered strikes and violence in the garment trades, began a series of labor articles which he believed could be "the most exhaustive newspaper work ever done on this subject."

In lighter hours he served the *Post* as a reviewer of New York's thriving German stage and its productions of Lessing, Schiller and Sudermann, popular comedies, and forgotten dramas like the one that opened at the Irving Place Theater on October 1, 1894:

> Like most so-called psychological drama and fiction, Paul Lindau's play, *Der Andere*, takes its central idea from psychiatry. It is mental disease, not normal psychical processes, which it illustrates, and it is no wonder that the psychologists and, indeed, all scientists, complain of the conceptions people get of science. For Art, in attempting to draw upon science for facts and inspiration, seldom goes beyond the most uninstructive and least beautiful of abnormalities. As an exam-

ple of this tendency, the play is interesting. After a tedious first act, it holds the attention closely without any other interest than the un-romantic adventures of a man in a somnambulistic state. He is a district attorney who in his lapses runs a criminal course, and in the play robs his own house. He picks the pocket of his fiancee, and gives the plunder to a young woman whom he meets in a dive. Hypnotic treatment cures him, and he is put under the care of his fiancee for a long vacation.

Steffens' youth, his upper-class manners acquired abroad, and even his English wardrobe, had not been held against him in the world of New York journalism; they had speeded his advancement. "There's the gentleman reporter," the president of the Board of Education said of him one day. The gentleman reporter carefully cultivated his acquaintance with the pivotal men of the city, was invariably polite and discreet, freely admitted his ignorance, his eagerness to learn, his gratitude for being taught. The inarticulate spoke, the secretive gave him their confidences, the men of action ruminated: he had begun to display, as a function of his personality, a peculiar life skill that was to make him a superb interviewer—a suspension of self and moral judgment, a total curiosity.

The old-style city reporter, colorful, tough, unschooled, socially marginal—"drunkards, deadbeats and bummers," according to President Charles W. Eliot of Harvard—was giving way to a new school of professionals when Steffens began his rise in journalism. Some reporters, like Jacob Riis, were reformers at heart. Others thought of their newspaper work—the daily reporting of actualities—as a stepping-stone to a literary career. "I think the same," Steffens wrote home, "but I act as if journalism were my sole aim, and to their questions about why I 'rustle' so much, I say merely that so long as I am at it, I am here for all there is in it."

"This is the young man's epoch," a time for drive and precocity, the novelist Gertrude Atherton was writing in 1895, the year Stephen Crane's *The Red Badge of Courage* made him a hero in New York and London at the age of twenty-four. (It was also the year Theodore Roosevelt, symbol and catalyst of a young generation, became Police Commissioner of New York at thirty-six.) Everywhere, it seemed, the young men were being promoted over the heads of their elders.

During the 1890s the generation of young reporters in New York was a college generation, even though the business community still believed that higher education hindered achievement by placing a false valuation on wit in place of work. Crane, who had gone to Lafayette and Syracuse, worked for the *Herald* and the *Tribune* while he was writing his first novels. David Graham Phillips, later a popular novelist and also author of *The Treason of the Senate*, the exposé that for Theodore Roosevelt epitomized everything that was wrong with muckraking, had come to Dana's *Sun* from Princeton in 1890 and was surprised to find that there were other college men on the staff. Dana himself, far from being prejudiced against these dudes and novices, said that he preferred to have even a prize fight covered by a young fellow who had read Tacitus and Horace.

The most flamboyant representative of the new generation was another of Dana's young stars, Richard Harding Davis, who came to newspaper work from Lehigh University and Johns Hopkins. The son of a newspaper editor and the novelist Rebecca Harding Davis, he had been born into both journalism and literature, and starting at the age of twenty-two, he conferred upon this once slightly seedy hybrid a considerable degree of dash, sartorial elegance and seignorial dignity. The reporter's desk was now recognized as the place where young writers were trained, where they learned to find and understand the raw materials of literature. "The daily newspaper," said Lorimer, "sustains the same relationship to the young writer as the hospital to the medical student. It is the first great school of practical experience." In that school, for the young sociologist and political scientist as well as the young novelist, the main study was the city, and the city was New York.

By 1900 a nation of seventy-five million people had absorbed nearly twelve million immigrants within thirty years. The immigrants had poured into the cities, where they joined masses of native Americans who were in the grip of an inexorable movement from the farms and small towns. Urbanization had become the distinctive fact of modern society, and its chief problem. With the shift of population from the grange to the tenement house came a degree of overexpansion and undermanagement that brought large cities to the crisis point: sanitation and health services were plainly inadequate; there was a constant fear of rioting and crime; the police used their night sticks against the people they were sworn to protect. Fed by immigrants streaming through Castle Garden and, after 1891, Ellis

Island, New York's East Side was the end point of all cities. With over five hundred people for each acre, nearly five times the average for the rest of Manhattan, the Tenth Ward was the most densely settled area in the world, and its ghetto was larger than Warsaw's. It was "the suicide ward" and "the typhus ward," the breeding place of the "white plague" of tuberculosis, epidemics of all kinds, crime, pauperism, alcoholism, sweated labor, hopelessness, and a frightful mortality rate. For years this had gone largely ignored or was "resisted" (in the psychoanalytic sense), except by a few determined observers, statisticians and reporters. For urbanization was democracy's Esau and its Ishmael, disinherited at best and at worst regarded with fear and loathing; the city ("enemy territory," as William Jennings Bryan saw it) was a place that had been despised for so long, and by so many different classes of people, from patricians down to populists, that in the end it became despicable, neglected for so long that it became negligible. At a time when the building of a public bathhouse could be denounced as a dangerous act of socialism, it could be said that as an agency of collective responsibility for the poor, the marginal, and the newly arrived, the American city had scarcely even begun to exist. By some bitter paradox a vast population was reliving in the cities some of the conditions of life on the harsh frontier.

Edward Bellamy, whose utopian novel, *Looking Backward,* galvanized the reform movement, compared urban society with the Black Hole of Calcutta. The "press of maddened men," he wrote, tore and trampled one another "in the struggle to win a place at the breathing holes." The streets of Bellamy's Boston of 1887 are black and fetid. Half-naked, "brutalized" children wrestle in the garbage. "I have been in Golgotha," Bellamy says, envisioning the ghettos and inner cities of America ninety years later. "I have seen humanity hanging on a cross."

In 1888, the year Bellamy published his book and James Bryce indicted "the government of cities" as "the one conspicuous failure of the United States," Jacob Riis, a forty-year-old immigrant from Denmark and already a veteran slum reporter, took the first of the searing photographs that brought to the uptown eye and conscience the indisputable facts of how the other half (in actuality it was closer to three quarters) lived: in filth and desperation. The following year Jane Addams opened Hull House in Chicago, and during the 1890s the infant science of American sociology, stirring chiefly at the University of Chicago and at Johns Hopkins, began to address itself to the nation's most urgent problem. "The city was the place where we had to begin," said Frederic C. Howe, one of the early urban sociologists. But if the city was a failure peculiar to democracy it could also be, as Howe argued, "the hope of democracy."

For writers too, just as much as for painters and photographers of the 1890s, reality meant the city, and the affairs of the slum poor became the subjects of fiction and human-interest journalism. Even gentlemanly practitioners like H. C. Bunner, Charles Dudley Warner, and Professor Brander Matthews of Columbia turned to the streets downtown for local color, for an exoticism and overtness they missed in the Protestant landscape. Returning from their visits to the ghetto, Chinatown and Little Italy, these writers generated a fair amount of picturesque literature that failed to recognize that the immigrants were the heart population of the future and, as far as their present exotic locales were concerned, wanted out and up as fast as they could get it. But other writers were turning to the city not just for that distinctively non-Anglo-Saxon magic and adventure that O. Henry summed up in the word "Baghdad," but for the materials of a literature of realism and concern. In the hands of the right man, it was believed, the struggles of the immigrant poor, the turmoils of New York City politics, the sagas of Boss Tweed, Jim Fisk, Oakley Hall and Boss Croker could be translated into fiction in the line of Ibsen, Zola and Tolstoy.

City life in the lower depths of the Bowery, the Tenth Ward, and Mulberry Bend had a certain hyperreality, it seemed. Success there was sweeter, but failure was more bitter—after these places there was nowhere else to go. The photographs of the time, by Riis, Alfred Stieglitz, Lewis Hine, and others, are marked by an unflinching but kindly and even lyric realism; their arriving immigrants, sweatshop workers, pushcart peddlers, children in condemned classrooms, boys playing one o' cat behind the gasworks are fixed in time like figures on a vase. They came to the city, and their future, defeated or otherwise, is now the past.

"When a man seeks his stuff for writing from low life he is at least sure of one thing," Steffens' friend Hutchins Hapgood said in his book *Types from City Streets*, "namely, that what he sees is genuine." But some writers were to find that this European emphasis, which was so alien to their own origins, could carry with it just as great a risk of falsity as what Hapgood called "overcivilized Henry James-ism." Subject matter was one thing, and point of view another, and much literature of the city was defeated by sentimentality, stereotypes instead of characters, dialect instead of dialogue, and in the long run a degree of remoteness from actuality suggested by the titles of Brander Matthews' books—"vignettes," "outlines," "vistas" —and by Hapgood's "types."

Still, there was the example of William Dean Howells, leader in the wars of realism, who used the life of the cities to depict the blighting touch of the capitalist ethic. There was the example of Howells' protégé, the Russian Jew Abraham Cahan, who wrote fiction about the sweatshops and the immigrant's climb but not without a certain regret for what was lost in the process of acculturation. Above all, there was the example of Crane, another of Howells' protégés. It was "on the Bowery," exploring the saloons and flophouses, that "I got my artistic education," Crane said, looking back on his novel of urban bafflement and defeat, *Maggie: A Girl of the Streets.* Following Crane, other writers starting out in the nineties—Theodore Dreiser, Frank Norris, Upton Sinclair—found their subjects in the materials of the sociologist and social worker, materials that city reporters like Lincoln Steffens dealt with every working day.

He had come back from Europe with the belief that the business of America was business, that the coming century was America's "by the right of might," as the Columbian Exposition at Chicago was supposed to show, and that the "giants," the great and representative men of the day, were "the masters, not of art and philosophy but of finance and industry." It was to these masters that the citizens turned for answers to their political problems. "The successful businessman was regarded by everybody as preeminently *the* good citizen," Theodore Roosevelt recalled in 1913. "The severe newspaper moralists who were never tired of denouncing politicians and political methods were wont to hold up 'business methods' as the ideal which we were to strive to introduce into political life."

As a Wall Street reporter during the seismic tumbles of 1893, Steffens covered the panic trading on the stock exchange, the gold crisis, the disintegration of trusts, the epidemics of defalcation and bankruptcy—within a year a quarter of the nation's railroads, representing forty thousand miles of track, passed into the hands of the receivers. But the masters, those of them that survived the panic, were masters still, titanic heroes of a cult of energy, and meanwhile the young reporter had won access to them. Steffens knew the canny market manipulator Russell Sage, reputed inventor of puts and calls, former ally of Jay Gould, and now fundamentally just a money-lender. He nerved his way in to see J. P. Morgan, who, from his office in the white-marble Drexel Building on Wall Street, single-handedly rehabilitated the railroads. Even in a bearish time, Morgan declared, "the U. S. is a bull country" where "for the long pull the bull side is the winning side."

Steffens became the willing pupil of James B. Dill, the sagacious corporation lawyer who drafted a certain ingenious statute in 1889. He thereby made himself the Hammurabi of holding companies and put the state of New Jersey, Steffens said, in the regular business of selling to corporations "not only indulgences but absolution." Steffens fondly remembered Dill as intelligent rather than sincere, a rogue outside but an honest man inside, who instructed his pupil in the workings of an autonomic system of pelf and power. "How can the closing of saloons hurt business in Wall Street?" Steffens asked him. Dill answered with a kick and a question: "Why does your mouth cry out when only your shin is hurt?"

Richard Croker, Tammany chieftain and virtual ruler of New York City, sketched in the same connection for Steffens. "Wall Street has its bosses just like Tammany and just like the Republican machine," he said. Government was not a matter of statecraft at all, it was a business, like any other, for when it came down to the real issues a politician might well ask, What's the Constitution among friends? Walking through Union Square with the young reporter, Croker said, "Everything is business." (As he was to tell an investigating committee, "Every man in New York is working for his pocket.") The former gangleader, who looked like Ulysses Grant and shared Grant's passion for quality horse flesh, had filled his own pocket well; he owned racing stables at home and in England, and these, like the rest of his fortune, were the rewards of what George Washington Plunkitt, the Tammany philosopher, called "honest graft." It was all a matter of seeing opportunities and taking them, Plunkitt said. "With all the grand opportunities all around for the man with a political pull, there's no excuse for stealin' a cent."

Soon Steffens was meeting other bosses, some merely greedy, some more intelligent and admirable than the reformers, more closely wedded to reality and more compassionate. From a shabby office in Boston's West End Martin Lomasney, for one, dispensed patronage, charity, advice, influence and fixes, and in return collected loyalty, obedience and votes. It was a fair exchange, as Steffens came to see it. Lomasney had started from the bottom, like Croker, had been a bootblack and a heeler and lighted city lamps along Nashua Street. He never forgot that the problems of his immigrant constituency were, first of all, food, shelter and jobs. "There's got to be in every ward somebody that any bloke can come to—no matter what he's done—and get help," Lomasney told Steffens. "Help, you understand; none of your law and your justice, but help." No one, it seemed, had ever stated the case for the neighborhood political boss of that era so humanely.*

The challenge to the reporter, Steffens said, looking back over his first dealings with these men, was to find the "unofficial, unresponsible, invisible, actual governments back of the legal, constitutional 'fronts.' " But he was scarcely even beginning to suspect that at issue was something more complex than a combat of bosses and reformers.

* Even Theodore Roosevelt, reacting against the "mental and moral thinness" of Eastern reformers—and also against their tendency to support "all good, and many goody-goody measures so long as they did not cut deep into social wrong or make demands on national and individual virility"—acknowledged the short-term and compassionate function of the bosses. Reacting in a more extreme way, Steffens heroized and sentimentalized them, even though in many respects they were just as conservative as the reformers themselves. (The bosses "never thought of politics as an instrument of social change—their kind of politics involved the processes of a society that was not changing," says Daniel P. Moynihan.) Steffens' tendency was shared by his friend Hutchins Hapgood, who, perhaps thinking of the exceptional Plunkitt, described "the Tammany man" as "manly, straightforward and kind, with a racy wit and a power of speech rare among the 'reforming' classes. Politically, he is corrupt; personally, he is good—richly, humanly good." Like the terms "boss" and "corruption," "Tammany man," which took in everyone from executive committee to ward heelers, was simply too broad and shifting to have any useful meaning. (Roosevelt: *Autobiography*, New York, 1913, pp. 151–53. Moynihan: "When the Irish Ran New York," *The Reporter*, June 8, 1961, p. 34. Hapgood: *Types from City Streets*, New York, 1910, p. 58.)

CHAPTER FOUR

Training Lobsters to Fly

I

TWO AND A HALF MILLION MEN WERE OUT OF WORK, three quarters of a million out on strike, in 1893–94, a year of violence and hardship. Jacob Coxey led his industrial army of the unemployed on the long protest march from Massillon, Ohio, to Washington and the Capitol lawn, where they were arrested for walking on the grass. President Grover Cleveland sent a regiment of the United States Army to Chicago to break the Pullman strike. A federal grand jury indicted Eugene V. Debs, president of the American Railway Union. In a powerfully argued book, *Wealth against Commonwealth*, Henry Demarest Lloyd, economist and social reformer, marshaled irrefutable evidence to show that power in America was passing from the people to the monopolies and giant trusts.

Absorbed in his work, the future radical Lincoln Steffens observed these tremors of upheaval without responding to them. His loyalty to things as they were was still unshaken. Politically he called himself a mugwump, or independent, and in 1894 he voted the straight Republican ticket. Josephine regarded his involvement in journalism with "genuine sorrow and fear." It represented intellectual decline, a lowering of the high goals they had set themselves in Europe. Evenings he was rarely at home, and when Josephine went with him, to the theater and to restaurants and cafés, they were rarely alone together. He sought out other journalists and writers. As an emancipated woman, and even at the price of loneliness, Josephine declined to have her own circle of friends. Emancipated people held friends in common, she believed. There was now even a certain implicit, implicitly hopeless competition between her and her striving husband, and it began to isolate them even further from each other. He could always throw himself into his work and into the life of the city, but she had neither career nor family. They did not feel they could afford a child yet.

As a writer, Josephine's chief success so far had been to sell a couple of pieces to *The Nation* about the status of women at European universities. She struggled with the novel she had begun in Paris when they were first married. As an article writer she was not qualified to deal with what Steffens told her were the issues that magazine editors cared about: labor, the trusts, finance, reform. To make the situation worse, as far as Josephine was concerned, one reform event, the appointment of a commission to investigate graft in New York City, threatened to absorb her husband's interest to the exclusion of nearly everything else.

II

DURING STEFFENS' TIME AT POLICE HEADQUARTERS, it began to seem that in the Reverend Charles H. Parkhurst, a kindly Presbyterian with a scholarly competence in Sanskrit and Greek and a hankering for thrills and power, Godkin and his *Post* may at last have found the man to slay the dragon of corruption.

Parkhurst, president of the Society for the Prevention of Crime and minister of the Madison Square Church, had given two celebrated sermons which signaled the opening of a campaign against Tammany Hall, the Police Department, and protected vice. From his pulpit he charged that under Croker and the other sachems of the Hall—"polluted harpies" all of them, "a lying, perjured, rum-soaked and libidinous lot"—New York had become an industrialized Sodom, where prostitution, gambling and illegal Sabbath carousing in the city's saloons were administered by the police through a wondrously intricate discipline of graft, bribes, blackmail, bought promotions and kickbacks. Parkhust insisted that he could prove that the city was "rotten with a rottenness which is unspeakable and indescribable" and sustained by the "connivance" and "purchased sympathy" of the police. New York lived under a "tyranny of crime," Tammany Hall being nothing other than "a commercial corporation, organized in the interest of making the most out of its official opportunities."

Parkhurst's targets—the brothel, the saloon and the gambling house—had been targets for reformers since the angels feasted with Lot and told him to flee the iniquities of Sodom. What was new was the connection Parkhurst established between vice and government. He had come to the startling conclusion that the politician was the natural enemy of the people and that vice was actually the policeman's stock in trade. "Our motto," he said about the work of his Society from 1892 to 1894, was "Down with the Police!"

When he came to write his autobiography, *Forty Years in New York*, Parkhurst followed the chapter about his "successful assault upon the Tammany interest" with one called "The Ascent of the Matterhorn." Apostle of action Christianity, he was as intrepid in the New York underworld as he was among the Alpine cols and peaks where he spent his summers. He had a certain imperviousness to ridicule which, along with his fervor, made him a dauntless investigator. Gotten up in loud, unclerical clothes he went on a four-night tour of the city's pleasure palaces, all countenanced and taxed by the police, and visited a thieves' saloon by the East River, a fan-tan parlor and opium den in Chinatown, and a sampling of brothels. During his stay in one of the fancier chambers of commerce, located only a few hundred yards from his own church, Parkhurst was treated by five naked ladies to what he preferred to describe as a "circus" or "a sort of gymnastic performance," which went on for about twenty minutes.

As he and his agents continued their raids on "protected vice," "the social evil," and the police, rumbles of an impending bipartisan investigation began to be heard from the state capitol at Albany. The rumbles were heard with some skepticism by the reformers, who had seen toothless investigations before (one as recently as 1890), and by observers like Steffens, who believed that the upstate Republican machine and the downstate Tammany machine together had too much of a stake in the existing system to want to do any serious tinkering with it. Thomas C. Platt, the Republican boss and the power behind the legislative committee which was sent down from Albany to "investigate" New York, appeared only to be playing at politics at the expense of Tammany; one of Parkhurst's congregants, Platt cared less about Parkhurst's crusade than he did about uncovering election frauds. Watching the state senators as they appointed an investigative committee chaired by a party stalwart, Clarence Lexow, Steffens was reminded of the politicians he had seen in the capitol at Sacramento when he was a boy. "They sounded alike, they acted alike. . . . I heard the same honest, cynical comments." Like most people he expected a whitewash.

Stung by derision and such low expectations as these, the Lexow Committee appointed an unswervable, even inquisitorial prosecutor, John W. Goff, and in March 1894, when the Committee met in the County Courthouse and called the first in a procession of 678 witnesses, several things quickly became plain: police reform was going to be the main issue in the November mayoral election, the Police Department was going to be raked over from superintendent to patrolman, and headquarters on Mulberry Street was going to be the city's center ring for months to come.

Wright, the *Post*'s city editor, had told Steffens that the job at headquarters was not only to report, "in a dignified way, without any sensationalism," the usual traffic in murders, suicides, rapes and burglaries, a category of news that Godkin ran only grudgingly. He was also to cover Parkhurst's often melodramatic activities along with the hearings themselves. At the start, Steffens doubted that he was up to the assignment. He was a new man, without the sources and contacts the older reporters had, and the competition for news at police headquarters was fierce. Moreover, he was caught in the middle of a wire-service war as well as the war between Parkhurst and the police. And so he was as frightened, he said later, as a man about to get up to make a speech. Soon, however, he found a tutor in Jacob Riis, the *Evening Sun*'s brilliant reporter who had been covering Mulberry Street for seventeen years. Riis focused on the problems of the city the same passion and patience with which he chronicled the dark ways of the poor in *How the Other Half Lives*. Investigating a routine Health Department report that mentioned "a trace of nitrates," Riis uncovered the fact that New York's drinking water was being contaminated by sewage and that two million people lived in daily danger of an outbreak of cholera; he forced the city to revise the entire water-supply system. He fought for strict building codes, for schools and clinics, for parks, "open spots that let the

sunlight into the slums." Riis had hot emotions, Steffens wrote in
1903; he was a reformer who "worked through despair to set the
wrong right." As a reporter, Riis "not only got the news," said Steffens, describing his own evolving sense of purpose as well, "he cared
about the news," and he cared in a way that was soon to go out of
fashion. "The day of scientific method has come," Riis told Steffens
in 1906, "and I am neither able to grasp its ways, nor am I wholly in
sympathy with them. Two or three times a week I am compelled to
denounce the 'sociological' notions of the day and cry out for common sense." During the 1890s Riis demonstrated to Steffens that the
reporter, as man of good will, had a social obligation: to make things
happen.

Most mornings on his way downtown Steffens called on Parkhurst,
by then one of the most powerful men in the city. Parkhurst was, in
theory, only an unofficial observer at the hearings, but through his
agents, he was one of the Committee's chief sources of information.
Steffens left after these morning visits with an improved picture of
what he was coming to call "the invisible government." ("Now I can
go into a strange city," he was to tell an interviewer in 1903, "and
with my knowledge of New York methods understand their peculiar
methods of corruption.")

Primed in this way, and soon known to be Parkhurst's man as well
as Godkin's, he was received coldly at headquarters by the superintendent, Thomas Byrnes, celebrated the breadth of the country as
"The Great Detective." Byrnes was the author of a standard reference book in his trade, *Professional Criminals of America*, the equivalent of a national rogues' gallery, and he was renowned for having
put so tight a police cordon around Wall Street that the more un-
sophisticated kinds of crime—holdups, pickpocketing, and petty confidence games—were virtually unknown there during business hours.
He was undoubtedly the most effective policeman in America. Still,
though there was little to go on, Steffens had begun to suspect, and
to investigate more or less on his own, the probability that Byrnes
was something other than what he seemed. The man who, as chief
executive of the Police Department, also commanded the ear of Tammany and the obedience of the city's criminals had to be giving and
taking something in return.

Parkhurst's crusade, as Steffens followed it, was a test of practical
and theoretical politics. "The word 'corruption' was big and under-

stood in the vocabulary of my day," Steffens recalled. "It meant diseased, politically," and it presupposed "an ideal state of affairs; an ideal described in American charters and constitutions" and possibly as false as it was misleading. What was the point of fighting "corruption" if in practice "reform" consisted chiefly of replacing "bad" men with "good" men? Wasn't it possible that, as far as the achievement of certain social and political objectives was concerned, a corrupt machine government could be more effective than a reform administration that merely meant well? And wasn't it also possible that "corruption," that term of absolute and categorical judgment, was in reality divisible and relative?* In order to be intelligent instead of merely sincere one might have to learn to distinguish between harmful and harmless forms of corruption, between those which defeated valuable objectives and those which actually furthered them. As a police reporter, Steffens had reason to believe that his future work and future materials were being set out for him.

III

LATE IN THE SPRING OF 1894, as the Lexow hearings were about to be recessed, the pattern of Steffens' life with Josephine was providentially interrupted. At the *Post* one day Steffens received word from the German consul in Naples that Johann Krudewolf had died of tuberculosis and—the most definite act in an indefinite relationship —had named Steffens in his will as executor and residuary heir. For Steffens this windfall did not arrive without shame and remorse. His friend, Steffens reflected, had not been much in his thoughts lately: Krudewolf's letters were about "me and my doings," Steffens' replies were about "my own selfish, healthy interest in my vivid, purposeless life." "You will always be loved more than you love," Josephine remarked sadly when he reproached himself.

To settle the estate, she and Steffens left New York for Lehe, the *petit-bourgeois* exurb of Bremerhaven, Krudewolf's birthplace. They

---

* "Talk about our corruption!" William James commented on the Dreyfus affair in 1899. "It is a mere fly-speck of superficiality compared with the rooted and permanent forces of corruption that exist in the European states. The only serious permanent force of corruption in America is party spirit." (*Letters*, Boston, 1920, Vol. II, p. 100.)

sailed at the end of June, spent a few days in London and in the countryside near Southampton, and then settled in Krudewolf's house in Lehe, now their own. By the end of the summer, Steffens had finished tending to the business of inheritance taxes, various small legacies, and a fund which Krudewolf, sentimental to the last, had set aside to tend the family graves and to pay for a monument with a portrait bust. Steffens himself was richer by a little over $9,000 in cash, with about $3,000 to come when some bonds were settled and the house and its furnishings sold. All in all, he now had a considerable stake for the time and, shrewdly managed, it would eventually permit him to buy his freedom from wage earning, just as Krudewolf had hoped. "I feel pretty well started toward being a capitalist," Steffens told his father, "and Josephine and I have concluded it will be safe to go ahead and have a family."

Strong in the reform faith, confident that he could make a name for himself in New York, Steffens came back in time for the resumption of the Lexow hearings in September. Soon he was spending evenings as well as days at his office, at police headquarters, with Parkhurst, at the County Courthouse. Even at the risk of professional disgrace he was determined "not to leave off till the Police Department has been reformed," he told his father. "Until now police matters have been treated in their bearing on politics; now we must turn the iron into the police vitals and some big men must fall. First or last must Byrnes come down. He has kept aloof from attack; now he must be investigated, and the results will be fatal to his reputation."

"I believed in the police force," Riis said, "while Mr. Steffens believed it guilty till proven innocent. Nothing escaped him. Publicity was his motto." After only a year on Mulberry Street the young reporter had taken on not only Byrnes but the entire upper rank of the Police Department. They included Byrnes's deputy, Inspector Alexander Williams, known behind his back as "Clubber" Williams and generally credited with having named the city's busiest red-light district "The Tenderloin." (He had been living on "rump steak" before, Williams said as he took command of the lucrative 19th Precinct; "I will have some tenderloin now"—by which he meant, as he subsequently explained to the Lexow Committee, "I got better living.") The heat of battle freed Steffens from the restraints the *Post* generally imposed on its reporters. He described Byrnes's superior, James J. Martin, president of the Board of Police Commissioners, as "formerly a street-car driver, now one of the Tammany Hall bosses" who were implicated in election frauds. Along with his brother Bernard, a police judge, Martin was "likely to be among the first of the gang to make way for decent officers." According to Steffens' account in the *Post*, Martin responded in a predictable way:

> "In view of your report yesterday," he replied, "I don't want to have a damned thing to say to you."
> This was said on a rising scale of anger, and as he finished his sentence he sprang up.
> "Was the report not accurate?" he was asked.
> Advancing in a threatening manner he shouted: "It was a damned lying report, and you get out of here. If you don't I'll kick your —————— out," at the same time putting his hand on the reporter's arm to push him. On being requested to keep his hands off he called the patrolman and ordered him to "put that man out of here." No resistance was offered.

Martin's "irritability," Steffens concluded, was "a clue to his feelings about the coming elections."

"Machine rule will be heavily struck, but no doubt will come in again," he told his father in the spring of 1894. "There is too much anti-machine and too little desire to reform the machine itself." The chief reformers, having organized themselves into a Committee of Seventy and declared their intention to unseat the machine, had nominated as a fusion candidate William L. Strong, a successful dry-goods merchant, bank president and corporate director. It was confidently expected that Strong would apply to the affairs of the city the business virtues by which he had amassed a personal fortune of about a million dollars. (It was at the counting table, the faith of the day ran, that philosopher-kings were to be trained.) But though Strong was honest he was also naïve, and his naïveté, as Riis and others soon observed, extended to his belief that he was politically sagacious.

In November, Strong was elected mayor by a majority of over 45,000 votes, and Boss Croker exiled himself to a squire's life in England. "It shows that there is some moral stomach in the community which will expel proven corruption," Steffens wrote home. For him, a mugwump who had voted the Republican ticket "almost straight" this time, the victory proved that independents could be the saving of city politics. Vindicated by the election, the Lexow Committee moved on from the small fry into the executive command at the Police Department. One captain confessed that he had paid $15,000 to be promoted from sergeant. Inspector Williams maintained weakly that his yacht and estate in Connecticut came from his successful speculations in Japanese building lots. And finally, despite charges by the *Post* that there had been a deal and that Byrnes would be subjected to only perfunctory questioning, the superintendent himself, the committee's final witness, spent four strenuous hours on the stand: he said he had made his fortune of about $350,000 from market tips given him by Jay Gould and others. All in all, according to Dr. Parkhurst, the victory of 1894 was a victory for the Ten Commandments, and reformers all over the country—pillars of the Citizens Protective Association and the City Club, the Law and Order League and the Committee of Public Safety, the Altrurian League and Good Government Clubs *A* to *Z*—hailed the advent of a "civil renaissance."

As reporter and participant, Steffens had been at the center of events, and his eyes had been opened to what was to be the great discovery of muckraking: the vast terra incognita that lay in the dark spaces bounded by public ignorance and official representations. To smell rats, investigate, expose—in a few years these were to be his personal as well as journalistic imperatives. ("What is being done in the police is the material of politics," he said. "My occupation is defined for some time into the future.") For the moment, though, Steffens could take pride in the fact that his independent conclusions about the police had been borne out by the Lexow hearings. " 'Lies' I have printed are proving true," he said. Parkhurst, Wright at the *Post*, and other newspaper editors had finally come around to Steffens' view and taken up the cry against Byrnes. When it was all over Steffens could figure that at the age of twenty-eight, after only two years in New York, he had become something of a power in the city. Parkhurst, who in a campaign speech had singled him out from all the other reporters, "has taken me in as his advisor," Steffens said in January 1895, "and I found myself the agent of the *Post*, the Committee of Seventy, Dr. P., and the reformers on an expedition to find a military man"—so the logic went—"for Superintendent of Police."

Meanwhile, he went on, "Dr. P., through me, has been getting an unofficial, secret audience with Mayor Strong, the doctor having asked to have one arranged. I got Mr. Godkin to invite both men to his house to dine, and Dr. P. and Mr. G. are to ask the mayor to send

74

for me afterwards for direct and explicit information of Byrnes. It is all very like a plot, but the principals to the intrigue are disinterested men." In the midst of this plot Steffens was also considering an offer, made him by certain "persons in power," of an appointment to the United States consular service, a traditional reward for public-spirited writers. The offer was conditional, he said, echoing the most approved mugwump sentiments, on the service being removed from the patronage system and "put on a civil-service-examination basis with nonpartisan appointments." Still, the consulate was one of several opportunities which he now had before him "for the gratification of my ambition and the building of a life."

IV

IT WAS WHEN HIS OWN RISE IN NEW YORK was inseparable from his faith in the simpler strategies of reform that Steffens identified himself and his fortunes as journalist with the coming man of power, Theodore Roosevelt. Eight years older than Steffens, Roosevelt had been in the public eye since 1882, when, almost directly out of Harvard, he was elected to the state legislature from Manhattan's 21st Assembly District. His peers in the Knickerbocker aristocracy shunned politics as being too dirty for a gentleman. Roosevelt, as he joked in his boyish voice, flashing the big teeth he was so proud of, was determined "to be one of the governing class." At Albany he began to demonstrate his genius for generating publicity, especially in connection with reform causes, and he presided over one of the several investigations of the New York Police Department that preceded the Lexow Committee.

So it was fitting that in May 1895, after a career as author and historian, rancher in the Dakota badlands, unsuccessful candidate for mayor of New York in 1886, and Civil Service Commissioner in Washington, Roosevelt should be appointed by Mayor Strong to be president of the bipartisan board of police commissioners. Earlier he had turned down Strong's invitation to become Street Cleaning Commissioner on the grounds that he had no qualifications for the job. As he implied to his friend Henry Cabot Lodge, this was not the sort of office he could "afford to be identified with," at least not if he hoped eventually to be President—and most men around him, including

Steffens and Jacob Riis, suspected that he did. But, for the time being, Roosevelt wanted to be Police Commissioner in the same way that other boys wanted to be policemen. "It is a man's work," he told his sister Anna. He looked forward to action and leadership, to the chance to prove once again that he was no longer a sickly boy fettered by asthma and poor eyesight. Reform, for Roosevelt, had begun with making himself over.

Oppressed by the spirit of business and by what he felt was a tragic waning of national purpose, Roosevelt pursued high adventure, hand-to-hand combat with the enemy, the frontier virtues. "The clamor of the peace faction has convinced me that this country needs a war," he told Lodge in 1895, when the United States was rattling sabers over British intervention in Venezuela. "Personally I rather hope the fight will come soon." He told Senator Mark Hanna in March 1898, "We will have this war for the freedom of Cuba, in spite of the timidity of the commercial interests." Still the frontiersman, in 1901, three weeks before he was summoned to Buffalo to succeed the slain McKinley, Roosevelt remarked to Steffens, "I always told you I was more of a Westerner than an Easterner." He was often self-contradictory and perplexing, but somehow he was never a mystery. His "abnormal energy" and "chronic excitement" made him appear to be "pure act," Henry Adams said. According to Steffens, Roosevelt "thought with his hips." "His life has been so sudden and his fighting so aggressive," Steffens wrote in 1898, "that most people think he never thinks, that every act is born of the impulse of the moment." The only "secret" Steffens could reveal about Roosevelt after three years of watching him was that most people were wrong about him— "He thinks before he acts." But aside from this one privileged opinion Steffens concluded that there was "no inside view" of Roosevelt —"The public man is the private man, and his friends have no advantage in acquaintance with him over strangers."

Roosevelt's friends, Steffens went on, never call him Teddy—"not even behind his back, neither among themselves nor in their hearts when alone." His friends and admirers agreed not only among themselves but also with strangers and his enemies that even when he had become President, Roosevelt's peculiarity still was that he had essentially a boy's mind. "You must always remember," said one of Roosevelt's closest friends, "that the President is about six." "Mr. Roosevelt is the Tom Sawyer of the political world of the twentieth century," said Mark Twain, who generally despised him. "He would go to Halifax for half a chance to show off, and he would go to hell for a whole one." To the people, whose hero he became, Roosevelt was a man on horseback; but, like the young Lincoln Steffens, he was also a boy on horseback taming the West, even though, according to his own account published in four volumes, the West had long since been won.

"We have no plans yet," Roosevelt told reporters when he arrived at police headquarters on Mulberry Street. "We will lose no time, however, in taking charge of the Police Department." In Steffens' *Autobiography*, Roosevelt appears as a comic stereotype of himself, an overgrown boy who bounds up the stairs and asks breathlessly, "What do we do first? Now, then, what'll we do?" Looking back on police days, looking back also on the failure of reform and on the diverging paths he and Roosevelt had followed, Steffens distorted his role. "It was just as if we three were the police board, T.R., Riis, and I, and as we got T.R. calmed down we made him promise to go a bit slow, to consult with his colleagues also." Roosevelt "knew nothing," Steffens said, claiming that he himself had taken on the responsibility of "instructing T.R. in the A B C of police corruption." But this was all retrospect.

In May 1895 Steffens had as high a regard for the new police commissioner as Boss Croker, who saw in Roosevelt a particularly ominous sort of reformer: this one had a feeling for politics and publicity. From his estate in Berkshire, Croker surveyed the political scene back home and said, "Roosevelt is all there is to the Strong administration and Roosevelt will make it or break it." Roosevelt's reputation survived Tammany's eventual rout of reform, and so did Steffens' respect for him.

Roosevelt too had a comparably adjustable recollection of Steffens. In 1913, when he published his own *Autobiography*, Roosevelt did not so much as mention Steffens in the course of a thirty-six-page chapter about the Police Department; the year before, in the rancorous aftermath of progressive politics, he privately referred to Steffens as either a liar or a lunatic. But in August 1895, after three months at Mulberry Street, Roosevelt felt differently. "He is a personal friend of mine, and he has seen all of our work at close quarters," Roosevelt wrote. He was recommending to the *Atlantic Monthly* an article Steffens had written about the police. "He and Mr. Jacob Riis have been the two members of the Press who have most intimately seen all that went on here in the Police Department. . . . As to Mr. Steffens' competency as an expert I can, myself, vouch."

Roosevelt had come to police headquarters as out of a whirlwind— a prodigy, a "freak," as Riis said reverently, who brought with him a "golden age" of high purpose and also of flamboyance. Having packed away his sombrero and buckskins and silver spurs, Roosevelt now appeared in pink shirts, and in place of a vest, he wore under his frock coat a broad silk sash whose fringes hung down to his knees. He patrolled the streets at night dressed in a bravo's black cloak and a broad-brimmed hat which still could never hide those eyes and teeth, and as watcher of the city's watchmen he struck terror and discipline into the hearts of men on the beat. Roosevelt looks "like a determined man," one editorial writer said after two weeks of the new commissioner. "He makes our policemen feel as the little froggies did when the stork came to rule them."

Roosevelt charged ahead with what Steffens described admiringly as a policy of "pitiless reorganization and absolute publicity." He ousted Byrnes and Inspector Williams, broke up old systems of graft and political preferment, rewarded merit and punished negligence, and moved on from purge to a general refurbishing. For the police to be honest, he reasoned, they had to do their job, which was to enforce laws, not some of the laws but all the laws, and this applied most of all to the Sunday-closing laws, which the saloonkeepers, the people, and the police had flouted for years. Roosevelt had nothing serious against drinking, but he was intoxicated with the same 180-proof moral absolutism that was the undoing of other reformers. As he saw it then, the life of the law was not experience, or even logic, but enforcement: law was the law. In Cincinnati the people had nearly rioted for their right to drink on Sunday. In New York, as the summer of 1895 grew hotter and drier, the people, who had only their saloons and beer halls on Sundays for refreshment, pinochle and political meetings, turned against Roosevelt and other gentry who, it was said, could always buy a drink at the Union League Club and plan other inequities to torment the lower classes.

Meanwhile, the Goo-goos grumbled and called for fewer political compromises, ever stricter enforcement, and that is what resurgent Tammany, knowing the temper of the voters, was not only willing but also determined to let the Goo-goos have.

The fact was that the people, with a natural appetite for inexpensive pleasures and short-term satisfactions, and also with a gaiety and humor the reformers never even acknowledged, grew tired of endless campaigns against rascality, endless scoldings from moralists at the other end of the social ladder who could not even get along with one another. Here, for example, was Theodore Roosevelt, who, accused by Parkhurst of making deals, came out with the statement that Parkhurst was "a goose," "an idiot" and "a dishonest lunatic." Viewed from below, reform was mostly stick and hardly any carrot. Within a few months after the victory over Tammany, the moral temperature of the city had dropped, as any ward heeler could have foreseen. The crusader Roosevelt was hamstrung by a bipartisan law that limited his authority; he was embroiled in squabbles with other members of the police board; he was under attack from the Democrats, the Good Government clubs and his own party. Perhaps there was no way a reform administration could win in the long run. It was like trying to stand a pyramid on its apex, one political sage observed.

All through the city government the same comedy was being played out and overshadowing some real achievements: pride restored to the police, clean streets, new bridges, parks rescued from neglect, the school system overhauled and enlarged, a new campus for the City College. Rebellious by nature and by definition amateurs, the reformers began to squabble among themselves and jockey for position. (The reformer "hasn't been brought up in the difficult business of politics," Plunkitt said, "and he makes a mess of it every time.") For a while, as Steffens wrote in April 1895, the promises of the new administration had whipped up "a mixture of hope and fear that made living here a delight." But after only four months in office the mayor had proven himself to be obstinate, slippery and confused, "a small man in a big place," who tried to please everyone and, not succeeding, became simply vindictive. Strong himself was to be so embittered by his one term in politics that he vowed never again to offer himself for public service. All in all, Steffens concluded, with the reform factions competing with each other, the fusion government "is a complicated and contradictory jumble of theories in practice of municipal administration which have but one end in common —the restoration of Tammany Hall."

Observing this likelihood, and having won from his work on Mulberry Street a national reputation for being incorruptible if not saga-

cious, Roosevelt looked for other opportunities. He stumped for
McKinley in the fall of 1896; and the following spring, after nearly
half a year of negotiations, he was appointed Assistant Secretary of
the Navy. "The end of the reign of Mr. Roosevelt in the Police Department is not the end of Rooseveltism," Steffens wrote in the *Evening Post* in April 1897. The men were going to miss him—for all his
melodramatics and even his mistakes he had been "dead square" with
them. "Mr. Roosevelt may disappear utterly from the board, and his
policy may be reversed, but his personality will persist as an active
influence in the force for a generation." Steffens was too hopeful by
far.

On Election Day in 1897 Tammany took over the city once again,
and it was a bigger pie this time, having been enlarged by charter to
Greater New York. Instead of "Onward Christian Soldiers" and
voices raised in support of the Ten Commandments, the crusaders
now heard the victorious slogan of Tammany's district attorney,
"To Hell with Reform." A peculiar transatlantic exchange took
place. Croker returned from England as from Elba and spoke what
he believed was an epitaph for the reformers, "They tried to stand so
straight that they fell over backward," he said; on election night, in
preparation for the sober business of patronage the next day, he celebrated with a vichy and bicarbonate of soda. And, sailing for England shortly after, Godkin, who had devoted half of his sixty-six
years to raising the level of public life, admitted that he was giving
up. Having once had "high and fine ideals about America," he was
now going to look elsewhere for something to sustain his faith in
humanity. "I have seen my last mayoral election and wish them God-
speed. I am tired of having to be continually hopeful; what I long for
now is a little comfortable private gloom in despair." "We all expected too much," he said. Finley Peter Dunne's Mr. Dooley arrived
at the same conclusion. "A man that'd expect to thrain lobsters to
fly in a year is called a loonytic; but a man that thinks men can be
tu-rrned into angels be an illiction is called a rayformer an' remains
at large."

Young men like Steffens read the lesson of 1897 less bleakly. What
had failed, he was coming to believe, was not reform itself but merely
the reforming tactics of an older generation that was moralistic,
scornful of politics, isolated from the people, and incapable of learning from experience. Honesty and high purpose were not enough,

Steffens now knew, one also needed realism, science, humor, compassion, a sense of the collective will and mood. The great clean-up of New York had not been pointless, only insufficient. In its return to power Tammany centralized and refined old techniques, eliminated middlemen and dilution, and, as Steffens wrote in 1898, built a "new, perfected system of blackmail and bribery." In short, "New York is New York again."

CHAPTER FIVE

"Getting up in the world"

I

BY 1897, AFTER FIVE YEARS ON THE *Post*, Steffens had become assistant city editor, a fair enough reward and a modest eminence,
but still, as it seemed to him in his hurry to move along and make a
name, really a dead end. When Wright, his immediate superior,
moved over to the *Commercial Advertiser* and offered him the job
of city editor there, Steffens accepted, even though this doddering
journal, which had seen better days during George Washington's
first term, was a step down from the *Post*. Under a new management
that, for a start at any rate, was willing to experiment and take
chances in order to jog the paper out of its torpor, Steffens was given
something he never had under Godkin: freedom and power to make
a new kind of daily journalism, personal, literary and immediate.

"The *Commercial Advertiser*, the good old grandmother of journalism, is still being printed. Why, God only knows," a trade columnist wrote soon after the move from the *Post*. "A Mr. Steffens is
the city editor. He wears on his chin a little downy fuzz he thinks
is a beard and he gets $25 a week. That is all I know about him ex-
cept that he used to be on the *Evening Post* and once had a story
printed in the *Chap-Book*. The men on the staff of the *Commercial
Advertiser* are each paid $10 a week, or less, and only college gradu-
ates are employed. When the good clothes their fathers furnished
them with when they left college to enter journalism become shabby

they are requested to resign, and the *Advertiser* gets more university men in their place." Speaking derisively for reporters and editors of the old school, the columnist at least acknowledged the unorthodoxy of what Steffens planned to do as a city editor with a staff of twenty.

There wasn't going to be any *Advertiser* "style," only personal styles, he decided at the start, putting Godkin behind him once and for all. After a few months he said, "I have the beginnings of one of the best staffs of reporters ever organized in this city." He was replacing "professional reporters" with young men from Harvard and Yale who, as he did, saw newspaper work as a stepping-stone to a literary career and were willing to cooperate with him in an experiment or, as he called it, a "conspiracy"—"to make a newspaper that shall have literary charm as well as daily information, mood as well as sense, gayety as well as seriousness." Among these young reporters were Hutchins Hapgood, soon to write a classic account of immigrant life, *The Spirit of the Ghetto,* and Robert Dunn, who came to the paper from Harvard after writing a blank-verse tragedy about incest for George Pierce Baker's drama seminar. Dunn saw no reason to apologize for the fact that he was now working for the *Advertiser* when one day his former philosophy professor, George Santayana, visited him amidst the litter of the city room and they went out for a lunch of snails, Camembert and red wine in a cellar restaurant on Nassau Street. Another novice, Guy Scull, a Rough Rider corporal who after being trained to meet newspaper deadlines was to be sent off to cover the Boer War, was for Steffens as good an example as any of what he, as city editor, was looking for and how he found it. "Hurry up," he'd say to Scull, "jam it, hard." And Scull, accustomed to leisure and a gentler prodding, would be forced to grind out a news paragraph that the two of them knew was not exactly right, was not as good as it could be.

> I guess he hated me sometimes [Steffens said], but I did make Scull write. That's what he needed. Someone at Harvard sent Scull to me. They told him I would take a mere writer. And I would. I wanted men who could write, so I passed the word that I would take no reporter on my city staff, no man who wanted to be a newspaperman; I wanted only fellows who cared to write—plays, poems, essays, tales. And Scull was this sort.

Of this sort, too, was Steffens' boldest appointment to the *Advertiser,* Abraham Cahan, the Russian-immigrant novelist, militant socialist, and future editor of the *Jewish Daily Forward*. While still at the *Post* Steffens had read and admired Cahan's first novel, *Yekl*, and bought an article by Cahan for the paper's Saturday supplement, an editorial transaction that was the start of a close relationship. After their first meeting Steffens took this exotic home with him to meet Josephine and her mother, and as he and Cahan walked uptown they talked about the passion they had in common, literature. At thirty-seven, when he accepted Steffens' invitation to join the *Advertiser*, Cahan had already been acclaimed by William Dean Howells as the premier realist of immigrant life.

Cahan's eminence and worldliness gave him a position of influence on the paper out of proportion to his duties there. He began as police reporter covering Steffens' old beat on Mulberry Street under the tutelage of Jacob Riis. Afternoons, when the paper had gone to press, Cahan, seated at the city-room table, led discussions of socialism and anarchism, the theater and Russian literature, discussions of the sort one heard in the immigrant cafés on Second Avenue and along Canal and Houston Streets. For Steffens and the others, Cahan provided their first systematic exposure to radicalism, to the ideas of Marx, Bakunin and Kropotkin, to a questioning of political fundamentals they had always taken to be unassailable. No wonder that Steffens, often smoking his pipe in silence during these after-work sessions, felt with satisfaction that Cahan was bringing not only a cosmopolitan and challenging mind but also the disputatious spirit of the ghetto into the editorial rooms of a newspaper committed to the interests of Republicanism and the financial community.

Cahan took us, as he could get us, one by one or in groups, to the cafés where the debate was on at every table and to the theaters where the audience divided: the realist party hissing a romantic play, the romanticists fighting for it with clapping hands and sometimes with fists or nails. A remarkable phenomenon it was, a community of thousands of people fighting over an art question as savagely as other people had fought over political or religious questions, dividing families, setting brother against brother, breaking up business firms and, finally, actually forcing the organization of a rival theater with a company pledged to realism against the old theater, which would play any good piece.

I rejoiced when this East Side controversy flowed over into my newspaper.

The spirit of the ghetto, which Steffens and Cahan urged the others to capture in their daily work, was in part the spirit of New York, already the largest Jewish city in the world. Cahan arrived on the *Advertiser* at a thriving time for Yiddish culture in general, a time, too, when other New York papers were also giving over ample space for the purpose of interpreting immigrant life and customs for their uptown readers. Steffens himself was as infatuated with Jewish life in the melting pot as Theodore Roosevelt and Owen Wister were with the Wild West. Josephine did not share this taste with him, and between them they reenacted the opposed currents of philo-Semitism and anti-Semitism which became conspicuous during the 1890s and the decade following. "As to the restrictions on the property," Josephine was to instruct some rental agents in 1909, "I will not let it to Hebrews; and you need not show any of that race about it, or entertain any offer from them for it." Steffens, meanwhile, had become "almost a Jew," he said: he had a mezuza on his office door, went from one East Side synagogue to another on high holy days, claimed to have made a practice of fasting on Yom Kippur, and even when he was on the *Post* permitted his journalism to reflect his enthusiasm for the ghetto. On September 17, 1896 he reported on "Yom Kippur on the East Side" for the *Post:*

> There were some men already in the synagogues. They had not yet drawn on the talith, but they were swaying gently, earnestly, back and forward as they mumbled, reading the book of prayer, and tapped their breasts. In the vestibules of the shules, the heads of the congregation set out the long table and arranged the baskets with the names in Hebrew of the cantor and members of the choir, each of whom receives contributions for his services on this day. At the doors of the synagogue the beggars were grouping themselves to be ready.

"The uptown Jews complained now and then," he wrote in his *Autobiography:*

> Mr. Godkin himself required me once to call personally upon a socially prominent Jewish lady who had written to the editor asking why so much space was given to the ridiculous performances of the ignorant, foreign East Side Jews and none to the uptown Hebrews. I told her. I had the satisfaction of telling her about the comparative

85

beauty, significance and character of the uptown and downtown Jews. I must have talked well, for she threatened and tried to have me fired, as she put it.

Steffens' city reporters were his protégés; his success depended on theirs. "All the fellows on my staff when I was city editor have made good," he was to say in 1911. "It's as near as I have been able to get to having children, and I have been pretty well satisfied so far." Even at the age of sixty, when he finally did become a father, he found that the experience, however long delayed, still had the effect of mellowing and extending his sensibility, rectifying some of the effects of a crippling one-way traffic in love. Substitute fatherhood as city editor was having some of the same effect now. True, some of his young college-bred reporters did not at first take to him, especially when he strolled into the office late, lighted up his pipe, in a few satiric sentences disposed of Boss Croker, whom he had just been interviewing, and then turned his attention to the stock ticker—"Anyone can make money on Wall Street," he said. "Even I." This little man with a shellac-colored beard trimmed in imperial style seemed pert and conceited, sometimes sophistical and too easily tempted to waste his finesse on politicians and businessmen. What was the use of all this paradox-playing and verbal fencing when one was dealing with the man who ran the whorehouses on Allen Street? "He'd talk one into a hole so glibly," said Dunn, "that I doubt the other fellow got Steff's point at all."

But these were first impressions. Soon Dunn found himself liking Steffens for his clear personality, his freshness, his enthusiasm, and his certainty that no problem was too big or too hard. Confidence was catching. More than this, Steffens' novices discovered that he had a quality of sympathy, a talent for inviting trust and spurring ambition, that made him a superb trainer of writers. "He was almost incredibly 'fresh' in the sense that he was palpitatingly alive to anything that had any quality or interest in it at all," Hapgood said; and Steffens himself, measuring his effect on his writers, was able to report after a year and a half, "It is a happy crowd I am working with." They were elated by their success, for now it appeared that the *Advertiser*, quixotic as it was by trade standards, could be pulled out of the red after all.

Steffens ran his city room on the belief that "the great struggle of a writer is to learn to write as he would talk." When there was time, he encouraged his reporters to talk their assignments first, and when he felt that he had got them excited enough to go for the heart of the story, he would say, "Good, now write it that way." (His own prose, when he came to maturity as a muckraker, was the equivalent of his staccato, stripped-down talk.) He was willing to forgive blunders, even to be amused by them, if he felt that the writer had looked at the news freshly, still saw red at a fire and felt pity at a disaster, searched for the odd fact and the revealing comment. When the Tammany-appointed superintendent of the Aquarium told Hapgood that *his* way of testing the water in the tanks was to see whether the fish died, Steffens ran the interview on page one. And to encourage similar recognitions of hidden news, Steffens assigned beginners to write atmospheric journalism about the difference between Seventh Avenue and Eighth Avenue, or between Fifth Avenue and Broadway, to describe old men on park benches, to interview derelicts and odd characters, and always to mix the news with the reporter's own feeling about the news.

Steffens wasn't interested in anything but writing, "the great, supreme passion" of his life during four years on the *Advertiser*, Cahan said. Politically he was still scarcely more radical than Theodore Roosevelt, who said that Tom Paine was a "filthy little atheist" and that Governor Altgeld was a traitor, and who feared above all "the evil spirit of revolution." As for Steffens, Hutchins Hapgood recalled, the "revolutionary instinct had not yet taken possession of him." He had been as eager as Roosevelt himself to fight in the war against Spain, and only his responsibility to Josephine stopped him from enlisting. He was a dissenter mainly insofar as he found himself, as "intellectual" and "artist," alienated from a business society. He was a reformer mainly insofar as he was still a moralist with a distaste for jobbery and party politics—"all fraud and buncombe, lying and thieving, disloyalty and selfishness." In 1900, when he was elected to membership in the 17th Assembly District Republican Club, he joined out of the most reluctant sort of partisanship, a belief that he would rather ally himself with "intelligent rascals" like the party of William McKinley, "the arch-American hypocrite," than with Democratic "fools," free-silver visionaries, and rabble rousers like William Jennings Bryan, spokesman for the have-nots and Markham's Man with the Hoe. In Steffens' city room the words "art," "realism," and "literature"—terms which were almost taboo on other newspapers—were part of the common discourse. After one of their evening walks uptown from Park Row, Cahan began to talk about Marx and socialism, but Steffens cut him off. "Drop it. Hang it, Cahan," he said. "Let's talk literature again."

It was his own writing, his own career beyond the city room, that chiefly occupied Steffens. As outside work he had often written for the *Post*'s Saturday supplement: local color and human-interest sketches of New York shopgirls, of Jews at religious observances and Italians at their street festivals, soft-news stories about a cruise on the floating hospital ship of the St. John's Guild, interviews with eccentrics such as "Captain" Jones, who wore a gold miner's sombrero and kept himself alive by combing the beach at Coney Island for lost money and jewelry. When Steffens moved to the *Advertiser* he continued working in this direction with a number of personal sketches, some of them rehearsals for the early chapters of his *Autobiography*. But his consuming interest was not in one form or another of newspaper and magazine reportage but in fiction, stories set in the Bowery, the ghetto, Little Italy, Chinatown.

In June 1896 the elite *Chap-Book*, champion of realism and *art nouveau*, had published a story by him about ghetto life and the pressures of Americanization. Later that year, after another story, this one about the Italians of Mulberry Bend, was published in the *Post*'s Saturday supplement he received a letter from Henry Holt and Company expressing interest in publishing a collection of his fiction, which, for a while, he thought of titling "The Human Various." The news of the Holt offer brought him the promise of another promotion at the *Post*, and with such encouragement he wrote a cycle of New York stories. But none made the impact of his first two, and several, according to Josephine, his editor as well as his copyist, were "pretty slight" or "almost too slight to correct at all." The most receptive market for his fiction, as it turned out, was *Youth's Companion*, the juvenile weekly, and by the time he submitted his book collection in 1902, Holt had decided that the market was glutted with "newspaper short stories" and "slum stories" written in frank imitation of one of the fads of the middle 1890s, Edward Waterman Townsend's wooden tales about a Bowery gamin named Chimmie Fadden.

Steffens had also been at work on a novel about Captain Max Schmittberger, one of the casualties of the Lexow investigations, and he talked about his book as an attempt to dramatize what was "good" in a "bad" man and to understand what had brought Schmittberger from small to big graft and then broke him from high command to a lonely beat in Goatsville. The trouble, in practice, was that Steffens' gift for systems and abstractions was not the novelist's gift, although it took him quite a while to find it out, and the living character eluded him. The novel was a tougher job than he had expected "but it goes," Steffens said early in 1900, and that was about the best report he would ever be able to render on the project. His confidence in himself as a writer was sustained by other sources altogether.

His article in the May 1899 issue of *McClure's Magazine* was as compelling as its subject, Theodore Roosevelt, who had, on his own responsibility, dispatched Commodore Dewey's Asiatic Squadron to destroy the Spaniards in Manila Bay and then led his Rough Riders in their celebrated charge up San Juan Hill in Cuba. Sporting a faded field uniform, the war hero declared, the summer day in 1898 when he and his regiment disembarked at Montauk Point, "I feel like a bull moose. I'm ashamed to be so sound and well." One by one, according to Steffens, Roosevelt's friends came to Montauk and whispered, "You are the next governor of New York." Boss Platt, who had the state in his pocket and meant to keep it there, also wanted Roosevelt to run, and Roosevelt was willing. He was not a mugwump; he had always believed in the Republican party; and besides, the campaign buttons were already made up.

Was he perhaps thinking of the Presidency? Steffens had asked him at Montauk.

"No, no. Don't ever say that again," Roosevelt told him. "I never sought an office. I always wanted a job, for I like work. Do you know, I have been thinking lately that I should like to have a professorship of history in some good college? I'd enjoy that sort of work." (A year or so later Roosevelt was not only running for the Vice-Presidency on McKinley's ticket—"He's gallopin'," Mr. Dooley said.)

"He is two personalities in one," Steffens reflected now that Roosevelt was settled in as governor in Albany and forcing his own terms on the Republican machine, "the first slow, reflective, open-minded;

the other quick, reckless and set. He gives time to making a decision; after he has settled upon a course, he ceases to be a man of thought and becomes altogether the man of action."

"A jim-dandy," "rattling good," S. S. McClure wrote to Steffens about the Roosevelt article. "I could read a whole magazine of this kind of material. We should have more of it. We will arrange our magazine so that this article will be the last thing to go into type, so as to bring it up to date as near as possible." McClure had already given him a contract to write a book-length biography of Roosevelt. The most brilliant editor of his day had discovered a new star.

Fresh out of Knox College and with $4 in his pocket Sam McClure had come East and left behind, once and for all, the lonely country boy the farm neighbors knew in northwestern Indiana. What emerged was the dazzling, mercurial and persuasive S. S. Mc-Clure, now forty-two, "the General" to his editors. He brimmed over with a thousand ideas and glittering schemes, seemed to live only in and for the immediate present and the near future, and he journeyed restlessly from continent to continent in search of the new, the real, the contemporary. (According to one wit, McClure was actively in the market for "a snappy life of Christ.") "He was a flower that did not sit and wait for the bees to come and take his honey," Steffens said years later. "He flew forth to rob the bees." "If he had been a woman," said one of his editors, "he would have been pregnant all the time." More and more frequently McClure was to suffer periods of exhaustion and collapse, bouts of insomnia, dyspepsia and arthritis, having burned himself out in the white heat of his enthusiasm, talk and projects, and then, like other neurasthenic press lords—Bennett, Pulitzer, Scripps—he traveled for the sake of the peace he found in ocean crossings.

On occasion authors could be found who withstood his charm and visionary enthusiasm—old Dr. Oliver Wendell Holmes had declared testily, "I will neither be lured nor McClured." But the young editor was to lure and win to his syndicate, magazine and, he hoped, publishing empire Robert Louis Stevenson, Anthony Hope, Rudyard Kipling, Mark Twain, O. Henry, Conan Doyle, Jack London, Booth Tarkington and, among the rising stars, Willa Cather, who was to become his managing editor and the ghostwriter of his autobiography. During the 1890s McClure's inflamed curiosity turned toward the world of contemporary fact. He wanted interviews and human documents, articles about industry, science, politics, labor, exploration, criminology. As the promoter of a new realism in magazine journalism McClure at one point tried to send Stephen Crane and an illustrator down to the ocean floor in diving suits. He had better luck sending Crane into the coal mines and Hamlin Garland to the steel mills and slums of Homestead, but he was distressed that their reports, as he charged, were marred by a flagrant prejudice against big business. It was a charge that he was eventually to bring against Steffens, and with considerable bitterness. But for the moment, Steffens too was being carried along on the flood tide of McClure's enthusiasm toward achievements as a journalist dealing in the facts of the booming and electric Now. Within a few years, and guided by McClure, he was to achieve some of the celebrity reserved for victorious politicians and heroes of the war with Spain.

II

DESPITE ITS FAILURES, THE AMERICAN CITY STILL HELD OUT THE PROMISE not only of life but of the good life; it was the place a man went to in order to become the person he wanted to be. Perhaps the congestion of the slums and the distance between the poor and the rich were after all a fair price for community and mobility, which is what drew men to cities. "Leisure is not alone for the rich nor for tramps," Steffens was writing in 1898:

> Go over to the East Side to the cafés of Second Avenue. On your way you will pass through some tenement house streets, where the women will gaze lazily at you over fat flesh folded up against their eyes by fists supported by naked elbows resting on the window sills. That is sheer, slovenly idleness, perhaps, but there is so much of it that anyone who walks among the other half with a mind unprepossessed by accepted notions of the life there will get distinctly the impression of plenty of time.
>
> You may make a detour, too, through Mulberry Street and see the great stalwart laborers of Italy lying half awake, bathing in the sunlight on benches, stoops and on the sidewalks. And they are not mere loafers. They are men who work in season. When they have nothing to do they do nothing calmly and pleasantly. Their women

gossip on their haunches in the alleys and on the curbs, while the children creep about in the gutters or play out under the horses' hooves. This also is not work and neither is it misery. It is only not your idea of living.

These and other urban pleasures—fishing off the East River piers, talk and laughter in the beer halls, cards in the scattered sunlight beneath the elevated—were all public, communal ways which preserved, Steffens said, "the graceful art of killing time without drawing a drop of blood."

Uptown the era of the bicycle had arrived. For the first time men and women in the mass were taking their exercise and their recreation together in freedom. Any fine day thousands of cyclists pedaled northward up Broadway, turned west, and followed Riverside Drive uphill to picnic grounds and to the Claremont Inn for cakes and iced tea or for supper. In the cool of the evening the cyclists flowed into the city again, a stream of darting and flashing lamps.

Steffens and Josephine, caught up in the same systolic rhythm, took long tours in and out of the city. They wheeled from the Hudson across lower Westchester and the Bronx to Throgs Neck on Long Island Sound, to Pelham Bay Park, and then to City Island, where they ate oysters, clams and lobsters at a hotel and napped by the water's edge before starting back home. "Our cyclometers showed tonight that we have made 39.75 miles," Steffens wrote to his father from Riverdale, where they were staying in a boarding-house. "Both of us are now as brown as berries." Often, loafing in the shade or on the beach after swimming, Steffens talked about the freedoms of his boyhood on horseback in California, talked about them "cheerfully, gaily, but without regret," recalled one of his cycling companions, John Barry, novelist and drama critic for *Harper's Weekly*. Infatuated with the life and promise of the city, Steffens, he said, "lived in the present."

They had moved in 1897 from furnished rooms to a seven-room apartment at 341 West 56th Street, just below Central Park and near the great bicycle arteries. The dining room was fitted out with a mahogany table and chairs and a mahogany sideboard which displayed, in a symbolic cultural mix, pewter, brass and pottery that they had bought in Europe, a samovar he picked up "among the East Side Jews," a silver tea service presented to Josephine's father during the Civil War. The parlor was dominated by a Persian rug and a bronze statue of Narcissus, both from Krudewolf's house in Lehe, and there was a library with new shelves and a rug-covered bench built in against the wall in place of a sofa. Eclectic, upper bohemian, cosmopolitan, this was a dwelling that reflected both taste and rising status. "We are getting up in the world," Steffens said shortly after they moved in, "and may some day have an elevator."

The Steffenses impressed people as an "interesting couple" who were literary, informed, and "given to eager talk about worthwhile things." Josephine was known to hold outspoken views and to be writing a novel about an emancipated woman. Somewhat in the background, but exerting a softening influence, was her mother, with whom Steffens continued to cultivate an understanding of considerable fineness. Now that they were settled, the Steffenses, previously accustomed to taking their friends out to restaurants, were serving home dinners, along with claret from Joseph Steffens' Sacramento winery, to "a mixed and interesting lot of people," Steffens said at the time. They were "mostly writers and artists, police officers and politicians," and included Captain Max Schmittberger (the hero of his novel), John Barry, and three members of the *Advertiser* staff, Abraham Cahan, Hutchins Hapgood and his brother Norman Hapgood, the paper's drama editor.

On evenings spent away from home there was the life of the theater in New York and afterward the Russian and Jewish cafés where Steffens sat by the hour and talked with Cahan, the poet Morris Rosenfeld, the visiting short-story writer of London ghetto life, Israel Zangwill, whom he took on a tour of the East Side. Or there was the banqueting clash of cutlery, the bedlam of voices, and the self-congratulating fellowship of the Press Club on Nassau Street or the Aldine, where one night Steffens consumed green turtle soup, boiled Kennebec salmon, terrapin Maryland style, and canvasback duck in honor of Mark Twain.

It was a booming period for Steffens, a successful city editor, a stellar magazine journalist, a man of some influence, to whom Theodore Roosevelt, at breakfast one morning, appealed for advice and editorial support. But these years were not at all kind to Josephine. Her novel had traveled in manuscript from publisher to publisher before it was tentatively accepted by a Boston house, which asked her to revise it completely. She did, and then, Steffens told his father, "she collapsed. It seemed as though she had held herself up by sheer will power till that job was done and then let go." Her doctors treated her for bronchitis or a possible tubercular condition and urged a milder climate, but Steffens was sure that "something else, something that lies deeper is the matter. She looks badly in her bed, poor girl, and all her interest in everything is gone."

With her mother she went to South Carolina to recuperate, leaving him for two months to lead a bachelor life in Greenwich Village. By the time she returned the Boston firm had decided against her book, and the manuscript began its travels again. When *Letitia Berkeley, A.M.*—the story of an American bluestocking in Paris who falls in love with a prig who offers to forgive her for a past indiscretion—was finally published in 1899, eight years after Josephine began, it had none of the impact she had hoped for, even though the book dealt with the relatively touchy subject of sexual "purity" before marriage and was denounced as "lecherous" by a Sacramento paper, one of the few to pay any attention at all. Along with her first novel—she never finished a second—some of Josephine's vital force vanished.

Letitia Berkeley, which deals with a woman much like Josephine who rejects a man much like Steffens, already implied a stagnation in their marriage. Coincident with the book's failure came a profounder disappointment. Prudently they had waited until the summer of Krudewolf's windfall, when Josephine was nearly forty, to "go ahead and have a family," but then year after year Josephine failed to conceive. "She is discontented with my barrenness to her," Steffens said in 1896, taking the entire responsibility upon himself, and for nearly thirty years he believed that he was sterile and was denied the fulfillment of "one of the deepest secret desires of my life." His belief, and hers, became an obscure hurt that lay between them, reason for him, and for her, to feel, as he now did, that he was a failure as a husband, a "dub," he said. More and more they came to live together in a resigned and affectionate sadness, a relationship stabilized by the presence of her mother, whom Steffens continued to adore. More and more, and eventually to the point of his own near-collapse, Steffens became absorbed in a life totally apart from

Josephine's—in his work at the paper, in the surrounding community of culture and ideas; in short, in the promise of the city, at whatever cost.

III

DESPITE STEFFENS' HIGH HOPES, BY 1901, his fourth year on the paper, the *Commercial Advertiser* was on its way to becoming "a perfectly conventional, dull and commonplace sheet," said Hutchins Hapgood. Its city editor, who had started out with such daring, was now, measured by his original aims, just "an interesting failure," a young man who seemed "strangely tired." The owners and managers of the *Commercial Advertiser* had grown conservative, and now that the paper was finally turning a profit they were no longer interested in supporting a city room conducted as a literary experiment and a writers' conference. They wanted more news coverage of a routine sort and fewer atmospheric essays. And at the same time, Steffens himself, occupied with his outside work, had less drive to fire up his reporters.

"We've got out of that man just about all there ever was in him," Steffens overheard someone at the paper saying. At the age of thirty-five he was on the verge of breaking down. "I have not been well for some time," he told his father early in May. "There have occurred to me some symptoms of nervous prostration"—his vision was impaired, he was at home, sick in bed. A few days later, when he came to the railroad station to meet Josephine on her return from one of her rest cures, he "collapsed," as she told his father. There had been too many pressures at one time: the newspaper, his novel, Josephine's illness, and climaxing all of these, Steffens had just received what had to be regarded as nothing less than a summons to join *McClure's Magazine.*

"Because I know and trust you I would like to have you here with us as one of the family," John S. Phillips, the general manager of McClure's burgeoning enterprises, said. On the prompting of Steffens' friend and personal sponsor, Auguste F. Jaccaci, the magazine's art director, Phillips had sounded him out over a long lunch and then offered him the job of managing editor at a salary of $5,000 a year. "We want you as soon as you can possibly arrange to come,"

Phillips urged, "the sooner the better; in one week rather than two."
It was imperative for the magazine that its star writer, Ida M. Tarbell,
should be freed at once from her office duties as acting managing
editor. In the balance was a position on the commanding mass magazine of the decade, a magazine that, with a circulation of 360,000
copies a month, offered Steffens power and prestige of a new dimension for him. Against it stood Steffens' certainty that he was already
worn out and that "really the question to be decided now is whether
to be forever a journalist, a publisher (with the magazine people,
who want me for that), or an author." Josephine compounded the
difficulty of making a decision. "I think myself he is too artistic in
temperament to be a wage earner," she told Steffens' father. "He has
not those qualities, or perhaps that lack of qualities, which makes the
average American the patient plodder, and provider of his own and
others' living." Also, she was in the grip of a smoldering xenophobia,
one of her responses to illness, disappointment, and city life in general. She opposed the move to *McClure's*, "because of the quality of
the men it will throw him in with." She had Jaccaci and McClure
himself in mind—"an Italian mongrel and a spavin American, whose
work as well as his own he will be expected to do." He needed a rest
at any cost, she said. And so everything was in question, the present
as well as the future; and all signs, as Steffens told his father, pointed
to at least "a temporary retirement"—"the crisis of our lives is upon
us."

The immediate crisis, at any rate, was soon over. Ida Tarbell and
Phillips agreed to wait until the beginning of October for Steffens to
join the magazine; to fill in until then, they summoned from California another journalist who wanted to write novels, Ray Stannard
Baker. Steffens was to have the entire summer off, and he was going
to use the time not just to rest but also "to prove that I am a writer
as well as an editor." At the end of May, Cahan, Hutchins Hapgood,
and the others on the city staff gave him a farewell dinner at the
Press Club. A month later, after a visit to his family in California, he
and Josephine were on their way to a lakeside cabin near Old Forge
in the Adirondacks. "Then for the novel," he said, "and a quiet
summer."

In time Steffens came to remember only his exhaustion. He slept
twenty hours his first day by the lake, he said, and nineteen the
second, and then came the canoeing and the hiking: "Nothing but

Reality meant the city. ABOVE: Hester Street around 1888, shopping center of New York's Tenth Ward, the most densely settled area in the world. (*Brown Brothers*) OVERLEAF: The Steffens (formerly Gallatin) house in 1880, now the Governor's Mansion, corner of 16th and H streets, Sacramento. (*From Thompson and West's History of Sacramento County, Oakland, 1880*)

Joseph and Louisa Steffens,
Lincoln Steffens' parents.
(*Courtesy Jane Hollister
Wheelwright*)

Lincoln Steffens, University
of California, Class of 1889.
(*University of California
Archives, Berkeley*)

Josephine Bontecou Steffens
in 1891.

Fall and Redemption of Minneapolis

M^CCLURE'S MAGAZINE

FOR JANUARY 1903

PUBLISHED MONTHLY BY THE S. S. M^CCLURE CO., 141-155 E. 25TH ST., NEW YORK CITY

S. S. McClure. He said that the January 1903 issue of his magazine (the cover is shown opposite) was "the greatest success we have ever had." It featured muckraking articles by Steffens, Ray Stannard Baker, and Ida M. Tarbell. (*Brown Brothers*)

Two muckrakers: Ray Stannard Baker and Ida M. Tarbell. (*Culver Pictures, Inc.*)

ABOVE: "Little Point," Steffens' country house at Riverside, Conn. (*Courtesy Josephine Young Case*)

Lincoln Steffens
at Union Square,
New York, 1914.

Christian soldiers, marching as to war: the paladins of muckraking, exposure and reform as depicted by the humor weekly *Puck* in 1906. Lincoln Steffens, helmeted, sits astride the warhorse at the right. S. S. McClure carries a crossbow in the foreground. Joseph W. Folk of Missouri marches at the left.

Two of Steffens' protégés: Walter Lippmann (ABOVE) and John Reed (BELOW) as undergraduates at Harvard. (*Harvard University News Office*)

"The public man is the private man," Steffens said about Theodore Roosevelt, "and his friends have no advantage in acquaintance with him over strangers." (*Brown Brothers*)

Mabel Dodge in Florence (ABOVE) and Taos (BELOW): a mingling of Récamier, waif, Venus'-flytrap, and sorceress. (*The Bettmann Archive*)

Lincoln Steffens around 1915. (*University of California Archives, Berkeley*)

Woodrow Wilson, with French President Raymond Poincaré, rides in triumph through Paris, December 1918. (*Culver Pictures, Inc.*)

LINCOLN STEFFENS' DAY NURSERY FOR REVOLUTIONS

Two cartoons by Art Young: from *Good Morning* (ABOVE) and *New Masses* (BELOW)

"I HAVE SEEN THE FUTURE AND IT WORKS"
LINCOLN STEFFENS

U.S.S.R.

STEFFENS REPORTS ON HIS VISIT TO RUSSIA.

Steffens with Jo Davidson, Hotel Crillon, Paris, May 1919. (*Courtesy the late Burnet Hershey*)

The second Bullitt mission, November 1933: Franklin D. Roosevelt says goodbye to William C. Bullitt, Ambassador of the U. S. to the USSR. (*Wide World Photos*)

San Remo, Italy, 1925. Steffens and Ella Winter with Sinclair Lewis. (*Courtesy Harcourt Brace Jovanovich, Inc.*)

Carlsbad, Germany, 1926. Steffens with Jane Hollister, Pete Steffens, and Ella Winter. (*Courtesy Harcourt Brace Jovanovich, Inc.*)

With Pete Steffens, Carmel, California. (*Photo by Edward Weston*)

Ella Winter. (*Photo by Sonia Noskowiak*)

Watercolor by Boardman Robinson, 1932. (*Courtesy Jane Hollister Wheelwright*)

dreamless nights and dreamy days. . . . I never woke up till three of my agreed-upon four months of vacation were gone." And when he went to work at *McClure's* in the fall, he said, invoking the rituals of rebirth to suggest that he came to the next step in his career as if waking from a long dreamless sleep, it was like "diving into the lake —and life. The water was cold." As a matter of fact, however, the crisis of the spring was still going on. His novel remained a failure that he preferred to forget, and soon after he came to the magazine he began to suspect that perhaps he was no more cut out to be an editor than to be a novelist.

Yet Steffens did have something to show for that summer, a formulation of attitudes which prefigured the work that was to make his name. "It had better not circulate much in Sacramento if you are running for Mayor," he warned his father about a forthcoming article in the October *Ainslee's Magazine*, "since it is against the business man in politics." It was also "against" his father and his father's world.

"Politics is a business," he wrote. His argument was laconic and slashing:

> Politics is a business. That's what's the matter with it! That's what is the matter with everything—art, literature, religion, journalism, law, medicine—they're all business and all—as you see them. Make politics a sport, as they do in England, or a profession, as they do in Germany, and we'll have—well, something else than we have now, if we want it, which is another question. But don't try to reform politics with the banker, the lawyer and the drygoods merchant, for these are business men.

The politician was simply "a business man with a specialty," a man acutely responsive to the law of supply and demand, which was something the reformers always overlooked, Steffens said. "They not only offer to the majority what the minority alone asks for, but actually give more than the few want," just as Mayor Strong had done when he "not only cleaned the streets" but "cleaned the town also." That's how reform became "a drug on the market."

"The commercial sense of profit and loss" ruled American politics, Steffens continued in his bitter argument. He had allied himself with other American moralists, from Emerson and Henry Demarest Lloyd to Thorstein Veblen, who decried a business society that appeared to be opposed to culture and intellect, unresponsive to humane and distinterested considerations, which was corrupt and corruptive. ("The trail of the serpent," Emerson had said, "reaches into all the lucrative professions and practices of man.") "The Struggle for Self-Government," as Steffens was to call it a few years later, appeared to be a losing one in 1901, and since the people were fundamentally as unwilling as the Tsar's subjects to govern themselves, "it is worthwhile looking straight in the face the fact that there is no marketable commodity more easily cornered than the people themselves. The people are a crop that costs little to harvest, and not the ablest men in the country go into the business." Junkmen and saloon-keepers, some with rich and even sweet personalities when they started out in the small retail trade of precinct politics, were brutalized by wholesale commerce. That astute coal-and-iron tycoon, Marcus Alonzo Hanna of Ohio, who had just engineered William McKinley, a businessman's President, into the White House for a second term, had no interest in "issues" at all, Steffens said. "Issues" did not stand for convictions; they were just commodities like any other. (Hanna was "technically not in politics at all," Thomas Beer was to write. "He spent money on politicians.") What Hanna and other party bosses wanted, and what they succeeded in getting, was "the management of the American people in the interest of the American businessman for the profit of American business and politics."

On September 6, as he stood among potted palms and bay trees at the Pan-American Exposition in Buffalo, William McKinley, the businessman's President of a bull country, was shot by the anarchist Leon Czolgosz, self-appointed champion of the working class. For a week or so it seemed that the President might live after all; the stock market stumbled and then picked up again. "McKinley is better. I sold stock on the recovery Tuesday and may be sorry," Steffens wrote to his father from the Adirondacks: "Roosevelt as a president would cause almost a panic."

For half a year Roosevelt had fretted under McKinley, complained that in accepting the Vice-Presidency ("not a crime exactly," according to Mr. Dooley, but "kind of a disgrace—like writing anonymous letters") he had actually "taken the veil." He even thought of going back to his lawbooks so that he could pass the bar examinations when his term ran out. On September 14, the "wild man" and "damned cowboy" hated by Wall Street was sworn into office at the age of forty-two. He was a young man's President. Within the week Steffens had cut his vacation short, packed up his futile novel, and left his lakeside cabin to report for work at *McClure's*.

Even so, Steffens soon began to suspect that the pattern of his last year or two on the *Commercial Advertiser* was going to be repeated. Working for *McClure's Magazine* was a business, like everything else, as he saw it. In what he was doing there was little room for prestige and creation; the title of managing editor was far grander than the actual duties. In a loose, catch-all way, he had absorbed everybody else's drudgery, just as Josephine had warned. McClure was now freer to comb the world for ideas and Phillips to run the business of the magazine, while Ida Tarbell and Ray Stannard Baker were working as full-time staff writers. Steffens, who had been impatient with the routine work of a newspaper and still wanted to follow his own career as writer, was now a desk editor: he wrote letters, he received visitors, he oversaw schedules, he handled the numbing flow of other people's writing—articles on the Shakespeare-Bacon controversy and prison reform, on perpetual motion and cosmic energy, on the trusts and prison reform and the causes of blindness in babies. "My dear Sir," he wrote to Theodore Dreiser, "I am going to hold the manuscript until I hear from you in reply to this letter, which is a plea for a better handling of a thing that is worth the best you can do."

After a few months of this daily traffic he began to think of quitting *McClure's* in order to take over the editorship of a small paper in Greenwich, where he had bought some land. "I feel ready to do something really fine in my own profession when the time and opportunity arrive," he said. "But there is no hurry." He had sounded the same note of hollow confidence as a student in Europe. It had become as obvious to McClure as it was to Steffens that the new editor was too impatient with routine to make a reliable administrator and also, perhaps, too New York-bound for a national magazine. He needed education, Steffens himself admitted, to find out who their readers were and how "the world is wagging, so as to bring the magazine up to date." He was echoing one of McClure's mind-expanding lectures. "Each editor is to regard himself as the whole world," Steffens was to tell his protégé John Reed a few years later. "Whatever will interest him involuntarily (not as an editor, but as a human being) will interest the rest of us human beings. That's S. S. McClure's rule for his manuscript readers, and it is founded on sound psychology."

Ida Tarbell remembered Steffens affectionately as self-confident, fearless, "incredibly outspoken"; he was "the most brilliant addition to the *McClure's* staff in my time." Yet she also remembered that he seemed bewildered in the fevered atmosphere that prevailed whenever McClure came back from one of his foraging expeditions. In cyclonic appearances at the magazine office McClure summoned his staff and brought forth creative chaos out of order by loosing torrents of ideas, notes, clippings. These were all evidences from the seething world outside, and he wanted them rendered into articles. Passionately, often despairingly, he told his editors that a national magazine edited from a suite of rooms on East 23rd Street in New York City was a stale and dying thing. He was quick to recognize the drooping morale of his new editor and to prescribe a cure. "Get out of the office," McClure told Steffens in December 1901, "go to Washington, Newfoundland, California and Europe. Meet people, find out what's on, and write yourself." From now on Steffens was to be a writer, not a manager, and he was to do his editing in railway cars and by telegraph.

On a trip to Washington he observed from his position of confidence with Roosevelt the anomaly that compelled "the most powerful constitutional ruler on earth" to waste his energies keeping open house for citizens and petty officeholders. ("The strain is beginning to be felt," he wrote in the lead article in *McClure's* for April 1902; "even Theodore Roosevelt is often weary.") But it was not constitutional leaders who interested Steffens as he traveled from city to city that spring, talking to politicians, businessmen and editors in Kansas City, Topeka, Chicago, St. Paul, Minneapolis, Duluth, St. Louis, Louisville, Cincinnati, Toledo, Cleveland, Pittsburgh. It was the bosses and the wielders of invisible power. He decided that he wanted to write a series of articles on the government and misgovernment of cities. "If I should be entrusted with the work," he told Ida Tarbell, "I think I could make my name."

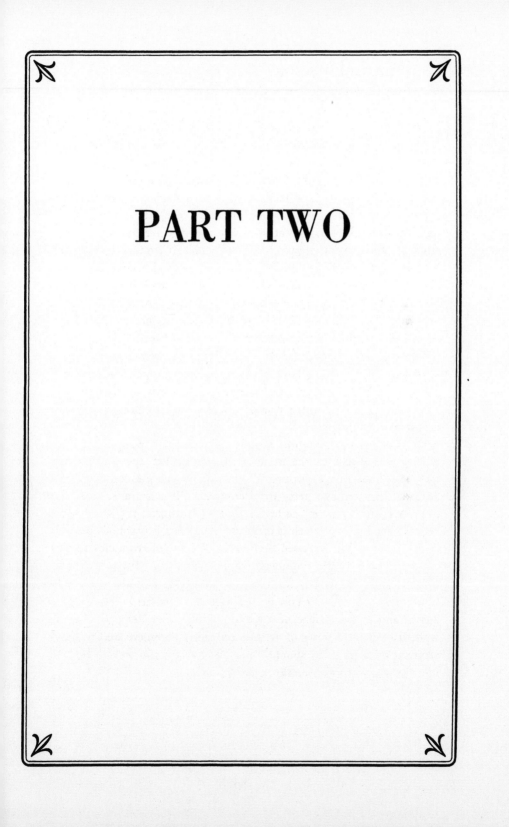

PART TWO

PART TWO

CHAPTER SIX

"American contempt of law"

I

"**M**cCLURE WAS RIGHT," STEFFENS was to tell an interviewer. "A man cannot be a successful editor who sits forever in his office." He had mapped out a route and then set out to discover the United States for himself, but wherever he went during the spring of 1902, it seemed, Steffens heard people talking and asking about one man. This was Joseph W. Folk, the young circuit attorney of St. Louis. He wired Folk for an appointment, took the sleeper from Chicago to St. Louis, and at noon the next day met him in a quiet corner of the lobby of the Planter's Hotel. At that moment, as it developed, Folk needed Steffens' help just as much as Steffens needed a story for his magazine.

"Mr. Folk really was an accident," Steffens was to write. Folk had become his city's chief law-enforcement officer by virtue of an alliance, as rare and fleeting as a transit of Venus, between reformers and machine politicians, and his entire subsequent career hinged on his chance reading of an item in a local newspaper. Within two years of their first meeting, and ultimately as a result of it, Steffens was the foremost political journalist of his day. He had been led, perhaps even driven, into muckraking by the work of exposure Folk had done in St. Louis. Largely because of Steffens' articles about him in *McClure's*, Folk was recognized nationally as "the champion prober" of boodlers, according to Mr. Dooley, who said that Folk pursued

103

his victims around the barn, back of the pig pen, and then into the house, where he pinned them with a pitchfork. Folk was elected governor of Missouri and for a while he even showed some promise of going all the way to the White House. "I wish you would tell Folk from me," McClure wrote to Steffens in 1903, "that he is the candidate of *McClure's Magazine* at the present moment for President." Within three years McClure was to publish four major articles, three of them by Steffens, about this new hero who reminded William Allen White of "the prince who broke through the thorn hedge and woke the sleeping castle."

Folk was thirty-two when Steffens met him, a reform Democrat and a former corporation lawyer who had made a success in his profession. He was thin-lipped and literal-minded, peremptory and impatient, even with the law itself. Some said that he was greedy for the spotlight, flirtatious, opportunistic, rigid, and self-seeking. He lacked color and verve, and even at the height of his popularity he inspired respect rather than love. In temperament he seemed hardly different from the other men whom Steffens had seen hitching their wagons to the star of reform and then going nowhere but out of office, always baffled by Boss Tweed's mocking challenge in the manner of Pilate, "What are you going to do about it?" That challenge was still to be answered, as Steffens (with McClure's help) acknowledged in the title of his first article about Folk, "Tweed Days in St. Louis."

St. Louis at the turn of the century was a demonstration of the worst that could happen to cities. In the forty years since the beginning of the Civil War its population had jumped from 160,000 to 600,000, making it the fourth largest of the nation's cities, but few of its agencies had kept pace with this growth. Spoilsmen flourished in the scramble and anarchy created by an outworn city charter. Franchises, concessions and public properties were openly traded, and from time to time the citizens heard of schemes to sell the city market, the courthouse, and the waterworks. Revenues flowed not into but past the city treasury, just as the Mississippi, flowing past the city, yielded the citizens for drinking water only a meager trickle, famously opaque and malodorous.

Other municipal services were no better. The "new" city hall could not, with much accuracy, be compared with Tweed's County Court House, which after ten years had cost the taxpayers of New

York $13,000,000 (the price of two Alaskas), but still it per-
sisted in remaining unfinished, the money for the interior walls
having been diverted to private uses along the way. Vermin infested
the city hospital and the courthouse. The streets were hummocky
and covered with garbage. Recently, St. Louis had been kept in
darkness for weeks pending payment of $175,000 in bribes. All in all
the situation was epitomized in the Tweed-like rejoinder which,
just before Folk came upon the scene, the Republican mayor, a
semiliterate, made to a group of citizens demanding street lighting in
their neighborhood, "You have the moon yet, ain't it? Well, what
more do you want?"

A former blacksmith, now several times a millionaire, had St.
Louis in his pocket. Edward Butler—Boss Butler—was a Democrat
who ran a bipartisan machine. By 1900, for a number of reasons,
including his determination to get his son elected to Congress, Butler
found it expedient to ally himself with a reform movement supported by the city's conservative businessmen. There was talk of "the
new St. Louis" and of a great exposition that, along with the Olym-
pic games of 1904, was to mark the centennial of the Louisiana Pur-
chase. In this climate of civic boosting Folk was elected circuit
attorney, and immediately after he took office he began a series of
prosecutions for election fraud. Still he was no maverick, as the
politicians were saying after this first scare died and Folk settled
down to routine business. He apparently was just what Butler had
believed him to be when he had him nominated, a "safe" candidate
whose promises to do his duty were part of the ritual of running for
public office and were to be received, White wrote, "strictly in a
Pickwickian sense." But Folk had only been biding his time.

His opportunity came one afternoon in January 1902, after he had
been in office a year. A newspaper reporter showed him a column-
and-a-half story in the St. Louis Star which, without naming names,
suggested there was a dispute going on between a group of city
legislators and a traction company over the passage of a street-
railway ordinance; at issue was the payment of a large sum of bribe
money that was supposed to be locked up in safe-deposit boxes at
two banks. Folk acted with the grim dispatch which was soon to
make him a figure of terror in St. Louis. Within an hour he gave
the sheriff a list of a hundred people to be summoned before the
grand jury. During the next few days Folk bluffed, bullied, and often

made threats that had no basis in law or fact. But he managed to force the president of the traction company to turn state's witness and bank officers to open locked boxes and turn over as evidence $135,000 in currency. The grand jury handed up indictments for bribery and perjury. Eventually Butler himself was arrested.

What Folk had done, said some observers who were reminded of the charge of the Light Brigade before Balaklava, was magnificent, but it wasn't politics. It did not show civic spirit either. Folk had no interest in the retail dealers in graft; instead, he went after the "better classes," the bankers, corporate officers, and businessmen. "Bribery is treason," Folk argued, "and the givers and takers of bribes are traitors." According to him, bribery was not random or local or a "mere felony," but part of a "revolutionary process" that was going on in all the cities and states. The problem of St. Louis, then, was really the problem of democracy; corruption anywhere and everywhere involved the transfer of power from the people to the powerful and made the visible government not much more than a ceremonial survival.

"When I set out to describe the corrupt systems of certain typical cities," Steffens was to write in 1903, "I meant to show simply how the people were deceived and betrayed. But in the very first study—St. Louis—the startling truth lay bare that corruption was not merely political; it was financial, commercial, social; the ramifications of boodle were so complex, various and far-reaching, that one mind could hardly grasp them, and not even Joseph W. Folk, the tireless prosecutor, could follow them all." At Folk's suggestion, Steffens had commissioned Claude Wetmore, a local newspaperman and author of South American adventure books, to write the story of the St. Louis exposures for the magazine. Then he headed back for New York. "It is too early to judge whether I achieved anything or not," he told Phillips after two days at the office. "I feel pretty well satisfied, and Mr. McClure wrote pleasantly to me about the reports I made him." Wetmore's manuscript, when it arrived at the end of June 1902, was a disappointment. Its author was an honest reporter, but he happened to live in St. Louis and he wanted to continue to live there. And so Wetmore steered a middle course, left out crucial names and facts, went easy on prominent citizens, went easy even on Butler, who was to come to trial that summer.

"I want this article taken seriously," Steffens told Phillips in desperation; and he rewrote it completely, sparing no local reputations, restoring Wetmore's diplomatic elisions, and introducing comparisons and parallels that related Folk and St. Louis to the larger context of a national problem and a theory of corruption. Wetmore objected. Why should he become a pariah in his own city? he asked. Steffens would have to sign the article along with him, he insisted, and bear the blame when, as it now seemed certain, the citizens of St. Louis would cry slander.

With "Tweed Days in St. Louis," published in *McClure's* for October 1902, Steffens made his bow as a philosopher of graft and as a muckraker. "I started our political muckraking," he said years later. It was a distinction that he was not alone and not altogether accurate in claiming. Nevertheless, "Tweed Days in St. Louis" represented a turning point for Steffens. McClure had sent his deskbound editor out to see the cities and the people, and the medicine had worked. At the age of thirty-six, Steffens at last defined himself in a way that reflected the imperatives as well as the accidentals of his personality and experience. He no longer signed himself Joseph Lincoln Steffens or J. L. Steffens, but instead—"for literary purposes," as he felt compelled to explain to his family—simply Lincoln Steffens, the final stage of an evolution: he had severed himself from his father in name and identity. Acting out of volition and necessity he had "chosen" (to the extent that it was a matter of choice) his distinctive mode, muckraking. Its innate mistrust of authority, constitutional fronts and concentrations of power, and its certainty that the reality was blacker than the appearance, corresponded to the unspoken assumptions of a boy on horseback, savage and would-be aristocrat. With "Tweed Days in St. Louis," the time, the place and the issue had joined.

It seemed that wherever Steffens now looked in the worlds of politics and business he could see signs of a restless, critical striving. In February 1902, to the consternation of J. P. Morgan and traders on the stock exchange, Theodore Roosevelt's Attorney General abruptly announced the government's intention to prosecute the Northern Securities Company, one of Morgan's creations, for violations of the Sherman Anti-Trust Act. "If we have done anything wrong," Morgan came to Washington to tell the President, "send your man to my man and they can fix it up." Morgan fumed, but Roosevelt declined to negotiate with him as if they were simply rival operators on Wall Street. With this decision died the conservative hope that for all his "radicalism" as governor of New York—his attacks on monopoly and "the wealthy criminal class," his commitment to social and labor reforms—Roosevelt would turn out to be Mark Hanna's President, in word and deed another McKinley. In July, Roosevelt was to speak out for public regulation of the trusts. It seemed that progressivism might be there to stay.

In May, John Mitchell, the thirty-two-year-old head of the United Mine Workers of America, called out his anthracite workers. Intellectuals and reformers like Henry Demarest Lloyd, pioneer muckraker and anatomist of monopoly, and the brilliant Boston lawyer Louis D. Brandeis declared their support of the strikers. What was at stake, they believed as they considered the terrible conditions the miners worked in as well as the terrible prospect of a winter coal famine, was not a private issue but the public interest. Mitchell himself was calm and dependable, somber, even ministerial, "a sound, conservative manager," Steffens wrote in *McClure's*, who had earned the respect of Wall Street and who sold his commodity, mine labor, in the same rational way Rockefeller sold oil and Havemeyer sold sugar. It had become time to question the stereotype of labor leaders as all horns, tail and bloodshed.

That summer and fall, while Roosevelt pondered his decision to intervene in the strike—not just break it, as his predecessors would have done—it had become harder than ever to believe what industrialist George Baer said in a letter that he regretted to the end of his days and that soon became part of American folklore. He had written that "the rights and interests of the laboring man will be protected and cared for—not by the labor agitators, but by the Christian men to whom God in His infinite wisdom has given the control of the property interests of the country."

McClure's responded to the critical temper of 1902. The October issue contained, in addition to Steffens' "Tweed Days in St. Louis," an editorial that announced the forthcoming publication of Ida Tarbell's serial *History of the Standard Oil Company*. "The public question which today stands first in interest, in importance, and in difficulty is that of the Trust," the announcement said—the Standard Oil Company was "one of the greatest and most far-reaching developments of our American civilization." The announcement enthusiastically promised that Miss Tarbell's series was "a great human drama, the story of thirty years of bitter, persistent warfare between the advocates of the two great commercial principles—competition and combination." That October another *McClure's* writer, Ray Stannard Baker, was out on assignment in the Pennsylvania anthracite fields and would soon report on the 17,000 workers who had refused to go out on strike; they were living in terror and starvation, having been closed out by Mitchell's United Mine Workers union just as the independents had been closed out by Standard Oil. McClure predicted that Baker's article, "The Right to Work: The Story of the Non-Striking Miners," would "undoubtedly be the most important publication of this winter."

From the start, there were a number of things about Steffens' work, however, that distressed and even angered McClure: his preoccupation with financial waste and political shenanigans, for one, and more than that, what appeared to be a blind prejudice against capitalism in general. One always had to distinguish between "organized capital" and "the sins of the capitalists," McClure argued, pointing to Baker's article, just as one had to distinguish between "unionism" and "the sins of the unionists."

The publisher had other grievances to air. "I have been thinking seriously of the attitude Steffens always takes in regard to the people, and I not only feel that he is wrong, but that such an attitude is discouraging," McClure wrote to John Phillips.

> In any event, the editorial policy of the magazine belongs to you and me. This is just as true of the editorial policy of the articles as it would be of editorials themselves. Steffens is not getting at the cause of the trouble by attributing it to cowardice on the part of the people, and therefore his articles will fail to help. The real cause of the trouble lies beyond them, in the passage of laws that render the people helpless. Steffens has a notion that the business man is a coward, and that the business man is to blame for political corruption, and he makes every fact bend to this notion. Now, he must disabuse himself of any predilections in the matter and write up things as they are.

On McClure's orders Steffens went back to Missouri with the assignment of writing a more even-handed sequel to "Tweed Days." He also was ordered to go to Minneapolis. There, said McClure, who had been following newspaper stories from the city for months, something "incomprehensible" had happened: a city of 200,000

Americans had actually voted criminals into office. McClure had a title ready, "The Shame of Minneapolis." He had a thesis, too, Steffens charged years later. "We had a pretty hot fight, and McClure won. What I went to Minneapolis to write was that democracy was a failure and that a good dictator was what is needed."

In October 1902, with "Tweed Days" being talked about everywhere, it seemed, Steffens was back in Missouri covering Folk's bribery prosecutions. Confident that he could do better outside St. Louis, Butler had won a change of venue to Columbia, seat of the state university and a couple of women's colleges. "What's the business of this town?" Butler had asked: "Education? That's a hell of a business." For all his cockiness, Butler was found guilty of bribery.

It seemed then, and for about a year after, until the conviction was set aside by the State Supreme Court, that Folk and Steffens had together won a great victory. A few weeks after Steffens' sequel, "The Shamelessness of St. Louis," appeared in the March 1903 *McClure's*, Folk reported that the tide of opinion had turned in their favor. "Nearly all of the daily papers have come to your view," he told Steffens, who, half a year earlier, had been denounced at a mass meeting as a liar. "Your article is bearing fruit. 'Folk Clubs' are being formed all over the city, and the state is commencing to speak. The machine is beginning to realize it has a big job on hand. I believe my theory and faith in the honesty of the majority will be justified." By the middle of April, enclosing a campaign button with his letter, Folk was asking Steffens to advise him in his campaign for the governorship of Missouri.

Steffens was a reform hero in St. Louis and, as a result of his Minneapolis article, something of a national celebrity. "The Shame of Minneapolis: The Rescue and Redemption of a City That Was Sold Out," published in *McClure's Magazine* for January 1903, was a stunning piece of revelational journalism. It described the intricate workings of a system of corruption that, Steffens wrote, "for deliberateness, invention, and avarice, has never been equalled." The Minneapolis bosses, as he showed, had franchised blackmail, theft, confidence games, crooked gambling and prostitution; they had, in fact, invited known criminals to come in and rob the people. No one could call him "liar" or cry "libel" this time: he had facts, figures, names, dates and documents enough to satisfy McClure himself.

At considerable risk, Steffens had obtained a key piece of evidence

that, until he reproduced it on the first page of his article, had been
known only to the Minneapolis grand jury. This was a ledger in
which the operators of a "big mitt" game—"swindling by means of a
stacked hand at stud poker"—recorded their earnings and also their
payments to city officials for the right to do business. Steffens then
tracked down the operators to their hiding place on the outskirts of
town and managed to coax from them an explanation of the ledger
entries. Finally, he linked his evidences together in a story that applied the lesson of Minneapolis to other American cities:

> Whenever anything extraordinary is done in American municipal
> politics, whether for good or for evil, you can trace it almost in-
> variably to one man. The people do not do it. Neither do the
> "gangs," "combines," or political parties. These are but instruments
> by which bosses (not leaders; we Americans are not led, but driven)
> rule the people, and commonly sell them out. But there are at least
> two forms of the autocracy which has supplanted the democracy
> here as it has everywhere it has been tried. One is that of the organ-
> ized majority by which, as in Tammany Hall in New York and the
> Republican machine in Philadelphia, the boss has normal control of
> more than half the voters. The other is that of the adroitly managed
> minority. The "good people" are herded into parties and stupefied
> with convictions and a name, Republican or Democrat; while the
> "bad people" are so organized or interested by the boss that he can
> wield their votes to enforce terms with party managers and decide
> elections. St. Louis is a conspicuous example of this form. Minne-
> apolis is another. Colonel Ed. Butler is the unscrupulous opportunist
> who handled the non-partisan minority which turned St. Louis into
> a "boodle town." In Minneapolis "Doc" Ames was the man.

Steffens went on to detail the story of Dr. Albert Alonzo
Ames, four-term mayor of Minneapolis; his brother Fred, who returned from army service to become Chief of Police; the Chief of
Detectives, a former gambler with contacts in the underworld; and
others who were put in charge of turning crime into a paying business for the Ames administration. "Even lawlessness must be regu-
lated," Steffens wrote.

> Dr. Ames, never an organizer, attempted no control, and his follow-
> ers began to quarrel among themselves. They deceived one another;
> they robbed the thieves; they robbed Ames himself. His brother be-

came dissatisfied with his share of the spoils, and formed cabals with captains who plotted against the administration and set up disorderly houses, "panel games," and all sorts of "grafts" of their own.

What finally wrecked the Ames machine was not internal dissension but a fearless opponent, a grand jury foreman named Hovey Clarke, who financed his own investigations, gathered his own evidence for the jury, and in effect took over the function of the public prosecutor. As a result of Clarke's work, Ames and his brother fled; others were caught and convicted largely on the testimony of criminals whom Clarke had bargained into turning state's evidence. During his short interim administration, the acting mayor, a well-to-do businessman, declined to cooperate with the gambling interests, and so there seemed to be some hope for Minneapolis, if no clear answers.

Can a city be governed without any alliance with crime? It was an open question. He had closed it only for the four months of his emergency administration. Minneapolis should be clean and sweet for a little while at least, and the new administration should begin with a clear deck.

"I ought to write to you that you have made a marvelous success of your Minneapolis article," McClure, completely won over this time, wrote to Steffens. "We fellows are so busy pushing things through that we don't stop to tell each other how much we think of each other's work. But I take this moment to tell you that you have been tremendously successful in this article." Glorious days seemed to be ahead for the magazine, for all of them. "I think it will probably arouse more attention than any article we have published for a long time."

II

FOR THE MOST PART, THE JANUARY 1903 *McClure's* CONTAINED WHAT subscribers and steady readers—about 365,000 each month—expected to find: four fiction pieces, a travel article about Abyssinia, an essay on careers versus marriage, a report on the work of a Viennese orthopedic surgeon, some vignettes and appreciations of English men of letters, a scattering of verse, many illustrations. Still, this single issue, from its frontispiece portrait of John D. Rockefeller to the editorial on the last page of text, was to be a controlling document in the history of journalism.

More than a third of the January magazine was given over to three carefully documented, soberly composed, and totally credible indictments (as they seemed) of life in a democracy: Lincoln Steffens' "The Shame of Minneapolis" (the lead article); Ida M. Tarbell's "The Oil War of 1872" (a chapter from her Standard Oil history); and Ray Stannard Baker's "The Right to Work: The Story of the Non-Striking Miners."

"How many of those who have read through this number of the magazine," the editorial asked, "noticed that it contains three articles on one subject? We did not plan it so; it is a coincidence that the January *McClure's* is such an arraignment of American character as should make every one of us stop and think." That subject was "The American Contempt of Law":

> All together, these articles come pretty near showing how universal is this dangerous trait of ours. Miss Tarbell has our capitalists conspiring among themselves, deliberately, shrewdly, upon legal advice, to break the law so far as it restrained them, and to misuse it to restrain others who were in their way. Mr. Baker shows labor, the ancient enemy of capital, and the chief complainant of the trusts' unlawful acts, itself committing and excusing crimes. And in "The Shame of Minneapolis" we see the administration of a city employing criminals to commit crimes for the profit of the elected officials, while the citizens—Americans of good stock and more than average culture, and honest, healthy Scandinavians—stood by complacent and not alarmed.

The articles had shown "capitalists, workingmen, politicians, citizens—all breaking the law, or letting it be broken," while lawyers and judges, the churches and the colleges stood by, either compliant or uncomprehending. "Who is left to uphold it?"

> There is no one left; none but all of us. Capital is learning (with indignation at labor's unlawful acts) that its rival's contempt of law is a menace to property. Labor has shrieked the belief that the illegal power of capital is a menace to the worker. These two are drawing together. Last November when a strike was threatened by the yardmen on all the railroads centering in Chicago, the men got together and settled by raising wages, and raising freight rates too. They

made the public pay. We all are doing our worst and making the public pay. The public is the people. We forget that we all are the people; that while each of us in his group can shove off on the rest the bill of to-day, the debt is only postponed; the rest are passing it on back to us. We have to pay in the end, every one of us. And in the end the sum total of the debt will be our liberty.

McClure and his writers had reached a sore point in the public mind and hastened the arrival of one of its cyclic moods of uneasiness, self-criticism, and indignation bordering on paranoia. Their articles confirmed a chronic though covert suspicion of concentrated power and wealth, and stirred fears of exploitation, disenfranchisement, conspiracy. The reader of *McClure's* for January 1903 now had what appeared to be evidence that he was steadily losing political and economic power and was fair game for labor as well as capital, two power blocs that, as Ray Stannard Baker said in a chilling phrase, were learning "to hunt together."

"I doubt whether any other magazine published in America ever achieved such sudden and overwhelming recognition," Baker has written. "We had put our finger upon the sorest spots in American life." The January number sold out almost immediately. From Washington, Roosevelt wrote to compliment McClure on his triumph and invite him to the White House, thus announcing the brief marriage—it was to last a little over three years—of muckraking and the Square Deal.

McClure no longer had reason to complain that his editors were isolated from the real news and the real temper of the country. Prodded and trained by him, they had demonstrated that journalism could be both dramatic and painstaking and that a magazine motivated by what Ida Tarbell called "righteous indignation" could serve the public and also make money. McClure wanted accuracy above all, he said, and to get it he claimed that he had to invent "a new method in magazine journalism"—he paid his staff writers "for their study rather than for the amount of copy they turned out," and in time they became authorities on their subjects: Tarbell on the trusts and giant corporations, Baker on the railroads, labor, and race relations, and Steffens on city, state and federal government.

McClure exulted over the January issue. "The greatest success we have ever had," he declared; and he foresaw a "great boom" for the magazine in months to come. Contrary to his expectations, contrary also to the legend and even the history of muckraking, the circulation of *McClure's* did not rocket; it recouped a loss, but at the end of a year the average monthly circulation was down slightly. What did show a spectacular increase was the amount of space that rivals and imitators—*Collier's, Cosmopolitan, Everybody's,* and other popular magazines—were soon giving to what was grandly called "the literature of exposure." Month after month, said Baker, the public "would swallow dissertations of ten or twelve thousand words without even blinking—and ask for more." By 1912 the "literature of exposure" had grown by nearly two thousand articles.

Magazines in the old days were very calming to the mind, said Mr. Dooley, whose creator, Finley Peter Dunne, was the comic philosopher of muckraking. "Angabel an' Alfonso dashin' f'r a marriage licence. Prom'nent lady authoresses makin' poems at the moon. Now an' thin a scrap over whether Shakespeare was enthered in his own name or was a ringer, with the long shot players always agin' Shakespeare. But no wan hurt. . . . But now," Dooley went on, "whin I pick me fav-rite magazine off th' flure, what do I find? Iverythin has gone wrong. Th' wurruld is little betther thin a convict's camp." There seemed to be nothing to read about but graft and crime. "An' so it goes," he said, "till I'm that blue, discouraged, an' brokenhearted, I cud go to th' edge iv th' wurruld an' jump off. It's a wicked, wicked, horrible, place, an' this here counthry is about th' toughest spot in it."

Muckraking, in its most general sense the investigation and exposure of wrongdoing, was as old as the expulsion from the Garden. During America's Gilded Age Henry Adams laid bare the workings of Wall Street and the Grant administration and Henry Demarest Lloyd wrote his pioneering exposé of Standard Oil. But in the main these were isolated ventures. What was new in 1903 was that muckraking served as leading edge of a political movement, progressivism, and that in place of the select group of readers Adams and Lloyd addressed in *North American Review* and *Atlantic Monthly* there now existed a mass audience created in part by an unexampled national prosperity and by a revolution in printing, publishing and communication technology.

In time muckraking entered a sort of Silver Age, and then, despite increasingly gothic revelations, readers began to suspect that there was less going on than met the eye. They had heard "Wolf" cried too often, and, prompted in part by Theodore Roosevelt's amply publicized change of heart in 1906, some began to say that muckraking was just another form of bread and circuses, probably useless if not downright unpatriotic. But during the five years or so following McClure's triumph scarcely an aspect of the national life escaped the harshest scrutiny. Government on all levels, business, finance, labor, race relations, urban life, the penal system—all were weighed and found wanting by magazines which each month had a combined circulation of over three million copies and which, on occasion, might reach twenty million families. To the extent that it created an informed and aroused citizenry, muckraking made things happen: new laws and regulations, new electoral procedures, social legislation, conservation measures, improved food and drug standards, wage and hour reforms, and, in general, a movement toward a publicly accountable system of social and governmental controls.

The muckrakers themselves achieved much of what they had set out to do: writing a literature of intense concern; applying art and science to present realities; recording not the official but the true, intimate history of their era. In doing this, they introduced a new range of characters and subject matter. Bosses, politicians, traction tycoons, cops, ward heelers, bagmen, manufacturers of tainted baking powder and addictive patent medicines, meat packers, quacks, gamblers, captains of industry, crooks, reformers—all of these and more, displaying only what Mark Twain called "that natural expression of villainy which we all have," were viewed in their native habitats of oil refineries, slums, red-light districts, city halls, saloons, sausage factories, cheap hotel rooms—settings that everybody recognized but nobody had really written about before in a family magazine.

It was only when the January 1903 issue of McClure's was about to go to press, Baker said, that the editors realized that three articles dealt with the same general subject, "The American Contempt of Law." But the editorial disclaimer—"We did not plan it so; it is a coincidence"—was candid chiefly in the sense that no one there had known much in advance that the articles would all be ready to run at the same time. According to the life patterns of McClure and his writers, the January issue represented a series of convergences which, in retrospect, even give it a certain predestined character.

Periodical journalism before McClure's time—venerable magazines like *Harper's, The Century, Atlantic Monthly*—spoke mainly for the values and culture of the Eastern seaboard. McClure and his group were outlanders. Their links to the vanished frontier and the struggle for economic survival were fresh and strong. During his boyhood in Indiana McClure's widowed mother had worked as a live-in domestic. When Ida Tarbell was born in a log house in Pennsylvania, her father was on his way to Iowa, looking for open land and a farm. Later, as an independent in Titusville, he and his partner had fallen victim to Standard Oil; the partner shot himself, and Franklin Tarbell went into debt. Baker was born in Michigan. His father, bankrupt as merchant and manufacturer, had gone west just as Steffens' father did when he rode across the plains from Illinois to find a clerkship in San Francisco. "He did not know, and neither did I as a boy," Baker wrote about his father, "that we were living on the 'last frontier.' There was no longer anywhere in America, or indeed in the world, for the ambitious or the discontented to go for free land, free forests, free rivers, for free opportunity." McClure and his writers, in an era when the average American did not go beyond the fifth grade in school, had all gone to college, but the colleges they went to—Knox, Allegheny, Michigan State, Berkeley—were remote from the East in spirit as well as in place.

The great depression that began in 1893 and lasted for about four years had the same formative meaning for Steffens' generation that a later, longer depression had for the generation coming to social awareness in the 1930s. The depression of 1893 dramatized corporate irresponsibility, the appalling gap between the rich and the poor, the failure of government to regulate an economy run wild. Instead of old, scattered patterns of reform it encouraged the rough and inconsistent unity of progressivism. Steffens, Baker, and Ida Tarbell were all starting out as writers in 1893, and that June, when the bottom fell out of the stock market and panic spread westward from Wall Street, S. S. McClure published the first number of his magazine.

Middle class, middle American, impatient with traditional wisdom, McClure and his writers shared a number of interests with each other and with other muckrakers. They revered sociology and science, but their stance and rhetoric were moralistic, evangelical, millennial, and echoed the pulpit as much as the laboratory, the lecture hall and the soapbox. Scolded by a critic for his "Jesus complex," Upton Sinclair replied, almost gratefully, that "the world needs a Jesus more than it needs anything else." His answer was consistent with the fact that the muckrakers claimed Jesus as the greatest of their remote antecedents, frequently cited Luther and among their immediate antecedents claimed W. T. Stead, the English editor and reformer who wrote *If Christ Came to Chicago*, a book that preached the social gospel and was published in the year of the great panic.

Many of the muckrakers had been exposed in childhood to the gospel Christianity represented by Steffens' grandfather and by Martha Neely, who wanted the boy to be a preacher. McClure's parents belonged to an evangelical sect called The Brethren, Baker was brought up on "the stern old Presbyterian Bible," and Ida Tarbell had knelt at the mourners' bench as a girl and knew herself to be a sinner. Such experiences left their mark even on the secularized adult. "Physical escape from the embraces of evangelical religion did not mean moral escape," wrote Frederic C. Howe, the urban reformer who was Steffens' close friend and ally.

> From that religion my reason was never emancipated. By it I was conformed to my generation and made to share its moral standards and ideals. It was with difficulty that realism got lodgment in my mind; early assumptions as to virtue and vice, goodness and evil remained in my mind long after I had tried to discard them.

Having settled in their minds the rival claims of Darwinism and orthodox religion, the muckrakers came to their work with a profound antagonism toward doctrinal and institutionalized Christianity (one favored target was Trinity Church in New York, the city's largest single owner of slum and whorehouse properties), but with a high moral and ethical purpose that they associated with the Prophets and the Apostles. Steffens' declared purpose in muckraking the cities was to awaken their Christian conscience, their *shame;* later, he and other critics of muckraking came to believe that the ultimate effect of these exposures and appeals had been simply to make the cities ashamed, not to make them better. The muckrakers yearned to find Christian solutions to social problems and believed in the practical utility of the Golden Rule. They also had a dangerous passion for strong leaders to bring Israel out of the house of bondage and to cast out moneychangers and devils. "Whenever anything extraordinary is done in American municipal politics, whether for good or for evil, you can trace it invariably to one man," Steffens (and McClure) concluded from the experience of muckraking Minneapolis. That one man often placed himself above the law, scorned codes, charters, the established legislative, electoral, and judicial process. In this respect, although they were dealing with "The American Contempt of Law" or (another *McClure's* catch phrase) "the degradation of Christian Citizenship," the muckrakers could be complicitly lawless: they recognized that democracy was slow to purge or reverse itself, and consequently they often looked with favor on strong men who set themselves above the law.

To the extent that one can speak of them collectively, the muckrakers stood at Armageddon, battling for the Lord, and in their dedication to moral absolutes they tended to see political and economic problems in terms of a timeless struggle for man's soul and to pay insufficient attention to the shifting character of institutions as institutions. They and their political counterparts spoke with fine theological inexactitude of sin, guilt, redemption, conversion, adopted revivalist techniques and were often grossly overoptimistic—the muckrakers expected too much of muckraking by itself alone. When Theodore Roosevelt decided that the time had come for him to part company with his journalistic allies, it was altogether fitting that he should go to a common well of inspiration, John Bunyan's *Pilgrim's Progress*, for his attack on the "Man with the Muckrake."

"Politics is a business," Steffens had written before coming to *McClure's*. "That's what's the matter with it! That's what is the matter with everything." Even in his first articles about St. Louis and Minneapolis this remained hardly more than an antipathy: "business" was something distasteful. As Upton Sinclair was to tell him, Steffens simply had not thought his data through to their logical (or ideological) conclusion; according to Sinclair, Steffens should have been able to see that the profit system was self-poisoning and that only socialism would work. Like the other principal muckrakers, Steffens began at *McClure's* relatively innocent of social or political theory and of any conscious left impulse except in the sense that not being "right"—not "celebrating things as they are," in C. Wright Mills's phrase—he could conceivably be described as "left."

As a group, McClure and his writers were centrists, like their hero Theodore Roosevelt, and beyond momentary indignations they had no serious designs on the existing order. Muckraking, McClure said, "was the result of merely taking up in the magazine some of the problems that were beginning to interest the people." Businessmen, bankers and solid citizens read and trusted *McClure's*, not only because it was generally reliable, but also because they believed that the magazine's target was the flagrant abuses within the system, not the system itself. The implicit achievement of muckraking, as Steffens later suggested, was actually to strengthen the system by alerting it to its own vulnerabilities. According to this view, muckraking was a fundamentally middle-class, loyalist strategy, despite dramatic appearances to the contrary; and its net effect was comparable to that of administering underdoses of antibiotics: warned and inured, the hostile organism becomes stronger than ever. "Th' noise we hear is not th' first gun iv a rivolution," said Mr. Dooley in the heyday of muckraking. "It's only th' people iv th' United States batin' a carpet." This social rug beating, according to one plausible interpretation, left political capitalism more secure than ever.

Steffens and his group were a home-grown product, as indigenous as Apaches and almost as isolated from ideology of any sort and from any countertradition to industrialism and the commercialization of American life. They tended to use conspiratorial personifications such as "the system," "the invisible empire," "the invisible government," "the Beast," "the interests," but this lexicon might have suited William Jennings Bryan just as well. What passed for a common body of theory and belief was a cracker-barrel mixture of the meliorism, service ethic, and Christian principles of the social gospel and values of the Republic traditionally attributed to the Founding Fathers. One could also detect traces of Abolitionist fervor, populist outrage, recollections of the Haymarket Square riots in Chicago, Homestead, Pullman, the Panic and Coxey's Army. In Steffens and a few others there were also elements of Debsian socialism and of another potent force that for a while seemed to be the wave of the future, the Single Tax creed of Henry George and his followers.

What Steffens conspicuously shared with McClure, Baker and Tarbell was not political belief; instead, it was a literary tradition that had begun to crystallize in the 1880s and 1890s and that brought these writers to politics, broadly defined. McClure, who had once made a stab at writing fiction, saw himself as a businessman-editor who shared the taste of the millions and was therefore able to anticipate and feed it. Still, he was as aware as any literary intellectual of what would soon be called critical realism. "It seems to me,"

McClure wrote, "that the scientific spirit of the times, when applied to literature, means a study of current product. By studying the present you see the animal growing, you see it developing. . . . You have the fun and the excitement of watching the gradual growth and the tendencies of the times." McClure had just founded a syndicate whose function, he said, was to "make the modern newspaper a complete and artistic reflex of modern life" by furnishing editors with the "results of the intellectual progress of the world."

Steffens, Ida Tarbell and Baker had all made the same commitments both to "the scientific spirit" and to literature when McClure recruited them for his magazine. Steffens, his work with Wundt and Charcot behind him, was working on short stories about slum life and a novel about police corruption. Ida Tarbell had planned to be a biologist and work with a microscope; her first article for McClure dealt with Louis Pasteur and the Pasteur Institute. Baker, an accomplished science reporter who wrote the first authoritative account of Marconi's wireless telegraph, had started a novel, but he was nagged by the suspicion that in order to write it he needed to know a great deal more about American business than he did. He was also nagged, as he remembered, "by the dissatisfaction I sometimes felt in trying to write fiction when the world seemed literally on fire with critical, possibly revolutionary movements." He believed that his mission as a writer was to make people "see and think, and thus fit them for living."

Would critical realism answer the question that paralyzed Henry Adams, a muckraker in Grant's Washington? How does one write "literature" about business and politics, two controlling institutions from which American intellectuals were alienated and excluded? What opportunities were there, in the age of McKinley and Roosevelt any more than in the age of Ulysses Grant, for the creative interplay of art, intellect and reality? The *McClure's* group of 1903 saw the answer in a concept of literature at truthtelling, as a way of applying science to experience. In their work a vagrant strain of grass-roots dissent and suspicion of authority fused with a definition of naturalism as a life force in literature and advocacy as a life force in journalism.

Just before "Tweed Days in St. Louis" came out, Steffens had a visit at the *McClure's* office from Brand Whitlock, one of the coming heroes of the progressive era. Whitlock, the son of a Methodist circuit rider and church elder, had thus far managed to combine literature and politics. His novel *The Thirteenth District*, also published in 1902, dealt with a political reformer who sold out the cause for a seat in the House of Representatives. Whitlock, former secretary to the fiery governor of Illinois, John Peter Altgeld, would soon be elected mayor of Toledo.

"I am going to do a series of articles for the magazine on municipal government," Steffens told him, and he joked that he knew nothing about municipal government—"That's why I'm going to write about it." In later years they would talk politics, but that afternoon, Whitlock recalled, "We had more interesting things to discuss." They talked about Mark Twain, whom they admired, despite his public love affair with the plutocracy, for his "right-mindedness" and "perfect Americanism," for his "democracy," his attacks on imperialism and colonialism.

They talked about William Dean Howells, whom Whitlock had just visited at Kittery Point, Maine. Howells had pleaded for clemency for the Haymarket anarchists and, at some risk to his standing in polite letters, had fought for Zola, when Zola was taboo in America, and for the young realists, among them Stephen Crane. They talked about Joseph Conrad, whose novels Steffens had been reading with an overwhelming sense of discovery. "He has seen everything," Steffens exclaimed, anticipating the direction of his own work and of the muckrakers as a group, "and he can tell it."

CHAPTER SEVEN

The Shame and Promise of the Cities

I

Do WE AMERICANS REALLY WANT GOOD GOVERNMENT?" Steffens asked in *McClure's*. "Do we know it when we see it?" His own observations, published during 1903 in six powerfully argued articles, suggested that the answer to both questions often was no.

Pittsburgh, which for some time had been describing itself as "Hell with the lid off," was now "angry and ashamed," he reported. It had shaken off the rule of one ring, but then another ring had taken over; the city tried to free itself, and so far it had failed. Philadelphia was no longer even trying; it was "corrupt and contented." Self-government there was dead, reform broken in spirit, a controlling oligarchy so firmly established in power that "nothing but a revolution" could recapture the city for the citizens. Under a reform boss Chicago was "half free and fighting on" (fifty years later an alderman greeted the election of Mayor Richard Daley with the observation, "Chicago ain't ready for reform yet"). Under Mayor Seth Low, the former silk merchant and president of Columbia University, New York had seen two years of honest administration. But in November 1903, Tammany took over the city once again.

For Steffens himself, 1903 had been a year of anxieties and quarrels. As a result of his Minneapolis article, a libel suit hung over the magazine, brought by a former county prosecutor who objected to being called a "politician." There was every prospect now, McClure grumbled, that "this man will stick us for at least two thousand dollars before we are through with him." The suit turned out to be a false alarm, but it had put a permanent fright into McClure. "Steffens' articles must never be rushed," he was soon telling Phillips. "His articles are far and away the most terrible stuff we can handle. The material is necessarily full of dynamite."* As far as Steffens could judge, McClure was more autocratic than ever. "I am not ordering you to go to Philadelphia at once and leave Pittsburgh," the publisher told him at one point, "but I am telling you what we think is best." Steffens' refractory answer to this was to stay put in Pittsburgh.

When McClure lectured Steffens directly there was a galling hint of the schoolmaster dealing with a backward student. "You must always remember that pictures are just as essential as text, and while you are collecting materials for the text collect pictures also," McClure told him in November 1902. Two months later there was another lecture. "Your narrative lacks force because you do not give proper emphasis to the things that should be emphasized," McClure said, and he recommended that Steffens study "the ideal method of writing . . . pursued by Alexander Dumas in his great D'Artagnan romances." Impatient with criticism, becoming prickly under accumulating pressures, Steffens clearly needed delicate handling if he was to go on with his work for *McClure's*. "We are paring it down to general points," Phillips wrote to him when the Pittsburgh manuscript came in; there were too many details, the story was too com-

---

* McClure and his muckrakers lived with the constant threat of lawsuits and were forced to devise certain defensive tactics. "Don't shoot all your ammunition at the first attack," Steffens told another journalist. "Hold back a few of the most damning facts. When the man you're after reads your stuff in print, he'll either feel relieved to find you haven't told the worst, or will be disposed not to start anything for fear you will find it out." McClure himself took a somewhat similar position. "When *McClure's* calls Tom Platt a moral leper," he once said, "*McClure's* understates the facts." The magazine had, in fact, called Platt a moral leper, and worse, and got away with it. William Allen White described him as "a dwarf on stilts," "a manifest type of hundreds of earthworms," a "senile," "cold-blooded, mousey, fidgety little man" driven by an insatiable appetite for "vengeance" and "the guile of politics." Platt's threat of "a libel suit for six figures" terrified White into a nervous breakdown but never came to anything. (Will Irwin, *The Making of a Reporter.* New York, 1942, p. 150. Ellery Sedgwick, *The Happy Profession.* Boston, 1946, p. 138. William Allen White, "Platt," *McClure's Magazine,* December 1901, pp. 144-53. William Allen White, *Autobiography.* New York, 1946, pp. 347-48.)

plicated to follow. "My dear Steffens," he added soothingly, "please trust me in this matter and don't worry about the article. I am not going to damage it severely. I shall handle it with great tenderness, though perhaps from your standpoint with considerable rigor. I shall make the operation as aseptic as possible."

With summer came other abrasions. After Philadelphia, Steffens had planned to move on to Boston. Here was "a virgin and rich field," he was assured by one of the editors of the Boston *Herald*. The people of this venerable city were simply "asleep," the editor said; and as for the rich and the influential, they were "almost totally lacking in public service." Here, it seemed, was the perfect situation in which to test a hypothesis Steffens had evolved in Philadelphia: that corruption was a function of age and not, as Godkin, Bryce and other patricians believed, part of the growing pains of lusty young cities like Chicago. If Steffens was right, Boston and Philadelphia only foretold the future of the others. But McClure, quite properly, was afraid that readers would tire of what now promised to be a steady diet of hopelessness. In place of Boston he held out for Chicago, which was at least fighting; and Steffens went, but only after another bout with McClure. Weren't they selling the truth short, or at least softening the truth, Steffens demanded, simply in order to sell more magazines? McClure answered him with unmistakable finality. "In regard to the point you have raised both in conversation and in your letter, as to how we shall not abuse our new-found power, all that matter you can trust absolutely to me. I do not believe that I will go wrong."

McClure was not often so imperturbable in his dealings with Steffens. The phrase "Enemies of the Republic," one of the editor's brilliant reductions of a complex situation to slogan size, had nearly been lost to the magazine by Steffens, who planned to credit it to Folk. McClure stopped him abruptly, warning of "a serious disaster." "The invention of that phrase I count as a most important thing," McClure told him. "I have a feeling of jealousy for *McClure's Magazine* very much like what the lioness has for her cubs." Close to one of his periodic breakdowns, McClure went abroad hoping to build up his strength for 1904—"the greatest year in our history," he predicted. "The only thing I ask of you this summer," he wrote to Steffens from London, "is not to subject me to any disagreeable surprises." A week later McClure was in a rosier mood. "I must tell you how tremendously pleased I am with your achievements, and with your plans for the future. I know of no young man who has such splendid opportunity of work in front of him as you have."

One such opportunity was unveiled to Steffens by Theodore Roosevelt, who, Steffens explained with satisfaction, "had resented my impersonal attitude toward him." Roosevelt, in fact, had reason to feel that this former confidant and present molder of public opinion had gone far beyond impersonality: here he was, booming a Democrat, Folk, as national hero and Presidential candidate, and following the trail of corruption into Republican cities. The President, Steffens told his father, "has asked me to write the most important things that are to be said next year; the account of his fight with capital and with labor. I was down to see him last week with Mr. McClure. We spent the evening, from nine o'clock to after midnight, going over the whole situation, and the next morning he gave an hour to going over with me the correspondence and documents that may be used."

Perhaps Roosevelt was too much in control for the article to have the objectivity that McClure liked to insist on. At any rate, the publisher soon had second thoughts. Earlier in the year he had planned to send Steffens abroad to write an article for which McClure already had a title, "If Tammany Came to London." Now he decided that the main work in front of Steffens for 1904 was to be a new series on American corruption, this time on the state level and with McClure's cherished title, "Enemies of the Republic." In March, McClure's book-publishing house was to issue the first series as *The Shame of the Cities*. Steffens could see a decisive year ahead of him. "I have to 'make good' once [and] for all," he told his father. "I feel that it is to be the crisis of my career."

Already he had a powerfully divided sense of how it felt to make good in America as a critic of the strategies and tactics of making good. "Somehow it scares me," he said about his success. In the correspondence and editorial columns of a thousand newspapers he could see his phrases cited day after day: everyone, it seemed, was talking about "the System." "You are the man best qualified to do it," the editors of *Collier's* urged. They wanted him to address himself to the question, Are we a nation of grafters? "If you ever think of making a change or if you care for money," a visiting London editor told him, "my own people will give you whatever you want either as a writer or as an editor." In recognition both of Steffens' work and of his new bargaining power in a competitive market, McClure had just given him a substantial raise, and there was even some talk now of starting a new magazine which he would edit and partly own.

Another career had opened. He was in demand as a speaker; he had invitations from all over the country. Undergraduates at Princeton and Harvard asked him to speak to them "along the lines of your recent *McClure's* articles." The president of Steffens' own university invited him to give a summer course of lectures at Berkeley on "the mechanism of present-day politics, or the present social situation, or anything you might choose to call it." He would be in distinguished company, Wheeler assured him. "A course of lectures by you on the topics such as I have suggested would fit in finely with the work in American History which is to be given by Professor [Frederick Jackson] Turner of Wisconsin, who is altogether the best man in the country in his field." On another level of recognition altogether there were several letters from a tobacco concern asking for permission to name a cigar after Steffens and to put his face and signature on the box. There were Roosevelt cigars already, even though the President did not smoke. Folk was on a label. So were Boss Platt, Henry George, Speaker Cannon of the House of Representatives, the actress Lillian Russell, and various heroes of the late war with Spain. "If you will only keep hammering the rogues a little longer," the cigar people persisted with Steffens, "it will not be long before we will be able to make you *truly famous*." Josephine enjoyed the humor of the situation. "Here is fame!" she said.

Often, though, she was troubled by what she believed was a self-deluding habit of his: in accounting for his success he made questionable claims to moral purism. "I won it without a sacrifice, without one single compromise," he protested—protested too much, for her taste. He had won success in a world of gain and loss, competition and self-serving, and that same world, along with its intricate code of incentives and strategies, was also his subject, his passion almost to the exclusion of others. Yet he believed that he remained disinterested through all of this, free of jealousy and competitive spirit, motivated in his craft by what he called "the art spirit." At the Holly House in Cos Cob, where on summer visits he lived in upper bohemia with painters and writers, "we talked art," he remembered, "and we had a contempt for people who talked business and politics." The spirit of the Holly House was reflected in the cut of his clothes, his beard, his flowing tie. "I am an artist, not a believer in issues," he told Mayor Tom Johnson when they first met in Cleveland. "I am writing as an artist."

Josephine now spent relatively little time with her celebrated husband as he traveled about on assignments or speaking tours. Still, beyond her function as his manager and professional adviser, she managed to play a more decisive role in his life than he was, at first, willing to acknowledge. Unbeguiled by talk of "the art spirit," she looked with a cool, unhooded eye on the cycle of competition and success. She served as the muckraking force in his internal affairs. Because of her, one particular occasion, trivial and impersonal on the face of it, became, as far as Steffens was concerned, invested with the urgency of revelation and religious conversion. Until his eyes were opened, he later confessed, he had been merely "righteous." "With all my growing contempt for good people, I was one of them. Unconsciously I wanted to be one of them." But after the crisis was over, he said, "I was never again mistaken for an honest man by a crook. . . . The politicians, the big, bad ones and the little, intelligent ones, they and the consciously corrupting business leaders have ever since acted with me upon the understanding that I was one of them. It facilitated my work; it explains much of my success in getting at the facts of a situation."

In Chicago, Steffens had turned up and then passed on to the others at *McClure's* evidences of collusion in the building trades between contractors and the labor unions. He also suggested that since similar things appeared to be going on in New York, *McClure's* had the basis for a major national story. As a result, Steffens claimed, Ray Stannard Baker wrote two sensational articles, "Capital and Labor Hunt Together" and "The Trust's New Tool—The Labor Boss"; readers scarcely had to go past the titles to thrill with fear and horror. Moreover, the timing of Baker's two articles put Steffens at a disadvantage. The first preceded by a month and overshadowed Steffens' own article about Chicago; Baker's second ran against Steffens' article about New York.

> When I got home [Steffens wrote in his *Autobiography*] my wife remonstrated with me for "giving away my ideas." I had not thought of that. My answer to her was that it didn't matter who wrote the

article; the important thing was to get the idea out. I was not only an article-writer; I was an editor, and—and, besides, Baker and my colleagues knew it was my idea. "Nonsense," she said; "Baker will never remember from whom he got the subject," and she invited him to dinner and asked him how he came to write that article. He told her the genesis of it, with no mention of me! She won, smiled, and I felt—yellow; whether with jealousy of Baker or humiliation at the defeat by my wife, I don't know. It was an old cause of friction between her and me: my habit of "telling all I knew" and her insistence upon my "career." The incident made me feel mean.

He had to acknowledge that, contrary to all his illusions about himself, he was in fact meanly envious of Baker, someone he thought of as his good friend, "a sincere, clear-eyed, sweet-hearted fellow" who was soon to visit Steffens' parents in California and tell them what a superb son they had, how generous and manly. "Baker has an absurd notion of 'what I am,'" Steffens warned his parents. Back on the road, heading for Missouri once again, Steffens had passed through a time of shaken identity and self-examination:

It was a hard day's work. The yellow was easy. I did have the streak. My professional jealousy may not have been dominant; absentmindedness covered it pretty well. But my wife, who had presence of mind, knew me better than I knew myself; and all she had to do was to scratch the surface and there it was: envy, jealousy, and all the rest. The only trouble I had was to face the yellow and call it yellow and say to myself that I was—what I was. It's odd that I hate to say it even now when I know that we all have some yellow and that it's only a matter of degree. But I did face myself down that day.

"I was having troubles with myself," Steffens wrote to Baker after he arrived in St. Louis. "Struck a 'yellow streak,' and it made me sweat burning it out with shame. Ever catch yourself at mean thinking?" The shame of the cities and the shame of the self had become indivisible.

II

"STEFFENS MEANS WELL BUT, LIKE ALL REFORMERS, he don't know how to make distinctions. He can't see no difference between honest graft and dishonest graft and, consequent, he gets things all mixed up." George Washington Plunkitt, the sage of Tammany Hall, was holding forth on the subject of Lincoln Steffens' book, *The Shame of the Cities*, published early in the spring of 1904. Plunkitt continued his discourse while having his shoes shined in the marble lobby of Tweed's County Court House. "The difference between a looter and a practical politician is the difference between the Philadelphia Republican gang and Tammany Hall. Steffens seems to think they're both about the same; but he's wrong. The Philadelphia crowd runs up against the penal code. Tammany don't." Plunkitt also looked back to the time when cities could count their money every night before going to bed. "I don't believe that the government of our cities is any worse, in proportion to opportunities, than it was fifty years ago," he said. "The old-timers had nothin' to steal, while the politicians now are surrounded by all kinds of temptations."

From Forest Row in East Sussex, James Bryce, who had once described the cities as the most conspicuous failure of American democracy, wrote to say that he regarded Steffens' book with "mingled feelings of admiration for the vigor and directness with which he tells his story and of regret to have such a story told." He hoped things were not really so bad as Steffens said they were.

Steffens' book "has done for American cities what De Tocqueville did for the country over a hundred years ago," said William Allen White. "Until very recently no one thought it worth while to go out into the wards and precincts of the towns and townships of this land and bring in specimens of actual government under actual conditions." *The Shame of the Cities*, White said, pioneered the scientific study of political reality.

Praising *The Shame of the Cities*, Medill McCormick, owner of the Chicago *Tribune*, declared that "Nothing has been printed which so well portrays municipal conditions in America." William Randolph Hearst, self-styled radical and socialist who was then in the hot grip of political ambitions in New York, invited Steffens to dinner. Joseph Pulitzer, Hearst's chief antagonist in the city's circulation wars, instructed his editorial writers to laud Steffens and thereby implicitly associate the *World* with the idea of "continuous public service."

Steffens had written a pioneer text on the American city. What he did "has never been equaled," Brand Whitlock was to say as the progressive era came to an end, and it "had a noble and splendid part in the great awakening of our time." He had depicted a functioning system that bore hardly any resemblance to what one read about in constitutions and city charters or was taught in civics courses. In doing this he epitomized what was best in muckraking: its realism, its strategy of understatement, its credibility. "I did no detective work," Steffens explained to an interviewer.

> I got corruption from corruptionists, bribery from those who bribed and were bribed. I interviewed successfully political bosses, politicians and business men. I find the latter class in every city largely responsible, most frequently in a criminal way, for bad conditions; encouraging and abetting them. From political bosses I got a great deal of help. I interested them by drawing comparison between the way "things" are done in their city and New York and other cities. None of these men are loth to tell something of what they know. As a matter of fact they have a strange pride in what they do. Besides they consider me "on the level" because I do not discriminate but expose them, business men and judges alike. Then I never tell all of the truth. I don't have to—one-tenth is sufficient to make any decent man rise feeling outraged.

In *The Shame of the Cities* Steffens went beyond exposure, and this sets him apart from most of the other muckrakers. So much of their work was simply and avowedly exposure that served its brief purpose and lived its brief life. Steffens' book too is of its time in the historically invalidated distinctions it makes between bosses and reformers, the machine and good government, and in its moralistic view of "corruption" as indivisible. ("The corruption that shocks us in public affairs we practice in our private concerns," he wrote in his introduction. "There is no essential difference between the pull that gets your wife into society or for your book a favorable notice and that which gets a heeler into office, a thief out of jail, and a rich man's son on the board of directors.") As an account of solutions, *The Shame of the Cities* wavers between hopefulness and despair. "The commercial spirit is the spirit of profit, not patriotism," Steffens declares; then he argues that since political leaders, like all good businessmen, have to be acutely responsive to the law of supply and demand, "all we have to do is establish a steady demand for good government." But how can there be a demand for good government if the people are supine and if "the spirit of graft and of lawlessness

LINCOLN STEFFENS

is the American spirit"? Over the entire book and its earnest search
for public and private virtue hangs, unanswered, the familiar question, "What are you going to do about it?"

Still, after seven decades, *The Shame of the Cities* remains a bold
and pertinent study of interest-group dynamics in a democracy. It
effectively demolished a number of cherished beliefs held by reformers from the Civil War on: that corruption came from the bottom
of the economic and social order, not the top; that it was part of the
growing pains of young cities; that it accompanied an immigrant
population who in a strange land reverted to innate lawlessness; and
that the businessman was the good citizen and the politician the bad
citizen. All of these, according to Steffens, were "hypocritical lies
that save us from the clear sight of ourselves." One is still impressed
by the centrality of the problems as Steffens stated them, by the
clarity of his analysis and the elegance of his demonstrations, and
also, not at all inconsistently, by the fervor both of his argument and
of his commitment to advocacy. In this last respect *The Shame of
the Cities* is part of a literature of social concern that goes back to
Edward Bellamy and Jacob Riis and which, during muckraking's
prime, included Robert Hunter's *Poverty*, John Spargo's *The Bitter
Cry of the Children* and, preeminently, Upton Sinclair's novel of
protest, *The Jungle*.

III

"I AM NO LONGER A POLITICAL ACCIDENT," President Theodore Roosevelt declared after he was elected in November 1904 with a plurality
of more than two and a half million votes. Folk was now governor
of Missouri. In Wisconsin, Robert M. La Follette was serving out his
second term in the state house, having proved himself in the course
of his battles with the railroads and the lumber interests to be the
real "head of state," as Steffens put it, "not just the head of the paper
government described in the Constitution." In the service of the progressive cause, public power had been invoked to curb private interests. And in Ohio, a state long in the grip of big business and the Republican satrapy of Senator Marcus Alonzo Hanna, something was
happening that verged on the miraculous and therefore suggested
that anything was possible.

"I never was a reformer," said Brand Whitlock, who the following year became mayor of Toledo. "I hate reformers." Reformers wanted efficiency, a sound business basis, law and order, and a thorough clean-up. They loved those cold terms and forgot what every precinct boss knew, that what the people wanted first of all was help. In Cleveland and Toledo, Steffens encountered and soon joined a remarkable group of political leaders, administrators and urban sociologists who believed that reform, as he had known it, was fundamentally negative. "The great problem is to make the government of a city human," Whitlock said. It was Whitlock who took Steffens to the city hall in Toledo to meet Samuel Milton Jones, the Tolstoyan evangelist and social reformer who, despite the opposition of Hanna and the city's businessmen, preachers and newspaper editors, had been mayor since 1897. "Everybody is against me but the people," he said.

Jones had been a day laborer in the oil fields, then a successful well operator who sold out to Standard Oil and moved to Toledo, where he made another fortune as a manufacturer of drilling machinery. For all his money, his hands remained as work-toughened as those of his employees. He also retained a bardic, visionary quality, which came from his reading of Walt Whitman but which people were apt to trace back to his Welsh origins. He ran his factory by the Golden Rule, which was painted on a large sign nailed to the wall; it was the only regulation he posted, and it replaced warnings, supervisors, time clocks, and even Golden Rule Jones's first name. During the depression of the nineties, Jones paid a living wage instead of the going wage, and he introduced an eight-hour work day, hot lunches at cost, vacations with pay, profit sharing, sickness and disability insurance. On Sundays, in the factory's Golden Rule hall or under the willow trees in the park and playground Jones gave to the city, there were concerts and addresses by outside speakers on themes of brotherhood, equality and the social gospel.

When he met Steffens, Jones talked less about politics and administration than about poets and prophets—"He was practicing what they preached," Steffens was to say—and he read aloud passages from *Leaves of Grass* and the New Testament. "I do not believe that we are to get very much relief from the evils that distress us by legislation," Jones said; in time, according to his scheme of things, society would regenerate itself and become a true commonwealth.

Later, as he walked along St. Clair Street to the railroad station with Whitlock, Steffens mused aloud, "Why, that man's program will take a thousand years."

Still, the first steps, at least, were visible in Toledo, even though the city's businessmen had opposed Jones and called him utopian, a socialist, and a traitor to his class when he fought for home rule and municipal ownership, expanded recreational facilities, lower transit fares, and a city administration free of party politics. According to the clergy, he was the tool of the liquor interests, because on Sundays he disregarded ordinances and (unlike Roosevelt as Police Commissioner) permitted the saloons to stay open, arguing that the people had earned their pleasures. He fought "police-court justice" as it was dealt out to gamblers, prostitutes and petty thieves; when he sat as magistrate he sometimes let them off. What was the point of punishing the victims of a system? he asked. He was often to be found visiting the workhouse and the prison. Vagrants came to his office for help. His answer to the cry for law and order was to abolish the practice of arresting "on suspicion" and to equip his police with canes instead of clubs. After seven years as mayor, Jones's spirit had become part of his city, Steffens was to say. According to Brand Whitlock there was a kind of poignant tribute to Jones's memory in the mere fact that on the day after his death stocks in the Toledo street railway company ran up a twenty-four-point gain.

By the time Jones died, in 1904, Steffens had fallen under the spell of another disputed hero in the Midwest. This was Tom L. Johnson, the steel and traction tycoon who became mayor of Cleveland in 1901. Jones had been a revivalist, sporadic and inspirational, sometimes merely eccentric. Johnson, on the other hand, Steffens said years later, "set the precedent for all businessmen and engineers in politics." At twenty-three Johnson took over the street railroad in Indianapolis. Soon after, he gained control of steel mills in Pennsylvania and Ohio, traction companies in Brooklyn, Detroit and Philadelphia. In Cleveland he battled Hanna for the street railroads and declined an alliance only because he was certain that in no time at all one of them would have to "crowd the other clear off the bench."

When he was still in his thirties and traveling back and forth on the train between Cleveland and Indianapolis, he stumbled upon the Single-Taxer Henry George's book *Social Problems*. Johnson liked to joke that he first thought *Social Problems* was going to deal with prostitution and venereal disease. It dealt instead with his kind of business, with street railroads, steam railroads, the use of land and resources. After *Social Problems* Johnson read *Progress and Poverty* and went to see Henry George at his little brick house in Brooklyn. George's dazzlingly simple economic creed had won him over. Land was the source of wealth, the argument ran, and so a single tax on land and land use, along with a forceful program of reform, was going to put an end to poverty and suffering. Johnson became George's friend and his political manager, and eventually he went into politics himself and served two terms in Congress. But, as he said, "The requirements of my work didn't square with my principles." As a single-taxer he supported free trade, but as a steel producer he supported protective tariffs. He liquidated his steel and railroad holdings, put his money into government bonds, and returned to Cleveland. In February 1901 the Democrats drafted him as a candidate for mayor. He pledged himself to "Home rule; three-cent fare; and just taxation," and he delivered more.

"When the history of America is written, if ever it is properly written," Brand Whitlock was to tell Steffens, "when the history of radicalism in America is written, if it can get itself properly done, Tom Johnson will tower high above all the other personalities it has flung up into the sky line. I should be really afraid to say just how great I think he is." Johnson's old enemy Hanna called him a "socialist-anarchist-nihilist." Roosevelt called him a "ruffian," an extremely undesirable person "from the moral standpoint." Steffens too, when he first came to Cleveland in the spring of 1902, had been prepared to dismiss Johnson as "a dangerous theorist with a dangerous ambition"—at worst, a demagogue, possibly an eccentric; at best just another businessman playing at reform. "My ambition," Johnson told him then, savoring the reporter's disbelief, "is to make Cleveland the first American city to get good government." Everybody had heard that one before.

"No man can finish a municipal reform job without going to the state," Steffens wrote, predicting what would remain for more than half a century a crucial issue for the cities, home rule. When Steffens saw him next, in the fall of 1903, Johnson was running for governor. One term as mayor had shown him that until the corporate charters were revised to give the cities broad powers to own utilities and levy taxes, "Privilege," Johnson's term for monopoly and special interests, would continue to rule. The Hanna forces swept Ohio that fall; it was not until 1910, as a result of Johnson's long fight, that the cities were granted a measure of autonomy. But in the meantime, though defeated for the governorship, Johnson was mayor still, and he went back to city hall more determined than ever, as he said scripturally, to make Cleveland "a city that is set on a hill." During the early months of 1904, Steffens was in Cleveland again, writing about Hanna for *McClure's* and still watching Johnson and his city for signs of wavering. "It seems to me," Steffens concluded, "that Tom Johnson is the best mayor of the best-governed city in the United States."

Johnson had shown that city government could be creative, humane and free of party politics. He revised the tax list, and with new revenues from utilities and businesses which had been systematically undervalued he began a program of public works and social services. He reclaimed the lake front from the railroads and converted it into a broad esplanade that became part of the city's park system; he removed the "Keep Off the Grass" signs. He was winning his fight for reduced transit fares and had vindicated the principle of municipal ownership by taking the waterworks out of politics and making it a model service, better run and cheaper than private enterprise. He sanctioned enlightened ways of dealing with the poor people and delinquents. His law department, under Newton D. Baker, his successor as mayor and later Woodrow Wilson's Secretary of War, was the undoubted best in the country. To run his police department Johnson had promoted a junior officer, a Republican. "There is absolutely no graft among the Cleveland police," Steffens reported. "Mayor Johnson is a good judge of men, and Cleveland has the best chief of police I have met so far."

Like Hanna, another strong man, Johnson had seen too much of legislatures in action to have much faith in them, and he had little respect for the law and the courts and most governmental machinery. He was, in effect, a benevolent dictator attempting to fulfill democratic ideals through undemocratic measures—these were the terms on which Steffens was later to understand and admire Lenin and, for a while, even Mussolini. Like other rich men in politics—Hearst, Jones, Altgeld, Mayor Hazen Pingree of Detroit—Johnson believed chiefly in himself. He was the undisputed head of Cleveland's Democratic machine, a reform boss who, like Folk, was not above demagoguery and borderline tactics. He dictated platforms and slates, expecting them merely to be ratified in convention, but, as his partisans said, if he was a boss he was a boss on the people's side. During his campaigns he set up in various parts of town a circus tent big enough to hold four or five thousand at a meeting. "We won't provide you with music or red fire," he told them; "we will promise you the truth." He told them that crime was the result of poverty and corruption was the result of privilege. The way to improve society was to restore equality of opportunity and so give people a reasonable chance to be reasonably good. He had no interest in "enforcing" Christianity, he said; he only wanted to make it possible.

Like Roosevelt, Johnson communicated energy, confidence, command. He also communicated to his closest followers a spirit that was revolutionary and messianic. Evenings and Sundays at his mansion on Euclid Avenue, Johnson eased his considerable bulk into a leather lounge chair and addressed his lieutenants and disciples. "There was in them a spirit I never saw in such fullness elsewhere," said Whitlock. "They were all working for the city, they thought only of the success of the whole." Steffens too was profoundly moved. "The best evidence of the 'goodness' of this government is the spirit of the men in it," he wrote in 1905. "They like their work; they like to talk about their work; theirs is a sense of pride and preoccupation such as I never felt in any other American municipal government."

Proud and preoccupied, Johnson and his group were breaking with a powerful covert tradition of mistrust of the American city as wicked, anomic and dehumanizing, the inevitable condition of industrial society.* Hostility to the city bred neglect and despair, and these in turn bred fresh hostility, a cycle as yet unbroken in America. Johnson's group accepted the realities of politics and the discipline of sociology, and they foresaw vast cities of ten or twenty million inhabitants. Still they celebrated urban possibilities in the accents of the Psalmist and argued that there should be higher goals for the city than just cleaning it up. They invoked the metaphors of social harmony and of a radiant abundant city that had stirred Aristotle and Augustine, and they remembered that the ultimate destina-

* The complementary belief in the peace and purity of the farmlands survived even the report of Theodore Roosevelt's Country Life Commission (1908) that "drudgery, barrenness and heavy drinking characterized rural regions."

tion of Bunyan's Pilgrim was not the agricultural landscape of Beulah Land but the Celestial City—"by reason of the natural glory of the City, and the reflection of the Sunbeams upon it, Christian, with desire fell sick." The new urban intellectuals were Pelagians in their denial of the original sin of cities and their belief that civic righteousness was a matter of will. They recognized urbanization as the dominant fact of their century; but instead of looking back to a vanished agrarian society they pointed to the role of cities in the advancement of civilization. They had come to believe that it was in the cities that the problems of democracy and industrialization would be solved.

One member of Johnson's inner circle was Steffens' close friend Frederic C. Howe. Howe had studied sociology at Johns Hopkins in the early 1890s. There, in a seminar on politics he heard James Bryce speak, with the scriptural weight of his authority, about the failure of the cities. In 1905 Howe published a book called *The City: The Hope of Democracy* and made it plain that what he learned under Johnson could serve as an answer to Bryce. "The trouble with our cities is not too much democracy, but too little democracy," he wrote; "not too little state supervision, but too much state supervision." Already he felt that the city had begun to resume some of the primacy it had in the days of Athens, Rome and the medieval towns. Urbanization along with the intelligent control of environment promised a new kind of society—"The city is the hope of the future. Here life is full and eager. Here the industrial issues, that are fast becoming dominant in political life, will first be worked out." More than half a century later, at a time when the coming American city is pictured as a cluster of garrison infracommunities separated from each other by sanitized corridors and places of terror, Howe's vision has a peculiar poignancy.

Howe was to look back on his years with Johnson as the greatest adventure of his life. On Steffens the influence of Johnson was just as powerful. "He cleared my head of a lot of rubbish, left there from my academic education and reform associations," he wrote in his *Autobiography*. "Honesty is not enough; it takes intelligence, some knowledge or theory of economics, courage, strength, will power, humor, leadership—it takes intellectual integrity to solve our political problems. And these Tom Johnson had above all the politicians of my day."

From boyhood on, Steffens had been without heroes; not his

father, none of his elders, none of his contemporaries could serve him as a representative man. Neither could Theodore Roosevelt, whose well-publicized rows with Wall Street had a taint of play acting, Steffens had begun to feel—the glove was iron, but the hand was velvet, conciliatory. If he had to, Steffens said, he would "characterize Mr. Roosevelt exactly, as I know him and he will not like that." Now a new spirit, combative and totally engaged, showed itself in Steffens' work and was reflected in the two books he published after *The Shame of the Cities*: *The Struggle for Self-Government* (1906), described in its subtitle as "an attempt to trace American political corruption to its sources"; and *Upbuilders* (1909), portraits of five men who had challenged "the system." Muckraking the states in 1904 and 1905 Steffens had described enemies of the Republic: in New Jersey the Pennsylvania Railroad and in Illinois Charles T. Yerkes, the transit promoter; in Missouri the captains of industry and in Wisconsin the lumber interests and the railroads; in Ohio Senator Hanna and in Rhode Island the millionaire Senator Nelson W. Aldrich, ally by marriage of the Rockefellers and, according to Steffens, well on his way to becoming "the acknowledged political boss of the United States," the nation's general manager. But there were heroes too, in addition to Folk, La Follette and the Midwestern mayors. Steffens' readers could now look to a band of "upbuilders" ranging from the gentle reformer Judge Ben B. Lindsey, of the Denver juvenile court, to the rough-and-tumble Francis Heney, who successfully prosecuted land frauds in Oregon and in 1906 began an investigation that turned San Francisco inside out and sent its political boss to San Quentin.

IV

"THE ARTICLE SETTLED THINGS. It was like the decision of a court of last resort," Governor Robert M. La Follette told Steffens soon after "Enemies of the Republic—Wisconsin" appeared in *McClure's* for October 1904. "I cannot but marvel at the amount you accomplish, the swiftness and accuracy of your work, and the depth of your soundings." La Follette said it was impossible to exaggerate the effect of Steffens' work on the elections that November.

The Wisconsin article succeeded in other ways as well. "It has sold out the magazine already," Steffens told his father. "We printed a heavy edition but should have had more." *McClure's* was now locked in a circulation battle with *Everybody's*, which was pulling ahead—half a million copies and more compared to about 370,000 a month for *McClure's*—on the strength of one of the lurid triumphs of the muckraking era: the publication, starting in August 1904 and promising to run almost indefinitely, of "Frenzied Finance" by the Boston plunger and manipulator Thomas W. Lawson. Lawson told his insider's story of how he and the Standard Oil Company had created a trust, Amalgamated Copper, which in five years "plundered the public to the extent of over one hundred millions of dollars. . . . It has from its birth to present writing been responsible for more hell than any other trust or financial thing since the world began." By the following spring, to the relief of the *McClure's* group, it seemed that the Lawson sensation had peaked, despite the reported infusion of $250,000 of Lawson's money for promotion and advertising. Newsstand orders for *Everybody's* had been cut back, Albert Boyden told Steffens in April 1905—"People are already tired of all that shrieking. I don't believe that there is any question but that he has shot his bolt." (There were widespread doubts now as to Lawson's plausibility, rumors that he had written his exposé in order to get publicity and settle old grudges.) Lawson's dubious triumph had made Steffens question his own purpose: Was his work too just a way of building business for a magazine?

That summer, his series on the states finished, he relaxed at Cos Cob with Josephine, swam, went sailing on the little sloop McClure had given him as a bonus, and began working on a new project. Fired up by some of Lawson's charges of chicanery and by news of an imminent investigation, McClure, after some hesitation, assigned Steffens to study the life-insurance business. More than ever he had doubts about the direction of Steffens' work, was troubled less by Steffens' scarcely disguised affection for political bosses and "realists" than by his hardening attitudes toward business in general. Back in 1903 McClure had protested that "Steffens has a notion that the business man is a coward, and that the business man is to blame for political corruption, and he makes every fact bend to this notion." A year later they had quarreled over the first article in Steffens' new series. The subtitle told all—too much, McClure believed: "THE

POLITICAL LEADERS WHO ARE SELLING OUT THE STATE OF MISSOURI, AND
THE LEADING BUSINESS MEN WHO ARE BUYING IT—BUSINESS AS TREASON
—CORRUPTION AS REVOLUTION." To make it worse, one of the "leading business men" whose activities Steffens described in detail was
the president of the Royal Baking Powder Company, a steady advertiser in *McClure's*. Steffens held firm, and McClure went off to
Europe grumbling that there were a number of things his writer had
in common with Napoleon. "All tyrants have short necks," he told
Mark Sullivan.

Writing from abroad, McClure shifted the battle to another sec-
tor. "Aldrich article is wrongly constructed and poorly worked out,"
he told Phillips after reading Steffens' Rhode Island manuscript. He
demanded that Steffens simplify it into "a study of Aldrich. How
he secures power in R. I. how he then robs his state & then how he
works for Rockefeller & others in the Senate." Obedient to McClure
this time, Steffens portrayed Aldrich as practically all horns and tail
and soon found himself caught in vigorous cross fire from the White
House. "I know nothing about the conditions in Rhode Island,"
Roosevelt told Steffens in June 1905, "but I did know it to be a simple absurdity to speak of Aldrich as 'the boss of the United States';
and such an absurdity has a sinister significance, for in my judgment
we suffer quite as much from exaggerated, hysterical and untruthful
or slanderous statements in the press as from any wrong doing by
businessmen or politicians."

This was the line Roosevelt was to take the next year when he
turned on muckraking generally, but in June 1905 Roosevelt had a
more specific reason to be outraged by Steffens. Once a supporter of
Roosevelt, Aldrich had now become leader of the Senate opposition,
and if he could be described as "the boss of the United States," then
by clear implication the President was still a "political accident."
There was altogether too much of this sort of poppycock and mis-
chievous sniping, Roosevelt believed, and from an old friend who
was also supposed to be a loyal Republican. "I do wish that you
would not repeat as true unfounded gossip of a malicious or semi-
malicious character," he protested. As he saw it, here was Steffens
exaggerating Hanna's power in the White House and Aldrich's in
the nation and booming Folk (a Democrat), La Follette (an insurgent), and Johnson (a "ruffian"), even going after a member of

Roosevelt's own Cabinet, Postmaster General Henry Clay Payne, the railroad man from Wisconsin. ("Poor Payne is sick either unto death or nigh unto death," Roosevelt told Henry Cabot Lodge in October 1904. "The attack on him in *McClure's Magazine* by Steffens was, I think, the immediate cause of breaking him down; and I am convinced that it is an infamously false attack." Payne died two days later.) Roosevelt remained outwardly conciliatory to Steffens, invited him to the White House, asked his advice, thanked him for an idea contributed to one of Roosevelt's 1905 messages to Congress; but on occasions his exasperation flashed out. "For me to follow such a line as you indicate would be simply silly," Roosevelt snapped, and in a letter of over two thousand words he demonstrated—to his own satisfaction, at any rate—that a suggestion Steffens made about campaign funds and "tainted money" was, in a single word, "nonsense." Writing to McClure in October 1905, Roosevelt sounded as exasperated as McClure himself:

> As I said to you and Steffens today, I think Steffens ought to put more sky in his landscape. I do not have to say to you that a man may say what is absolutely true and yet give an impression so one-sided as not to represent the whole truth. It is an unfortunate thing to encourage people to believe that all crimes are connected with business, and that the crime of graft is the only crime. Put sky in the landscape. . . .

Listening, then, to outer as well as inner voices, McClure reconsidered the wisdom of assigning Steffens to write about life insurance. It was all too clear, for example, what Steffens would make of the scandal-ridden affairs of the Equitable Life Assurance Society of the United States, whose controlling stockholder—custodian of the nest eggs of six hundred thousand policyholders—had recently given a $200,000 costume ball at Sherry's in New York and charged it to the company. Steffens was going to look for a "system." "If a public, non-profit, trust business is as bad as the life insurance," he reasoned, "what must be the condition of some of the private businesses that are run only for profit? This line of inquiry seemed to frighten businessmen." It frightened McClure, who, with Phillips, read what Steffens had written so far, told him it wouldn't do, and late in 1905 took him off the assignment. Half a year of work gone to waste; such were the drawbacks of being someone else's man.

V

FOR PROGRESSIVES THE NOVEMBER 1905 ELECTIONS SEEMED to promise a new era. "We, the American people, carried ourselves at last," Steffens declared, "and the beginning has been made toward the restoration of representative democracy in all the land." In Cleveland, Tom Johnson was reelected by the largest plurality of his career. In Toledo, Brand Whitlock, whom Steffens had urged to run for mayor and now called "the most advanced leader in American politics today," won out over the Republican candidate. Robert M. La Follette was elected Senator from Wisconsin. In Philadelphia and Cincinnati, in Ohio and New Jersey, the bosses had been toppled. From all over letters and telegrams of congratulation hailed Steffens for his three years' work on the cities and states and the part he had played in making Election Day "the people's day." "I think you more than any other one man may take credit for the result of the elections wherever 'boss or no boss rule' was the issue," wrote the future Chief Justice Harlan Fiske Stone, then a professor of law at Columbia. From the governor's office in Jefferson City, Missouri, came a letter that summed up all the rest. "It must make you feel good to look over the election returns and to know the important part you had in bringing about these results," Folk wrote. "You started the revolution."

CHAPTER EIGHT

"The Man with the Muckrake"

I

As 1906 opened, "revolution" was a word that Americans were hearing with increasing frequency and in contexts of factuality, hyperbole, irony or alarm. Half a world away the Russia of Nicholas II had been torn by strikes, uprisings and reprisals, rehearsals for the fury of 1917. Theodore Roosevelt feared that the same spirit of dynamite and bloodshed was infecting his own country. The Immigration Act of 1903 had been a response to Roosevelt's insistence that "anarchists" and "all active and passive sympathizers with anarchists" be excluded from American shores. Nonetheless, a former governor of Idaho had just been assassinated, in a manner distinctly anarchistic, with a dynamite bomb, allegedly the vendetta work of the Western Federation of Miners. One of the Federation's leaders, Big Bill Haywood, had founded the dread Industrial Workers of the World; he described its organizational meeting in June 1905 as "the Continental Congress of the Working Class" rising in revolt against its "Capitalist masters."

President McKinley's assassin, Roosevelt often said, had been incited not only by anarchist manifestoes but also by editorials written on direct orders from William Randolph Hearst—"the most potent single force for evil we have in our life," Roosevelt said of Hearst, "a sinister agitator." Demagogues, socialists and "lurid sensationalists," Roosevelt claimed, deliberately exaggerated the sins of capitalism in order to build up "a revolutionary feeling" and raise the spectres of the red flag, class warfare and the barricades. In his new book, *The Struggle for Self-Government*, McClure's man Lincoln Steffens addressed an ironic epistle dedicatory to the beleaguered Tsar, telling him that the easiest way to put off a revolution in Russia was to give his people exactly what Americans now had—the illusion of a representative democracy without any of the realities. What sort of nonsense was this?—where was "the sky in the landscape"? Viewed against the background of 1906, Roosevelt's cherished function as reformer, political realist and mediator was in jeopardy. "To use the terminology of Continental politics," he was to say, "I am trying to keep the left center together."

Steffens had come to Washington that January with a commission from the McClure Newspaper Syndicate to write a series about the federal government. He also had, in the absence of a Freedom of Information Act, a ukase from the President addressed "To any officer of or employee of the Government":

> Please tell Mr. Lincoln Steffens anything whatever about the running of the government that you know (not incompatible with the public interests) and provided only that you tell him the truth—no matter what it may be—I will see that you are not hurt.
>
> T. ROOSEVELT

But even such carte blanche, as Steffens called it, turned out to be of little use. Federal officials, he told Roosevelt a year later, "think their information is for the President and not for the press and the people"; the "public interests" were best served by silence. Steffens had been shrewdly disarmed, even shackled, by his indebtedness to the President, who continued to lecture him on the difference, in harm done, between retailers of "gossip and hearsay," partisans, demagogues, and simple obstructionists, on the one hand, and on the other, in Roosevelt's blandest phrasing, men who are "improperly sensitive to the influence of great corporations." Roosevelt was just as persistent in scolding Steffens for his refusal to recognize the expediency, even necessity, of compromise and concession. "As a matter of fact," he added pointedly, "I have come a great deal nearer getting what I wanted than, for instance, Governor La Follette in Wisconsin came to getting what he wanted in the matter of legislation and appointments."

Largely as a result of Roosevelt's sponsorship and tutelage Steffens' project of muckraking the national government turned out to be surprisingly mild in its revelations. Editors complained that his weekly reports lacked color, detail, exposure—everything that his magazine work had led them to expect. "You ought to put someone on the rack every week and compel him to defend existing conditions in Washington," Charles H. Taylor, Jr. of the Boston *Globe* told him. "The articles are very good as they stand, but they might have been written by someone else than Lincoln Steffens. What we want is the true Steffens brand." Attacking from another quarter, *The New York Times*, in an editorial, chided Steffens for personifying "The Sudden School" of journalism and quoted with approval the advice Speaker of the House Cannon was supposed to have given him about the labyrinthine mysteries of Washington. Having smoked eleven cigars in the course of their interview, Cannon placed a paternal hand on Steffens' shoulder and said, "I'd have you devote twenty years to study before beginning to write."

Even so, Steffens was the publicly recognized leader of a movement that was at the peak of its influence at the beginning of 1906. The insurance companies and the railroads were under fire. So were the liquor trust and the patent-medicine industry, exposed by Samuel Hopkins Adams as "The Great American Fraud." According to Adams, Mark Sullivan and others, the public, hoodwinked by labels, advertising, endorsements, and a hired press, was being turned into alcoholics and drug addicts. This work of exposure was splendid, Roosevelt could reason as he hounded Congress for regulatory powers, so long as he determined where reform had to end and expediency begin, so long as he was leader and not captive of the mighty army of crusaders for the public interest. As the humor magazine *Puck* depicted this army, Steffens on a war horse and McClure armed with a crossbow are in the forefront—behind them, in an array that stretches into the far distance, follow Baker, Adams, Tarbell, Johnson, Folk, Lawson, and a thousand others marching under the banners of the popular magazines and the daily press. Suddenly, as two great explosions shook the ground and sent sheets of fire up to the crimson sky, the President decided that this army was marching not with him but upon him.

Upton Sinclair's novel *The Jungle*, serialized during 1905 in the socialist weekly *Appeal to Reason*, had already had a national im-

pact when Doubleday, Page and Company published it in book form
at the end of January 1906. "What *Uncle Tom's Cabin* did for the
black slaves," Jack London told the twenty-seven-year-old Sinclair,
"*The Jungle* has a large chance to do for the white slaves of today."
He correctly judged Sinclair's purpose, but not his effect. For *The
Jungle*, dedicated to "the workingmen of America," was only sec-
ondarily intended as an exposé of the meat-packing industry. It was
an ideological novel; it preached the cause of labor and the coming
victory of socialism. What one heard in the slaughterhouse was
really "the hog squeal of the universe," Sinclair wrote, the cry of the
oppressed and the defeated. Sinclair depicted capitalism as an order
imposed by those who possessed power to enslave those who did not,
and in the course of his narrative he touched on practically every
social or political issue raised by the muckrakers: municipal corruption, the decay of representative democracy, the trusts, child labor,
consumer exploitation, the connection of crime with poverty, the
industrial city as Golgotha.

"I aimed at the public's heart," Sinclair said ruefully after his book
had been out for nearly a year, "and by accident I hit it in the
stomach." Instead of reforms in working conditions for the benefit of
workingmen, he saw government enforcement of reforms in meat
packing for the benefit of the packers themselves. What had happened was consistent with the tangled history of muckraking. Readers of *The Jungle* were not aroused by Sinclair's pictures of wage
slavery's hell or of socialism's New Jerusalem so much as they were
by his disclosures of a horrendous traffic in adulterated meat products, tubercular, festering beef, cholera-ridden swine, poisoned rats,
and even human remains rendered as lard. ("I haven't been able to
ate annything more nourishin' thin a cucumber in a week," said Mr.
Dooley. "A little while ago no wan cud square away at a beefsteak
with betther grace thin mesilf. Today th' wurrud resthrant makes
me green in th' face. How did it all come about? A young fellow
wrote a book." According to Dooley, even Theodore Roosevelt, the
glass of fashion among carnivores and the most bloodthirsty of
American Presidents, was now a vegetarian.) "The things you tell
are unbelievable," Steffens said when Sinclair had complained he was
having trouble finding a publisher for *The Jungle*: "I have a rule in
my own work: I don't tell things that are unbelievable even when
they are true." But the public believed what Sinclair wrote, investi-

gations confirmed it, and in the ensuing outcry for a complete skin-
ning out and evisceration of the beef trust, it was forgotten that for
twenty years or more it was the major meat packers themselves,
eager for a share of the export market at a time when American
meat had a bad name, who had pressed for federal regulation, especially of their smaller competitors and suppliers: an exposé of the
meat-packing industry was implicitly an exposé of federal delin-
quency. By June, when Roosevelt signed into law a Meat Inspection
Act which also had the approval of the big packers, he might have
had an uneasy feeling that under pressure from a number of quarters
he was in danger of becoming his own assistant for Congressional
affairs. "Tell Sinclair to go home," he appealed to the publishers of
The Jungle, "and let me run the country for a while." Meanwhile
Sinclair had come to realize that the President was interested in
food legislation but not, with any immediate prospect of action, in
structural reform or in "the workingmen of America."

Sinclair, Steffens and other members of what Roosevelt was beginning to think of as "the lunatic fringe" claimed that he was going
too slowly. But according to the Senate he was going too fast. The
Senate had become a place where reform bills, like old elephants,
went to die. Roosevelt's message to Congress at the end of 1905
challenged the rights of business to set its own prices, keep its books
private, and deal with labor unilaterally. The need of the day was
government intervention and regulation, as the muckrakers demonstrated in article after article; yet the Senate stood firm against
Roosevelt. "It was a chamber of traitors," Steffens remembered from
a winter of watching from the press gallery, "and we used to talk
about the treason of the Senate." Congress was the common council
for big business, he reported to the San Francisco *Bulletin*: "Speaker
Cannon knows of it, Senator Aldrich admits it, nobody denies it."
This was the sort of journalism that Roosevelt could not abide. It
was hysterical, he charged, absurd and sinister; it confused reform
and revolution, and it made politics impossible.

Now, in the February issue of *Cosmopolitan*, newly under the
ownership of William Randolph Hearst, Roosevelt read the editorial
announcement of a series by David Graham Phillips, author of three
muckraking novels about the Senate. Phillips was not writing fiction
this time. According to the announcement, which alluded to "iniquitous figures," "the cruel and vicious spirit of Mammon," and the

imminent resignation of Chauncey Depew of New York, "The Treason of the Senate" was to be "the most remarkable story of political corruption ever told in print." Hearst's hand was evident in this promotional lure, in the choice of writer and subject, and in his close editing of the series. The first articles exceeded Roosevelt's blackest expectations. "Treason is a strong word," Phillips wrote,

> but not too strong, rather too weak, to characterize the situation in which the Senate is the eager, resourceful, indefatigable agent of interests as hostile to the American people as any invading army could be, and vastly more dangerous; interests that manipulate the prosperity produced by all, so that it heaps up riches for a few; interests whose growth and power can only mean the degradation of the people, of the educated into sycophants, of the masses toward serfdom.

He went on to particularize the careers of Depew (a man of "greasy conscience," "greasy tongue," and "greasy backbone") and of Nelson Aldrich, "boss of the Senate" and therefore chief traitor. Even the insurgent Albert Beveridge of Indiana, critic of his fellow senators, believed that Phillips had gone too far. If Phillips was at all representative of the muckrakers, plainly the time had come for Roosevelt to disavow some of his allies.

Roosevelt tested out his next move on the occasion of a Gridiron Club off-the-record speech on March 17. He spoke hotly and recklessly of a group of writers who, he explained by an extended reference to John Bunyan's *The Pilgrim's Progress*, were concerned only with "that which is vile and debasing," with "the filth of the floor." (This particular reference to Bunyan may have been suggested to Roosevelt by an item in *Collier's* for February 10, 1906, "The Man with the Muckrake Improved.") Roosevelt named no names in his speech, but in a letter to his Secretary of War, William H. Taft, he confided that he had been thinking of Phillips, Upton Sinclair and Thomas Lawson and also the writers for *McClure's*, *Cosmopolitan*, and *Collier's*—his list was practically a directory of what from then on would be known as muckraking.

As he sifted the reactions to his speech, Roosevelt volunteered under pressure a series of evasions. Steffens came to him dismayed and reproachful—the President had attacked a group of writers who helped make him a reform hero. ("*You're* the chief muckraker,"

Speaker Cannon was supposed to have muttered to the President after the Gridiron Club speech.) Now Roosevelt told Steffens that he had had no intention of generalizing. Of course he had Lawson and Sinclair in mind, but Phillips most of all, and he had spoken out as he did in order to "comfort" Depew, "poor old Chauncey Depew," who, after all, had been one of Roosevelt's sponsors for the governorship and was in enough personal trouble already without being called a "traitor." As Steffens, with an obviously hollow casualness told a reporter a few weeks after this audience with Roosevelt, "He said he didn't mean me." Through his emissaries Roosevelt even made several attempts to persuade Phillips that he hadn't meant him either, but Phillips ended up being persuaded only that the President was an opportunist, and nothing more. Ray Stannard Baker told Roosevelt that the muckrake speech, in effect a Presidential bill of attainder, was a threat to one of the self-preserving functions of a democracy—"the letting in of light and air." "Even admitting that some of the so-called 'exposures' have been extreme," Baker argued, "have they not, as a whole, been honest and useful? And would not a speech, backed by all of your great authority, attacking the magazines, tend to give aid and comfort to these very rascals, besides making it more difficult in the future not only to get the truth told but to have it listened to?" In reply Roosevelt was as disingenuous as he had been with Steffens. "I want to let in 'light and air,' but I do not want to let in sewer gas." This time he explained that it was the Hearst press that he had in mind and not exposure journalism in general. And it was precisely because so many people misinterpreted him on this point, Roosevelt said, that he was going to repeat his speech publicly and for quotation so that it could be reported, and understood, in full.

On April 14 the ruffles and flourishes of the Marine band announced a Presidential performance to representatives of the three branches of government, the foreign diplomatic corps and reporters primed by a month of buzzing and speculation. Roosevelt had come to lay the cornerstone of a Congressional office building. He had also come, it was clear, to bury a movement.

"In *Pilgrim's Progress*," he declared, "the Man with the Muckrake is set forth as the example of him whose vision is fixed on carnal instead of on spiritual things."

Yet he also typifies the man who in this life consistently refuses to see aught that is lofty, and fixes his eyes with solemn intentness only on that which is vile and debasing. Now, it is very necessary that we should not flinch from seeing what is vile and debasing. There is filth on the floor, and it must be scraped up with the muckrake; and there are times and places where this service is the most needed of all the services that can be performed. But the man who never does anything else, who never thinks or speaks or writes save of his feats with the muckrake, speedily becomes, not a help to society, not an incitement to good, but one of the most potent forces of evil.

To writers like Steffens, whose targets were wealth and power, there was a deal of mischief in the antic way Roosevelt cited allegory for his purpose. The Man with the Muckrake, by whom Bunyan intended the single-minded pursuit of worldly goods and rewards, had been stood on his head. But with the sort of promiscuous violence that was to be seen again a few days later in the San Francisco earthquake, Roosevelt went on to assault men with muckrakes for their "gross and reckless assaults on character," their dedication to "financial or political profit," their vision of "the whole world" as "nothing but muck." The ultimate effect of their work, he said, was to create "a morbid and vicious public sentiment," "a mere crusade of appetite against appetite." Then he moved on to other matters, and by the end of his speech, having already placated the business community by disavowing legislative programs that might possibly be born in such a state of "hysterical excitement" and "violent emotionalism," Roosevelt made peace offerings to the progressive left; he proposed federal supervision of interstate business and a federal inheritance tax to curb "fortunes swollen beyond all healthy limits." What he took away with one hand he gave back with the other.

A few conservative papers attacked Roosevelt's reform proposals as "socialistic." The Hearst press, predictably, mocked him for being afraid that "too much light on corruption impairs the public eyesight" and said that his speech was "full of platitudes." But in general Roosevelt had reason to believe that he had recaptured public loyalty away from the muckrakers and that the people would now quickly tire of what had become a national habit of self-excoriation. He convinced a number of publishers that investigation and exposure, watchdog functions of a democratic press, were contrary to the public interest and the public desire and were therefore likely, in the future, to prove to be poor business as well as poor policy.

"It was a great day while it lasted," said the New York *Sun*, certain now that the muckrakers were on the way out, "but it became too hot." As a Western paper put it two years later, carrying repudiation through to its ultimate logic, the way to clean up politics is to get rid of people like Lincoln Steffens. The humor magazine *Life* conceded that Steffens and Phillips had "armed hundreds of thousands of readers with fighting knowledge" but said that these writers had now succumbed to commerce—"Exposure is the kind of a job to be done to an accompaniment of prayer and fasting. When it begins to be remunerative and excite enthusiasm it is time to go slow." This was a temperate version of the line taken by Ellery Sedgwick in an editorial for *American Magazine*. Motivated by "circulation, and the money and power that circulation brings," the muckraker—"always hoping for the worst"—was not an agent of Roosevelt's kind of progressivism and reform but of schemers like Hearst and Debs.

Soon Secretary Taft too took to the warpath, while Roosevelt, in public and private statements, continued to pursue the enemy.* Shun "hysteria" and "wild vindictiveness," he told a crowd of Oyster Bay neighbors standing around in a rainstorm on July 4. "It is a poor trick to spend nine tenths of the time in saying that there never was such iniquity as is shown in this nation, and the remaining tenth in saying that we are the most remarkable nation that ever existed." The term "muckraker" was on everyone's lips now.

The President's assurances and his Square Deal slogan no longer meant anything, said Baker. "I could never again give him my full confidence nor follow his leadership." He, Steffens and Ida Tarbell had been lumped together with sensationalists; Roosevelt had sacrificed "a fine and vigorous current of aroused public opinion."

* Even the luckless Maxim Gorky, victim of a public scandal which broke the day of Roosevelt's speech, found himself caught up in the President's wrath. Roosevelt refused to receive him at the White House, arguing that Gorky's "domestic relations"—the woman he was traveling with while raising money to overthrow the Tsar was not his wife—epitomized "revolt against the ordinary decencies and moralities." As Roosevelt viewed him, Gorky was "the very type of fool academic revolutionist which tends to bring to confusion and failure the great needed measures of social, political, and industrial reform." (Joseph Bucklin Bishop, *Theodore Roosevelt and His Times*, New York, 1920, Vol. II, p. 112.)

Neither could Steffens ever again believe that Roosevelt was a reformer in the White House or anything other than "a careerist on the people's side." He was in Cleveland when the storm of Roosevelt's "Man with the Muckrake" speech broke in the newspapers. "The longer I live," he told a reporter there, swallowing his consternation, "the more I feel that the individual is not so much to blame as the system of corruption which has grown up about us." He had begun to think in structural terms. Soon, for want of any better tactic, he and Baker tried to make the best of a bad setback by embracing the title of "muckraker" as if they had sought it from the start, but they never managed to purge it of its connotations of negativism and defamation; in the war of words Roosevelt had prevailed. But as Steffens went about the country during the fall of 1906 lecturing on graft, he flung the President's speech back at him and rang desperate changes on a by-then familiar theme:

> If muck were mere muck, then I, for one, would be for leaving the makers of muck to our official muckrakers, the men we elect to represent us and protect us from crime. But we have left the muck to the muckers and they have raked it, yes, they have raked it in. They have failed us, our representatives have. They do not protect us from crime; they protect crime. They stand for muck. Why? Because muck isn't mere muck. It's money, easy money.

II

THE NOVELIST WILLA CATHER WAS A FAVORED CONTRIBUTOR TO *McClure's* and a member of its editorial staff from 1906 to 1912. In more ways than one she possessed an insider's view of the uneasy harmony that prevailed between the magazine's chief editor and his muckrakers: McClure's friend and in time the ghostwriter of his autobiography, she knew him well enough, she once said, to be able to write "better and truer McClure than McClure himself." "He had built up about him an organization of which he was somewhat afraid and with which he was vastly bored," she said in a short story. "He found he could take an average reporter from the daily press, give him a 'line' to follow, a trust to fight, a vice to expose—this was all in that good time when people were eager to read about their own wickedness—and in two years the reporter would be recognized as an authority. . . . The strangest thing was that the owners of these grave countenances, staring at their own faces on newspapers and billboards, fell to venerating themselves."

There was just as much resentment on the other side. During the spring months of 1906 the spirit of revolution reached into the offices of *McClure's,* and the group of writers described by a contemporary, Ellery Sedgwick, as "the most brilliant staff ever gathered by a New York periodical." Reporting the progress of an uprising at *McClure's,* the *Times* and the *Herald* linked it with Roosevelt's speech. They said the muckrakers were having a falling out over whether to press on toward the eye of the storm or take in sail. Roosevelt's attack may have made the writers edgier than usual, but their uprising had less to do with Roosevelt than with McClure himself. He had returned from a European rest cure with a project that in their judgment smacked of megalomania and even downright J. P. Morgan-ism. "He started on a big fool scheme," Steffens reported to his father, "of founding a new magazine with a string of banks, insurance companies, etc., and a capitalization of $15,000,000. It was not only fool, it was not quite right, as we saw it."

As they—writers who were by now acutely alert to the ways of Standard Oil, Amalgamated Copper, the meat-packing industry, the railroads, and the insurance business—saw it, McClure had got the wrong religion and wanted them to go about spreading it. ("No man and no employer buys my mind, when he hires my pen," Steffens said, "and I shall not sell my liberty for any price.") McClure was proposing nothing less than a horizontal communications trust that, in addition to magazines, an expanded book-publishing house and a newspaper syndicate, was also going to sponsor a correspondence school through which, presumably, the people would be educated to bank their money with McClure and buy their life insurance and even their housing from him. The entire scheme was "not only impossible but wrong," Ida Tarbell recalled, the disordered product of a state of "mental and physical exhaustion" brought on by McClure's chronic indigestion, insomnia and arthritis. Years of restiveness under his autocratic and mainly absentee editorship boiled up into mutiny, and while Ida Tarbell and Phillips tried to reason with McClure, Steffens briefly entertained an offer from Hearst of $20,000 a year and half profits to edit a new magazine. There had been other such rows at the office before—they had all been settled somehow.

This time there was no compromise. "I own a majority of the stock, and I am the editor," McClure said, with absolute conclusiveness, to the press on May 4; and he shook off with annoyance the suggestion that the strife had anything to do with Roosevelt. On May 10, haggard and unbelieving, McClure witnessed the last stages of the revolution. Phillips, Ida Tarbell and several others submitted their resignations and walked out, and it was understood by everyone that Steffens and Baker, both of whom were away on assignment, would go with them. Soon this group recruited William Allen White and Finley Peter Dunne, raised about $400,000 in cash and pledges, and on July 2 the newly formed Phillips Publishing Company, with Steffens as vice-president and shareholder, took formal possession of the *American Magazine*, a ten-cent monthly hobbled by debt. Steffens had invested $10,000 of his own money. They stood to make a fortune now, if the magazine succeeded, Josephine said.

In a year or so Steffens would regret that he had gone into the magazine at all. But that summer he and his partners celebrated their freedom from McClure's house of bondage, as they now saw it. There was a spirit of picnic and honeymoon about the enterprise; affections, loyalties, professional comradeship had never seemed quite so strong before and never would again. They dealt with each other as equals: " 'We' were all to edit a writers' magazine," Steffens said. "We" were "a goodly company." They revered Ida Tarbell for her tact, intelligence, force—"a lady," said Dunne, "but she has the punch." For her, Steffens, nine years younger, stood for beauty as well as brains, audacity, confidence. "I often loved him for the gifts of sympathy he had," Baker said, "and the moments of generous courtesy." Baker described him as "a kind of Socratic skeptic asking deceptively simple questions." An "honest" man, William Allen White was to say, "thoroughly, beautifully, effectively and courageously honest."

Along with a tacit acceptance of Roosevelt's appeal for more sky in the landscape, a new sense of adventure showed itself right away in the announcement of the *American* as "a magazine of joyous reading." "It will reflect a happy, struggling, fighting world, in which, we believe, good people are coming out on top." Reform was in the saddle, and the *American*, reborn in the sunlight of the progressive era, was going to be "the greatest thing" of its kind, Steffens said then; "sincere, but good-natured; honest, but humorous; aggressive, but not unkind; a straight, hard fighter, but cheerful. . . . Every man in this whole country who is for better things is with us."

Meanwhile, during the summer of 1906 Steffens was busy with work that he still owed McClure (who now referred to him as "our friend, the enemy"), with a piece about William Randolph Hearst for the *American*, with preparations for a lecture tour. He was also busy sailing his sloop and fixing up a house that he and Josephine had just bought at Riverside, Connecticut, in what was coming to be an enclave of the rich. "Little Point" was an eighteenth-century farmhouse, built out and improved, with a barn, a sandy beach, and a view of open water, boats, and Cos Cob across the harbor. The New Haven trains rattled distantly over the railroad bridge upriver. Steffens had had his eye on Little Point for some time, and for the next five years it was home.

III

"HE HAD DISCOVERED THAT THERE WAS ROOM AT THE BOTTOM," Steffens said about Hearst in his *Autobiography*, "and with sensational news sensationally written and pictured, he did reach for and get the people. He was a demagogue; he was pro-labor. I cannot describe the hate of those days for Hearst except to say that it was worse than it is now."

A rich man who talked about Jeffersonian democracy and used the power of the press to set the poor against the rich, labor against capital; a strong, cold, isolated man, unmoral, without fervor except for political power—in 1906 these were some of Steffens' reflections on the enigma of Hearst, candidate for governor of New York that year and, if he had his way, President of the United States in 1908. As Upton Sinclair judged him then, Hearst was another Lincoln, a true radical, "the man of the coming hour."* For others, Hearst was

* Sinclair said this in *The Industrial Republic* (1907) and lived to regret it. In 1932 he said, "I have never reprinted this book because of the embarrassing fact that I had prophesied Hearst as a radical president of the United States. He really looked like a radical then." (*American Outpost: A Book of Reminiscences.* New York, 1932, p. 185.)

merely a symptom. "He has been given to the American people," the liberal publicist Herbert Croly was to write, "for their sins in politics and economics." But so little was actually known about the man, so much conjured up out of fear and loathing—invocations of Antichrist, Nero, Caligula.

In such a climate of discussion, Steffens discovered, it was impossible to write about Hearst temperately, not to say sympathetically, without being thought of as a lunatic, a dupe, or a paid agent. His interview article, "Hearst, the Man of Mystery," published in the *American* in November 1906, turned out to be a test of consensus editing at the magazine. The others had expected an exposé and an attack; instead, Dunne said angrily, Steffens' article might just as well have been written by Arthur Brisbane, Hearst's chief lieutenant and editor of the New York *Evening Journal*.

Steffens had spent two evenings with Hearst in Chicago, sat with him on the train to New York, interviewed him twice after that. Hearst's reputation for inscrutability was well-founded, he discovered. His cold, narrow-set eyes told nothing; his somber smile told nothing. His strength was in reserve for himself: he volunteered nothing, scarcely seemed to care whether he was believed or understood. Yet he was generous with his time, answered questions willingly. There was a certain community between Hearst and Steffens —they were nearly the same age, both had the air and manners of gentlemen, both had come East from California derisive of conventional heroes, and, in the same way that muckraking and yellow journalism had now been lumped together, both of them, rightly or wrongly, were reputed to be radicals.

Steffens came as close as any journalist did to penetrating Hearst's "absolute self-sufficiency." It was partly a matter of suspending one's identity and never relaxing one's ego, of remaining receptive in a value-neutral way but delicately in control. He had a rule for interviewing, Steffens wrote in his *Autobiography*: "never to let the interviewed get started on a speech; he will say only what he wants you to say, not what he himself thinks; and he will dominate." Steffens was the best interviewer he ever encountered, Hearst said.

He had opened up surprisingly, even to the point of admitting that often his own papers failed to rise above sensationalism. "I think that part of the fault for the failure is mine," he said. "If I had stuck to one newspaper, I might by personal direction in detail have made a newspaper to suit me exactly. But I went off starting other papers in widely separated places, and, of course, I can supervise all of them only in a general way. I can't give myself to any one." It was clear, though, that Hearst himself was eventually in command and that he was not, as many people believed, just a playboy who had hired Brisbane to do his thinking for him. But he was not simply the most powerful press lord of his day; he also wanted to be President and said that he would be to his day what Jefferson, Jackson and Lincoln had been to theirs. "I mean to restore democracy in the United States," he said almost placidly, without apparent emphasis. But it was understood that the operative word was not "democracy" but "I." "Mr. Hearst is not part of the general reform movement," Steffens wrote. "He simply has a movement of his own. This isn't democratic, this is plutocratic, autocratic." Hearst was going to give the people democracy the way Andrew Carnegie gave them public libraries.

Tom Johnson, Frederic Howe and Newton Baker, sitting by the fireplace in the mayor's Cleveland house, were full of praise for the article. It was "brilliant," they said, the best thing Steffens had ever done. It explained Hearst, and more than that, it pointed out "the weakness of any attempt to *give* democracy instead of enabling and helping the people to achieve it for themselves. . . . We shall know democrats now both by what they say and how they want it done." The election results that November seemed to be a vindication of this: Hearst was beaten by the Republican Charles Evans Hughes, who had become, by virtue of his investigation of the insurance business, yet another hero of the age of muckraking. Roosevelt, celebrating Hughes's election as a "victory for civilization," came closer than the Cleveland Democrats to an accurate reading of where Steffens himself stood on the issue of Hearst. For he sensed Steffens' paradoxic admiration for strong men and bosses, men like Johnson, for example. That Hearst article, he said to Taft, "tho faintly condemning him, is in reality an endorsement." As a matter of fact, Steffens told Whitlock just before the election, he intended to vote for Hearst.

IV

HEARST'S FATHER, STEFFENS WROTE, had been "one of the five or six men who got the most (which is saying a great deal) out of the first hurried exploitation of the rich, virgin resources of California the golden." More and more, though Steffens had got a great deal out of the East, he felt the pull of California the golden, wanted to settle there again one day. It was a matter partly of winning over Josephine, who had never seen the Pacific Coast and was happy now where they were, settled at Little Point with a mother too infirm to travel. For Steffens, though, the East was beginning to be a place of restraints.

In his journalism, even under the new freedoms of the *American Magazine*, he enjoyed at best a compromised independence; the editorial arguments about his Hearst article made it plain that the days of picnic and honeymoon were over. In order to further their business interests, he claimed, the others were pressuring him to rush his material, to scant the details and concentrate on the headlines. What counted was timeliness; all the research and writing in the world, Phillips told him, amounts to nothing "if we don't get the material into the magazine when it needs it." Phillips had a point. It simply wasn't "practicable" for Steffens to follow one story for six months or, worse, for him to confuse writing about Francis Heney and San Francisco, for example, with helping Francis Heney solve the problems of San Francisco. It was an impossible conflict. Steffens' power may have gone to his head, as Phillips believed, but he undeniably had power. He was a public figure whose arrivals and departures were noted in the local press, a name to be invoked in the furtherance of good causes, some of them more newsworthy than workable— with Mark Twain and President Mitchell of the United Mine Workers, he was on the governing committee of something known as the People's Lobby, a coalition that, it was hoped, would be to Congress and national politics what Dun and Bradstreet was to commerce. Steffens had the confidence and, in many cases, the gratitude of reform leaders all over the country who regarded him as a one-man committee of public correspondence and a force in politics; in Colorado ten thousand reprints of his article about Judge Lindsey were being circulated as campaign literature.

In January 1907 Steffens started for California with Josephine. She was enchanted with what she saw as the train bore west from Denver through the highlands of New Mexico to Arizona and the coast. On a motor trip with E. W. Scripps, the newspaper publisher who lived in misanthropic splendor at Miramar, his ranch near San Diego, she and Steffens even scouted some land that was for sale. They would think about it—thought about it too long, Scripps told them a few months later; the land boom was on. Meanwhile, from Scripps, an intermittent mover in progressive politics who valued Steffens as "an intellectual aristocrat," they heard once again the nagging paradox of leadership in a democracy. "One great, honest, fearless man," Scripps was to say, thinking simultaneously and indiscriminately of Roosevelt, Tom Johnson, Kaiser Wilhelm and the secret ballot, can overcome "all the forces of combined evil."

But after the visit with Scripps the mood of their trip changed. It rained all the time, Steffens recalled—rained in California, rained in Oregon. "The rain is waiting for me," Josephine said two years later when Steffens proposed another trip to the West. Ill with bronchitis, Steffens testily poured out his grievances in a letter to Phillips which drew an injured response. "You haven't confidence in us, and that is everything," Phillips wrote. "I could very easily by comparison show that you have had more out of this magazine than anybody else in proportion to what you have put in." Soon Josephine too was ill and depressed. She was already planning to go home alone when, at the beginning of April, she was called East to her father's deathbed.

Instead of opening up a new life for them their trip West reinforced the pattern of the old and pointed to its future: a resigned remoteness from each other, separations during which she was less a wife than a business manager. The decline of their marriage and their long childlessness he blamed on himself. He could always measure his regret against the exhilarations of being out in the world, active and powerful, but for Josephine there was only the sense of loss; she was husbandless as well as childless.

"My husband has become famous, but at a high price," she reported to the lawyer who had handled their affairs in Germany. "He is practically never at home. He is constantly traveling and then writing. He is known as a great political writer—he writes only about politics and is very radical, practically a socialist. . . . He's just coming back from California where he had to go once again. I expect him for Christmas. A few days at home, and then away he goes again."

Steffens, she wrote in a biographical sketch that she prepared for his lecture tours, had turned from exposure to

> the constructive side of his subject. Having made his demonstration he is ready now to draw his conclusions, and to give his opinion as to a cure. That cure he believes is the American himself, as a voting man. Mr. Steffens is an optimist; he is also a good American, too. He believes that the people will do right, even the grafters themselves, if they can be made to see the wrong and how to right it. And it is along this line of his work, its constructive side, that Mr. Steffens is now working, in print and on the platform.

"Let's talk socialism," he was now saying; and when he suggested to Ida Tarbell that they turn their magazine into "a Socialist organ" she stopped being a lady for once and told him what she thought of the idea. Prescribing cures was not the function of the *American Magazine*, as his associates saw it; prescribing cures was propaganda.

Paradoxically, at least by way of his new stress on cures rather than symptoms, he was now closer to Roosevelt than to his own colleagues on the magazine. A year had passed since Roosevelt's public disavowal; the dust had settled. "Fighting dishonesty as you are," Steffens wrote to him in March 1907, "you are doing more than all the rest of us so-called muckrakers put together to show the American people that the cause of graft and the result of all our corruption is simply misrepresentation in government, and that the cure is to regulate, to control, or, if these fail, to own those businesses which find it necessary to their success to corrupt men and cities and states and the United States." (Soon Steffens would be proposing this clause to Roosevelt as a plank in the 1908 platform of the Republican party.) As a matter of fact, he now said playfully, it was Roosevelt who seemed to be looking down at the muck: "You ask men in office to be honest, I ask them to serve the public."

From time to time they celebrated a fragile alliance. Friday, August 23, 1907—last glimpses of the politics of confidence and good hope, a mood of summer: Steffens went by launch from Little Point across Long Island Sound, remarkably undefiled, to Oyster Bay, then by car to Sagamore Hill where Roosevelt came out to greet him, took him into the study, where he had been dictating, and talked frankly and trustingly about Heney and reform Republicanism, about the iniquities of Wall Street. "If it should come to a choice between the business good and the enforcement of law against law-lessness," Roosevelt declared, "I will let the prosperity go," such as it was. The stock market had crashed in March, soon there would be a run on the banks, panic, and failures. All this showed just how skittish was a prosperity founded upon speculation, stock jobbery, and just plain water—someone had asked for a dollar in cash, the joke went, and the whole economy collapsed.

At lunch with his family and a few guests, Roosevelt ate enor-mously and fast (food and company had a way of making him "almost drunk," Steffens wrote) and talked all the while. Now it was his next message to Congress, Wall Street once again, the history of the Mongols, the problem of Puerto Rico and, with some urgency, the Japanese. They were rumored to be preparing for war, the President indicated, glancing to the lower end of the table where his wife sat flanked by two of his admirals, but the jingo fools in Japan would likely be brought to their senses not only by diplomacy but by a Pacific "practice cruise" of the entire United States Navy.

More of a menace than the Japanese, or even the muckrakers, if one judged the ferocity with which the President pursued his next subject, were "nature-fakers" (another Roosevelt epithet that stuck) like Jack London, Ernest Thompson Seton and the Reverend William J. Long, writers of outrageous animal fiction who were bamboozling the children of America into believing, for example, that bullfrogs ate barn swallows, that wolves had the stoic dignity of Marcus Aurelius and could actually penetrate to a caribou's heart on the first bite. After lunch, out on the veranda, the torrent of talk went on two hours longer, and then it was time to go home.

CHAPTER NINE

"Out of the muck"

I

ROOSEVELT, THE MOST CONSPICUOUS FIGURE IN A YOUNG MAN'S ERA, had become President at the age of forty-two. As he himself turned forty-two in April 1908, Lincoln Steffens looked on his own life with satisfaction and puzzlement. Within the limits of his profession he had achieved fame along with a certain hankering for power—he had made his fame, after all, as a student of power. He had achieved, too, a certain distinctive presence. This short, delicately built, nervous man dressed fastidiously and now wore a bristling mustache, a closely trimmed beard that gave him a European air, a fringe of hair down over his forehead. He had direct blue eyes, which flashed out from behind steel-rimmed spectacles, and a disarming smile. His conversation was soft-spoken, quizzical and audacious.

In contrast to the October day in 1892 when he landed in New York with a sinking heart, a hundred dollars from his father, and the knowledge that the time had come for him to stay put and hustle, he was now modestly well off, thanks to Krudewolf, his own skill as an investor, and Josephine's inheritance, about $25,000, from her father. There were not many other magazine writers who kept a country place with three servants near Greenwich. Not many critics of the "system" had been so well rewarded by it. This was one of his vulnerabilities: the morality of success, if one followed its trail, led to a secret hurting place. All along, it seemed, he had been asking the same question: How does one come to terms with a society in which the price of success seemed almost necessarily to be a compromised morality? Muckraking had examined this morality and, largely because it had, in fact, "succeeded," muckraking itself was now associated with venality, power-grabbing and malicious disruption. For Steffens, aware of his own "yellow streak," the same question of integrity kept coming up over the conference table at the *American Magazine*. Consensus editing was irksome and frustrating. So were the bitter exchanges with Phillips, conflicts of ego with ego. So was Steffens' suspicion that the hope of financial success was dictating to his fellow editors a policy of excessive tact. So was his sense that his function as a critic of the system was at odds with his part-ownership of the magazine he wrote for. Never again, he was coming to decide, would he go to work where his money was.

At the beginning of March 1908 he resigned from the *American* and arranged to dispose of his stock. At the age of forty-two—public moralist, messiah-at-large (as some joked about him), or simply "expert on politics" (as Josephine described him in publicity releases)—Steffens believed that his real work and success were still ahead of him. "Before I die," he told his sister Laura, "I believe I can help to bring about an essential change in the American mind."

He was now certain that muckraking in itself had run its course and led to no solutions. "We Americans have been out on a man hunt," he wrote in June 1908, perhaps for the wrong man. It was even possible, as Steffens urged in a paradox that was becoming as habitual as eating and smoking, that the bad man who knew what he was doing was potentially a more useful citizen—realistic, intelligent, unflinching—than the good man who could not help deluding himself. "The whole hunt, the hate and the spirit of vengeance upon men, whether of the law or of the mob, is wrong," Steffens now argued, voicing progressivism's belief that sin was really a problem of sociology; the cause of Adam's fall was not Adam or Eve, or even the Serpent, but simply the apple. "It is things, not men, that hurt us; it is bad conditions, not ill will, that make men do wrong." Muckraking, it seemed, had only been a way of shouting at society, and this was pointless, especially now that one had to shout louder and louder to get people to listen, much less to do something. Muckraking itself had become an easy target, as Steffens saw in a *Saturday*

Evening Post parody called "Contaminated Constantinople" by "Blinken Biffens," author of "Benighted Budapest" and "The Sin of Sacramento." (The important thing for "the compleat muckraker" to bear in mind, the parodist said, is that "every man who is 'out' is a reformer. Only the 'ins' are corrupt.")

In 1908, as he moved into what promised to be a new phase of his career, Steffens no longer believed in arraignments but solutions proposed in the faith that "man has only to tackle a problem to solve it somehow." As he told Roosevelt, he wanted to propose "a new and a broader base for political criticism. . . . I want to see our public men required to announce their remedies for our evils, and by these, and afterwards, by their records, judged, defeated, or re-elected." The remedies were to be found not in the courts or the laws, which only punished but did not prevent crimes against democracy, nor in government regulation, which presupposed the existence of good government, but in *politics*, and through politics to reforms of society that would eliminate or at least isolate the causes of corruption. Without the apple even the Serpent was powerless; the American political prayer, Steffens said, ought to be "Deliver us from temptation." The answer for him was a loose socialism founded on Christian ethics rather than Marxist doctrine; how could there be class warfare if the Golden Rule was applied in daily life? "When the old parties offer no choice, choose the Socialist party," he said in October 1908 endorsing Morris Hillquit as a candidate for Congress from New York. Steffens had already published in *Everybody's* an admiring interview with the party's candidate for President, Eugene Debs. From his campaign train "Red Special," Debs gratefully acknowledged his support. "You have written from and have been inspired by a social brain, a social heart, and a social conscience, and if you are not a socialist I do not know one." But it didn't much matter whether he was a socialist or an anarchist or whatever, Steffens was saying. The important thing was to support third parties, to experiment with almost any alternative to plutocracy, to "do something for the common good and quit being just plain hogs." In this spirit of good hope he entered upon a series of trials of brain, heart and conscience.

II

WITH HIS FRIEND THE BOSTON MERCHANT, civic patriot and social philosophizer Edward A. Filene, Lincoln Steffens for a while shared a belief in what Alexis de Tocqueville had called "self-interest rightly understood." This was not a lofty principle, Tocqueville warned. "It does not aim at mighty objects, but it attains without excessive exertion all those at which it aims."

Filene's father, an East Prussian Jew, had come over in the exodus of 1848, and the democratic faith of 1848 lived on in his son. By doggedness and applied intelligence Filene came to terms with a limp, the result of an accident in childhood, and a skin condition that made him hide from sight as an adolescent and, he said, prevented him from going to Harvard. His maimed and cheerless personality fed itself on platitudes, jargon, flattery and instant obedience; but a few people, like Steffens, found him attractive not simply because he was rich and useful but also because he was an object of study, a coelacanthine oddity in the natural history of commerce.

Filene had taken over the family business and with his brother made it into one of the most profitable department stores in America. His celebrated "Automatic Bargain Basement" demonstrated the way enlightened self-interest could be applied to the problem of distribution. Filene sold, at a reduced price, merchandise that he would otherwise have carted away. The customers picked up bargains in the basement and then went upstairs to buy other things at full price. Advised by a fellow heir to the ideals of 1848, his attorney Louis D. Brandeis, Filene applied the principle of enlightened self-interest to his eight hundred employees, whose loyalty and earnings, by design and profit-sharing, were so bound up with the success of the store that, as a next step, he planned to turn William Filene's Sons into a cooperative owned and controlled by the workers, an example of what Brandeis was calling industrial democracy.

The workers never did move to take over the store, as Filene wanted them to. Instead they used their voting power for settling small issues, such as hours and holidays, and eventually it was his board of directors who ousted Filene from control, not his workers. You couldn't even give power away, it seemed. "Maybe your life shows, among other things," Steffens told Filene many years later, "that Mussolini is right when he says that the people don't want to govern themselves, that they want George to do it." As Filene might have conceded, the failure of his experiment proved that self-interest, except in confined areas like the Automatic Bargain Basement (where one also saw jungle law in action as well as herd behavior), was not a lofty principle and perhaps not even a reliable one.

In 1908, however, heartened by his success as an innovative merchant, Filene was active in the Boston City Club (which he founded), the Chamber of Commerce, the Good Government Association, and similar organizations intended to confront what had to be called, pure and simple, the Problem of Boston, a problem of waste, corruption, decay, and erosion of civic purpose. Along with its physical and institutional fabric the mind of the city had begun to go. According to a recent visitor, H. G. Wells, Boston's mind had simply "filled up," like the Back Bay, and decided there was nothing more to be learned. Frightened and outnumbered by the Irish, who were already so established at city hall that they could afford to feud among themselves for power, the Yankees found comfort in fitful reform movements and in a cultural life that had become merely Hubbish. The official culture professed classical and Christian ideals; politics and business were something else altogether. "Boston has carried the practice of hypocrisy to the nth degree of refinement, grace and failure," Steffens was to write. "New England is dying of hypocrisy." When Filene and the Good Government Association decided to recruit Steffens as a sort of pathologist, the extent of the damage to Boston had already been revealed, in unwelcome detail, by an investigative body, the Finance Commission, appointed, in one of his rare moments of political napping, by the Democratic mayor and future dynast, John F. Fitzgerald. Fitzgerald spent the next two years out of a job.

"It will take time," Steffens had written in 1903, "to evolve masters of the (in America) unstudied art of municipal government—time and demand. So far there has been no market for municipal experts in this country." Five years later, partly through his own work as muckraker, there *was* such a market. All through the first half of 1903, and even before Steffens resigned from the *American Magazine*, Filene had been offering him the job of municipal expert. According to the terms that he agreed to in July, Steffens was to spend a year in Boston, on a salary of $10,000 from the Good Government Association, writing, in greater depth than he had ever been allowed before, an account of the Problem of Boston and, at the same time, proposing ways to solve the problem. He was no longer just an investigator and observer. Now, as he saw it, he was taking an active role in practical politics.

"It's the biggest piece of work I ever attempted," he told his father, "and I have a dim hope that it may lead to the establishment by me of a profession, a new calling; that of a city manager or municipal architect. For I think other cities will want, as they need, that sort of service." At the beginning of October Steffens moved his household—including his mother-in-law, servants, a dog, a cat, and a bird, together with seventeen trunks—from Little Point to 25 West Cedar Street, an old house on Beacon Hill.

Soon after his well-publicized arrival, the Boston papers were hailing him as the city's "most interesting immigrant" and even a savior perhaps come in time, said the *Post*, "to save Boston from the pit which our own people have digged for our city." More skeptical editors described him as having become "an exponent of the theory that deodorization is better than muckraking," a writer who was now motivated by the desire to get good copy and "help the cause of good government cover itself with medals." At a meeting with the press at the City Club, Steffens declared that he had come to Boston looking not for exposure but for "good." "I know of no instance in history where prosecution has proved successful in reform movements. What interests me in Boston is that practically everyone wants to see the thing made right. I have doubts about mere good will, but it ought to be tried somewhere. If it will succeed anywhere, it will here." Trailing such rosy clouds, he set off on a fall and winter season of interviews, sociological and statistical tours, lectures, speeches, receptions and dinners—glimpses of the total life of the city, preparations for what he called his experiment in "constructive politics."

When Brand Whitlock passed through Boston in February 1909 he found Steffens smiling, buoyant, and at the top of his form. They went to a dinner at the City Club, where, according to Whitlock, three or four hundred men discussed the city charter, recently revised, "in a lofty and wholly unintelligent and inefficient way"; then on to the Lincoln Centenary Exercises at Faneuil Hall, where Steffens, introduced as "the Nation's Teacher of Civics," spoke for ten minutes on the sovereignty of the ballot; and finally, at a late supper, Steffens played the role of Socrates and drew from Whitlock, for the benefit and disorientation of the solid citizens at the table, "anarchistic and shocking replies." "I am trying to educate Boston," Steffens explained. He even mischievously proposed a new sort of seminar to President Eliot of Harvard as they walked through the Yard one day. He planned to instruct students in the practical ways of bribery, he told Eliot, but it wasn't his function to deter them. "Oh, no," he said. "I don't mean to keep the boys from succeeding in their professions. All I want to do is to make it impossible for them to be crooks and not know it. Intelligence is what I am aiming at, not honesty." This was too much for Eliot, despite forty years he had spent opening Harvard to the winds of contemporary life. He bowed politely and went on his way.

Nevertheless, Steffens managed to establish a gadfly relationship, informal and unofficial, with Eliot's students. Two of them in particular, Walter Lippmann and John Reed, were to say that their lives had been changed as a result. In almost every point of temperament the two were mirror opposites: Lippmann was to win the trust of men in power and drift out of socialism into eminence; Reed, demonstrating "an inordinate desire to be arrested" (according to Lippmann), was to ally himself with revolution and be buried under the Kremlin wall.

> More than any one man Lincoln Steffens has influenced my mind [Reed said in 1917 just before he went to Russia]. I met him first while I was at Harvard, where he came loving youth, full of understanding, with the breath of the world clinging to him. I was afraid of him then—afraid of his wisdom, his seriousness. . . . Being with Steffens is to me like flashes of clear light; it is as if I see him, and myself, and the world with new eyes. I tell him what I see and think, and it comes back to me beautiful, full of meaning. He does not judge or advise—he simply makes everything clear.

Walter Lippmann, too—another member of a Harvard group that included, among its writers, T. S. Eliot, Alan Seeger, Conrad Aiken and Heywood Broun—responded to Steffens as a bringer of light. He explains people to themselves, Lippmann said, explains even "powerful conservatives" to themselves. "Never after do they exercise their power with the same unquestioning ruthlessness." Encouraged by Steffens, Lippmann led the Harvard Socialist Club, organized a discussion course in politics, economics and the problem of poverty, and in general helped to introduce what Reed called, "for lack of a better name, the manifestation of the modern spirit."

> The college political clubs which had formerly been quadrennial mushroom growths for the purpose of drinking beer, parading and burning red fire, took on a new significance. The Club drew up a platform for the Socialist Party in the city elections. It had social legislation introduced into the Massachusetts legislature. Its members wrote articles in the college papers challenging undergraduate ideals, and muckraked the University for not paying its servants living wages. . . . All over the place radicals sprang up, in music, painting, poetry, the theater.

"There is not enough intellectual curiosity in your college," Steffens told Reed, recalling his own career at Berkeley. "There is very little in any American college." In talks and informal meetings Steffens was now urging experience, open criticism, student power. Sixty years before Cambridge's university community finally generated a radical analysis called *Who Rules Harvard?* Steffens put the question to Reed and the other editors of the *Harvard Monthly* and suggested that here was a chance "for a very interesting controversy and for the leakage of some light. . . . It will be significant, I think, to enquire and report whether it is a monarchy, an aristocracy, or even a benevolent oligarchy. . . . Ask the student body editorially why they are so content to be unrepresented directly in their college government; whether their indifference doesn't show how and why they will neglect politics after graduation; and whether it doesn't show that, if we had had good kings, we all would still be monarchists."

At dinner with Professor William James in January 1909, Steffens outlined the plans for Boston. "We are seeking out the biggest and often the most selfish men in the community," he explained as a corollary to his belief that "big men like big jobs." "To them we are holding out the vision of the great things that might be done with a city"—the "big men" were to take on the "big job" of finding practical solutions to the problems of municipal government. (Professor James, a recent convert to socialism, was skeptical.) "Boston—

1915," as the grand scheme was called when it was unveiled at a City Club dinner in the spring, was supposed to be a timetable for six years of civic uplift and improvement. By 1915, according to projections, the city, its business and industry, and its people were all to have been persuaded by a vigorous propaganda and education campaign that self-interest and the public interest were not only compatible but inseparable. Meanwhile, the people were to be given a glimpse of the promised land at an exposition that Filene planned for November. According to *The Survey*, a generally cautious journal dedicated to social problems, Boston's businessmen were joining the movement "with the zest of a group of schoolboys turned loose in an apple orchard." The New York *Sun* said that the Boston atmosphere was "charged and surcharged with hot air and civic righteousness," and Lincoln Steffens, diverted from his work in the muckfields, was now "stricken with the uplift fever" and had become "one of the most ardent and forceful workers in the cause of banners, oratory and welcomes home."

Content so far, Steffens summered at Marblehead and on Filene's yacht. But already there were intimations of trouble, and he tried to reason them away: "I am always in doubt at this stage of the game," he now said. His Boston report was not going so fast as he expected. And now he was less secure in his new profession of municipal doctor whose job it was to treat symptoms and support vital functions while busying himself with a diagnosis that was supposed to lead to nothing short of a cure. He still believed in cures—"In social as in physical life," he was saying in 1909, "there is a cause for every effect . . . and to stop the fever you must remove the cause." But "mere good will" was not working out. Neither was "Boston—1915." Its parent, after all, was Filene's Good Government Association, a coalition of the Chamber of Commerce, the Merchants Association, the Associated Board of Trade, and other such groups. Filene believed that these could become progressive and innovating forces, but the fact was that Boston's organized business interests, when all was said and done, were prepared to support only the standard brands of reform.

"Boston—1915," drawn up by a committee on which Steffens had only an outsider's voice, ended up as another attempt (in H. L. Mencken's phrase) "to bring on Utopia at an inside price." The plan skirted any serious examination of the economic order, refused to consider a rise in the tax rate, drew back from even the moderate heterodoxy of municipal ownership, and, according to Steffens, failed to appeal to the natural leaders of the community.* "Boston—1915," he said, had fallen into the hands of "heelers" rather than "principals."

Shuffling through Filene's Exposition at Copley Square in November, the citizens of Boston were treated to movies, an Italian marionette show, statistical charts, displays of model housing of the future, and a demonstration, put on by the Massachusetts Institute of Technology, of advanced methods of garbage collection. Elsewhere, however, the Good Government Association had been reenacting a familiar tragicomedy. Having pushed through a new city charter that increased the power and term of the mayor, the businessmen reformers nominated James Jackson Storrow, a patrician investment banker, to run against John F. Fitzgerald, who, as "Honey Fitz," had returned from political exile. Storrow, a Protestant of enormous wealth and chilling rectitude, proved to be tongue-tied and inept in public discussion, and his supporters blundered into dividing the voters of Boston along religious lines. Filene sent an urgent appeal to Steffens. "Is there any of the material you have gathered that can be used for the fight? Help—as quickly as you can." It was already too late.

Defeat in Boston was only part of a tide of reform defeats in the 1909 elections. In his third book, *Upbuilders*, published that summer, Steffens had written a farewell salute to the politics of good leaders ("new-style Christians," he thought of calling them) and good hope. The people of Cleveland, he told Tom Johnson, "may have made you sick, as they have me. But they have not disturbed my confidence that in the long run the people will go right more surely than any individuals or set of individuals. I believe, for example, that they will reelect you at the next election." But that November, after eight years, during which he had made Cleveland "the

* The plan's statement on transportation, an example of innocuousness trailing off into the comic, called for "public deliberations between the transportation interests and the public, represented by men who best understand Boston's needs in transportation, advised by experts familiar with the latest improvements at home and abroad, these deliberations to be guided by the assumption that the true interests of the transportation companies and of the public are identical." ("A Plan for a Boston Plan," *The Survey*, Vol. XXII, No. 10 [June 5, 1909], p. 396.)

best-governed city in America," Johnson was defeated. Broken in
health and in fortune, he returned to private life doubting whether
he had accomplished anything of value. In San Francisco Heney
was defeated as district attorney: three years of heroic work as an
investigator had gone for nothing, it seemed; Heney was now just a
scapegoat. Reform was beaten in Jersey City, in Philadelphia. "All
my friends who ran were beaten this year," Steffens told his father.
The only exception was Brand Whitlock, and he was already tired
of politics and within two years would leave elective office for good.
Shortly after the November defeats he came to visit Steffens at
Little Point, and together, Steffens recalled, "We spent the time
grieving over our losses." The people were stupid and gullible, Whitlock complained; above all, they were ungrateful. "The people
should not be grateful," Steffens reminded him later. "As Dooley
said, when Hennessey had remarked that republics were ungrateful:
'Yes. That's why they are republics.' If the people were grateful,
they would be corrupted by the magnificent gifts to them of Rockefeller, Carnegie, *et al.* If they were grateful, they would stick to a
leader after his usefulness was over."

Aside from Whitlock's survival there was small consolation to be
found in politics. In Washington, William Howard Taft was proving an embarrassing successor to Roosevelt. As far as progressives
were concerned Taft was no leader at all but instead, in the description supplied by the Iowa insurgent, Senator Jonathan P. Dolliver,
"a large, amiable island surrounded entirely by persons who know
exactly what they want." Two magazines had asked Steffens to "do"
Taft. He said, "No, leave the man alone; he is doing himself better
than anybody else can."

Despite all his divagations, Roosevelt, it was clear, really had been
holding the left-center together, and now that he was gone, off
shooting animals in Africa, a time of scattering and waste had arrived. Steffens' own activities were increasingly centrifugal. He still
believed in politics and political leaders like La Follette, but he was
coming to suspect that maybe only revolutions solved problems. He
was president of the Liberal Club, a Greenwich Village association
of "radicals," "rich anarchists," and "intellectuals" who, nonetheless, managed to blackball Emma Goldman when she was proposed
for membership. More strongly than ever Steffens was drawn to
gospel Christianity and to practical applications of the Golden Rule;

but at the same time, out of loyalty to Tom L. Johnson, he served as publicist, fund raiser, and tactician in the thinning ranks of the single-taxers. What was needed, he told Johnson, was an issue that "would crystallize all the sentiment of the American people today and give a common point to all the now separate fights that are being waged."

During the fall of 1909 he tried his hardest to bring the scattered leaders together again. E. W. Scripps, then in the grip of his intermittent ambition to form a party of "liberals and patriots," was willing to offer Miramar, his San Diego ranch, as a conference site at Christmas and to pay for time and travel. But after Steffens had completed the intricate arrangements necessary to bring twenty or thirty public men to the same remote adobe ranch-house on the same day, Scripps changed his mind. As he warned Steffens' earlier, he was acutely susceptible to "nervous disorders" and the "black beast of neurasthenia"—so much so, he said, that "I have not been reading your articles or following you up closely because, Steffens, your writings generally have a depressing effect upon my spirit and induce a feeling of pessimism."

This, in itself, had been hard enough to take, but now that Scripps had abruptly decided to cancel the conference the impression remained that whether he had done this for clinical reasons or out of simple cussedness, he had behaved in a "scurvy" way. Steffens was left with the chore of writing letters of apology all around and the conviction that rich men, though they were sometimes usable if rarely reliable, suffered from megalomania, stinginess, and violent moral contortionism. Here was that millionaire visionary, E. A. Filene, for example, agreeing, through his secretary, to contribute all of $100—anonymously—to La Follette's campaign fund, while Scripps himself, in a gassy discourse on the topic of "Statesmanship and Poverty," argued that money sapped motivation and therefore he wasn't going to contribute anything at all. It was enough to make a man vomit.

Nothing was going right that fall and winter. Steffens was ill with a throat infection. A favorite dog was run over by a car near Little Point and killed, and Josephine's grief was more than that of a childless woman desperately attached to a pet; it was ominously overwrought. "My dear Lincoln," she wrote, "I mourn him and I miss him so cruelly, that I cannot keep the tears back from my eyes or keep my voice steady." She was not consoled by Thomas Lawson's gift to them of a pedigreed bullpup named Frenzy, a reminder of the heyday of speculation and muckraking. Then, on the last day of 1909, fire broke out at Little Point and destroyed two rooms. It was depressing to live with the smell of smoke and wet char.

Meanwhile Steffens' Boston book, to which, in a more hopeful time, he had given the title *Boston, A Promise*, dragged on despite letters from Filene's committee accusing him of procrastination and broken promises. By the spring of 1910 he was already seven months late in delivering his manuscript. He was worried, sick with bronchitis, and losing weight. Maybe he would never finish the book. "Maybe Boston will finish me." The book withered away into inconsequence: a couple of articles published in 1914, by which time hardly anyone remembered what all the excitement had been about; a pile of useless manuscript that turned up in Filene's office years later. "What my committee expected," Steffens told Upton Sinclair, "was an exposure of the political conditions, which I simply could not go into; it was such an old story"—the same story everywhere, in cities, states, the federal government, the national structure of power and capital. Perhaps, as he planned to show in an altogether different book he was now working on, only Jesus had the answer— "I find that Jesus saw what we see; he understood, as his disciples don't, the evils, their causes; and he had a cure."

Steffens' bafflement in the world of events was reinforced by a period of withdrawal, itself an effect as much as a cause. A long time ago, in his Steffens grandfather, he had observed this slow drifting into immobility and silence. "Rather early," his own father too had begun to "retire," Steffens said, using another word for "withdraw." As for himself, it was not his own style to be concerned with the shadows or even the bright places of his inner space, yet he was soon to acknowledge that "something happened to me about the time I was half-way along in my Boston book. It lasted till Josephine died, and then for a year, so that some people thought it was her death that did it. I know better. I know they were wrong." He failed in Boston, he said, because this was a job for men of action, not for intellectuals. Toward the end of his life, he was to tell a Tom Mooney rally that an intellectual is someone who "can't *do* a damn thing." He was echoing Lenin then, but he was also carrying on the same process of confounding his inner and his outer life, of rendering a psychological state in ideological terms.

At Little Point during the early months of 1910 Steffens wasn't *doing* much of anything. Absorbed in New Testament studies in preparation for the book he hoped to write sometime, he led an uneventful life which was altogether satisfactory to him. He was as out of things as he wished to be, semiretired, semiwithdrawn, at the age of forty-four and with no pressing need to go out and earn money. Josephine, already suffering from what was later diagnosed as Bright's disease and beginning to decline into chronic invalidism and terminal illness, had a more poignant sense of time passing than he did. With all the force she could muster, she described to him the nature of his Christianized nirvana, so nicely provided for. She said that it was "like dying." "And I could see that it was," Steffens later wrote, his cadence still conveying the depth of his depression, "but I thought—I would not have dared say it—that dying was not so bad. It was the pleasantest and perhaps the most serviceable thing I had ever done."

III

"WHAT I HAVE DREAMED OF DOING IS TO WORK UNDER YOU," Walter Lippmann wrote to Steffens in May 1910; Steffens had come out of his semiretirement and joined the editorial board of *Everybody's Magazine*. "Can you use me in your work? There is no position I should go at with more eagerness, because there is no kind of work that appeals to me as much as yours does. Money does not happen to be an important consideration for me at the present time. Opportunity to work and learn is the thing I am looking for." The editors of *Everybody's* were skeptical, but Steffens, faced with a new opportunity to exercise his faith in the young, took on this twenty-year-old beginner and was not disappointed. "Lippmann, the student I was challenged to make a writer of in a year," he said in 1911, "is not only writing articles for the magazine, he is now one of the editors." Only five years after he came to work for Steffens, having meanwhile had a taste of practical politics and written two books, Lippmann had established himself as a public philosopher; in the eyes of Theodore Roosevelt, he was "the most brilliant man of his age in all the United States."

As Steffens' researcher at first, Lippmann worked out of Little Point and lived nearby. Together they muckraked Greenwich and at a town meeting at the end of December 1910 demonstrated, with charts and supporting evidence, that this select community, whatever beliefs it had held about itself, was in reality as riddled with privilege as any, and as much in need of change. Lippmann worked, unavailingly, on the Boston book as well, but mostly he traveled through the East and Midwest collecting data in support of what he later described as Steffens' "bold and brilliant guess" that the business world had its own forms of political organization and that "American sovereignty has passed from our political establishment to the national organization of money, credit, and centralized business."

"We were looking not for the evils of Big Business, but for its anatomy," Lippmann said. "We found that the anatomy of Big Business was strikingly like that of Tammany Hall: the same pyramiding of influence, the same tendency of power to center on individuals who did not necessarily sit in the official seats, the same effort of human organizations to grow independently of legal arrangements." The undisputed ruler of "the money power" was J. P. Morgan, whose firm, according to Lippmann's notes, held directorships in thirty-nine banks, which had nearly a billion dollars out on loan. Again, though, one had to stop at Tammany's question. What are you going to do about it?

If the question was the same, the answers, at least, should have been different. Through Steffens, Lippmann was meeting the Old Guard of muckraking and reform: Heney, Spreckels and Fremont Older; Tom Johnson, Newton Baker and Frederic Howe; Brand Whitlock. They sought out Steffens in New York or at Little Point and clustered around him. As Lippmann viewed them, in belief even more than in age they belonged to another era of history. He was beginning his career armed with a certainty most of them had not yet acquired; the political problem was one of freedom and control in an industrial society, not of greed or deflected morality.

The invisible government is malign [Lippmann was to write in 1913]. But the evil doesn't come from the fact that it plays horse with the Newtonian theory of the constitution. What is dangerous about it is that we do not see it, cannot use it, and are compelled to submit to it. The nature of political power we shall not change. If that is the way human societies organize sovereignty, the sooner we face that fact the better. For the object of democracy is not to imitate the rhythm of the stars but to harness political power to the nation's need. If corporations and governments have indeed gone on a joy ride the business of reform is not to set up fences, Sherman Acts and injunctions into which they can bump, but to take the wheel and to steer.

The solution lay in mastery, not in drift, and to that end, Lippmann concluded, the work of the muckrakers had been a waste, a descriptive, historical exercise that dealt with conventional acts and could have been performed almost as well by a couple of graduate students brought over from Germany.

Lippmann was to recall that Steffens seemed "too whimsical for a permanent diet," too paradoxic, literary and abstract; the series of articles on the banking monopoly did not really get "down to grips with anything," Lippmann said. He was not alone in feeling this. "We have been the blind leading the blind," Steffens himself confessed in December 1910, after Lippmann had been with him for about five months, "but we have led, and not so very far astray, and we are beginning to see the light. I suppose some young fellow like Lippmann will expose us some day, and I say, let 'em expose us. No one can throw more dirt on some of us than we have eaten in our private humility." Since *The Shame of the Cities*, it seemed, history had been passing him by, and at times, with his wife, Josephine, dying before his eyes, he saw his work as an array of outworn tactics and unsupported hopes. Josephine slipped downward each day, but she still believed that she would recover and made plans for the future. "Her willful, able mind, her strong character—these hurt her now," Steffens told his sister Laura. "She is so hard to manage." In anger and grief she died on January 7, 1911.

There were other deaths in Steffens' circle around this time: his mother; Josephine's; Tom Johnson, worn out at fifty-six; and in February 1912, the retired banker Joseph Steffens, who, like his father before him, "drifted very gradually into physical quiet and absolute silence." Steffens took these losses as they came, but Josephine's death "knocked me down," he said, "knocked me out." After nineteen years of marriage he discovered that he was helpless at the small details of living. He had to face up to his own inadequacy, his dependence on her, and also to her compensating fervor and strength, her penetrating awareness of him, even of his unspoken and unacknowledged thoughts. As in the other love relationships of his life, he had received far more than he had given; it was not fair, it was shameful, yet what could he have done about it?

He found among Josephine's papers, along with an unfinished novel, a diary that she had been keeping, "partly for me, I think." The diary made it clear to him that he had thought very little about her all those years and that she had always known this. He had been a failure as a husband, and "an ass" for finding out only when it was too late. The diary was her way of settling accounts with him—"an epoch-making revelation of me to me," he recalled, "one case where a man got his, really saw himself done to a turn." He had never been able to muckrake himself, she had done it for him once again, this time with finality. And, together with her novel, the diary made all too plain the hollowness of their marriage, the hollowness of middle-class life in general, with its insistence on conformity at the expense of vital impulse. Society was made up of "legitimate grafters," he was soon to say, generalizing from the devastated recognition of himself at the age of forty-five.

A month after Josephine died, Steffens was amazed to see that his grief had not abated. "It deepens and grows," he said in a mood of self-scrutiny, "and with the increase of pain goes the process of idealization and of penitence." Out of idealization and penitence came a reinforced belief in the spirit of gospel Christianity, in innate goodness, and in retrievability. "I, a muckraker and a pessimist, a reporter who went forth 'looking for evil and found it, of course,' lots of it—I have come up out of the muck believing that Christianity will work; that we can trust mankind; that liberty and reason, education and patience and kindness; in brief, that faith, hope, and charity would save the world. And I mean now. I mean right here in the United States in this year of our Lord, 1911."

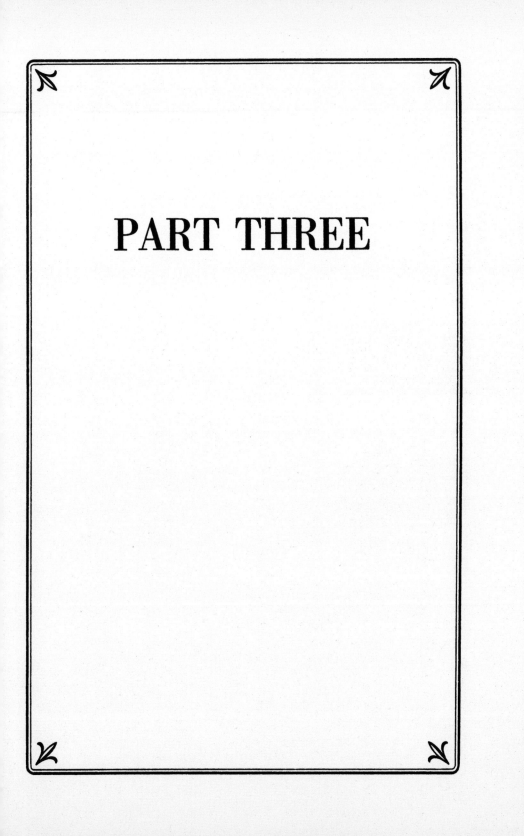

PART THREE

CHAPTER TEN

"Somewhat like handling dynamite"

I

"DEAR MR. STEFFENS," WALTER LIPPMANN WROTE from Topeka, Kansas, in mid-April 1911.

> Before I left I wanted badly to tell you a little of what this year with you has meant to me. . . . Writing it down while you weren't looking on makes it a little easier. You often asked me whether the year had been worthwhile. Lord, if I could tell you and make you believe it. You'd know then why "Everybody who knows you loves you." You gave me yourself—and then you ask me whether it has been worthwhile. For that I can't write down my thanks. I shall have to live them.
>
> But whenever I understand a man and like him, instead of hating him or ignoring him, it'll be your work. You've got into my blood, I think, and there'll be a little less bile in the world as a result. You opened your wonderful experience to me. It was like letting loose a hungry man in Park & Tilford's. You gave me a chance to start.

To take Lippmann's place as companion in Steffens' loneliness came John Reed, back from European adventures and looking for a job in New York during the spring of 1911. At first as a favor to Reed's father, and then for the sake of Reed himself, Steffens got him hired as an assistant editor on the *American*, gave him advice about writing, lent him money from time to time, guided him out of an engagement he had contracted with a French girl. At the end of the summer, after trips to California and Europe and on the point of assuming, briefly, the editorship of an evening newspaper, the New York *Globe*, Steffens moved into two front rooms at 42 Washington Square South, the ramshackle establishment, kept by frowsy land-ladies, where Reed and some Harvard friends lived in what Reed celebrated as "Anarchic Liberty."

Steffens' friend Hutchins Hapgood visited the house at Washington Square and remembered "the large generous room of the old-fashioned kind, and the young lusty poet so full of life that it was one of my extraordinary experiences, contrasting so with the paternal, amused, and hopeful Steffens. I also felt a little annoyed at Reed's Gargantuan gall and his three-dimensional self-confidence." In the discourse of the Village, and in his own image of himself, Reed was a Poet, even though his talent was not really for poetry but instead for passionate reportage—"Wherever his sympathies marched with the facts, Reed was superb," Lippmann said. Like Scott Fitzgerald, born ten years after him, Reed was a Young Man from the Provinces who came to New York dazzled by what Fitzgerald was to call its promises of "fantastic success and eternal youth." For a brief period in the Village Reed could have declared, along with Fitzgerald, "I had everything I wanted and knew I would never be so happy again." In time, both as romantic hero and dedicated agent of the social revolution Reed achieved the same symbolizing preeminence for the radical decade of the Village as Fitzgerald did for the succeeding speakeasy decade of Fifth Avenue and the Island.

With John Reed and his group Steffens, in middle age, lived once again in the country of the young. Recognizing that many of the things he stood for—muckraking, grass-roots politics, the reform urge, a belief in good men rather than economic forces—by now belonged to a prerevolutionary past quickly fading into a hollow joke, he offered the young an open mind, encouragement. What do you want to do? he had asked Reed. "I said I didn't know," Reed recalled, "except that I wanted to write. Steffens looked at me with that lovely smile: 'You can do anything you want to,' he said; and I believed him. Since then I have gone to him with my difficulties and troubles, and he has always listened while I solved them myself in the warmth of his understanding." In the "clear light" of Steffens' presence, Reed saw himself with "new eyes."

What Steffens cherished in Reed was curiosity, freedom from conclusions, freedom from defeat; through Reed it sometimes seemed that he could reenact his own life. "I had never seen anything so near to pure joy," Steffens said in 1920, looking back to the beginning of a period of nine years during which he and Reed shared the spirit of revolt that came to the Village and together witnessed industrial violence in America, the breakup of Europe, revolution in Mexico and in Russia. "If only we could keep him so, we might have a poet at last who could see and sing nothing but joy. Convictions were what I was afraid of. I tried to steer him away from convictions."

Yet, as Reed explored the city, much as Steffens had once done, he formed some of the convictions that remained intact when he lay on his deathbed in a Moscow typhus ward in 1920. He wrote:

> I couldn't help but observe the ugliness of poverty and all its train of evil, the cruel inequality between rich people who had too many motorcars and poor people who didn't have enough to eat. It didn't come to me from books that the workers produced all the wealth of the world, which went to those who did not earn it. . . . All I know is that my happiness is built on the misery of other people, that I eat because others go hungry, that I am clothed when other people go almost naked through the frozen cities in winter; and that fact poisons me, disturbs my serenity, makes me write propaganda when I would rather play—though not so much as it once did.

When 25,000 silk workers went out on strike in Paterson, New Jersey, in 1913 and the millowners opposed them with armed force, Reed covered the encounter for *The Masses*—he called his first report "War In Paterson," and for a while after he was advertised by his magazine as its "jail editor." Then, fusing art and social protest in one spectacle, Reed staged in Madison Square Garden a great Pageant of the Strike. The Paterson millworkers took part, and it ended triumphantly, with the singing of the "Marseillaise" and the "Internationale."

Toward the end of 1911 Lincoln Steffens responded to a similar industrial war in Los Angeles. His conduct in that war reflected certain traits—soon to be observed in the American role at the Paris Peace Conference—of the national sensibility and style: a conflictive juggling of Christian and political imperatives, a sense of redemptive mission, a tendency to declare purposes on a lofty level of moral abstraction, a tendency also to regard innocence as a positive virtue and sincerity as an instrument of policy. Given its representative nature, it was only fitting that Steffens' role in the McNamara trial should have provoked a national response and ended in allegory.

II

FOR TWENTY YEARS, MAJOR GENERAL HARRISON GRAY OTIS, publisher of the Los Angeles *Times,* had battled the labor unions and kept them out of his city. Consequently, in October 1910, after a dynamite explosion destroyed part of the *Times* building just as a general strike was threatened for Los Angeles, Otis accused the unions of waging warfare by murder as well as terror—twenty bodies were found in the wreckage. In editorials that were echoed and amplified across a country already fearful of class conflict, Otis vowed that the supposed dynamiters, "Unionite murderers" who had committed "The Crime of the Century," must surely hang and the labor movement in general be held accountable. The following April, acting on information from William J. Burns, the detective who had made his fame in the San Francisco graft investigations, police in Detroit and Indianapolis arrested the secretary of the International Association of Bridge and Structural Iron Workers, John J. McNamara, and his brother James. Burns himself extracted from another member of their union a confession so incriminating that the prosecution seemed to have a perfect case. The McNamara brothers were charged with dynamiting and murder, and were extradited to California for trial.

"Murder is murder," declared Theodore Roosevelt, America's most influential private citizen. The Colonel's gift for disarming simplisms of a Solomonic cast had improved with time and with freedom from Presidential responsibilities. "The question of organized labor or organized capital, or of the relations of either with the community at large, has nothing whatever to do with this issue," he wrote in *The Outlook,* the weekly magazine of which he was contributing editor. "All we are now concerned with is the grave and vital question of fact whether or not the accused men have been guilty of murder, and of murder under circumstances of peculiar foulness and atrocity."

On the other side, Samuel Gompers, President of the American

Federation of Labor, protested Roosevelt's "insidious indictment of organized labor" for standing by the McNamaras. Labor and socialist leaders claimed that the impending trial, about which Roosevelt, Otis and other public voices were waxing so bloodthirsty, had less to do with alleged murder than with a conspiracy to stop the unions in Los Angeles. Some labor spokesmen argued that Otis and his agents had framed the McNamaras, the object being to cover up the fact that the explosion had really been caused by leaking gas, proof of the callous irresponsibility of management. In any event, there was little doubt expressed, on the labor side and among liberals in general, that the McNamaras were innocent. Gompers had visited the brothers in jail, heard John swear his innocence, and then, after a fervent handclasp, went forth to raise a legal defense fund of a quarter of a million dollars. He engaged the services of Clarence Darrow, who had never yet lost a client to the executioner and was determined to protect this record, perhaps at any cost. One of Darrow's assistants was Job Harriman, a former preacher turned lawyer, who was now the Socialist candidate for mayor of Los Angeles. On October 11, 1911, the McNamara brothers were led handcuffed to trial. It was soon plain from the wrangling within the courtroom—after a month only eight jurors had been chosen—and from the publicity and hysteria outside that labor was indeed on trial and that the function of the jury, if a jury ever was empaneled, would be less one of determining the facts than of refereeing a confrontation of class interests—or, as the Otis camp saw it, of "followers of the Red flag and the forces of law and order."

As he followed the McNamara case from England and Europe that summer, Steffens made certain characteristic assumptions that ran counter to current liberal belief. He and the Scotsman Keir Hardie, leader of the Labour party, agreed that in all likelihood the McNamaras—or their union, at any rate—were guilty. This sort of labor violence was an old story; during the past five years there had been close to a hundred similar dynamitings that implicated the Bridge and Structural Iron Workers. Why not cut through the issue to the bone and deal not with guilt but with causes?

"I don't have to wait for the verdict to know the truth," Steffens was soon saying. "I want to assume that organized labor has committed the dynamiting and other crimes charged against it, and raise the question: Why?" Justice could be done, he reasoned, only if such acts of violence were examined not as murder, as Roosevelt would have it, but as issues in economics and psychology that would have to be tried in the public mind as well as in the courtroom. "Only the press can try it," he said in November, for the rules of evidence forbade any discussion before a jury of causes, conditions and precedents. By this time Steffens' interest in the McNamaras had brought him to Los Angeles on assignment from the New York *Globe* and a syndicate including the Boston *Globe*, the Chicago *Daily News*, the Kansas City *Star*, and the San Francisco *Bulletin*. He had a national forum for what was going to be a gamble involving journalism, social analysis and his own reputation. "I am to write for my newspapers," he told his father, "the situation back of the McNamara trial; not the trial itself, but the cause, consequences, and the significance thereof. It's a delicate job, somewhat like handling dynamite, but somebody has to tackle it hard; why shouldn't I be the McNamara of my profession?"

During a weekend court recess in mid-November Steffens and Darrow went south to stay at E. W. Scripps's ranch. The publisher met them at the depot and drove them to Miramar for two days of sun and rest. But over drinks and dinner followed by coffee and brandy out on Scripps's patio assorted ideas came together in a chemical reaction eventually generating much perturbation, heat and regret. Darrow arrived at Miramar with the sure prospect of defeat. He had failed, in his own investigations, to breach the evidence against the McNamaras; on his own, he had even turned up fresh evidence against them; and, in desperation, hoping for a hung jury and a mistrial, he made some ambiguous gestures that were to lead, twice over the next few years, to his trial on charges of attempted bribery and influence of jurors. Now, here was Steffens, who had interviewed the McNamaras in their cell that week, asking for permission to write about them on the assumption that they were guilty; he had even talked to them about changing their plea. Darrow, too, was approaching the same stage in his reasoning. It was tragic, he had to agree with the other two, that the case could not be tried on its true issues, not as murder, but as a "social crime" that was in itself an indictment of a society in which men believed they had to destroy life and property in order to get a hearing.

With a child's pride of performance, Scripps drew from his pocket the manuscript of one of the "disquisitions" with which he was in the habit of regaling friends, editors, family and himself. A few years later, seeking consolation for the loss of a son, he proved in one of these disquisitions that through his remaining heirs, and in about 2,500 years, there might be as many as eight hundred million living descendants of E. W. Scripps, each one, presumably, just as pleased with himself as their forebear when he made this calculation. The disquisition he now read to Steffens and Darrow was called "Belligerent Rights in Class Warfare"—just an exercise in ideas, he assured them, a bit of radicalism.

According to Scripps the McNamaras had committed a selfless act of insurgency in the unequal warfare between workers and owners; after all, what weapons *did* labor have in this warfare except "direct action"? The McNamaras were as "guilty," in a jury's sense, as John Brown had been "guilty" at Osawatomie or Harper's Ferry, but did "guilt" have any meaning in those circumstances? "Workingmen should have the same belligerent rights in labor controversies that nations have in warfare. There has been war between the erectors and the ironworkers; all right, the war is over now; the defeated side should be granted the rights of a belligerent under international law." And unless these rights were recognized, Scripps went on, the country would be lucky if it escaped with nothing more drastic than socialism.

Exactly right, Steffens agreed. The only way to avert class struggle was to offer men a vision of society founded on the Golden Rule and on faith in the fundamental goodness of people provided that they were given half a chance to be good. He had been moving toward this vision for years, especially in the aftermath of Josephine's death. Standing between labor and capital and grossly miscalculating the bitterness and duration of their enmities, he now believed that economic issues could be mediated through benevolence. As a Christian, he believed, too, in the blessedness of peacemakers, and he was willing to offer himself as mediator, hero or scapegoat.

In this maelstrom of social theories, Clarence Darrow, who was responsible for the lives of his clients and not for the adjudication of philosophic issues, discovered his solution: a settlement out of court, an amnesty. Darrow, as he said, valued Steffens for "his intelligence and tact, and his acquaintance with people on both sides." Now Steffens was to go out among the city's businessmen and reformers, labor leaders and politicians, in search of a compromise that, as Darrow saw it, would combine at least the appearance of benevolence with the realities of horse trading. Darrow still had some bargaining power. Found guilty by a jury and sentenced to death, the McNamaras, in the absence of a confession, were likely to become martyrs to the labor cause and therefore more dangerous dead than alive. The unions stood to gain, and it was probable that Harriman would be elected the first Socialist mayor of Los Angeles.

By the end of November 1911, by means of what Steffens claimed was Christianity in action but others saw as a hard bargain or a sellout, a series of secret agreements were reached among the prosecution, the defense, the court, and the opposed representatives of business and labor. "I negotiated the exact terms of the settlement," Steffens later wrote. "That is to say, I was the medium of communication between the McNamaras and the county authorities." The brothers were to change their plea to guilty but offer no confession; the state would withdraw its demand for the death penalty, agree to impose only moderate prison terms, and also agree that there would be no further pursuit of other suspects in the case; and, as token and instrument of a new era of industrial peace to come, industry and labor would participate in a joint conference.

Side by side, as Steffens saw them, labor and capital stood guilty—one of committing a crime, the other of inciting to crime. The McNamara settlement was an "experiment in good will," he said, risking all for his faith in self-interest liberalism and the Golden Rule. This experiment was going to "put the ancient controversy between labor and capital on a new and clearer basis forever." He had hoped to stab the world with an idea, offering himself as sacrifice, if necessary, and the day the McNamaras changed their plea to guilty, December 1, he had had a long swim in the Pacific before breakfast and dressed as if for a wedding. It was the morning of his life. Later he felt joy and power returning to him after what now seemed a long time of inactivity. His role in the settlement of the case had become public knowledge, he heard his name spoken in the lobbies and streets, reporters crowded around him, his story was on front pages everywhere. It was like "the olden days" in St. Louis and Minneapolis and Chicago—"I'm famous again. I'll use it to make people think. They'll listen now, and I can do something."

As the day of sentencing approached he also felt an undercurrent of premonition, and then he felt downright fear. He had felt it first in the courtroom the day the McNamaras pleaded guilty. A moment of shocked silence passed before the reporters ran to their telephones, and then, as the spectators stumbled out and the news spread through the streets, there was cursing and weeping and cries of anger, a sense of menace, rage and broken hopes that chilled him to the heart when he walked to his hotel. It was dangerous to make people think, to tamper with their idols. "The public is too fiendish," he was already saying in anticipation of the worst. "It makes me sick." Labor itself, shocked, betrayed, and set back ten years and more by the worst blow it had ever received, was now crying for the blood of the McNamaras. The Sunday before sentence was to be passed, the churches too turned on the dynamiters and on the peacemakers as well. "The sermons of that black Sunday turned the tide against us," Steffens said. "The Christian churches would not recognize Christianity if they saw it." What he heard now, swelling and echoing across the country, was the cry of "a lynching mob," and this is what he also heard in the courtroom on December 5.

Speaking, it seemed, for "the public," Judge Walter Bordwell denounced Steffens' peacemaking efforts as "repellent to just men," a shameful attempt to make "heroes" out of "murderers." Bordwell disavowed the existence of any settlement or compromise, suggesting instead (as Steffens recalled) "that the case had been terminated to save costs to the county." He concluded:

> The duty of the court in fixing the penalties in these cases would have been unperformed had it been swayed in any degree by the hypocritical policy favored by Mr. Steffens (who by the way is a professed anarchist) that the judgment of the court should be directed to the promotion of compromise in the controversy between capital and labor.

Then Bordwell sentenced James McNamara to life imprisonment at San Quentin and John to fifteen years at hard labor. "You see," James McNamara said to Steffens as the brothers were led handcuffed out of the courtroom. "You were wrong, and I was right. The whole damn world believes in dynamite."

Steffens' principled intervention proved to be a disaster, and to the end of his life he worked to secure a pardon or parole for the McNamaras and, by extension, for himself. In his own terms, he had been "sincere" rather than "intelligent." He had wholly misjudged the ferocity of the opposed forces. Occasionally he rescued some comfort from the ruins. "What I am really up to is to make people think," he wrote to his sister Laura as he traveled homeward from Los Angeles on the Overland Limited. "I am challenging the modern ideals; not the conduct of bad people, but the ideals of the good people. And every time I can confront the busy world with what it thinks it thinks, I do it. The McNamara incident was simply a very successful stroke in this policy. It was like a dynamite explosion. It hurt; it may have killed some and it may land me in Coventry if not in San Quentin." And, far from being cowed by his failure, he went on that January to Lawrence, Massachusetts, where the I.W.W. had struck the textile mills. "You can't weave cloth with bayonets," the strikers taunted the owners, and the girls marched under the slogan, "We Want Bread, and Roses too." Steffens planned to make a general study of labor in the United States and England. "The real war," he was sure, "is going on under politics, in the industrial field, both here and abroad."

Champion of a desperate cause, Steffens did succeed, to some extent, in doing what he had set out to do: make "people think." Olav Tveitmoe, West Coast labor leader and prominent ideologue of dynamite, came looking for him in Los Angeles. "I will show him there is no Golden Rule," he said menacingly, "but there is a Rule of Gold." After two hours of talk in Steffens' hotel room Tveitmoe took a different view. "Lincoln Steffens is O.K.," he said. "He understands the law of gravitation, and he is the first man I have met that has no Pope."

Steffens' morally impassioned question about the nature of a society in which men used dynamite to assert their interests was argued in editorials and sermons; it became the subject of a magazine symposium, "The Larger Bearings of the McNamara Case"; and out of the symposium grew a Presidential commission charged with exploring the "crucial boundary line between industry and democracy."

According to Emma Goldman, however, the whole thing had been a farce and had only served to disclose "sickening timidity" and "childish credulity," "the appalling hollowness of radicalism in and out of the ranks of labor, and the craven spirit of so many of those who presume to plead its cause." For once she and Roosevelt were in agreement about something. "It seems to me that Steffens made an utter fool of himself," Roosevelt said. "By George! I take a certain grim satisfaction in remembering that I wrote the 'Murder Is Murder' editorial about the McNamaras last summer."

As he suspected, Steffens had become the McNamara of his profession, a sort of pariah even among friends, who now made fun of him as "Golden Rule" Steffens, the man who believes that lions will not act like lions when they lie down with lambs. (The Golden Rule works best "among equals," Walter Lippmann commented and suggested that labor remember that if it turns the other cheek, "that cheek will be smitten without much compunction.") Max Eastman, the young philosophy instructor at Columbia who was soon to become editor of *The Masses*, had heard all the Christian preaching he ever wanted to hear from his parents, both of them ministers. "A very brilliant and boldly inquiring reporter," a man of genuine kindness and candor, he was to write of Steffens. But in the immediate aftermath of the McNamara affair Steffens appeared to be merely a "sanctimonious" imitator of Christ, "an old-maidish fuss-budget" who should have been transmitting his "kindly and disastrous sentiments" about practical Christianity to a Sunday-school class; instead he betrayed "the class struggle" by acting as go-between for capitalists and so-called labor leaders, most of them frauds.

When Steffens published his *Autobiography*, he claimed, in the retrospect of nearly twenty years of unavailing effort to atone for the disaster, that even Reed had turned against him. "Jack Reed, 'my own boy,' wrote a fierce poem, 'Sangar,' denouncing me." One sentence, three charges of betrayal, none of them wholly reflecting what happened. Reed, it was true, had not been able to embrace Steffens' creed, but still, with friends uptown at the Harvard Club or in the Village, out of loyalty but with only a certain hollow conviction, Reed had argued in his defense and generally lost. Finally, as he said, he had succeeded in "converting" himself to the gospel of industrial peace governed by the Golden Rule. He was carrying a copy of a newspaper with an account of Steffens' "experiment in good will" when Eastman ran into him on Waverly Place in the Village. "Have you seen this?" Reed said. "Yes," Eastman answered, "and I think it's absolute bunk." According to Eastman, Reed was indignant—"I think it's the greatest stuff ever printed in a newspaper." Soon afterward he wrote his poem.

On a soft winter night, with fog and warm rain muting the outlines of Washington Arch and promising a green Christmas, Steffens took him to dinner, and, afterward, over a bottle of wine, Reed read the manuscript poem to him. It was a romantic allegory in which Steffens, to whom the poem was dedicated, figured as Sangar, a soldier hero leading his army to repel the Huns. In the midst of the battle Sangar cries out for peace in Christ's name, breaks his sword, and stands as peacemaker between the two armies. His own son kills him, shouting,

> *Father no more of mine!*
> *Shameful old man—abhorr'd*
> *First traitor of all our line.*

And at the end of the poem the warrior's soul ascends:

> *Oh, there was joy in heaven when Sangar came.*
> *Sweet Mary wept, and bathed and bound his wounds,*
> *And God the Father healed him of despair,*
> *And Jesus gripped his hand, and laughed and laughed.*

Neither Reed nor Steffens, that evening or during Reed's lifetime, seemed to have any doubts about the intention of the poem as a tribute, even though, along with hero worship and beatitude it invoked repudiation and a murderous anger, all suggesting that Reed, in spite of his "conversion," was saying something else that neither of them wanted to acknowledge then, to themselves or to each other: Sangar is slain by his own son ("Jack Reed, 'my own boy' "), and whatever Sangar's welcome in heaven, he was dead on earth, useless in battle, anathema to the young. But on Christmas Eve, 1911, "Sangar" seemed neither "fierce" nor a denunciation. It was a good poem, Steffens said, he was pleased by the dedication, and over the next year their relationship deepened as Steffens continued his efforts to lead his protégé toward liberty and self-expression—"I'll only try to make you feel free and the world wide-open." In turn, Reed sent the poem to Harriet Monroe at *Poetry* with a note explaining that its subject was Lincoln Steffens' "magnificent try for peace during the trial of the McNamaras." "Sangar" was published in *Poetry* at the end of 1912; then as a pamphlet by itself; again in Reed's collection *Tamburlaine;* and finally, after Reed's death in Moscow, Harriet Monroe said in an editorial in her magazine that "Sangar" was about Reed as well—"His dream was of a peaceful, co-operative world," she wrote. "In the fight for his dream he died."

Well, Steffens hadn't died, but he was one of the war wounded, and he carried the scars to his grave, one in a long succession of American champions of desperate causes. Walt Whitman was as much to the point as Reed:

I play not marches for accepted victors only, I play marches for conquer'd and slain persons.

Have you heard that it was good to gain the day?

I also say it is good to fall, battles are lost in the same spirit in which they are won. . . .

Vivas to those who have fail'd!

When the uproar had subsided Steffens was not left altogether without influence, admirers or a future. "This little, Machiavellian, itinerant preacher went up and down upon the earth shaking it in his own way. . . . Steff's delicate music undoubtedly had its share in collapsing the civilization of the twentieth century." So he was to be described—along with his "power over people" and the plain gold cross that he had taken to wearing on his watch chain as a "souvenir" of Los Angeles—by Mabel Dodge. She was the young and wealthy matron who had given Reed the impetus for his Pageant of the Strike. Her "evenings" at her salon at 23 Fifth Avenue were, for a year or two before the European war broke out in 1914, the focus of a ferment and variety unknown in America before then. "Really," she said, "the Evenings were, in the first place, Steff's idea."

CHAPTER ELEVEN

Winds of Change

I

"THE DAYS ARE WONDERFUL AND THE NIGHTS ARE WONDERFUL and the life is pleasant," Gertrude Stein wrote in "Portrait of Mabel Dodge at the Villa Curonia." The grateful subject of the portrait had it printed and bound as a pamphlet, which then served as one of her passports to avant-garde when, in 1912, at the age of thirty-three, twice married, widowed the first time and bored the second, she decided it was time to leave Florence and seek purpose in New York. Despite the days and the nights and the life, Mrs. Dodge had discovered an old enemy, neurasthenia—in its various aspects of angst, accidie, melancholia, ennui, black dog—standing at the door of her pleasure dome in the sweet hills above the Arno. She moved into 23 Fifth Avenue, a stodgy building on the corner of Ninth Street inhabited, on its ground floor, by General Daniel Sickles, who encapsulated an appalling amount of ancient history, having murdered his wife's admirer in 1859 and survived both a trial and the battle of Gettysburg. He was very old. In her own apartment on the floor above, Mrs. Dodge set about eradicating comparable vestiges of the century of General Grant and the Widow of Windsor. She had the woodwork painted white, the walls covered with white paper, the tall windows hung with white linen. A white porcelain chandelier hung from the living room ceiling, a white bearskin rug lay in front of the white marble chimney piece. In place of brownstone tonalities she introduced the lucent and favoring light of the Modern.

Fearing the return of boredom once the renovations were completed, Mrs. Dodge concluded on the advice of her psychiatrist that if she were truly to "*live* mentally," she would have to send her husband away; and soon, in the boil that she generated, Mr. Dodge, a wealthy New Englander who dabbled in architecture, was hardly missed. As a matter of fact, in order to "mitigate his negative effect upon me," she said, Dodge had encouraged her in her ambition "to know everybody. . . . I wanted, in particular, to know the Heads of things. Heads of Movements, Heads of Newspapers, Heads of all kinds of groups of people. I became a Species of Head Hunter, in fact. It was not dogs or glass I collected now, it was people. Important People."

The "fresh and sparkling" whiteness of the apartment at 23 Fifth Avenue provided the background for Mabel Dodge's celebrated "Evenings," a domestic equivalent, on a busier scale, of Gertrude Stein's Paris Saturdays at 27 rue de Fleurus. "All sorts of guests came to Mabel Dodge's salons," Lincoln Steffens recalled in 1931, "poor and rich, labor skates, scabs, strikers and unemployed, painters, musicians, reporters, editors, swells; it was the only successful salon I have ever seen in America. By which I mean that there was conversation and that the conversation developed usually out of some one theme and stayed on the floor."

Her apartment also set off Mabel Dodge's elusive but compelling personality, in which were mingled Récamier, waif, Venus's fly-trap, and even sorceress; some of her intimates believed she was able to generate psychic phenomena, haunt houses, project "forms and sounds of abysmal woe." ("When she isn't shining," Steffens said of her power to communicate misery, "she's a wet, cold, cloudy day.") It was agreed that she was not conspicuously beautiful or witty or well-informed. She was not even talkative but on the contrary, as she confessed, suspicious and shy, "aloof and withdrawn," and sometimes, in her white dress with a chiffon wrap, she greeted her guests with "the merest mask of cordiality," sat quietly in her armchair and simply listened. But neither was she, on the one hand, a sort of receptive principle, or, on the other, merely Bounty, as one might have guessed from her wealth, her chauffeured motorcar, her nurse-companion, the midnight suppers of turkey, beef, ham, cheese and first-rate liquor served in the dining room by her staff of Italians.

Given this riddle, her friends competed with one another in trying to establish just what she was or was not. Hutchins Hapgood, through whom Steffens met Mrs. Dodge, said that she seemed to lack some rooted and self-sustaining quality. "She is like a cut flower," he remarked to Steffens; the suggestion of traumas and displacements tacitly invoked a new spirit, Freudianism, which had just come to the Village. "You attract, stimulate and soothe people," Steffens told her at tea one afternoon. "You make them think more fluently, and they feel enhanced. If you had lived in Greece long ago, you would have been called a *hetaira*." Clearly there was something extraordinary about her, "something going on, or going round, in Mabel's head or bosom," Max Eastman said, "something that creates a magnetic field in which people become polarized and pulled in and made to behave very queerly." Eastman's was perhaps as good a key as any to what made Mabel Dodge's Evenings work.

They had begun inauspiciously, and even disagreeably for her, when Carl Van Vechten, apostle of jazz and negritude, captured a pair of entertainers from Harlem and asked Mrs. Dodge to invite some people for them to entertain. But she had not yet been liberated by her several ventures into psychoanalysis and a series of love affairs. She found Van Vechten's entertainers coarse, leering and embarrassing. She invited Steffens to devise another scheme. "Why not organize all this accidental, unplanned activity around you, this coming and going of visitors, and see these people at certain hours? Have Evenings!" he told her. "All these different kinds of people that you know, together here, without being managed or herded in any way! Why, something wonderful might come of it. You might even revive General Conversation!"

Under this arrangement Mabel Dodge's apartment became a trading place for art, ideas, revolution, bohemianism and experiment, an opulent white cave through which the winds of promised change whistled and howled, but with little bitterness. Among the remarkable qualities of the Village was a spirit of concert, gaiety and insurgence, a kind of radical innocence that had a brief flowering before the war. Antagonists dealt with each other in relative amity; they shared a commitment to rebel against an irrelevant past and a middle-class present, to build an indivisible future in which the arts and socialism would nourish one another. "We shall have no further part in the factional disputes within the Socialist party," said an editorial in *The Masses*, the "*popular* Socialist magazine" that was the distinctive voice of the cultural entente forming in the Village. Its editors, Max Eastman and John Reed, described *The Masses* as "a revolutionary and not a reform magazine; a magazine with no dividends to pay; a free magazine; frank, arrogant, impertinent, searching for the true causes; a magazine directed against rigidity and dogma wherever it is found; printing what is too naked or true for a moneymaking press; a magazine whose final policy is to do as it pleases and conciliate nobody, not even its readers."

The bohemians had not yet split with the revolutionaries, the artists still embraced both art and radical change, and it was possible to be a Marxist and a Freudian. *The Masses*' mood of insurgency found other expressions in Reed's Paterson Pageant, in Alfred Stieglitz's gallery at 291 Fifth Avenue, and in an event in which Mabel Dodge also took a characteristically proprietary interest, the exhibition staged by the rebel Association of American Painters and Sculptors at the Sixty-ninth Regiment Armory in February 1913. With an abandon verging on a state of religious possession, Mrs. Dodge described the Armory Show, which introduced European modernism and "The New Spirit" to a shocked America, as "the most important public event that has ever come off since the signing of the Declaration of Independence." Theodore Roosevelt clearly preferred the Navajo rug in his bathroom to the Armory painting by Marcel Duchamp he called "A naked man going down stairs." He dismissed Futurism as "only a smirking pose of retrogression" and spoke darkly of "extremists," "the lunatic fringe," and the "power to make folly lucrative" which had been demonstrated in the previous century by P. T. Barnum. Even so, as Roosevelt acknowledged in a troubled way, the Armory Show implied a militancy that went far beyond painting and sculpture.

"It seems as though everywhere, in that year of 1913," Mabel Dodge recalled, "barriers went down and people reached each other who had never been in touch before; there were all sorts of new ways to communicate, as well as new communications." Ezra Pound had begun to talk about a Risorgimento in America, an awakening that "will make the Italian Renaissance look like a tempest in a teapot."

By contrast with this vitality, national politics seemed impossibly slow, petty, irrelevant, something one had to suffer through while the real issues—"the real thing," Steffens said—emerged. Roosevelt appeared to be wasting his energy in a feud with Taft, bay window of a Republican party that, according to Roosevelt, once spoke for the ideals of Abraham Lincoln but was now "a whited sepulcher inhabited by second-story men." Meanwhile, the Colonel himself, Steffens complained, was "mussing up the whole Progressive situation" by playing Prince Hamlet and saying that he either would or would not seek nomination for President. "The most to be hoped from President Wilson," Steffens said when the 1912 elections were all over, "is a few laws that won't do much good; some more prosecutions that won't do much harm; and—this is best—the splitting of the Democratic party in two."

For Steffens the message of 1913 was freedom—to think, act, speak, experiment, change. In Mabel Dodge's salon one heard, for the first time in America, serious and informed discussions of the ideas of Freud and Jung. Lippmann's *Preface to Politics,* published that year, was praised by Freud as a pioneering practical application of psychoanalysis to social problems. On various occasions at 23 Fifth Avenue—once with A. A. Brill, the psychoanalyst and translator of Freud's *The Interpretation of Dreams* and *The Psychopathology of Everyday Life*—Lippmann expounded the new psychology along with what he believed to be its implicit demand for codes of behavior based on psychological realities, on understanding and introspection rather than restriction and taboo.

> Freud has a way of revealing corners of the soul which we believed were safe from anybody's knowledge [Lippmann was to say]. From anthropology through education to social organization, from literary criticism to the studies of religions and philosophies, the effect of Freud is already felt. He has set up a reverberation in human thought and conduct of which few as yet dare to predict the consequences.

At one and the same time psychoanalysis offered a system of therapy, an instrument of self-exploration, and a radical critique of society.

Freud's ideas reverberated through the Village. Max Eastman was writing articles about psychoanalysis for the popular magazines. The playwright Susan Glaspell remembered this as a time when "you could not go out to buy a bun without hearing of someone's complex." With her husband, George Cram Cook, she was to write a clearly labeled Freudian satire, *Suppressed Desires* (1915). Floyd Dell found psychoanalysis "helpful to me in my love life and literary work." (He was celebrated for the freedom of expression he achieved in both.) Mabel Dodge's neurasthenia was mitigated in a Jungian analysis with Smith Ely Jelliffe and a Freudian analysis with Brill. And despite his tendency to shy away from introspection, the effect on Lincoln Steffens—who, like Freud, had been exposed to Charcot in Paris—was considerable if inconsistent. "I remember thinking," he recalled of the psychoanalytic evenings at 23 Fifth Avenue, "how absurd had been my muckraker's description of bad men and good men and the assumptions that showing people facts and conditions would persuade them to alter them or their own conduct." Freudianism confirmed his suspicion that middle-class morality was unreliable, at the very least, because it had no relation to actual behavior or desire. How useful, after all, were distinctions between good and bad, permissible and forbidden, if these distinctions disregarded motives that were unconscious, contrary and lawless? How was it possible to be guided by enlightened self-interest if it could be shown that the self often craved painful resolutions that went beyond the pleasure principle and even the survival instinct? The future lay in the direction of self-awareness, new codes of conduct. "Don't suppress," Steffens was to say. "One of the few discoveries of our day of personal use to us is that of the danger of over-repression, over self-control; a new sort of tyranny, the mis-rule of one's self."

The Village also heard the advocates of sexual freedom, liberalized divorce laws, and "birth-rate control," an awkward phrase originated and then, in a shortened and more memorable form, put into circulation by one of Mabel Dodge's guests, the socialist and feminist Margaret Sanger. "She made love into a serious undertaking," Mabel Dodge recalled. "She was the first person I ever knew who was openly an ardent propagandist for the joys of the flesh."

Such propaganda worked. "The speech of your body to my body will not be denied," John Reed said to Mabel Dodge during the summer of the year of liberation, 1913. After their bodies had spoken in a Paris hotel room, he whispered, "I thought your fire was crimson, but you burn blue in the dark." When they returned to New York in the fall he moved in with her. The relationship was too proprietary on her part to last. Even after he had acknowledged his dependence upon her "selfish, selfish love," Reed, with the help of Lincoln Steffens, whose intervention was welcomed at other times during the affair, got himself hired as correspondent for *Metropolitan Magazine* and the New York *World*, went south of the border, and joined Pancho Villa's rebel band. Reed's move from Mabel to the Mexican revolution was another demonstration of the seamlessness of freedom in sex and politics.

The cause of women's suffrage, in 1913 still seven years away from being constitutionally ratified, seemed to Steffens so imperative that it was difficult for him to argue its justice in public without falling back on the rhetoric of dynamite. ("Let the women destroy buildings, let them destroy anything they want to destroy," he told a meeting at Cooper Union in January 1914. "Forms of force are all wrong, but all are necessary.") The vote for women, he warned, was merely preliminary to more sweeping kinds of liberation. "Women are in error," he was to write, "in asking for what men have. In the first place men have not what they want or need, and in the second place women have some peculiar requirements, which they can only get when they make the double fight: women's rights for women as such and human rights for women and children AND men."

The sexual revolution was not always treated with Margaret Sanger's preferred degree of seriousness. At Mabel Dodge's one night, with a stenographer hidden behind a screen and taking down the proceedings, Steffens introduced an Evening given over to the topic of "Sex Antagonism." The first speaker was Hutchins Hapgood, drunk when he started and even more confused as he stumbled through the ideological thickets of feminism and the socialist-labor movement. "The problem is," he declared, meaninglessly, "How get the heat without the lie." "Quite Steinesque," Steffens said when he read the stenographer's transcript.

Steffens shared Mabel Dodge's taste for staging vivid confrontations and encounters. It seemed, often, as if Don Juan and the Commendatore's statue were about to sit at the banquet table again. At 23 Fifth Avenue declared if not mighty opposites were brought together, uptown and downtown, society people and revolutionists, the establishment and its enemies, law and disorder. One evening the editors of *The Masses* exchanged views with the editors of the pluto-cratic *Metropolitan.* "All of a sudden the guests were telling each other what they thought of each other," Mrs. Dodge recalled; Reed's assignment to cover the Mexican revolution was one of the after-maths of the exchange. Another Evening witnessed an encounter between anarchists and I.W.W.'s, on the one side—advocates of industrial violence, boycott, sabotage, "direct action," and class war-fare—and, on the other, the socialists, reformists, believers in elec-toral and legislative change, whose spokesman, on this occasion, was William English Walling, the rich intellectual who had spent two years in Russia studying the revolutionary movement and knew Lenin and Gorky. The other side was represented by people who were under surveillance by the Justice Department and the "Radical Bureau" of the New York City Police Department: Emma Gold-man, editor of *Mother Earth,* the anarchist magazine that from time to time spoke of the day when blood would flow in the city streets; her partner and sometime lover, Alexander Berkman, who, applying the anarchist doctrine of "propaganda of the deed," tried to assas-sinate Henry Clay Frick during the Homestead strike in 1892; and Big Bill Haywood, soon to be sentenced to twenty years' imprison-ment for sedition, national secretary-treasurer of the I.W.W., and a star performer at more than one of Mrs. Dodge's Evenings. It was the role of Walter Lippmann, then working toward a divorce from socialism, to draw Haywood out in discussion; in the left center of the spectrum hovered Steffens, a Christian anarchist who was com-ing to believe in revolutions but dreaded the thought of blood.

The "Dangerous People," as Mabel Dodge called them, never did succeed in making a clear statement of their positions to Walling and the socialists, and on that score the Evening was not a success. Still, it reflected the spirit of the Village as well a phenomenon that in time came to be known as "radical chic." In 1886 Henry James had observed it against a London background in his novel *The Princess Casamassima.* Now, in New York, with Mabel Dodge as the Princess, James's story about the symbiotic yoking of riches and revolution, champagne and dynamite, was being reenacted Evening after Eve-ning and generating, as Tom Wolfe wrote in 1970, "the delicious shudder you get when you try to force the prongs of two horseshoe magnets together." On one occasion, when the topics were free speech and help for the unemployed, Mrs. Dodge's drawing room was decorated with a red banner, and her guests—Haywood, Emma Goldman, Berkman, Steffens, Lippmann, and about two hundred people in evening clothes, some of the women smoking gold-tipped cigarettes—were joined by workers in work clothes drifting back from a protest meeting that had been ringed with mounted police. "I.W.W. Throng Are Guests of Society Folk on Fifth Avenue" was the headline in a Washington newspaper.

Certainly, this sort of mingling sent shock waves of consternation racing through conventional society. It could even be argued, with some historical basis, that Haywood and his Dangerous People were obeying Bakunin's instructions to anarchists: infiltrate the great world, compromise the rich, use them for their money. Nonetheless these supposedly dangerous transactions across class lines were mild in their effect. "They talk like goddam bourgeois," the anarchist Hippolyte Havel said in disgust of all the participants in the Haywood-Walling Evening. On the part of Mabel Dodge and her uptown friends there was a degree of frivolity and self-consciousness in their traffic with revolution, a certain infatuation with radical style rather than radical action. "Playing" was the deliberately ironic word that Lincoln Steffens used in his *Autobiography* to summarize his own activities with "Reds and Liberals" before the war. The rich made satanic heroes out of Wobblies and anarchists, exaggerated their menace and their effectiveness, and then, as one might have expected, the rich moved on to other entertainments, without embarrassment, just as Mabel Dodge once ordered the chauffeur to take her and Reed, miserable and mortified, on a limousine trip through the ghetto and the Bowery. It was "nature" and "art" that claimed her interest after 1914—"I did not feel in the mood for Evenings any more."

The Dangerous People themselves suffered a perceptible blunting of purpose. Their exposure to the rich was like Lenin's exposure to Beethoven's *Appassionata*—"It affects your nerves," he told Gorky, "makes you want to say stupid nice things and stroke the heads of people who could create such beauty while living in this vile hell." According to Steffens, Big Bill Haywood, after meeting capitalists for the first time face to face and as social equals, had trouble speaking out with the old passion against foes of the working class. Instead he talked more "like goddam bourgeois." His contribution to the workers of Dublin, when he visited Ireland in 1913, proved to be a lesson in nothing more violent than how to boo the police.

Yet on Steffens just as much as on Reed—both starting from positions closer to a middle ground in the class war—the Village and the salon years had a polarizing effect. "When I go to an I.W.W. or an unemployed meeting and talk a bit on the quiet to the police, they let the agitators talk," he said in March 1914. "Yesterday at Union Square, I got the cops to stand by and let Emma Goldman, Berkman, and others urge to looting of stores and then lead 1,000 men up Fifth Avenue." He had drawn upon his credit with the Police Commissioner and the Chief of Police. But in times of trouble this was credit easily exhausted. Two weeks later Steffens had a different story to tell.

> I was sick at heart last night. I was in Union Square yesterday, and saw the unemployed clubbed. I've seen such things for 20 years now, but I can't get used to it. It lifts my stomach every time I see a policeman take his night stick in both his hands and bring it down with all his might on a human being's skull. And then, when he does it, the crowd come about me and ask me if I won't make a complaint against the cop and have him fired! As if I could!

Friends warned him that he was hurting himself "by appearing so much among the unemployed, the Anarchists, and the I.W.W.'s," warned him that he was "coming to be regarded as one of that bunch." But he wasn't worried now. Power and confidence had begun to return to him as memories of the McNamara debacle faded. During the early months of 1914 the *Metropolitan Magazine*, through a panel of judges that included Andrew Carnegie and Jack London, awarded him first prize in a competition for the best answer to George Bernard Shaw's article "The Case for Equality"; parts of his Boston book were coming out as articles; he had just sold a short story, "The Dying Boss," to *McClure's* for $1,300. "All the editors are bidding for my stuff now, and I'm in demand as a speaker. I don't yield to the latter often, but, when I do, the papers give me space," he reported to one of his sisters. "I'm being listened to again, and in much the old way. I seem to be able to arouse feeling and stimulate thought. What more can I ask? I don't have to be careful either. I'm expected to be radical now, so I'm free of the incubus of caution."

II

ON FIFTH AVENUE SOON AFTER JOSEPHINE DIED STEFFENS MET HIS Berkeley sweetheart and former fiancée, Gussie Burgess Nobbes, a teacher in the music department at Hunter College. He had not seen her since he left for Germany in 1889. Since then she had married; now she was separated from her husband, an invalid, who refused to give her a divorce. From Steffens' point of view as well as hers the intervening years had treated her harshly—she was inclined to insomnia, bouts of depression and anxiety. Still, something of the original attraction remained, and they took up again where they had left off. For years they were to live together, irregularly—during vacations at Provincetown, Nantucket and Martha's Vineyard, summers in Europe. Their relationship had an abated quality; they were like an old married couple setting up housekeeping again. Neither of them had many illusions about the other, and when they broke up for the second and last time, they reenacted old patterns of trust and rejection.

Gussie, her emotional recognition of him fixed in their Berkeley years, was not much impressed by his fame. "It isn't glamorous or anything like that with her," he said, "nor is it her voice or her intellect with me." There was a vein of scold in her now, a hint of prudishness—she detested "vulgar" stories—and when he chided her for "inefficiency," she answered, "Never mind, Lennie dear. I've discovered lots of chinks in your armor, and so we're square." She "saw through him," by his implicit invitation, just as Josephine had, and in other respects their relationship was comparable to his rational first marriage. It was lacking in the least hint of "infatuation." "She is neither pretty, nor very young (about 43), nor brilliant, and I am reasonable and clear," he told Laura, who did not at first know the lady's identity. "I mean I have not lost my head."

With his sisters he was at first secretive and then defensive. He depended upon their approval; he now realized that all through his marriage he had been "kept out" of the family because of a chill between his sisters and Josephine. With this in mind, when he took up with Gussie again he went out of his way to be conciliatory with them, tried to entice Laura to New York "to show her and interest her in the things, the people, and the life I lead," offered to do whatever was necessary to get back in the family and stay there. He answered their accusations, or at least insinuations, to the effect that, nearing fifty, he had become "weak." If this was true, he argued, perhaps it was something "like the change of life in women"; the process had begun even before Josephine died, at about the time that he got stuck in his Boston book, and so it was "all wrong" to point to his affair with Gussie as the cause. At other times, when the needle of his sister's response moved from provincial disapproval to downright outrage, he began to regard his liaison with Gussie, innocuous as it was by Village standards, as an insurrectionary act.

"Social position not only does not count with me as it counts with you," he told his sister Dot Hollister, now married to a Santa Barbara County cattle rancher of conservative principle and upper-class loyalties, "it counts the other way. Society is made up of the legitimate grafters, the very people we want to abolish. How, then, can I care to be one of them? And thinking [them] wrong on everything, what regard can I pay to their opinions?" "Respectability" was holding back the world, he said; it was time for a "simultaneous, worldwide assault upon it." Still, assuming that in time Gussie could work out a divorce from her husband, he had every intention of remarrying. "I must. I always get into trouble when I live alone. I did as a young bachelor, and I have now again."

Trouble came in the ample form of Mary Austin, author of *The Land of Little Rain*, novelist, playwright, and mystic of the deserts and Indians of the Southwest. They had met in California, first at Carmel. There she wore long priestess robes and was given to meditating in a tree house. On occasion she took down her knee-length hair and spoke throbbingly about her need for a grand passion; she was one of the features as well as one of the terrors of the Carmel community, western seacoast of Bohemia, founded by Jack London and George Sterling. Without reckoning the consequences, Steffens, who had a taste for large women, had turned the light of his personality upon her, told her about his early life, his marriage to Josephine and how it had trailed off into nothingness and invalidism. Perhaps it was he who was destined to be Mary Austin's grand passion. She was dazzled, she wrote, by his "personal charm and his destiny," and on his part he was no less admiring. In her work she had "got" the desert, captured it for literature, Steffens wrote in a tribute in the *American Magazine* in June 1911 after seeing her in California that spring. Soon after, by then in her middle forties, she was in the East determined to "get" Steffens as well, to capture and ingest this man who had engaged her so thoroughly and then skipped away across the continent.

She was to be seen at Mabel Dodge's, dressed in prairie-colored satin, or patrolling Fifth Avenue, Gramercy Park and Greenwich Village, or stationed on the upper decks of buses and in the corridors of Carnegie Hall, but she was generally in pursuit of Steffens and hoping to penetrate a protective cordon of his friends. According to some of them, she hired a detective to track him. It was through inadvertency, however, that Mary Austin, apartment-hunting one day, came upon him in a situation which implied domestic intimacy with Gussie, and she was sorry that she had. Her anger lasted for years. "I killed a man this morning," she was later to say to Mabel Dodge in Taos. She had just finished a novel, *No. 26 Jayne Street*, published in 1920, in which she portrayed Steffens as a philanderer and a fraud, a man who stood for change, "almost any kind of change," and so was not a revolutionist at all but merely "a lover of revolutions," one who spoke of them "with the slightly overripe accent of infatuation."

For Mary Austin's thinly veiled character, as for Steffens himself, the European war was a welcome event. "My theory was false, of course," Steffens later conceded. "My theory was that the inevitable war would bring on the inevitable revolution."* He had gone abroad that summer to muckrake England and Europe, or at least to confirm his belief that what he had seen in America was, as befitted a young country, only an earlier stage of decay within capitalism.

* This was current theory in revolutionary circles. In *The Bolsheviki and World Peace* Leon Trotsky predicted that "the general economic exhaustion in Europe will affect the proletariat most immediately and most severely. The state's material resources will be depleted by the War, and the possibility of satisfying the demands of the working masses will be very limited. This must lead to profound political conflicts, which, ever widening and deepening, may take on the character of a social revolution, the progress and outcome of which no one, of course, can now foresee." Steffens wrote the introduction to the American edition (1918) of Trotsky's book.

"The same system of corruption which reigned in all American cities, states, and business corporations dominated Europe, too," he was to write. "There was some law at work, parallels of identical forces which made the social problem one and the same problem everywhere." From the retrospect of the 1920s, he could well believe that Western civilization was going the way of Rome, Egypt and China.

In June 1914, that civilization, as Steffens saw it in England, presented a different face: gaiety if not promise. It was intoxicating to watch "the outward signs of the high life"—society, racing, theaters, the crowds; to live in a house in Regent's Park and be carried away to a musical weekend in Berkshire; to shop at Liberty's, "one of the most beautiful sights in the world," and to get a new wardrobe on Savile Row; to talk with Wells and Chesterton. Just to ride the bus, walk the holiday thoroughfares, watch the fashionable women "buying, buying, buying" was like being at a pageant. About the only fear one noticed had to do with the possibility that domestic politics, the exceptionally savage struggle between Liberals and Tories, might spoil a brilliant London season. In a high mood Steffens left for the Continent the day after Archduke Franz Ferdinand was murdered at Sarajevo, and he was in Italy writing, "at peace" with himself despite the rumble of ultimatums, when war was declared at the beginning of August. "I stayed where I was till I had finished off my work down to the last period." Then, toward the end of the month, he joined Gussie in Florence, traveled with her to Venice, where they boarded a Greek ship. Despite the cockroaches and bedbugs, they enjoyed a three-week voyage home by way of the Adriatic, Greece and the Greek Islands, Italy again, and then the Mediterranean to Gibraltar and the open sea.

"There was a moment," Walter Lippmann wrote after the war, "when the picture of Europe on which men were conducting their business as usual, did not in any way correspond to the Europe which was about to make a jumble of their lives." Lippmann had sailed for England a few days after Sarajevo, spent July in London and in the Lake Country where the Webbs and Shaw were running a Fabian summer institute, and then was "astonished and rather annoyed" to have to cancel plans for a walking trip because the German frontier was closed. He had been "totally unconscious" of the world he lived in, he said with deliberate exaggeration; it was only then that "I began to take foreign affairs seriously." A little over a year later, as one of the editors of *The New Republic*, Lippmann was denouncing Woodrow Wilson's timidity and urging that America enter the war against the Central Powers.

Steffens was to follow a different course. "The war was not the thing to watch," he was soon saying—not if one were interested in causes rather than symptoms, in the future rather than the present; not if one wanted to remain unaffected in judgment by the "spirit of passionless shooting into the dark." "The war psychology" and "the war hysteria," "patriotism" and "preparedness"—these, as he suspected, were going to confound dissent with sedition, inaugurate a period of repression and abridgment of Constitutional guarantees. In wartime, Randolph Bourne was to write, "the State becomes what in peacetimes it has vainly struggled to become . . . the inexorable arbiter and determinant of men's businesses and attitudes and opinions." Like Bourne, Steffens did not believe that the war would make the world safe for anything. He was going to be a "peace correspondent," not a war correspondent. "I did not therefore go to the front," Steffens wrote. "I went to the rear. I decided to make a study of revolutions."

III

THE SHIP THAT IN NOVEMBER 1914 BROUGHT LINCOLN STEFFENS TO Vera Cruz and the Mexican revolution replicated a world at war. "All the passengers aboard out of Havana were bound for Mexican ports and—Americans, Germans, and Latins—they all had interests in Mexico," he wrote. "They didn't mix, however. The battle lines in Europe separated the Germans and English, and the revolutionary groupings of Mexico cut up the Mexicans on deck. The sun, doubling at us from sky and sea, drove us all back into the neutral shade of the awning, and I, as an American, tried to cross all boundaries."

Four years had already passed since Emiliano Zapata, sometime dealer in horses and mules, raised the cry of "Land and Liberty" and a revolutionary force overthrew the dictator General Porfirio Díaz, but the country remained torn by civil war. Half a dozen military chiefs contended against one another, having in common, for the most part, only a hatred of the United States that went back to the annexation of Texas and California. ("Poor Mexico," Diaz said, "so far from God and so near the United States.") Two administrations in Washington had responded to what were considered threats to American investments in Mexico. Taft sent twenty thousand troops to the border. Wilson sent the Marines to occupy Vera Cruz and was angry when the Mexicans protested as an invasion what he had intended only as a friendly landing. "We Americans can't seem to get it," Steffens reflected, "that you can't commit rape a little." "Our right to be in Mexico," he was to say, "is about as good as Germany's to be in Belgium"; if America was partly the cause of Mexico's disorders, then it was hypocritical for Americans "to force ourselves on them as the cure."

Mexico remained so problematic that it was possible for outsiders, aligning themselves with different factions, each to believe that what he saw was prototypal. For some, the revolution was just another sombrero riot that had to be quelled because it interfered with business. For others, like Steffens, it was " 'the' revolution," a glimpse into the world's future.

Jack London, for example, came to Vera Cruz with the Marines. Having also come a long way from radicalism he spoke out for American intervention, American business, and the superiority of Anglo-Saxons to mestizos—blood would tell, and therefore "Mexico must be saved from herself." Ambrose Bierce came south as an admirer of Pancho Villa, the peon marauder regarded by many as being little better than a chicken thief. John Reed first saw insurgent Mexico from Presidio, on the Texas bank of the Rio Grande, late in 1913—"Toward evening, when the sun went down with the flare of a blast furnace, patrols of cavalry rode sharply across the skyline to the night outposts. And after dark, mysterious fires burned in the town." Then he waded across the river to join the revolution and Villa, whom he extolled to American readers for his "extraordinary native shrewdness," his "reckless and romantic bravery," his audacity as a guerrilla Napoleon. Mexico liberated Reed—"taught him to write," John Dos Passos said. Mexico also prepared him for Russia, just as it prepared Lincoln Steffens.

Steffens and Reed differed "very practically" in their understandings of Mexico, Steffens said. One saw revolution as a column of horsemen against the sky, armored trains, organ cactus; the other saw it as a drudging process which was not military nor even political, but instead economic. Dazzled by action and the poetry of struggle, Reed romanticized Villa and dismissed the constitutionalist leader Venustiano Carranza as only a reformer, a malevolent, pig-headed man driven by egotism. Steffens too, for his part, erred in placing all his hope in Carranza and writing off Pancho Villa as an "illiterate, unscrupulous, unrevolutionary bandit" who appeared determined to provoke America into warring with Mexico.

It was difficult to be certain of anything. One of the great up-heavals of the century was taking place, yet Mexico offered no pattern for revolution. Socialists who came to observe left in dismay and confusion. This revolution "was not according to Marx," Steffens said. "It had occurred not in a highly capitalized country, but in a backward country with an undeveloped industrial system, among an unorganized, illiterate people who knew nothing of socialism and little of labor unions. It had no clearly defined socialist purposes; it was all mixed up—politics, economics, civil wars, graft." But, if the Russian revolution itself was to be found wanting in historical logic, here, in Mexico, there was no Lenin, no Bolshevik fraction to seize power where it lay in the streets. Among its congregation of feuding rebels, there was only a sort of Kerensky in the person of Carranza, according to Steffens, "a mere indignant gentleman once," who had been "converted by the radicals about him and by events."

The Carranzists trusted Steffens. He was interested in revolution, not in business; he was an important journalist who had the ear of men of power in Washington, and he was willing to serve as spokes-man for the revolution. "I'd do almost anything for Mexico," he said, and within his powers he did, making repeated attempts to persuade Wilson to recognize either "Carranza or nobody," even though the Carranza regime still governed only by decree.

For three months during 1915 and 1916, traveling south from Piedras Negras on the border to Mexico City and then east and west between Tampico on the Gulf to Manzanillo on the Pacific, Steffens saw Mexico with the Carranza government. "It was like a trip across the face of the moon," he wrote of the war-wasted landscape. The First Chief of the Revolution governed from a military train convoyed by other trains which carried troops and artillery. He kept on the move in order to show his government to the Mexican people and, not incidentally, as he explained to Steffens, to keep his govern-ment away from foreign lobbyists. He knew it was time to move on, Carranza said, when his Mexicans began to talk "as if they had heard American money talking." The idea of a government on wheels was a good one, Steffens decided—"only, if our government were to keep ahead of our corruption, it would have to be a very fast train and make no stops."

Carranza and his circle were slow and blundering, they lacked "competence, executive and organizing ability, and economic understanding," Steffens said, and they were resigned to a long struggle. A new constitution, adopted in 1917, provided the legal basis for land reform and for state ownership of oil and mineral rights. But three years later Carranza fell, and civil war went on as usual. "The revolution had not run its course," Steffens was to say, "so a revolutionary party of labor and unsatisfied leaders and followers rose up against Carranza, caught and shot him, and went on." By the time peace finally came to Mexico at the end of the 1920s, the revolution had claimed nearly a million lives.

"What you don't understand, I think," Carranza had told Steffens, "is that this is an economic, not a political revolution. You keep asking us to establish peace first, then set up a constitutional government, and then enact our reforms. I can understand why you want that. That is the way you did it." But this revolution was not going to follow the American pattern nor was it going to repeat the mistakes Mexico had made in the nineteenth century—"We want to establish an economic democracy and then we will have a political democracy."

In the retrospect of Steffens' career, Mexico served as rehearsal for another revolution; in the retrospect of his country's history it served, for good or for bad, as one of the levers that pried America out of neutrality and into the First World War. On March 22, 1917, eleven days after he gave *de jure* recognition to President Carranza and his constitutional government, Wilson recognized the new provisional government in Russia, and on April 2, stung by recent disclosures that Germany had offered to support a Mexican military invasion of the border states, Wilson delivered his war message to Congress. By then Steffens was on the North Atlantic bound for Russia and, at the age of fifty-one, for the great adventure of his life.

CHAPTER TWELVE

"Man in the mass"

I

IN MARCH 1917 IT BEGAN TO SEEM THAT LIBERALISM, shaky in America, reeling in Europe, and ultimately one of the casualties of war, might be vindicated in vast and backward Russia, a country that, according to Marxist theory, was scarcely ready for a socialist revolution. Lincoln Steffens and some other early observers warned that the Russian revolution was "in its first phase only" and that a "re-revolution," of some unspecified sort, would have to follow. They had in mind the historic lesson of France after 1789: great upheavals rarely stay within appointed bounds; days of liberation are followed by nights of terror in which the revolution devours its children. It was prudent to defer judgment. "If the world wants to know what's happening in Russia at the present time," the American correspondent William G. Shepherd was to cable from the capital city of Petrograd that spring, "the world must wait until it stops happening."

Through the jumbled instrumentalities of food riots and strikes, and the refusal of the Petrograd garrison to support the police against the demonstrators, the Tsar was overthrown. A week later the United States extended recognition to a government that was not only provisional but also, as time soon proved, powerless and largely illusory. The ongoing revolution, Steffens said, was to leave "high and dry" this "bourgeois-democratic regime" of manufacturers, businessmen, professors and lawyers. (As John Reed pointedly noted in *Ten Days That Shook the World*, the Constitutional Democrats who composed the provisional government were "the great party of *political* reform, roughly corresponding to the Progressive Party in America.") This official or paper government, Steffens went on, "functioned in the air, while the revolution flowed on, turgid, underneath them." The countervailing power, a second government of "revolutionary democracy," lay with the Petrograd Soviet of the Workers' and Soldiers' Deputies, an unwieldy congress that was neither workable nor representative. With the provisional government and the Soviet locked in struggle, Russia, far from moving in the direction of a stable republic, as American recognition implied, was on the verge of an irreconcilable civil war intensified by foreign interventions.

But it was easy to dodge reality in the elation with which the news of the Tsar's overthrow was greeted in America. Secretary of War Newton Baker casually threw a foot up onto his desk, pulled his pipe out of his mouth and, just as if he were celebrating one of Tom Johnson's victories in Cleveland in the old days, exulted to Steffens, "Well, I guess this king business is pretty near over." Another old friend, Abraham Cahan, who years earlier had fled Tsarist anti-Semitism, was equally jubilant. "We can no longer distinguish between the Russian government and the Russian people. Both are one in soul and spirit. We now love both." And Woodrow Wilson, who at the scriptural eleventh hour was spared the mortification of offering to make the world safe for democracy while standing shoulder to shoulder with the Autocrat of all the Russias, was in a state of thanksgiving almost trancelike when he came to the matter of America's Eastern ally in his war message to Congress on April 2, 1917. "The autocracy that crowned the summit of her political structure, long as it had stood and terrible as was the reality of its power, was not in fact Russian in origin, character, or purpose," said the former professor of history and political economy, ignoring the plain facts of both. "And now it has been shaken off and the great, generous Russian people have been added in all their naïve majesty and might to the forces that are fighting for freedom in the world, for justice, and for peace. Here is a fit partner for a league of honor."

Of course, the problem that was soon faced by a series of Western missions blind to the ultimate thrust of the revolution and the mood of the people was how to keep as partner in this league of honor a country that after three years of fighting had suffered more than five million casualties and two million desertions and had no gains at all to show for them. Russia's industry and transportation were paralyzed, her social and political structures lapsing into anarchy. Meanwhile, the front-line soldier had become convinced that what was at issue in this conflict were territorial arrangements that had nothing to do with "Peace, Bread and Land."

It was partly a matter of chance that Lincoln Steffens, student of revolutions, found himself on the way to Petrograd at the end of March 1917. He went over as observer, reporter, unofficial liaison and go-between, a Tom Sawyer-ish role he was again to play as a member of the Bullitt mission to Russia two years later. In Washington on March 22 Steffens ran into someone he had known since the days of muckraking and the *American Magazine*, Charles R. Crane, the plumbing-fixture millionaire turned reformer, philanthropist and slavophile. At a time when the incumbent United States minister to Russia, David R. Francis, was qualified for his post chiefly by his success as a grain merchant and his popularity as Democratic governor of Missouri, Crane was among the few Americans who had some knowledge of Russia. He had lived there, and among the evidences of his continued interest was his endowment of the chair of Slavic Studies at the University of Chicago. As the largest individual contributor to Wilson's 1912 campaign and as vice-chairman of the Democratic finance committee, Crane also was in a position of influence at the White House—in April 1917 Wilson was to appoint him to the official mission to Russia headed by former Secretary of State Elihu Root. The previous month, as Crane started out for Russia with the as yet unofficial backing of Wilson and the State Department, he invited Steffens to come along.

Steffens leaped at the chance. "It's my story. There's no American in Petrograd now, Crane says; only two English writers; and none that understands the fundamentals," Steffens explained to his family; and on March 27, a few hours before sailing from New York, he reckoned up the advantages of going over with Crane, even though he knew that Crane, as a former president of the Municipal Voter's League of Chicago, tended to see the revolution as another example of reform in action—sound and honest businessmen (the provisional government) had replaced the Tsar's corrupt administration. Crane believed, as he told Steffens, that "the Russians are a strong, gentle people with a genius for cooperation and centuries of experience in local self-government and community ownership"—in Russia, as well as in America, the cure for the ills of democracy, at least until Lenin took over, was going to be more democracy rather than less. "He knows everybody. He is 'the friend of Russia' in the U. S.," Steffens said about Crane. "He has entertained all the great Russians, including Milyukov, whom he has had as his guest here and in Chicago. And all the great radicals have had his aid. He (and I with him) will walk into the inner circles of the new government and the new radical party; into the old court group and the new nobility. I will be able to get the whole story up to date, and be in the next phase of it personally."

The Norwegian ship *Christianiafjord* left from a Brooklyn pier on March 27 carrying, among the businessmen, couriers and agents in first class, Steffens, Crane, and William F. Shepherd. Shepherd had been present in Vera Cruz when the Marines landed, was sunning himself in Washington Square when fire broke out at the Triangle Shirtwaist factory a block away, and was now, like Steffens, going to Russia with a commission from *Everybody's Magazine*. At pierside before sailing they listened to speeches and manifestoes in Russian, the singing of the "Internationale" to the waving of red flags made of squares of tissue paper fastened to canes. "It created uneasy stirrings in your mind," Shepherd said—it was a strange political demonstration to be taking place on American soil. In second class, as a fellow traveler (in his own phrase), was Leon Trotsky, homeward bound with his family after years of exile, three months as lecturer and editor in New York, and a farewell from the city's socialists the night before. That November, on his thirty-eighth birthday, he would stand with Lenin at the head of the victorious Bolsheviks, confident that the long-awaited "permanent revolution" had begun at last. But now, and especially after the *Christianiafjord* passed beyond sight of the Statue of Liberty, floodlit during this last week of American neutrality, Trotsky was somber, spoke little, reflected the anxiety that prevailed as they neared the British naval blockade at Halifax. "Wait," Trotsky and his group said when Steffens tried to draw them into conversation, "let's wait till we get by Halifax."

"Sorry to go now but opportunity too great to miss," Steffens had wired to Laura three days before sailing. Here was the opportunity of his life; he was certain of it, and he was not going to let it go, but still his mind was filled with "self-accusing and self-defense," "doubt and suffering," an inescapable sense of wrongdoing. In San Francisco his sister Lou lay paralyzed after a stroke in January. Clearly he belonged with her, he knew, and yet the stronger pull on him now was to go east, to Russia, obeying that iron law of his personality which put his hunger to take in the world above his allegiance to anyone. "It seems to me I must be there," he told Laura. "If I have done what you wouldn't have done, forgive me, and help me to forgive myself."

Steffens had arrived at a painful intersection of private and public experience, of the claims of love and the world. His view of history was bound up with his view of himself, and in measurable ways his "self-accusing and self-defense" colored his response to the revolution: he came to the revolution, as he knew he would when he started out, in search of forgiveness for himself. The "future," as he was soon to call the new order brought in by the Russian revolution, was going to "work"—it had to. After so many years, after he had discarded so many premises, the "future" was going to make him whole again and bring him a measure of certainty.

In Steffens' personal understanding of it, the upheaval he witnessed in Russia was redemptive, exculpatory, cleansing, and it had universal applications. For other students, with greater historical justification and also with a longer perspective in time, that revolution was not prototypical and not even representative; it was a series of random events finally dominated by Lenin, a great strategist who recognized a unique opportunity, moved into a political vacuum and, as he said, picked up power where he found it, lying in the streets. Steffens was struck not by the Russian-ness of the revolution, but by what he believed were its lessons for the West and its universal aspects; revolutions proceeded as ineluctably as the planets in their orbits, he said. Still, the way he described the revolutionary future owed less to Karl Marx than it did to the free-floating strain of messianic Christianity that bound Steffens to his grandfather the preacher.

" 'The Millennium first; then the Messiah.' Thus the Russian prophecy. Hence the Russian revolution," Steffens wrote in *The Nation* at the end of 1918, a year after Lenin came to power. He wrote under the pseudonym "Christian," John Bunyan's Pilgrim. "The revolution in Russia is to establish the Kingdom of Heaven here on the earth, now; in order that Christ may come soon; and coming, reign forever. Forever and ever, everywhere." John Reed, whom Steffens had tried to convert to Christian anarchism, caught some of the same spirit during the ten days of Petrograd in November 1917—"I suddenly realized that the devout Russian people no longer needed priests to pray them into heaven."

Steffens did not think of himself as "expressive" or demonstrative, he wrote to his dying sister; and only rarely—in grief or depression —did he turn inward and toward the past. But now, bound for Russia, he relived the childhood terror that had gripped him when Lou, whom he adored, had been so sick that he expected her to die. Every day the boy had searched in the doctor's face for some sign that would give him reason to hope. "How I used to cry, and how silently," he remembered. This time a continent and more away from him instead of upstairs in their father's house in Sacramento, his sister again hung between life and death, and again he was helpless to help. Josephine, too, was in his thoughts now, for like Lou, who had struck off on her own and gone to study in Europe and at Johns Hopkins, Josephine had lived an unfinished life—her death had been tragic, he said, "because she wasn't done. She hadn't had what she wanted so deeply to have." Steffens went on to use a metaphor that related his private grief to a continuum of violence and upheaval: the Russian Revolution; industrial warfare; the McNamaras and their dynamite; the bomb that exploded at the Preparedness Parade in San Francisco in July 1916 and, as Steffens was to see in Petrograd, made Tom Mooney an international labor martyr; and, in other senses closer to him, the bombing of the Governor's Mansion in Sacramento, the old Steffens house. "I don't like these unfinished lives," Steffens now told Laura. "There's something violent, even criminal about them and they wound, like a bomb."

At Halifax, after days of inspection, British naval police boarded the *Christianiafjord* and removed Trotsky to an internment camp. It was at Halifax, before the ship was finally cleared to sail for Norway, that Steffens learned by cable that his sister was dead. He had expected it—the dread had grown on him all through the voyage. He returned to his metaphor about unfinished lives, unwhole personalities. "It is a wound, and wounds do heal," he said. "I wish I could make myself sure of it."

II

FROM CHRISTIANIA THE AMERICANS TRAVELED BY TRAIN ACROSS NORway to Sweden and then north from Stockholm toward the Arctic Circle. A horse-drawn sleigh carried them across the frozen lake to the frontier at Tornio, where a startling red flag flew over the wooden customs house. A red flag was lashed to the smokestack of the train that took them to Petrograd. They entered the city at midnight, were driven from the Finland Station over icy streets that felt like a battlefield, past buildings with Tsarist machine-gun emplacements still on the roofs, past the smoke-stained walls of a burned courthouse, the gutted headquarters of the secret police. There were Red Guards on the Alexandrovsky Bridge over the Neva and at the intersections, but otherwise the city seemed deserted and its mood unfathomable. "What we knew was worse than nothing; it was just a lot of disconnected, contradictory flashes of scenes. The picture on my mind," Steffens wrote soon after, describing his midnight arrival in Petrograd, "was like one of those post-impressionist paintings you can make nothing of, or an anarchist's nightmare; a terrifying vision of an ignorant, brutal people hungry for food and hungry for vengeance, loose, free—free to wreak their will; who had, as a matter of fact, done very little killing and plundering so far; who had, indeed, up to now, shown astonishing self-restraint and even good judgment; but, then, they had only half done their work and were waiting, panting to finish it."

In Petrograd, once the most luxurious city in Russia, Steffens and Shepherd shared a cold hotel room, meager food, and the task of untangling events. Everything Steffens learned about Rasputin's murder and the last months of the old regime seemed to suggest that it was not revolutionists who "make a revolution" but blundering rulers—revolutions were made by Pharaoh, not by Moses; by the Tsar, not by Marx. (From his exile in Switzerland, Lenin, caught off balance by the first upheavals of 1917, had at first argued, along somewhat similar lines, that the Russian revolution had been provoked by foreign embassies.) But once the revolution had started it belonged, in its early stages at any rate, to the people. That spring in Petrograd the people, debating the course of their revolution, enjoyed a freedom of speech—dangerous speech, pacifist or Bolshevik or even openly pro-German—never known before or since in Russia (and, ironically, in view of the model the Russians at first saw in the American republic, no longer permitted in America in 1917). What the Russians believed in, Steffens learned in street conversations through his interpreter, was not just liberty, "a right," but license, "an impertinence"—"License is the impudence of some son-of-a-gun, who has no right to live on earth anyhow, to say some damned thing that is true."

It was Russia that was then the freest country in the world, said Lenin, back from exile in mid-April; but he pointed to the drawbacks of freedom. He addressed the crowds from the balcony of the Kshesinskaya Palace, liberated from the Tsar's mistress and now headquarters of the Bolshevik party. From a distance of twenty years and more, his recollection colored by his knowledge that history had proved to be on Lenin's side, Steffens set down the substance of the speech:

> Comrades, the revolution is on. The workers' revolution is on, and you are not working. The workers' and peasants' revolution means work, comrades; it does not mean idleness and leisure. That is a bourgeois ideal. The workers' revolution, a workers' government, means work, that all shall work; and here you are not working. You are only talking.
>
> Oh, I can understand how you, the people of Russia, having been suppressed so long, should want, now that you have come to power, to talk and to listen to orators. But some day, soon, you—we all—must go to work and do things, act, produce results—food and socialism. And I can understand how you like and trust and put your hope in Kerensky. You want to give him time, a chance to act. He means well, you say. He means socialism. But I warn you he will not make socialism. He may think socialism, he may mean socialism. But, comrades, I tell you Kerensky is an intellectual; he *cannot* act; he can talk; he cannot *act*. . . . But when the hour strikes, when you are ready to go back yourselves to work and you want a government

that will go to work and not only think socialism and talk socialism and mean socialism—when you want a government that will do socialism, then—come to the Bolsheviki.

"Bolsheviki!" Shepherd said, seizing on the word for his cabled stories. "It sounds like all that the world fears. Can't you see it in the headlines?"

"Now that the dam is broken," an American observer was told, "the flood of language never stops." Day and night one heard this torrent of argument, oratory and propaganda, and not on street corners only. One heard it also at the Tauride Palace, where the great hall in which the Duma used to meet was now stripped of seats and desks and packed from wall to wall with the members of the Petrograd Soviet along with their cooking and sleeping gear. This council of workers and soldiers was "the invisible government of Russia," "a life-and-death convention," Shepherd reported. It was there and not in the offices of ministers of state that he and Steffens witnessed revolutionary sovereignty attempting to shape itself into existence. "The first time I went to the immense hall where the first Soviet met," Steffens wrote, "I was halted, as by a blow, by the stink of the mob inside, and I could see the steam rising, as from a herd of cattle, over those sweating, debating delegates. They lived there. Once inside, they stayed inside. They cooked and they ate there, and you saw men sleeping in corners and around the edges of the hall. No hours were kept. When delegates were tired, they lay down, leaving the majority to carry on; and when they were rested, they woke to keep the endless, uninterrupted debate going. . . . Watching that mass meeting of delegates was like seeing the historical development of human government out of chaos."

He was to remember this for the rest of his life as an antidote to the lessons of reform back home. He was stirred, too, by the moral spaciousness of Petrograd that spring. A revolutionary transformation of morale prevailed in the capital city of the revolution. There was a world to win. "A great, strong, young people," he wrote, were "in a state of exaltation." May Day, 1917, had been preceded by rumors that the next stage of the revolution—the terror and the bloodbath—was about to begin. Yet the day brought instead peace and festival, processions and songs. Soldiers and civilians mingled in the cold sunlight. Red flags hung from the buildings along the icebound Neva, the aristocratic boulevards were thronged with workers, slum dwellers, families. Honking their horns in celebration, armored cars moved slowly through the crowds. The holiday ended, like holidays in cities which had not known revolution, with crying babies and parents too worn-out to care. "Some of us who lived with the Russians in their joy," Steffens wrote, "will never again lose our belief in the possibilities of human nature in the mob; of man in the mass."

He was present at the American Embassy when a "red mob," a delegation from the Petrograd Soviet, gathered outside the front door and demonstrated for the release of Tom Mooney. "Muni!" said Ambassador Francis. "Who or what is Muni?" Correct and cautious, Francis put the demonstrators off with a promise to communicate their views to Washington. He explained to Steffens and Shepherd that his sole business was to deal with the provisional government, not with the Soviet, which, in diplomatic terms, did not even have a shadow existence. But it was becoming clearer each day that the provisional government and the Soviet, the paper power and the revolution, were growing farther apart, hopelessly split on the issues of the war and of what were rumored to be Russia's secret treaties with the Allies.

On May 5, after some sporadic street fighting, Milyukov, the historian turned foreign minister, was ousted, and the cabinet was reorganized, with the silver-tongued lawyer Alexander Kerensky as war minister. Like Milyukov, Kerensky was charged with carrying on a war when the army and the public were clearly tiring of the war. This was the situation that Kerensky explained to Steffens in two long interviews and that Steffens, in turn, was asked by Crane and Ambassador Francis to explain in Washington as soon as he could. "The Russians can be made to fight, but only by an act of the Allies," he was to tell Wilson's adviser Colonel House in June, reporting on "a condition in Russia which you and the President should know."

> In a highly exalted state of mind, the effect of the revolution, they think that if all the Allies would reduce their purposes (or raise them) to a demand only for permanent peace (no punishments; no compensation; no extension of territory; and a promise to let the questions of the sovereignty of the lesser nations be answered by the lesser nations), then we could have peace. And if we couldn't, if

Germany refused to hear on this basis, then—the Russians would fight.

It may be an illusion, but the Russians think they are asked now to fight, not to achieve idealistic ends, but to carry out certain secret treaties among certain of the Allies. Whatever it is, illusion or fact, this belief and the psychological condition of the Russian mind are facts which should be and can be dealt with, if understood.

For the chance to "state to someone in authority my understanding of the matter," Steffens told House, he had come "a long way," had come more than halfway around the world, in fact. He reached home in June after traveling across Russia and Siberia to Vladivostok and Japan and from there across the Pacific to Vancouver, Seattle and Washington. Steffens is "a *great* friend of President Wilson and very important, probably the outstanding American journalist," Crane and Francis had told Boris Bakhmetieff, who was leaving for the United States to negotiate war credits for the provisional government. And so Steffens became a passenger on Bakhmetieff's ambassadorial train to Vladivostok, was given a bedroom in the Ambassador's private car, and sat in on meetings in the main drawing room with the mission's engineers, economists and diplomats. It was like the Carranza train all over again, a long journey through a devastated land and punctuated by occasional rifle fire, except that Steffens was now beginning to suspect that the Mexican revolution had not gone far enough: instead of abolishing, as the Bolsheviks promised to do, the "privileges" that had produced a capitalist class, Carranza merely took them away and then handed them over to his revolutionists. Soon it became all too plain to Bakhmetieff and other representatives of an increasingly beleaguered provisional government that Steffens' sympathies lay with their enemies. His views were "completely unacceptable to us." He was even arguing the Bolshevik position that what was important for Russia was not that the war with Germany go on but that the revolution go on toward its next stage of "literal socialism, the dictatorship of the proletariat," or, as Steffens later conceded that it was in fact, "the dictatorship of one man." Bakhmetieff had caught himself a tartar.

In Washington on June 26, Steffens had an afternoon appointment with Wilson at the White House and laid before him Kerensky's appeals for a restatement of aims. Wilson, not altogether a stranger to secret diplomacy, declared that he had no direct knowledge of secret treaties and so could scarcely ask his Allies to repudiate them. "But the way he said it and what he meant was clearly understandable to me," Steffens was to say in his *Autobiography*. "He evidently knew what I was talking about. He knew of these secret treaties, not as an ally, not officially as a party to the making of those treaties, but only as I and the public knew of their existence." That December, with the Kerensky government overthrown, the Bolsheviks began publishing the secret treaties to the world, and by the time Wilson restated his aims, in the Fourteen Points of January 1918, the Russians were past believing the truth of anything he said.

Nearly two years later, after having made a second attempt to interpret Russia to Wilson, Steffens would be overwhelmed by a sense of utter defeat; by then he had seen the "Future," and it was a matter of life and death to him whether the West understood the purposes of the new Russia. But in 1917, as a messenger from the provisional government, his heart was not really in his mission, any more than his heart was with the immediate issue of keeping Russia in the war. He felt little rancor as he left Washington—he still believed in Wilson's sincerity. "Another chapter is done," he wrote to Laura. "I've been here two days, have seen the President and all I sought; done all I promised and more for the Russians," having also presented the official position in a long magazine article, "What Free Russia Asks of Her Allies." By then there were other pulls on him: "Every unpopular cause, everybody in any trouble." Steffens had defined his wartime occupation.

III

STEFFENS CAME BACK FROM RUSSIA TO FIND THE UNITED STATES so transformed by its own war propaganda that almost any cause, with the exception of the war, was likely to be unpopular. "Rage is developing, the war rage, which is the I.W.W. spirit of force, raised to the nth power," he told Senator La Follette in August 1917. "That is war insanity. They know it in Europe. It is as dangerous as madness and as unapproachable to reason. Doctors, not statesmen, must deal with it." The national state of mind had become "as raw as a wound." What he had seen is by now a familiar story, the embattled democracy victimized by its own propaganda, the individual will bent to the momentum of war. Inevitably, Steffens himself is to a certain extent swallowed up in the collective history of the time.

The President, arguing that in wartime the office of commander in chief is necessarily autocratic, moved quickly in the direction of a government by the executive or, as some claimed, a dictatorship dedicated to his avowed policy of "force without stint or limit, force to the utmost." The Congress, in turn, impatient with procedural safeguards, passed a series of espionage, trading-with-the-enemy, and sedition acts which were broadly interpreted and harshly enforced, gave the government unprecedented powers over speech, opinion and assembly, and established severe penalties for the utterance or publication of "libels" on American policy and the American form of government, the armed forces, the flag, and the military uniform. The Bill of Rights itself became an unpopular cause. "When a nation is at war," said Mr. Justice Holmes, "many things that might be said in times of peace are such a hindrance to its effort that their utterance will not be endured so long as men will fight."

As Walter Lippmann was to point out after the war, it was impossible to have propaganda without some form of censorship; it would have been equally pointless to have censorship without propaganda. This was the function of the infinitely resourceful George Creel, who had moved on from progressive causes of one sort or another to bigger game and on April 14, eight days after the United States declared war on Germany, was sworn in by President Wilson as Chairman of the Committee on Public Information. Through a swiftly improvised machinery of pamphlets, handouts, managed news, celebrity tours, stunts, public-speaking programs, and other devices of publicity, ballyhoo, persuasion, engineering and saturation, Creel's Committee packaged and sold the war to the American people and, in turn, a warlike American people to the world.

The Committee did its work so well that when peace threatened even Creel's peace propaganda, though mounted on an equally grand scale, was too little and too late to slow the juggernaut. "The country shows no preparation for peace," Steffens was to say in October 1918, three weeks before the Armistice. "It is bloodlusty; thinks not at all of peace terms and has no opinions. Of course it hasn't. We have not been allowed to discuss that subject." Public opinion, as Steffens learned from his experiences as a peace lecturer, had not only crystallized on the issue of the war, it had metastasized. Wilson was to come to the peace conference leaving behind him a nation still deliciously wedded to its war aims.

Selling the war was "a plain publicity proposition," according to Creel, "a vast enterprise in salesmanship, the world's greatest adventure in advertising." Some years later Steffens was hardly surprised when Benito Mussolini, on short notice, was able to call out a hundred thousand Roman citizens to roar approval of his sudden invasion of Ethiopia. For Steffens had seen the United States transformed within a few weeks in 1917 from determined, official, and even principled neutrality to an infatuation with carnage, militarism, and enforced unanimity of opinion and a belief in the kinship of Christ and Mars. In 1916 Steffens had been an active Wilson supporter, member of a blue-ribbon group of writers and publicists whom Creel recruited to work in the Presidential campaign. Now, however, when Creel sent Ernest Poole, the head of the Committee's Foreign Press Bureau, to ask if they could count on Steffens to interpret America's war purposes to the Russians, Steffens said no, they couldn't. "No use. The demand is for liars and lying."

Aliens, radicals, spies, anarchists, dissenters, pacifists, socialists, conscientious objectors, strikers, labor organizers, suffragists—the distinctions were erased. Heartsick, Steffens witnessed mass arrests, disruptions of public meetings, deportations, the peremptory dismissal of college professors for various heterodoxies and the persecution of plain citizens for having German-sounding names, the suppression of radical publications, the jailing of Eugene Debs for alleged violations of the Espionage Act. Said John Reed in September 1917, "In America the month just past has been the blackest month for free men our generation has known. With a sort of hideous apathy the country has acquiesced in a regime of judicial tyranny, bureaucratic suppression and industrial barbarism, which followed inevitably the first fine careless rapture of militarism."

"War is essentially the health of the state," said Randolph Bourne, another of the nonjuring young intellectuals and still the most trenchant of them more than half a century after his death in 1918 at the age of thirty-two. ("If any man has a ghost, Bourne has a ghost," Dos Passos was to write.)

War is the health of the state [Bourne repeated]. It automatically sets in motion throughout society those irresistible forces for uniformity, for passionate cooperation with the government in coercing into obedience the minority groups and individuals which lack the larger herd sense. The machinery of government sets and enforces the drastic penalties, the minorities are either intimidated into silence, or brought slowly around by a subtle process of persuasion which may seem to them really to be converting them.

He noted "the cardinal fact of our war—the nonmobilization of the younger intellectuals."

The hysteria born of the war lingered, like Randolph Bourne's ghost, far into the peace. "I hated the new state that had arisen, hated its brutalities, its ignorance, its unpatriotic patriotism, that made profit from our sacrifices and used its power to suppress criticism of its acts," Frederic C. Howe wrote in 1925. He could also look back on the long battle, side by side with Tom Johnson, for a free city, a City on a Hill, in Cleveland; he saw now that the new men of power created by the war were infinitely more dangerous than the old corruptionists who in the end had taken over Cleveland again. "My attitude toward the state was changed," he said of his experiences in wartime. "I have never been able to bring it back. I became distrustful of the state. It seemed to want to hurt people; it showed no concern for innocence; it aggrandized itself and protected its power by unscrupulous means. It was not my America, it was something else. And I think I lost interest in it." Another survivor, Gilbert Seldes, also looking back from 1925, believed that one hundred years of intellect, science and creative force had been undone in ten. What sort of serene faith did the intellectuals have, he asked, that it gave way so suddenly?

The spirit of 1913, the year all things seemed possible, had been crushed by the iron persuasion that the war with Germany was ideological, apocalyptic, preemptive. Symbolic of the change was the fate of *The Masses*, that journal of "fun, beauty, realism, freedom, peace, feminism, revolution." *The Masses*, distinctive voice of the insurgency of 1913, became, Max Eastman said, "a kind of spearhead for the native American resistance to our intervention in the European war." The magazine was successively banned from the newsstands, banned from the mails, and finally, in December 1917, shut down altogether after the government indicted its editors under the Sedition Act.

Socialism itself, the creed of 1913, showed misleading signs of health in 1917, a sort of deathbed remission of terminal symptoms. Having immediately condemned the war as "a crime against the people of the United States and against the nations of the world," the Socialist party won strong pacifist support in the big cities. But soon, and with quick results, the government invoked its new powers, and the party's intellectuals left to become supporters of Wilson and the war. Old-line socialists like William English Walling, Charles Edward Russell, John Spargo, Robert Hunter and Jack London were certain that the war would eradicate German militarism. So were some of the muckrakers whom Creel recruited for his Committee—Ray Stannard Baker, Ida Tarbell, Samuel Hopkins Adams.

John Dewey, along with Walter Lippmann, Herbert Croly and Walter Weyl of *The New Republic*, reasoned—"realistically" and "pragmatically"—that in time of war the world outside Plato's cave is the world of action and that almost any strong policy is preferable to a neutral one. They suspended their attempts to frame broad strategies and instead became tacticians and functionaries for the men of power. Structural critics were absorbed into the infrastructure of the war; social engineers became mere conductors; historians acted as salesmen for government policy and vouched for the authenticity of forged documents allegedly proving that Russian girls had been "nationalized" and that Lenin and Trotsky were on the payroll of the German General Staff. The results of this mass defection of the intellectuals—they "scurried to Washington," Dos Passos said—still remain to be reckoned. In the eyes of Lincoln Steffens and Randolph Bourne, the intellectuals permanently disqualified themselves; having failed to oppose the war and then having gone on to promote it, they were not likely to be of use when peace came.

"Only in a world where irony was dead," Bourne wrote in June 1917, "could an intellectual class enter war at the head of such illiberal cohorts in the avowed cause of world-liberalism and world-democracy. . . . We have had to watch in this country the same process which so shocked us abroad—the coalescence of the intellectual classes in support of the military programme." In that time one had to look far and long for an honest man and, having found him, did well not to publish the association.

On the issue of the war Lincoln Steffens had parted company

with the majority of his contemporaries. As before, he was in league with the generation of John Reed and "the younger intelligentsia." In September 1914 Reed wrote, in *The Masses*, that the Austro-Serbian conflict was "a mere bagatelle—as if Hoboken should declare war on Coney Island—but all the Civilization of Europe is drawn in." He explained this, in Marxian terms, as "a clash of Traders"—the European war was not, and never should be, "our war."

A few months later, along with Robert Dunn, another of Steffens' protégés, Reed figured in what came to be seen as a sinister incident. Correspondents on the Western Front, they visited the German front lines one night in February 1915, and after having been encouraged by a fair amount of champagne, each of them fired, from a borrowed Mauser, a couple of rifle shots "high into the air," Dunn said, but in the general direction of the French. "Be it on our heads, we did it," Dunn reported, indiscreetly, in the New York *Post*. "Both fired twice, turn and turn about, wicked, full-fledged franc-tireurs. . . . That Reed should have done so, with his scorn of force and soldiering, is sufficient, if sophistical, excuse for me."

In the resulting uproar, during which Theodore Roosevelt declared that if he could have his way he would have Reed and Dunn "shot on sight," Steffens offered a characteristic interpretation. "It would have been 'discreet' to suppress any mention" of the episode, he wrote to the *Post* editor.

> But Dunn mentioned it; of course he did; he couldn't help it. And he shouldn't have helped it. And neither should you have cut it out, as you wished you had. It is one of the most significant facts reported from the front. It shows that you, and I, and Dunn's critics would fall in the trenches into the spirit of actual war; the careless spirit of passionless shooting in the dark. Dunn says it means, and he suggested in his "story," that this spirit is so passionless that the trenches are the place to start the movement to end the war!

Even at the end of March 1918, when the Germans launched the great spring offensive that threatened to smash the Allied lines, Steffens felt not "the slightest tendency in myself to hate the Germans." "That hideous battle in France" was "just one welter of the victims of ignorance, greed, and false virtue . . . militancy and superstition." The Kaiser to catch and kill was not the one in Germany, he said, remembering what muckraking had revealed about the good citizen. "Everybody has a little Kaiser in him."

IV

ELECTION DAY, NOVEMBER 6, 1917, was quiet in New York City and in some respects hardly different from elections Steffens had been seeing there ever since he started as a reporter twenty-five years earlier. Reports from the Western Front told of hand-to-hand fighting between Americans and Germans; stock prices on Wall Street tumbled; and Morris Hillquit, running for mayor on the Socialist party's peace platform, was to capture twenty-two percent of the city's votes. Pretty much as predicted, however, the Tammany candidate won handily over the incumbent reform mayor, and the prospects for an orgy of patronage were bright. The victor was John F. Hylan, a judge of the King's County Court who had been hand-picked from obscurity by the former horse-car driver and saloonkeeper Boss Charles F. Murphy, apostolic successor to Boss Croker. (Croker, having worked long and hard for his own pocket, was living out his last years as sportsman and country squire in Ireland, the owner of a racing stable that had already sent a winner to the Derby at Epsom Downs.) In Hylan's political lineage as well as in the systolic, tidal rhythm of reform and reaction, Election Day 1917 was like the old days all over again. Back from the polls, lulled by familiar sounds from the billiard room and the bar at the Players' Club on Gramercy Park, Steffens took his leisure and wrote some letters. "We rather expect Tammany to win."

In Petrograd that day John Reed witnessed the shaking of a world. He cabled to Max Eastman:

THIS MORNING I WAS AT THE SCENE OF THE DISPERSAL OF THE JUNKERS DEFENDING THE WINTER PALACE BY THE SOVIET TROOPS IN THE AFTERNOON I WAS PRESENT AT THE OPENING OF THE ALL-RUSSIAN ASSEMBLY OF SOVIETS IN THE EVENING I WITNESSED THE ASSAULT ON THE WINTER PALACE ENTERING WITH THE FIRST BOLSHEVIK TROOPS.

By the next day, while voters in New York were reading about Hylan's commanding plurality, the Bolsheviks, voting with their feet, had overthrown the provisional government, and Lenin was on his way to becoming absolute ruler of Russia. It would be a long time before anyone in America was at all sure of what had actually happened or was at all prepared for what might happen next. "Believe Russian crisis temporary," *The New York Times* declared on November 10. "Washington and Embassy Officials Expect Bolsheviki Rule to Be Short."* The *Times* also reported that Lincoln Steffens, in a lecture at Washington Irving High School the evening before, had told his audience that the Russians were not seeking a separate peace with Germany; this statement, at that time, was accurate. A week later, beginning to measure the pandemic confusion generated by one stunning event in Russia, Steffens noted a shortage of "direct, believable news from Petrograd." There was only rumor, but "the rumor says that the Bolsheviks are on top, or, anyhow, the Soldiers' and Workmen's Council. This makes the Allies hot, but it's good news for Russia. They don't go back; they go on."

The intellectual entente of 1913, already smashed by the war, received its death blow in the Russian revolution. That hopeful alliance had in part been held together by a shared rejection of bourgeois allegiances. Now, it seemed, one either went with the revolution and the proletariat, or, rejecting them, went back to the middle class. One was either a rebel or an accomplice. With alarming urgency and apparent finality one had to decide whether this "re-revolution" was the second coming or the catastrophe of modern times, a wedding or a funeral, a stage in an inexorable process or just a tragic fluke, an attempt to realize age-old dreams of abolishing war, poverty and suffering or a reversion to the blackest of tyrannies. One had to take sides, disregarding the possibility that perhaps

* "No other note appeared more faithfully and with emphasis so certain," Walter Lippmann and Charles Merz wrote in their study of how the Russian revolution was reported by *The New York Times*, the newspaper which represented for them the best but also the most typical in American journalism. "In the two years from November, 1917, to November, 1919, no less than ninety-one times was it stated that the Soviets were nearing their rope's end, or actually had reached it." The conclusions Lippmann and Merz arrived at supply part of the context for Lincoln Steffens' generally unavailing attempts to explicate the revolution for the American public: "From the point of view of professional journalism the reporting of the Russian Revolution is nothing short of a disaster. On the essential questions the net effect was almost always misleading, and misleading news is worse than none at all. Yet on the face of the evidence there is no reason to charge a conspiracy by Americans. They can fairly be charged with boundless credulity, and an untiring readiness to be gulled, and on many occasions with a downright lack of common sense." ("A Test of the News," *The New Republic*, XXIII, August 4, 1920, pp. 3, 10.)

everyone would turn out to have been wrong. (There was no room for "so-called Socialist compromisers," Trotsky said. "They are so much refuse which will be swept into the garbage heap of history.")

"The impact of the Bolshevik revolution on the American left wing was stunning," said the historian Theodore Draper. "It was as if some left-wing Socialists had gone to sleep and had awakened as Communists. The Bolshevik Revolution had a dazzling, dreamlike quality." As in dreams, old problems, including the nagging problem of how to make a minority revolution, suddenly appeared to have been solved. Lenin had shown how a minority party, disciplined, ruthless, and brilliantly led, could bypass politics, time, inertia, and mass persuasion, seize power, and, having seized it, hold, consolidate and threaten to extend it to the ends of the world. And the old, depressing process of "Socialists and Radicals going into office and being 'sobered by the responsibilities of power'" no longer held true, Steffens said in January 1918. The days of "compromise and surrender" were over—Trotsky and Lenin, in power, were "as red" as they had been when they were exiles.

Using a familiar phrase of the time, Steffens, like many others, described the Russian revolution as an "acid test." He said it burned "President Wilson himself and almost all liberals, Socialists, Americans." It burned away John Reed's exuberance. He came back from Russia as a Communist party organizer and ideologue. The revolution burned Lincoln Steffens too, and its effects were both immediate and delayed. For him, the grace of the Petrograd revelation of spring 1917 had been followed by the pain of a negative conversion —he was compelled to discard his entire accustomed structure of belief. His defense mechanisms, in the language of depth psychology, had crumbled, and his response to this loss—which was also his attempt to repair the loss—was a severe depression. The revolution "seemed to me to require a complete change of mind, just, for example, as Einstein's relativity does. Nothing that I used to think could stand in the face of that Russian experience," he said in 1926. "I could not have talked fast enough to anyone to mention in a flash as I 'saw' it the details of the wreck of my political philosophy in the war and the revolution *and* the threads of the new, and better, conceptions which lay mangled but traceable in the debris." In the course of this "psychological revolution," he followed the family pattern and fell into a period of brooding silence and isolation, a panic state marked by "a kind of thinking that is inexpressible in words. It is rapid, wide, and confused; it takes in apparently unrelated subjects so far apart that it gives me a pain in my stomach." But this was a delayed effect. The trauma of the Bolshevik revolution had taken a few years to travel all the way through to the cortex of his belief.

"The world is fighting on perpendicular lines, but the real division is along a horizontal line," Steffens wrote a month before the Armistice. "For it's a class war, or it will be at the peace conference." As a pacifist in both the class war and the military war, he had spent the war years in the forefront of unpopular causes. In a time of the growing victory of illiberalism and therefore with largely negligible degrees of success, he worked in Hillquit's mayoral campaign and for woman's suffrage, served as character witness for Emma Goldman and Alexander Berkman when they went on trial for conspiring to obstruct the draft, interceded on behalf of the *Masses* editors with Colonel House (who received Max Eastman amiably enough at Beverly Farms and dined with him tête à tête, the net result of which was that the Attorney General moved to bring the case to trial again). In general, Steffens attempted to introduce tolerance in the place of "patriotism" and to work out the terms of "an amnesty in the class war."

Among the new Russians Steffens was known to be one of the few Americans capable of explaining their revolution at a time when the word "Bolshevik" conjured up a vision of the antichrist wearing a German uniform. "Trotsky is not pro-German," Steffens wrote in a syndicated newspaper article which also served as his introduction to Trotsky's *The Bolsheviki and World Peace*. "He isn't a patriot at all. He is for a class, the proletariat, the working people of all countries." Steffens followed the same line of argument on the lecture circuit during 1918. "It jars all hearers, even the radicals, but it goes," he said of his talk. "It's Bolshevism, straight, the science, the technique of revolution. It explains the inevitability in such crises of autocracy, minority government; the abolition of liberty, etc., etc."—he was still minimizing, as John Reed no longer did, the bitter finalities of the struggle. Steffens' function, as he saw it—even though William English Walling and others were now describing him as an out-and-out Bolshevik agent—was to interpret, not propagandize; he was convinced that there could be no peace until what had happened in Russia was understood as one way—there might be others—of rejecting a social order that seemed bent on war.

"It is only here in the U. S. that no clear opinion is forming upon peace terms," Steffens noted in February 1918, a month after Wilson proclaimed his Fourteen Points. Having been identified as a publicist for the Bolsheviks, Steffens met with little success as a lecturer on "The Price of Permanent Peace." He had enrolled himself as an un-official agent of Wilson's peace policy even though, as Colonel House told him, he could expect no support or even acknowledg-ment from the Administration. As a matter of fact, House warned, he might be arrested or even lynched. As Steffens traveled from city to city, lecturing from platforms where often the red flag and the American flag were displayed side by side, he found that House had not been far from the truth. Now there were sheriffs and police-men in the audience, federal agents taking stenographic notes, threats, newspaper squibs and rumors denouncing him as a German propagandist "glorifying the bolsheviki and deriding the war aims of the United States and her allies."

The war psychology was more intense than ever. "The least word out of tune brings a question from the audience, a sort of flaming sword of a question." In dealing with "the war-mad," the "truly sick," he said, one had to learn not to give pain, but this was some-times impossible. "RUMOR HERE STEFFENS PRO-GERMAN. IF SO LECTURE WILL NOT GO HERE," a clergyman in Peoria wired, to which Steffens replied, mocking the lurid but by then pan-demic confusion in the public mind, "RUMORS ABSURD. MY LECTURE IS ON THE RUSSIAN REVOLUTION." After the lecture in Peoria he reported, "I'm not arrested yet." At the South Broad Street Theater in Philadelphia uniformed police censors stand-ing in the wings interrupted his lecture and threatened to arrest him if he uttered any further criticisms of Allied policy. He shrugged his shoulders, went on with a more cautious talk, and afterward reported once again, "Not arrested yet."

The lecture tour came to an abrupt stop in his home state. An edi-torial in the April 26 San Diego *Sun* denounced his efforts to propa-gandize for "the spirit of Bolshevism at its worst, of unmitigated anarchy." Fired up by the editorial and by responses from an en-raged citizenry, the San Diego chief of police and federal representa-tives confronted Steffens in his room at the Coronado Hotel and told him that no man who criticized the government as he did could be allowed to speak in San Diego. "I have been criticizing the United States Government for twenty-five years," Steffens answered, but it was futile to argue. He cancelled his San Diego talk and soon after cancelled the rest of his lecture tour. It was cruel and pointless, he decided, to go on talking peace to a people at war.

"One clog in your peace machinery," Steffens had told House in February 1918, "is the failure of Trotsky and the Russians to believe in the sincerity of President Wilson." (According to Karl Radek, the Bolshevik spokesman, the President was the "prophet of American imperialism," and his Fourteen Points, in the course of which Wilson pledged himself to the withdrawal of Allied forces from Russia and to Russian self-determination, added up to "a very deliquescent program of political rascality.") The Russians, Steffens went on, regard the United States as "a plutocracy; it is part of the capitalistic system. Therefore the head of it can't mean literally what Mr. Wilson says. He must be playing some game." "I think some way must be found to dislodge this doubt," Steffens told House, and that way was John Reed, "because he seems to have the confidence of Trotsky & Co." On February 25, supported by House, he cabled an open message to Reed at Christiania:

TROTSKY MAKING EPOCHAL BLUNDER DOUBTING WILSON LITERAL SINCERITY. I AM CERTAIN PRESIDENT WILSON WILL DO WHATEVER HE ASKS OTHER NATIONS TO DO. IF YOU CAN AND WILL CHANGE TROTSKY'S AND LENIN'S ATTITUDES YOU CAN RENDER HISTORICAL INTERNATIONAL SERVICE.

STEFFENS

But Reed now saw the revolution in a different light than Steffens. The revolution was not something with which the West would have to find an accommodation; it was the first stage of a battle to the finish. And so when Steffens once again played Sangar the peacemaker, this time with the blessings and cooperation of George Creel and the State Department, there was no ambiguity in Reed's response; having come from Steffens and not from a revolutionary leader like Big Bill Haywood or Eugene Debs (both under indictment by the federal government), Steffens' cable appeared to Reed to be merely ridiculous.

By June Reed was more tolerant. "I think you must have been suffering a good deal," he told Steffens, "perhaps more than anybody." On the face of it Reed had fared worse. Indicted with the other *Masses* editors and certain that he did not have "the ghost of a show," Reed gallantly came home at the end of April to stand trial. At pierside he was met by federal agents, who spent hours searching his person and his cabin for revolutionary propaganda and ended up confiscating his notes for *Ten Days That Shook the World*. In Philadelphia, he was arrested for conducting a street meeting and charged with inciting to riot, inciting to assault and battery, and inciting to seditious remarks. So there he was, living by the Hudson River at Croton, in a community which he sometimes referred to as the Mount Airy Soviet, depressed, physically ill, "blocked," he complained to Steffens, "unable to write a word of the greatest story of my life and one of the greatest in the world." He bridled when Steffens suggested that Walter Lippmann could use his influence to have the notes returned. "I wouldn't ask Walter L. for anything for the whole world." (Lippmann was then in charge of "The Inquiry," a study group appointed by Wilson to deal with the problems of the peace.)

Reed, now a party Communist and organizer, had found certainty in Russia—"Something like dreams-come-true," he told Steffens—and the rift between these two survivors of the Village entente, mentor and protégé, had become as wide as the oceans and continents that separated them on Election Day in 1917. In Reed's eyes, Steffens had been left behind by history; for all his revolutionary sympathies, Steffens remained only a rebel, a liberal gripped by the deadly habit of seeing both sides of the issue and therefore unable to commit himself in action. "Go on—the limit," the Communist party and the world revolution, Reed was to say to him the last time they met. He had finally voiced the repudiation and anger that had been merely covert in "Sangar." "Why don't you join us? We are trying to do what you used to talk and write about."

In the summer of 1918, with Allied troops moving into Vladivostok, Archangel and Murmansk to support the enemies of his revolution, Reed had little use for Steffens' counsels of patience, his cool diagnosis of events. "Jack, you do wrong to buck this thing," the older man said, trying to argue Reed out of his bitterness. "In the first place, the war was inevitable; in the second place, the consequences of the war, its by-products, are normal and typical; and in the third place, the public mind is sick. This last is what I learned in my experiences with it. I gave pain. I tried to speak always with the consciousness that an audience was in trouble psychologically, and I was just as tender as I could be. And I often did my job without hurting them very much. But sometimes I saw that what I had said cut like a surgeon's knife into a sore place, and I was sorry. Really, I think it is wrong to try to tell the truth now. We must wait. You must wait. I know it's hard, but you can't carry conviction. You can't plant ideas. Only feelings exist, and the feelings are bewildered. I think it is undemocratic to try to do much now. Write, but don't publish."

CHAPTER THIRTEEN

"I have seen the future"

I

"IT HAS NOT BEEN FORGOTTEN THAT I SPOKE FOR PEACE when there was war; many communities will not read, hear, or heed me," Steffens said years later. He was describing the "punishment" for his "dangerous experiment" with public opinion. But along with the punishment there came a reward for his services to Wilson's administration. Early in June 1918, a little over a month after he was closed down in San Diego and virtually ridden out of the city, Steffens asked Colonel House for permission to attend the peace conference when the time came, and through House's direct intervention Steffens sailed for France a few days before hostilities stopped on the Western Front on November 11.

Collecting this "reward" proved to be a nerve-racking business. At a time when prominent citizens like former President Taft and former President Eliot of Harvard were being turned down when they applied to go to Paris, it was a near and remarkable thing that Steffens was allowed to leave the country at all. It took the combined efforts of House and George Creel to dislodge Steffens' passport from the State Department. Meanwhile, the French and the English threatened to deny him a visa; they had the idea, Steffens said, "that I sympathize with revolutionists and am prejudiced against Imperialists other than Germans." Naval and military inspectors at the New York Customs House on November 7 reviewed his entire history, called up various misdeeds, cited his speeches, lectures and views as having been consistently socialist, pacifist, pro-German. Toward the end of these proceedings Steffens invoked the authority of Colonel House and this time, to his surprise, all difficulties "faded" for the moment. "I got my pass to the dock and the last visé of the United States."

Steffens' "punishment" took other, more durable forms: blacklisting and an underground professional existence the beginnings of which he sometimes traced to the time when he played peacemaker in the McNamara affair. In 1904, in the blaze of recognition that followed *The Shame of the Cities*, he had every reason to believe that he was the foremost political journalist in the United States. There had been more demand for his work than he could possibly meet. Now he even found it difficult to get a by-line for his few assignments—"nothing but anonymous stuff, editorial in character," he complained. Just before the war ended in 1918 Max Eastman and his sister Crystal, joint editors of *The Liberator*, successor to the defunct *Masses*, offered to send him abroad as a correspondent. He declined. He still hoped to be a persuader instead of writing for the Eastmans' already committed audience. "Not yet," he told the *Liberator* editors. "I may have to publish in the radical magazines, but I'll not do so till I'm excluded from the middle-class magazines."

He just barely missed being excluded. For ten years he had been an editor and writer for the staunchly middle-class *Everybody's*. Less than a month before the Armistice, however, Steffens was told that the magazine's management and ownership were unalterably opposed to the idea of having him represent them at the peace conference. He frightened away advertisers, Howard Wheeler, the editor, told him; he was now altogether "too radical." (Soon, in the hysteria that followed the Armistice, *Everybody's* stood in the forefront of alarm, denouncing Russia's "murderous anarchy" and alerting Americans to a "Bolshevist infection," which, it was rumored, was being spread by a propaganda fund of half a million dollars in Moscow gold sent over by Lenin and Trotsky.) Steffens managed to hammer out a compromise. "They wanted my ability, my connections, my experiences—everything but my name," he told his family. "When I had that established I struck them hard. I offered to write anonymously or under an assumed name. They were flabbergasted. They hemmed and hawed, and finally they said they would have to talk it over. Wheeler said I won."

Steffens was standing at a New York pier in the slow inspection line that separated him from the gangplank of the French liner *Lorraine* when someone clapped him on the shoulder from behind. His heart pounded wildly; he was certain that at this perverse, last moment the detaining hand of government was being laid upon him. He spun around only to find not an official but instead a Village acquaintance, the sculptor Jo Davidson, on his way to France to make portrait busts of the Allied leaders. "If you ever do that again, I'll kill you," Steffens said. "Don't you ever do to anybody what you did to me."

Later, in the ship's bar after sailing, Steffens' mood lifted as he shared Davidson's stories and his enormous pleasure in drink, food and human company. They were in mid-ocean when news of the Armistice came over the radio, and in the celebration the French captain ordered the *Lorraine*'s outside lights turned on. It never occurred to anybody, the sculptor later considered, that there might be a U-boat nearby that had not got the news or preferred to ignore it. In Paris, at the Hotel Chatham off the Place de l'Opéra, he and Steffens, friends for life by then, moved into the only vacancy, the bridal suite adorned with golden Louis XV furniture, golden cupids and golden garlands, emblems not only of the old civilization wounded in the war but also of the awaited arrival of tranquillity, the arts of peace and Woodrow Wilson.

In the mid-term elections that fall, Wilson, rashly dissolving his wartime coalition with the Republicans, went to the people to ask for a vote of confidence, and the people vigorously denied him. Now the Republicans controlled the Congress, and the President's enemy, Henry Cabot Lodge, was chairman of the Senate Foreign Relations Committee. Wilson's "leadership has just been emphatically repudiated," said another enemy, Theodore Roosevelt, speaking, as it turned out, not just for himself in the last few months of his life, but for a reunited party leadership that was soon making overt attempts to discredit the President in Paris. "Our allies and our enemies and Mr. Wilson himself should all understand that Mr. Wilson has no authority whatever to speak for the American people at this time," Roosevelt said, enjoying the taste of battle that had been denied him during the war. "Mr. Wilson and his Fourteen Points and his four supplementary points and his five complementary points and all his utterances every which way have ceased to have any shadow of right to be accepted as expressive of the will of the American people."

Abroad, those same points and utterances, magnified through Creel's propaganda, had transformed Woodrow Wilson from warrior in the White House to spokesman from Sinai, prince of peace, bridegroom of Europe. On December 14, seated with the French President in an open state carriage banked and bedecked with flowers, Wilson the Just rode in triumph through Napoleon's victory arch and down the Champs Élysées as two million people cheered him. No man in history had ever had such an ovation, and after other triumphal progresses and entrances, in London, Milan and Rome, it was clear that, whatever was going on back home, among the masses on the European side of the Atlantic Woodrow Wilson was the most admired man in the world. People burned candles before his picture, named him in their prayers, it was said and duly repeated.

"I really believe," said Lloyd George, "that at first the idealistic President regarded himself as a missionary whose function it was to rescue the poor European heathen from their age-long worship of false and fiery gods." The conference and the horse trading had not started yet, and it was still possible for Wilson to talk about peace unilaterally, intransigently, in terms of the powers of light and the powers of darkness, and on his preferred level of moral and political abstraction, a level so high that objections and tactical realities perished for lack of oxygen. Embarked on "the world's highest adventure," Wilson appeared to be "winning"—" 'in principle,' " Steffens said at the end of December. Other Americans in Paris were not prepared to endorse even this guarded analysis. En route to Europe aboard the *George Washington*, an audacious young American diplomat, William C. Bullitt, had badgered Wilson into admitting that his plans for the League of Nations he had proposed in Point Fourteen were still vague, certainly preliminary to a draft constitution for the League. In other respects as well, members of the American mission were troubled by Wilson's lack of a definite program. Firm in the faith that a vindictive peace would lead to an early war, Wilson was all too content to rely on broad principles and let the specifics take care of themselves. (Wilson "could write Notes from Sinai or Olympus," John Maynard Keynes said. "But if he once stepped down to the intimate quality of the Four, the game was evidently up . . . like Odysseus, he looked wiser when seated.")

Ten thousand civilians having some sort of business with the conference poured into Paris along with five hundred and more correspondents for newspapers and magazines. Ray Stannard Baker was there as Wilson's press chief; Ida Tarbell had come over for the *American Magazine,* and William Allen White for the McClure syndicate; the muckrakers of 1903 were brought together once again in the expectant churning of the peace conference. Still there was not a great deal for Steffens to do but see old friends, practice his French, spend occasional afternoons with a secretary or shopgirl in an apartment on the Avenue de l'Opéra lent him by the admiring correspondent of the New York *Sun.* Life in Paris was mostly a matter of waiting, questioning and listening in crowded lobbies and press rooms and at American Commission headquarters in the Crillon, where Colonel House treated him with conspicuous attention. When Steffens fell ill with the flu and bronchitis, friends and visitors continued to bring him the news, or what passed for news. Legendary reporter, private observer, informal liaison man with the Russians and with revolutionary movements in general, Steffens was already well established as a tutelary figure in his profession, someone to whom other journalists rendered accounts. "I looked up to him as a demi-god," recalled Herbert Bayard Swope of the New York *World* "and wondered if ever by some convulsion of nature I would be able to call him by his first name."

Paris was a chaos of gossip masquerading as history. Caught in this disordered information system—itself a cause of the failure of Versailles, Lippmann claimed when it was all over—correspondents in search of news relied on rumors, handouts, leaks, vagrant interviews and just plain lies. Perhaps, despite Wilson's talk of "open covenants of peace, openly arrived at," publicity and diplomacy were fundamentally incompatible. Skeptical and experienced reporters like Steffens and Baker, at home in the labyrinths of governmental and corporate politics, fared no better than novices, sometimes worse and without even knowing it.

Here, for example, was a correspondent who had got wind of the secret conference on board the *George Washington* and cabled a story to the effect that Wilson had no concrete proposals at all to make regarding the League of Nations. The fact was, Steffens innocently assured the reporter as they talked in the Crillon lobby, that Wilson's draft constitution for the League had been ready for months. How did Steffens know? Why, House had told him this back in New York, and besides, Steffens added, all you have to do is ask the person standing not ten feet away, Baker, the President's spokesman. And Baker, perhaps almost as innocently as Steffens, assured them that a draft was indeed ready, seeming proof, as Baker claimed, that Wilson, contrary to what his detractors were saying, had come to Paris prepared. Baker had taken on the job with Wilson believing that nothing would be withheld from him. Two years later, when Wilson opened his papers to him, Baker, by then Wilson's biographer, was shocked by what he learned he hadn't known.

> What an ignoramus I had really been! Every third document I turned over revealed wheels within wheels, the tortuous fatuities of secret discussions that I had known little or nothing about. I soon began to discover that the President himself, to say nothing of Lloyd George and Clemenceau, did not begin to know all that was going on in that cave of winds.

II

IN THE EARLY MONTHS OF 1919, STEFFENS SAID, "nobody but spies and armies" could get into Russia. The country was torn by counter-revolutions that the West supported through military interventions, and after the waning of a shadowy plan to invite the warring factions to meet on the Turkish island of Prinkipo, a sanitary two thousand miles from Paris, the peace conference went about its business in the conspicuous absence of representatives of the "fit partner for a league of honor" that Wilson had saluted less than two years earlier.

Out of the veiled transactions of Paris there emerged, in mid-February 1919, a characteristic scheme. Its origins were as cloudy as its purposes, its method of execution and its outcome.

With the support of the British, but without the knowledge of the French, the Americans decided to send to the Bolsheviks an emissary who, depending on the view one took of him, was a negotiator or an observer or merely a courier and either had an official existence or did not. Steffens was one of several who proposed the idea of some sort of diplomatic mission. "You are fighting them, hating them, and all of a sudden you invite them to a parley," he said to Colonel House about the Bolsheviks at the abortive Prinkipo meeting. "What for? Why, if you want to deal with them, don't you do as you would to any other government?" Among others who were proposing a mission to Russia were the young diplomat William C. Bullitt and Lord Northcliffe, the British press magnate. As Steffens learned in January 1919, Northcliffe wanted to send in a fact-finding group which presumably would bring back reliable information about the stability and future of the beleaguered Bolsheviks—was Lenin's government going to be around long enough to have to be negotiated with at all? This appears to have been the official American understanding of the mission when it was finally authorized. "Sir," Secretary of State Robert Lansing informed Bullitt on February 18, "You are hereby directed to proceed to Russia for the purpose of studying conditions, political and economic, therein, for the benefit of the American Commissioners plenipotentiary to negotiate peace."

Formerly of Rittenhouse Square, Yale College, the Philadelphia *Public Ledger*, and Creel's Committee, Bullitt was now twenty-eight and an information attaché of the American Commission. But he brought to his junior post at Paris the certainty, which was not without some basis in fact, that he was born and bred to be a leader and sit in the councils of the mighty. Lansing had not reckoned on Bullitt himself, who, upon accepting an assignment that he had vigorously sought, proceeded to display his characteristic audacity.

First, he appointed as an unofficial member of the mission Lincoln Steffens, a known Bolshevik sympathizer and publicist. Bullitt's superiors might be outraged by the choice, but his reasoning at this point was unanswerable: he needed Steffens to vouch for him. American and British expeditionary forces were fighting on the counterrevolutionary side in Russia; as far as Lenin's government was concerned the West had already declared war. Whatever John Reed might think, the Russians trusted Steffens, knew that he was on their side and that he believed they were there to stay. As Bullitt joked with a newspaperman in Paris, Steffens even looked like a Russian.

Next, Bullitt consulted with Lloyd George's chief secretary, Philip Kerr, who equipped him with a confidential memorandum of terms

Kerr believed the West would be prepared to discuss in order to achieve a workable relationship with the Soviets. Bullitt, in turn, interpreted this memorandum not as mere background, but, along with some rather elastic, last-minute instructions from House, as tacit authorization to negotiate with Lenin.

Dispatched in darkest secrecy from Baker's "cave of winds," the Bullitt mission was a risky proposition from the start, an experiment in personal diplomacy at a time when public opinion on the Russian issue was so volatile that, as Bullitt and Steffens soon discovered, it was possible to travel East as a legate and return to the West as a leper. Other aspects of the mission's collective personality and style —excited and freewheeling, passionately indiscreet, possessed of transcendent certainty—derived to a large extent from the interaction of Bullitt and Steffens. One was an aristocrat fueled by careerism and idealistic fervor, the other a partisan of the revolutionary future who in Russia two years earlier had been soul-stirred by the redemptive vision of government emerging out of chaos. The separate accounts which Steffens and Bullitt wrote of their mission to Russia, released to the Senate Foreign Relations Committee in September 1919, were so similar in sympathies and conclusions as to be either interchangeable or simply redundant. ("As to Bill Bullitt," Ezra Pound was to tease Steffens in 1934, "did any of his brain go into that report or was it Linkie Linkie Linkie all the way?")

As they left Paris, Bullitt and Steffens believed that they had been presented with a unique opportunity to make history by mediating between the West and the revolution. It was an opportunity that might never come again. "I am full of our project," Steffens told Gussie, "expecting something good of it, something decisive and climactic." "The firmness of the man's enthusiasm made my heart ache when I met him first," Ramsay MacDonald said of Bullitt. "A young man of great heart, integrity, and courage," said Lenin. Steffens recalled that on the way into Russia Bullitt and an assistant "skylarked, wrestling and tumbling like a couple of bear cubs all along the Arctic Circle. A pretty noisy secret mission we were."

In Petrograd, as dark and forbidding as when Steffens arrived at midnight two years earlier, they were greeted with the harsh question, *"Sind Sie bevollmächtigt?"* ("Are you empowered to negotiate?"). It was not clear at first that the Russians, who assumed that

Steffens was in charge, would be willing to deal with Bullitt at all. Finally, Grigori Chicherin, Trotsky's successor as foreign-affairs commissar, came to Petrograd, looked them over, was convinced that they were competent and sincere, and brought them to Moscow, once again the Russian capital.

Steffens' interview with Lenin, as he was to report it in conversations and in several written forms, provided Westerners an alternative to the popular image of an Oriental despot, a ruthless utopian, and a cold-blooded trickster who, in the distinction George Orwell made thirty years later, did not establish a dictatorship in order to safeguard a revolution but instead made a revolution in order to establish a dictatorship. In the view that Steffens helped popularize, Lenin was a great moral personality. By contrast with Woodrow Wilson—"a mere sailor" adrift on seas of compromise and accident —Lenin was a "navigator" who had set a course for the future. He had decided, as he told Steffens, that "in the long run of history it will have been better for us to have tried out Marx to a finish than to have made a mixed success." Lenin exercised an absolute dictatorship, Steffens was to report, and in fact "is farther removed from the people than the Tsar was, or than any actual ruler in Europe is." But this dictatorship was merely evolutionary, Steffens sincerely believed, a stage on the way to economic and then political democracy—like the terror, the suppression of personal liberties, the absolute subordination of the individual to party and state, dictatorship was a birth pang of the revolution and would pass.

In his excitement, Steffens, an admirer of strong leaders, had put aside his skepticism about the face value of political utterances and also put aside the lesson he learned as an interviewer; this time his subject dominated, and Steffens said what Lenin wanted him to say. The Russian terror, the killings and the secret police, Steffens explained, stood between the peace commissioners in Paris and an acceptance of the revolution. "Do you mean to tell me," Lenin demanded, "that those men who have just generaled the slaughter of seventeen millions of men in a purposeless war are concerned over the few thousands that have been killed in a revolution which has a conscious aim: to get out of the necessity of war—and armed peace?" Then he became resigned. "But never mind, do not deny the Terror. Don't minimize any of the evils of a revolution. They occur. They must be counted upon. If we have to have a revolution, we have to pay the price of it."

In Steffens' view, Lenin, a quiet, open, visionary and inquiring man in shabby clothes, was "an idealist, but he is a scholar, too, and a very grim realist." On the basis of what he knew and had been told Steffens claimed that Lenin—a "liberal . . . the greatest of liberals"— had, with the utmost reluctance and only after an attempt on his life, yielded to other Bolshevik leaders and sanctioned the use of terror against the opposition and the establishment of the Cheka as "protector" of the revolution.

Bullitt too reported that Lenin stood "well to the right in the existing political life of Russia" and represented the side of reason. "He is a very striking man—straightforward and direct, but also genial and with a large humor and serenity. There is already a Lenin legend. He is regarded almost as a prophet." At a time when the Communist Third International was meeting in Moscow to proclaim a program of world revolution, Lenin appeared to be interested primarily in solving domestic problems of survival. As a consequence of the Allied blockade, Bullitt reported, "every man, woman, and child in Moscow and Petrograd is suffering from slow starvation." Corpses were common sights in the streets. Contrary to the reports of luxury and carousing that were current in Paris, Lenin's food ration was no different from that of a soldier or workman, and Steffens recalled that Chicherin, Lenin's Talleyrand, developed the habit of calling with a question just as the Americans were sitting down to a meal made of the canned goods they had brought in with them. "Yes, Mr. Chicherin," Steffens said to him one evening. "Come right in. Supper is about ready."

"The destructive phase of the revolution in Russia is over," Steffens and Bullitt were to report. "Constructive work has begun." Despite famine, epidemics of typhoid, typhus and smallpox, a harsh winter, and a shortage of fuel, Russian morale was high—higher, they thought, than it was among the masses of people in London or New York. Civil order had been restored; crime and begging had virtually disappeared. "All meetings of workmen during work hours have been prohibited, with the result that the loafing which was so fatal during the Kerensky regime has been overcome and discipline has been restored in the factories as in the army." Even the trains were beginning to run on time, a claim that was soon to be made for other postwar states.*

"The organization of life as we know it in America, in the rest of Europe, in the rest of the world," Steffens wrote, "is wrecked and abolished in Russia." In its place was the evolving, infinitely promising "future," a new economic and scientific culture. The peace commissioners in Paris believed that Bolshevism was only a temporary and abnormal condition and would soon give way to a constitutional democracy. But that was not the case at all: under Lenin, Bullitt said, Russia had regained its equilibrium. "No government save a socialist government can be set up in Russia today except by foreign bayonets, and any government so set up will fail the moment such support is withdrawn." The Soviet system of government had become for the Russian people not only the instrument of their revolution but "the symbol of their revolution," and so, as Bullitt was to conclude, "No real peace can be established in Europe or the world until peace is made with the revolution."

In the interests of this peace he was bringing back with him a Russian proposition to which the Allies were asked to respond by April 10: in substance, Lenin's government pledged itself to respect the status quo in non-Bolshevik Russia and to assume a share of Russia's war debts in return for Allied pledges of an armistice and a peace conference, the lifting of the economic blockade and the withdrawal of occupying forces. The Russian proposal, which Bullitt jubilantly cabled to Wilson and House from Finland on March 16, presented, he told them then, "an opportunity to make peace with the revolution on a just and reasonable basis—perhaps an unique opportunity." As Steffens said, the proposition "seemed to us more than fair and not to be rejected." Nearly fifty years after the Bullitt mission returned from Moscow, the diplomat and scholar George Kennan described the terms for this negotiated peace as offering "the most favorable opportunity yet extended, or ever to be extended, to the Western powers . . . for the creation of an acceptable relationship to the Soviet regime."

* "In spite of the necessity of firing with wood," Bullitt noted, "the Moscow-Petrograd express keeps up to its schedule." The railroad, built during the 1840s by an American (the painter Whistler's father), was now administered by an American, Bill Shatoff, a former I.W.W. leader in Chicago, who had become commandant of Petrograd.

"William Bullitt, who went to Russia for the American mission, returned today," Herbert Bayard Swope of the New York *World* cabled from Paris on March 25.

> He was instructed to say nothing for publication, in conformity with the new efforts to hide the peace proceedings under a veil of secrecy. In spite of this restriction, it may be said that he and Lincoln Steffens found conditions in Moscow under far better control than had been pictured, and their reports will tend to show a degree of permanency and stability in Russian affairs which puts a new face on the Russian situation.

This was significant news from Paris, where each day reports from White Russian sources, faithfully accepted as gospel by the French press and Western diplomats, told of Bolshevik defeats, heavy losses, Trotsky's Red Army in full retreat, the government falling.

Steffens' response to the promised land was evident between the lines of Swope's guarded story. Steffens had rushed over to Jo Davidson's studio to pick up his typewriter, and there he met Bernard Baruch, the capitalist whom Lenin wanted to bring to Russia to develop industry and natural resources. Baruch, sitting for a portrait bust, said, "So you've been over into Russia." And not for the first time, far from the last, Steffens replied, "I have been over into the future, and it works," by which he meant, in part, that the Bolsheviks were not a bad dream but real and there to stay. According to Bullitt, it was on the train to Stockholm, days before they even made their first contacts with Bolshevik agents and set out for the Russian frontier, that Steffens had begun to rehearse his celebrated mantra. In its perfected form—"I have seen the future, and it works" —it would ring in Western ears for the next two decades.

Like the hedgehog, Steffens now knew one thing for a truth, knew it with certainty and passion. "It was like a trip into the future," he wrote home. "I could write a mile and not tell all that makes me glad these days. I have seen the future; and it works." The Columbia historian James T. Shotwell, exposed in Paris to Steffens' electrifying gospel, found it persuasive. "As between extreme nationalists as they paint themselves and Bolshevists as Steffens paints them," Shotwell decided after dining with him on March 28, "give me Bolshevists." Steffens' newspaper friends, jealous of his adventure and also angry with him because he was compelled to withhold some of its details, soon began to feel a trifle derisive toward the future and the wonderful tidings he brought back from it: he was the Ancient Mariner, and they were wedding guests. "I have seen the future, and it works," he said once again, this time to Swope, William Allen White, Arthur Krock, and four or five others seated as a kind of frogs' chorus in the deep leather chairs of the Crillon lobby. He went on with his Marco Polo tale, which they had already heard or heard about, and came to one of the several social miracles he had seen in Russia. "Gentlemen," he declared, "I tell you they have abolished prostitution." Apparently it was Swope who broke the silence that followed this announcement. He held up his hand and said, "My God, Steff! What did you do?"

Pleading a headache, on March 26 Wilson broke an appointment to hear Bullitt's report. A few days later he was too preoccupied with his clash with Clemenceau over the Saar to give much thought to a chancy scheme brought back by a brash young man—at a time, moreover, when it seemed probable that the Bolshevik problem was going to solve itself; Admiral Kolchak's White Russian forces were rumored to be at the gates of Moscow. Meanwhile, Lord Northcliffe, who proposed the mission in the first place, had made what amounted to a one-hundred-and-eighty-degree turn. In the *Daily Mail* one of his chief editorial writers thundered against conciliation with the Soviets and denounced Lenin as a "sinister fanatic" who would go to any length to accomplish "the ruin of ordered democratic civilization." The cry was taken up in Northcliffe's *Times* and in other English papers. Rebuffed by Wilson, Bullitt had managed to have breakfast with Lloyd George, who was affable enough but feared for his political future and cited the *Daily Mail* editorial as proof that inflamed public opinion had made it impossible to negotiate with Moscow. Soon after, Lloyd George's Secretary of State for Foreign Affairs, using the traditional techniques of démarche, protected his government's flank and rear by professing official ignorance of the Bullitt mission.

House too had been shaken by the *Daily Mail* editorial. He was all for abandoning direct dealings with the Russians and substituting a food-relief program administered by Herbert Hoover. There seemed to be only one way to salvage the work of the Bullitt mission, and that was to persuade Hoover to combine Russian relief with economic initiatives, or, as Steffens put it, "to take the blooming philanthropy out of the thing and make it a simple proposition to stop fighting on both sides and begin to trade." He had his chance at lunch with Hoover on April 7. Hoover was angry and hostile, was dead set against any sort of parity for the revolution, and might just as well have written the *Daily Mail* editorial himself. The only way to deal with the Russians was to treat them as starving beggars and no more than that, he seemed to be saying, and besides, "Can those Communists make a go of their fool system?"

How far into the future are you willing to look? Steffens countered. What is your standard for "making a go of it"? "Suppose," he went on, "that after two or three hundred years of the communistic system, the world should break out into a world war, kill off twelve millions of men, and then come to a peace conference as incompetent, sordid, and warlike as this, would you say that Bolshevism was a go?"

But in general, with Hoover or anyone else in power, such arguments were unavailing, especially as coming from Steffens, suspect, tainted, and now, as he claimed, under surveillance from spies, detectives, and the Secret Service. According to *The New York Times*, an agent of the U.S. Department of Justice had identified him, somewhat superfluously, as a Bolshevik sympathizer and an admirer of Trotsky. "Wilson sees Russia by Steffens' eyes," the New York *Tribune* said, and, picking up the metaphor as well as the totally false impression that Wilson was having anything at all to do with Steffens or Bullitt, the *Sun* claimed that Wilson was bound to have "defective vision" if he relied for his views of Russia on "socialistic amateurs." *Collier's*, once among the paladins of muckraking, now denied that Steffens ever was, in any respect, a reliable source of information. "His reports are too highly charged with genius to be satisfactory to the humdrum seeker for the facts," a *Collier's* editorial said. "He is an artist, a distinguished and successful painter, after the style of Doré, of the woes of mankind. If Mr. Wilson imagines that this eminent illustrator of the political and social 'Inferno' will condescend to tell him what is really going on in Russia to the dispassionate eye . . . he will suffer a great disappointment."

By April 16, a week after the Russian offer expired, the Bullitt mission and even Bullitt's breakfast with Lloyd George were public knowledge. But in Commons the Prime Minister conceded only that "there was some suggestion that a young American had come back from Russia with a communication," and then he shifted the burden of embarrassment to Wilson. "It is not for me to judge the value of this communication, but if the President of the United States had attached any value to it he would have brought it before the conference, and certainly he did not." Outraged by the recognition that all along he had been no more than a passenger in a trial balloon, Bullitt decided to resign as noisily as possible. The failure of his mission, as he saw it, had fused with the larger disaster of the Versailles settlement; a League of Nations was to be charged with the task of enforcing a vicious and punitive treaty in which Bullitt claimed he could see "at least eleven wars."

As for Steffens, he had seen too much of the war spirit at home to be shocked by the failures that he witnessed in Paris: the failure of Woodrow Wilson, righteous and principled, a liberal reenacting the old, sad confrontation of the reformer and the boss, virtue and intelligence; the failure of a moral culture that discoursed passionately but unscientifically about liberty, democracy and fraternity, that sincerely desired peace, but with equal if unacknowledged sincerity desired things that were impossible to have without war. "We are going to have a League of Nations, weak, wrong, capable of great abuse; and we shall get a peace also, full of dynamite which will burst into war," Steffens said in mid-April. The Council of Four had hammered out their agreements in bitterness and bargain. "So they have failed. They have the appearance of success, but—they have failed. And it does not matter. The problem will be solved. Other, newer men, with a fresher culture—the men I have seen lately—they will have their turn now."

A few weeks later Steffens listened to Bullitt and his friends arguing the tactics of protest. To Bullitt and other young idealists on the American Commission—Adolph Berle, Jr., Christian Herter and Samuel Eliot Morison—Steffens had served as a kind of elder brother. This time, asked for advice, he preferred to remain silent. In Berle's possibly melodramatic recollection of what took place at the end of a long evening in May, over coffee and brandy at the Crillon Bullitt lifted a bouquet of flowers from the table and with his fine sense of occasion—he claimed descent from both Fletcher Christian of the *Bounty* and Patrick Henry—he awarded yellow jonquils to those who proposed to stay on with the commission and work from within. To rebels who, like him, planned to resign and make what they believed was a public sacrifice of their careers in government, he awarded red roses. Bullitt had expected that Steffens too would be for taking the heroic course. "And I would have been in the old muckraking days," Steffens reflected. Now he knew too much for roses. "I had seen the Russian Revolution, the war, and this peace, and I was sure that it was useless—it was almost wrong—to fight for the right under our system; petty reforms in politics, wars without victories, just peace, were impossible, unintelligent, heroic but immoral." He could only explain to Bullitt's young men how he felt; there was no point to arguing.

Bullitt, determined to "break all bounds," began what was to become his lifelong vendetta against Wilson with a hotly aggrieved letter of resignation.

> It is my conviction [he concluded] that if you had made your fight in the open, instead of behind closed doors, you would have carried with you the public opinion of the world, which was yours; you could have been able to resist the pressure and might have established the "new international order based upon broad and universal principles of right and justice" of which you used to speak. I am sorry that you did not fight our fight to the finish and that you had so little faith in the millions of men, like myself, in every nation who had faith in you.

In the ensuing boil of recrimination against Wilson and the treaty, Bullitt was widely quoted as saying that he intended to "lie on the sand and watch the world go to hell." Others shared his mood. "To bed, sick of life," Harold Nicolson wrote in his Paris journal that June. For William Allen White Versailles represented "the peace that passeth understanding." John Maynard Keynes resigned in despair over a Carthaginian settlement dictated by an "outrageous and impossible" treaty—"We are at the dead season of our misfortunes. Never in the lifetime of men now living has the universal element in the soul of man burnt so dimly." Yet for Lincoln Steffens at the age of fifty-three it was possible to hope that this "peace that was no peace," that was built on the ruins of the old culture, might turn out to be prelude to an age of creative change all over Europe. He might live to see the advent of the future. "I would like to spend the evening of my life watching the morning of a new world."

"*La séance est levée!*" Georges Clemenceau said in the Hall of Mirrors at Versailles on June 28, and it was all over but the aftermath. Steffens was not among the American journalists who competed for the privilege of witnessing the signing of the peace treaty. He had no interest in spectacles, he told Swope, who, as an act of tribute, had finagled a press pass for him; and besides, it was his time of day for a bath. A gloomy quiet descended upon Paris as the peacemakers and their entourages packed up, leaving the restaurants and lobbies suddenly empty. That evening Woodrow Wilson, who had arrived as a messiah and had been cheered by millions, slipped away for home from the Gare des Invalides with a minimum of ceremonial farewells.

PART FOUR

CHAPTER FOURTEEN

Moses in Red

I

ACCORDING TO A CARTOON IN ART YOUNG'S SATIRIC WEEKLY, *Good Morning*, Lincoln Steffens, who stayed behind in Europe after the others went home, was busy "running a day nursery for revolutions." Expatriate, and in a limited sense political exile, he lived among the ruins that stretched from Paris to Berlin and beyond. The European battleground and wasteland had become a sort of limbo between the eve and the morning of a new world, between Egypt's house of bondage and the promised land.

> We Americans made a great mistake having that brief period of muckraking [Steffens now concluded]. It set back our death more years than we devoted to it. It protracted the age of folly; did harm, and no good. . . . Since our muckrakers did not know and therefore did not tell us what actually was the matter, but only taught us morality, they stretched out the age of honest bunk.

Liberalism and reform seemed to be dying, and the West—along with "our old culture"—seemed to be in decline, having spent the best of its blood, youth and spirit to save "an old bitch gone in the teeth," Ezra Pound wrote, "a botched civilization."

For Steffens even the Carpentier-Siki boxing match he went to with Filene in September 1922, when Mustapha Kemal's Turks were on the march against Greece and the world sat on the edge of war, became a parable of a failed culture, of "man put to the test and almost always failing." (It was also, it now appears, a parable of the end of empire.) That evening in Paris, Georges Carpentier, the French champion and a national idol, went down to a shocking defeat, knocked out in six rounds by an unknown fighter named Battling Siki, a Senegalese who had got his training as a boxer while serving in a territorial regiment. Siki, "the underdeveloped man, fresh from the jungle," should not have stood a chance in a ring with the skilled and polished Carpentier, Steffens wrote, straying far out of his field to moralize the encounter.

In the ultimate sense it was not Siki who won, it was the culture of capitalism, Steffens said. "What a great thing it would be if some of our financial and political champions could be put to an obvious test like pugilists are. Watch Siki when Montmartre and his friends and the girls and the wine and the vanity and the glory have had a few rounds with him." Six months later, having gone a few rounds with celebrity and taken to strolling the boulevards with a lion on a leash, Siki lost his title to another ephemeral winner.

Other champions were put to the test at the Lausanne Conference, convened that November to settle the Turkish crisis. The guiding spirit of the conference, as Steffens judged it from the point of view of a special correspondent for International News Service, appeared to be Émile Coué, the French pharmacist who, having stumbled by accident on the therapeutic effectiveness of placebos, came to the conclusion, he explained in his international bestseller, *Self-Mastery Through Conscious Auto-suggestion*, that believing will make anything so. With a simple formula, the equivalent of "Close Sesame," one could liquidate the physical and spiritual ills of mankind including aches and pains, night terrors, constipation, insomnia, psoriasis, premature ejaculation, and presumably the larger problems that arise between nations and classes. Coué's formula, "*Ça passe*," represented a mingling of science and faith that was particularly seductive for a generation that had heard enough of "*Ils ne passeront pas*."* Along with Thomas Alva Edison, Lord Curzon, the British foreign secre-

---

* Even Soviet "Socialist realism," a literary device that treated "the present as though it did not exist and the future as if it had already arrived," was "a kind of Couéistic propaganda," according to the historian Louis Fischer. (*The God That Failed*, Richard Crossman, ed. New York, 1963, pp. 205–6.)

tary who served as presiding officer at Lausanne, was among the
countless thousands who faithfully intoned the panacean creed,
"Every day, in every way, I'm getting better and better"; and, as a
matter of fact, he was one of Coué's chief publicists. Curzon instructed the Lausanne delegates, who had their minds chiefly on oil,
to "speak more of peace," Steffens reported—"They must not forget
that was the purpose of the conference, and he advised that they
mention at least the word in every speech they make."

Against the background of such exercises in the optative mood,
Benito Mussolini at Lausanne was as challenging as a knife. Like
other reporters—including Ernest Hemingway of the Toronto *Star*,
who eventually decided that Mussolini was "the biggest bluff in
Europe"—Steffens came away at first with a distinct if imprecisely
proportioned impression of bluster and power. Wearing a frock
coat, gray trousers, and his renowned white spats, Mussolini strode
through the crowded hotel lobby like a conqueror. He stared scorn-
fully with white-rimmed eyes at some peasant women who proffered
flowers and then, turning on his heel and giving what appeared to be
his entire attention to a small open book he held in his hands, he
waited by the elevator obliviously but with a contemptuous smile.
"Mussolini had registered Dictator," Hemingway said. Upstairs, still
pretending to immerse himself in his book (a French-English dic-
tionary, which he held upside down and then ostentatiously reversed), he kept his interviewers waiting before he flared out at
them and declared that despite all representations to the contrary,
peace was not the important concern at this peace conference. Loot
was, and if loot was to be divided, he was there to get a fair share of
it for Italy. And as for his own role as dictator, Mussolini, who only
a month earlier had led a successful revolution from the right, saw
no need at all to justify himself to liberals. "He despises the old game
of politics and diplomacy, democracy as we pretend it is," Steffens
cabled. "He has risen into an empty throne by dint of his contempt
for the present type of government and his knowledge that the
people have lost all hope and respect for it."

"We have seized power, we possess power, we will use our
power," Mussolini said, with his contemptuous smile. "What will
you do if the opposition becomes strong?" someone asked. "Whatever is necessary," Mussolini replied. "Would you dissolve parlia-

ment?" "Dissolve them, shut them up, shoot them—whatever is necessary." "But to get to the spirit of that answer," Steffens cautioned in his report, "you must know that Mussolini was laughing. He regarded the question as absurd."

"Of late I have been feeling that I might stay here forever," Steffens wrote from Paris in 1919. "I like it; I feel that I might understand it; and here I am myself understood. I seem to speak the language of Europe." He lived abroad for nearly eight years after Versailles. From time to time he went home, to see Gussie and to lecture, but he was not a welcome figure in the America of Warren G. Harding and Calvin Coolidge. He was not welcome in the British Empire either, as he learned when he was denied a visa to go to India and observe Gandhi's nonviolent revolution.

"I don't see how I can ever afford to go home," he told Owen D. Young, soon to be chairman of the board of General Electric. Young, who had been renting Little Point from Steffens since 1915, finally bought the place from him in 1920. He paid $35,000 in the form of a seven-percent mortgage note, which yielded Steffens just what he wanted for the now-homeless life he had in mind, not lump sums of cash but a steady interest income. With $2,450 a year from Young's note and about as much from other investments, Steffens lived well on American dollars in inflationary Europe. At the spas of ruined Germany he was greeted with the deference accorded a prince of commerce and a prince of the Almanach de Gotha, took the waters, strolled, listened to music. For sun and privacy, when Gussie came over to see him, there was the Italian riviera. For creative ferment there was Paris. He was used to Paris, and he liked it. He wore a soft black velour hat, silk shirts with long, Byronic collars, and tailored suits sent over from London, and amidst the *apéritifs* and cigarette smoke, the steady talk about art, music, literary experiment, and the money politics of the French, he functioned as a kindly gadfly of the sidewalk cafés, genial, fraternal, admired, assured, and enviably leisured. "His life is a charming enigma," a newspaperman in Paris said. "To great financiers he is a harmless radical; to radicals he is a harmless reactionary. Both worlds find him elusive: a spectator but not an actor in the drama of their shock and conflict."

The future might be in Russia, but as Gertrude Stein said, "Paris

is where the twentieth century is." For Americans the spirit of the
prewar Village had revived after contact with French intellectual
and artistic life. It was in Paris, the capitalist hell, rather than in
Moscow, the socialist heaven, the Steffens felt most at home, as comfortable in Gertrude Stein's apartment on the Rue de Fleurus as he
was in the cafés of the Latin Quarter or, wearing an evening cape
and a silk hat, in the grand foyer of the Opéra.

At thirty-five an expatriate in search of cosmopolis and a "laboratory of ideas," Ezra Pound translated himself from London to Paris
in 1920, a move that was a turning point in the cultural history of
the decade. It was to Pound, as well as to Jo Davidson, that Steffens
owed his introductions, chiefly casual, to James Joyce, who was to
be seen sitting silently at his restaurant table; to "the cubist writer"
(as Steffens called her) Gertrude Stein, who, while Davidson
modeled her in clay as Buddha, composed a portrait of him in words;
to the composer George Antheil and the enterprising Ford Madox
Ford, who invited Steffens to write for his *Transatlantic Review*.
Yet the bond between Pound and Steffens had little to do with the
distinctive life of Paris. They were to share a more than passing
admiration for Mussolini and for Major Clifford H. Douglas, the
originator of the Social Credit theory. Despite their sophistication
and internationalism, they belonged to a straggling, authentically
native succession of grass-roots radicals (of the right as well as of
the left) and cracker-barrel sages, men with a populist hunger for
drastic solutions and an inclination to spend their time and spirit
cussing out the government and the banks while awaiting the arrival
of the messiah.*

The Irish-American critic Mary Colum recalled being "dragged"
by Pound to someone's apartment to hear Steffens talk about revolution, and although she found his performance of an "appalling
dreariness," Pound listened to it with "rapt attention, his eyes glued
to the speaker's face, the very type of a young man in search of an
ideology, except that he was not so very young." Fragments of

* Pound seemed to be continuing an old conversation by the pot-bellied stove
in a letter he wrote to Steffens from Rapallo on March 26, 1927. "Is there any
solid conservative review that will take an article on the rise of bureaucracy and
the general gone-to-hellness of Murkn. life, administration, irresponsible govt.
by pimps and placemen etc. Either from YOU (you ought to write it) or from
me who might . . . Or praps you're for having things rot as quickly as possible
so that the dead fish will revolute (i.e., turn belly side up)."

Steffens' talk, among them his account of riding on the Carranza train in 1915–16, are quoted in one of Pound's early Cantos, and in 1944, when the poet was a captive of the American army and living in a solitary-confinement cage made out of metal air strip, Steffens reappears at the end of *The Pisan Cantos* as a quasi-Virgilian figure

> thru the barbed wire
> you can, said Stef (Lincoln Steffens)
> do nothing with revolutionaries
> until they are at the end of their tether

Among the younger men Steffens saw in Paris, Ernest Hemingway appeared to him to have the surest future, the most buoyant confidence, and the best grounds for it. Steffens had first been impressed by Hemingway's cabled reports and had asked to read his literary manuscripts; and when they were at Lausanne together he volunteered to send Hemingway's race-track story, "My Old Man," to *Cosmopolitan*. When the valise containing Hemingway's manuscripts was stolen from the Gare St. Lazare that December, "My Old Man," safe in transit between New York and Paris, and one other story remained all that Hemingway had to show for a couple of years of work, his nest egg, or, as he joked, his own *Das Kapital*. Steffens ran into Hemingway frequently at Gertrude Stein's; at the office, above a wine cellar on the Ile St. Louis, of William Bird's Three Mountains Press, which published Pound as well as Hemingway; and at the apartment at 8 Place du Palais Bourbon where Bird—wine expert, bibliophile, newspaperman, and confidant of Joyce—provided, Steffens said, a place for "rebels to conspire and play in."

Altogether recovered in spirits, William Bullitt, too, was in Paris again. At the elegant house which he rented from the novelist Elinor Glyn he settled down to enjoy the wines, the parties, and a new life. In conclusion of an affair that had some of the superheated quality of his mission to Moscow he had divorced his wife and married Louise Bryant, John Reed's widow. In 1924 he was about to become a father for the first time, and this is what he and Steffens often talked about over drinks and dinner.

They also talked about the book Bullitt was working on, a thinly disguised autobiographical novel (dedicated to Louise Bryant and published in 1926, with some success, as *It's Not Done*). In it he settled a number of old scores—with Philadelphia society of Rittenhouse Square and the Main Line; with American responses to the Russian revolution ("They've all become atheists," one of the characters says, "and I'm for blockading them and starving them and killing them till they return to their senses and become Christians again"); with postwar America, which seemed to have nothing to look ahead to except "Communism"; and, of course, with Woodrow Wilson, the self-anointed savior who let everyone down. Martyr to the Revolution, the unmistakable figure of John Reed, Bullitt's predecessor, appears in the novel as the hero's illegitimate son by a first love, a substitution or displacement of role that might have been of interest to Freud when Bullitt came to see him in Vienna.*

One of the characters in Bullitt's novel says, "I seem to see a capering virgin heifer with a blue face, a yellow back, and a buttoned-down tail, who nevertheless exudes perpetually a stream of immaculately conceived milk and answers to the name 'America.'" From the distance of his European exile Steffens could hear, with a certain knowing approval, similar voices—Sinclair Lewis, for one, and H. L. Mencken, Van Wyck Brooks, Lewis Mumford, and the other contributors to Harold Stearns's gloomy symposium, *Civilization in the United States*. These writers detailed their country's failures in spirit, culture, intellect, communal meaning, and morality, private and public, her makeshift ideals and catchpenny opportunism,

---

* Psychoanalysis merely exacerbated Bullitt's hatred for Wilson. Bullitt's testimony before the Senate Foreign Relations Committee in September 1919 did considerable damage to Wilson in his effort to mobilize the American people behind the Versailles treaty. Later, Bullitt collaborated with Freud on a "psychological study" of Wilson (published finally in 1967) which was so venomous and foregone in its conclusions that the speculative insights of depth analysis take on the form and function of a handy length of lead pipe. In one respect, at least, the collaboration of Bullitt and Freud, which has the historical curiosity of a two-headed calf or a Push-me-pull-you, was ideal: Freud's antipathy to Wilson equaled Bullitt's in intensity and complemented it in national perspective. "The figure of the American President, as it rose above the horizon of Europeans, was from the beginning unsympathetic to me," Freud confessed at the outset of the book. "This aversion increased in the course of the years the more I learned about him and the more severely we suffered from the consequences of his intrusion into our destiny." Freud, of course, was speaking as a subject of the defeated Austro-Hungarian Empire. (Sigmund Freud and William C. Bullitt, *Thomas Woodrow Wilson: A Psychological Study*. Boston, 1967, p. xi.)

her obsession with motorcars, advertising, high-colonic irrigation, sleeping porches, success, the rights and wrongs of Prohibition, the sport of evading it, and, as Lewis wrote, "suburban bacchanalia of alcohol, nicotine, gasoline, and kisses," the dream of "eternal cabaret."

There was worse and there was more to be said. In simplest terms, Steffens claimed, his country had gone crazy. It was panicky and quick to violence, and he had no intention of going home for good until they made the jails more comfortable. During the Red Scare of 1919 and 1920, Wilson's Attorney General, A. Mitchell Palmer, was sending out the agents of his General Intelligence Division to raid and round up, by the hundreds and thousands, suspected communists, anarchists, radicals, and aliens in general. The American Legion called for the removal of eight thousand "disloyal teachers." Until Harding released him on Christmas Day 1921 and invited him to the White House, Eugene V. Debs—according to Wilson "a traitor to his country"—remained prisoner number 9653 in the Federal Penitentiary at Atlanta, even though nearly a million people had voted for him for President the year before. Emma Goldman, Alexander Berkman, and other "undesirables" were deported. As a long reflex of the hysteria which, born of the war, ended up poisoning the peace, the anarchists Sacco and Vanzetti began their seven years of remaining life in prison.

"It all looks to me as if our people were trying to imitate what they think Bolshevik Russia is," Steffens said at the end of 1919, and when, over the next few years, he returned to the United States briefly for lecture tours, to see his family, to try to sell his work, to remove his things from Little Point, and to support such lost causes as a general amnesty for political prisoners, he found his impressions from abroad confirmed at first hand. The magazines remained closed to him, and when he lectured his way west—his subject, on one occasion, the tide of revolution, and his sponsor an organization called the Red Star League—he met with resentment and harassment that increased so steadily that again he doubted he would be able to reach San Francisco a free man. In Sacramento, once his home, he was surely not welcome. He was "a Radical and a Red of the deepest dye," said the owner and editor of the powerful Sacramento *Bee*. "The proper place for Lincoln Steffens is in jail."

II

IN SEATTLE ONE EVENING EARLY IN 1921 Steffens sat in a dingy basement café talking with Anna Louise Strong, a reporter for a local labor newspaper. She had just heard him lecture about Russia. "I'd give anything if I could go there," she said. "Why don't you then?" Steffens answered with the calmness and soft smile that were as mesmerizing then as they had been years earlier when he told John Reed, "You can do anything you want to do," and Reed believed him. At that moment in Seattle Anna Louise Strong began to change worlds; Steffens "set me free," she recalled. In the autumn she crossed the border into starving and pestilence-torn Russia, and as far as the ideology of a lifetime was concerned she never came back.

She saw Steffens again when he was in Moscow in September 1923 on a short trip with Jo Davidson and Senator La Follette. His faith in the Soviets had not been shaken by what seemed to many a backward step: in his New Economic Policy Lenin had reinstated small capitalism (even to the extent of recognizing prostitution as a legitimate form of private enterprise). But "the big points are that the Bolsheviki have yielded nothing," Steffens wrote to Gussie from Moscow. "They are on their course, proceeding as they began, and they intend to see it through ruthlessly. That's the first good news. And the second is that their policy is working. Conditions are amazingly improved and their state machine of federated industries is pulling out of the hole of war, famine and corruption."

Again, the future was already here—"Russia is an oasis now of hope in a world of despair"—and he was certain that it would remain. Still, Anna Louise Strong and other Americans Steffens talked to in Moscow—Bill Haywood, Max Eastman, Bill Shatoff, Albert Rhys Williams—had every reason to ask him why, with the exception of this brief (and, as it turned out, last) visit to Russia after an absence of four and a half years, he seemed content enough to stay behind, out of action. The Russians, he was to tell Upton Sinclair in 1926, are "disgusted with me. They blame me for the Bullitt fiasco and for being able to state their case and yet staying out of the Communist Party." They were harder on him than they were on Emma Goldman. Deported to Russia, she fled from Russia shattered in belief; the hoped-for "miracle" had turned out to be a "phantom" and worse, a nightmare of repression and bureaucracy from which she was grateful to escape. The title of the book she published in 1923 told it all, *My Disillusionment in Russia*. (She had been "a Methodist sent to a Presbyterian heaven," Steffens told her, "and naturally she thought it was hell.") Bertrand Russell, who welcomed her to England, had undergone the same negative conversion. He had gone to Russia in 1920 "hoping to find the promised land." Stifled and horrified, he left—"I lost all power of balanced judgment."

John Reed, dead of typhus in Moscow on October 17, 1920, and buried in the Kremlin wall, never did say unequivocally what it had been like for him at the end. At their last meeting, Reed had blazed at Steffens for remaining an accomplice of the old order.* "He met me on the street," Steffens said, "and gave me hell for not getting into it and doing something." Steffens claimed that *his* Jack Reed, poet and celebrator of life, had altogether ceased to be the "free soul" who despised priests, cant and bureaucrats of utopia or of any other place. Instead, he was hard, intolerant, clinched for a fight, unquestioning, disciplined. So Steffens believed. A week or two after Reed's death, writing out of grief, guilt, and a nagging sense of his own failures and abdications, Steffens was certain that Reed had become living and dying proof that "all roads in our time," including poetry, "lead to Moscow."

> You see, in Moscow, in Soviet Russia, where there are lice and hunger and discipline and death; where it is hell now; they see— even a non-communist can see, something to live or to die for. They can see that life isn't always going to be as it is now. The future is coming; it is in sight; it is coming, really and truly coming, and soon. And it is good. They can see this with their naked eyes, common men can; I did, for example. So, to a poet, to a spirit like Jack Reed, the communist, death in Moscow must have been the most wonderful thing in the world: a vision of the resurrection and the life of Man.

* Even before the Bullitt mission proved to be a failure, Reed was derisive of Steffens' part in it. When, after a month as a well-kept secret, news of the mission broke in the Western press, Reed wrote to Louise Bryant from Croton: "Did you see that President Wilson has sent Lincoln Steffens, Bill Bullitt, and two or three of that sort to Russia on a destroyer to investigate the Soviets?" (March 21, 1919. John Reed Papers, Houghton Library, Harvard University.)

For Louise Bryant and Max Eastman, there had been nothing visionary about Reed's death in the typhus ward. It was not a sacrifice but a waste, the result of cynical neglect on the part of Lenin and others, who later said they had been too busy to see that Reed was cared for properly. Even from the confused stories that surrounded Reed's last months it was clear that Steffens' version of Reed as a willing martyr to the revolution was not altogether sound; it represented, in part, what Steffens was compelled to believe, for his own peace.

In Reed too, as in Emma Goldman and Bertrand Russell, the values of the old culture had risen up in protest, as if to anticipate the time when *Ten Days That Shook the World* would be suppressed in Russia and its possession made a criminal offense, because Reed had omitted to mention Stalin as being among the heroes of November 1917. Leaving the United States for the last time, Reed had been sad and reluctant; he wanted to settle down to poetry, he said to Susan Glaspell and her husband, but he had "promised too many people." Once again in Russia, he broke with the Comintern, resigned from the executive committee, quarreled bitterly with Radek and the demagogue Zinoviev, and in all this he showed no patience at all with the first virtue of a party Communist, discipline. At the end, when he turned his face to the wall, his imagination must have begun to dwell once again in Europe's romantic hells, the scenes of a young man's discoveries of the world. "You know how it is when you go to Venice," Reed said to Louise Bryant as he lay dying in Moscow. "You ask people, 'Is this Venice?'—just for the pleasure of hearing the reply."

Steffens remained behind among the damned, content to serve the future in his own way—not in the vanguard but far back, in "the second line," as an intellectual convert, a broken or tired liberal who was still captive of the old culture and its un-Soviet values of freedom, ease, patience, skepticism. "Life is not so serious as the Russians see it," he said. Rentier and expatriate, Steffens was moderately certain that capitalism, as he knew and depended on it, would fail in the long run, but, as Keynes once remarked in a different connection, "In the long run we are all dead." In the short run Steffens intended to remain a pacifist opposed to the class war, a conflict so costly that he believed that some other solution would have to evolve, a third philosophy that discarded established tactics of force and countercommunism and perhaps even the idea of democracy. Looking at Russia from the condemned playgrounds of Europe, he conceded that he was no better prepared for the future, no less "harmless," than Russell or Emma Goldman. Perhaps heaven and hell were the same place after all. "To those who are prepared, it is heaven; to those who are not fit and ready, it is hell." Depressed and torn he could say and believe this while knowing that others who had gone all the way, gone the limit, would condemn him for being not even a witness to history—one who gives testimony—but simply a voyeur.

Steffens made an attempt to rationalize his dilemma in a historical fable or parable, *Moses in Red*, published as a book in 1926 and, if ever remembered, quickly forgotten. (In keeping with Steffens' theocentric reading of history in *Moses in Red*, the entire printing of the book, except for about four hundred copies, was destroyed in a warehouse fire construable as an Act of God.) It was the story, he said, "of the Revolutionists who do not go through, who don't like the Promised Land." Looking for absolution from history, Steffens succeeded only in coming up with desperate answers, fevered optimism, and a ticlike string of paradoxes. His intricately conditioned response to the events of 1917 in Russia trapped him into the certainty that the Bolshevik revolution was a sovereign stereotype that illuminated all historical time. Like the Russian revolution, he argued in *Moses in Red*, the exodus of the Children of Israel from Egypt took its impetus not from Moses but from Pharaoh. But once set in motion revolutions moved as inexorably—and predictably—as the stars in their courses. The Bolshevik terror, repression, the police state—everything that sickened the Western mind—these were the doing not of revolutionary leaders but of the laws that governed the revolution of Moses and the revolution of Lenin. "Not Lenin, but Nature required the excesses of the Russian revolution; or, if you please, God." Terror was divine in origin and therefore "right" (a proposition Steffens might have had some difficulty defending if he had lived long enough to reckon up the toll of Stalin's purges). Drawing a partial self-portrait through the figure of Moses, Steffens externalized his own split as the horizontal time structure of the Biblical story of Exodus—the forty years that Moses and the Jews spent in the desert cleansing themselves of "the ethics of slavery" and absorbing instead "the fresh morals of the desert." Steffens was resigned to not crossing over Jordan into the future. Perhaps he really didn't want to. He was too old, too incurably liberal, not fit and ready, and therefore he was "ruined," he said. He was able to recognize salvation but was beyond being saved.

CHAPTER FIFTEEN

A New Life

I

ONE DAY AROUND LUNCHTIME IN APRIL 1919 Steffens answered a knock at the door of his bedroom at the Chatham in Paris. A young English girl, Ella Winter, had come to deliver a dinner invitation from her employer, Felix Frankfurter. Steffens was still in his dressing gown, but he asked her in, and for an hour or so, she was to remember, he talked "as I'd never heard anyone talk," winningly and intimately, and with a constant ironic challenge both to her middle-class and distinctly Victorian upbringing and her education as a Fabian socialist at the London School of Economics. He was drawn right away by her youthful vitality and by a certain passionate, headlong intensity which reminded him of Jack Reed in the Village. Entertaining this strong, handsome girl, with her big eyes and intense black hair, Steffens was also excited by a distant flutter of adventure, flattered by her interest in him and by her awe. As seen through Ella's eyes, he was one of the knowledgeable people, men of the world, whom Frankfurter had told her to make a business of meeting as she started off on a career in politics or economics. She and Steffens met casually a few times after this first encounter. Later there were long walks along the Seine at night. By the time the peace conference ended and Ella went back to London in June, it was clear that some powerful bond had been established.

Ella Winter's father, a German-Jewish businessman who had him-

272

self and his family baptized as Lutherans, moved from Nuremberg to Melbourne, where Ella was born in 1898, and finally, in 1910, to London. For Ella, who looked up to older men from childhood on, her father was "the God-being" of her life—"I was certain I could never marry anyone but my father," she later said. She was twenty-one when she met Steffens, he was fifty-three. At first, in an attempt at self-deception that was briefly successful, he considered himself not as a lover at all. Acknowledging the difference in their ages, he favored some more acceptable role, father or brother figure, mentor, or simply friend. She was to be his protégé or pupil, and he called her "boy," or, a name he gave her and which she accepted during all their time together, "Peter," for Peter Pan, perennial polymorph. The name must have had subliminal associations for Ella, who had been brought up on Dr. Heinrich Hoffmann's children's classic, *Struwwelpeter* (sometimes rendered as "Slovenly Peter"), for her childhood nickname, "Fidgety Philip," had been drawn from that same cruel and fantastic book. Her family, who had once hoped in this way to check her impulsive nature when she was young, her tendency to lurch rather than move, had every reason for downright consternation when her new friend, Lincoln Steffens, came to spend the autumn months of 1919 with her in London.

He engaged her as his secretary, and although he was two and a half times her age and his domestic status as well as his "intentions" remained an enigma, he was with her practically night and day. He was passionately involved, to a degree he had not felt for many years if, indeed, ever before. Nevertheless, in its nature as well as its intensity, their relationship remained anomalous. Ella Winter, realistically, had begun to take into consideration the prospect of marriage to a much older man and of early widowhood; Steffens was scarcely thinking about marriage at all.

He went back to Paris and awaited, with some trepidation, the arrival from America, early in January 1920, of the steamship *Rochambeau* bearing a melancholy and chronically aggrieved Gussie. She had managed to resign herself to their long separation by reasoning that Europe was good for him, but she felt lonely and depressed nonetheless. Ironically, it was in the hope of cheering her up that Steffens asked her to come to Paris in the first place. Now, compelled to face up to the implications of the months in London, he was "appalled," he told Ella, "at what has happened to me." He expected, as he told her, that in time the Gussie affair would end in some sort of benign friendship. But meanwhile, as a self-styled monogamist who considered himself in effect married to Gussie, he was committed to the older woman at the risk of losing the younger. "What is to *become* of us?" was his Christmas greeting to Ella. "What *is* to become of us!" It seemed to him that all his life with women, ever since his days at Berkeley, he had generated hurt. Now, like the statesmen who, try as they did, only made a hash of the peace, he was to find over the next four years no evenhanded way of untangling his tangled affairs.

"She knows about Us," Steffens told Ella soon after Gussie arrived in Paris. "I didn't tell her at first; she was too ill. But, Lord, I can't conceal anything like that, and she's a woman. There was something the matter. She felt it, of course; said nothing for a few days, and then asked. I told her the story. She took it as you said she would, and as I knew she would. And now she wants to be my friend. Like you. So I'm going to be a lover completely surrounded by friends." This was whistling in the dark. "It was a terrible thing I did," he reflected. "Certainly I can do fierce things to those that love me." Ella was just a "little, passing fancy" of his, he almost believed, and he was going to put her behind him. "I'm going to destroy all your letters, Peter, before I leave here, wherever I go," he wrote from Paris. "For, while it is all right to commit crimes, it is a mistake to leave a record of them." Then he traveled south to rejoin Gussie, having been given, by her apparent willingness to release him once again, "a fresh sense of the true nobility that is in her" and a fresh determination to make the best of what they had between them.

Nevertheless, he continued to write to Ella, and his letters had a muzzle velocity that belied what he liked to think of as a tutorial relationship with "a young genius" who was on her way to a brilliant future and who ought also to be giving some thought to finding a suitable husband her own age. On the surface this was the way things stood for about three years. Pursuing her career under his remote guidance, Ella taught for a while at the London School of Economics, worked for H. G. Wells when he stood, unsuccessfully, for Parliament, studied at the Psychology Laboratory at Cambridge, and prepared herself for the task she was soon to undertake and capably perform, her translation of Wolfgang Köhler's founding work in Gestalt psychology, *The Mentality of Apes*. She also made a break with her family's strict morality and had a brief, unsatisfactory affair with her father's physician in 1923, the year Steffens' accommodation with Gussie came to an end.

That summer Steffens and Gussie traveled down the Italian coast from Genoa to Naples and Sorrento, where they spent three weeks quietly together, swimming, reading in the sun, dining alone at the same small table every night. He had almost stopped drumming his fingers and chain-smoking cigarettes, habits which always annoyed her. She had never seen him so calm, so free from the compulsion to dazzle and perform, and she was pleased with his plan to stay abroad indefinitely, finish his book about Moses and revolutions, and then, as she had been encouraging him to do, start on his autobiography, the story of his "life of unlearning." Gussie was too sensitive for him by far, too touchy; and yet, as he rationalized, "she is used to me now and I can settle down and feel more at home with her than anybody I know. I never have to play up to any expectations. No use. She knows me and accepts me as I am. So it's all good for me."

Still, something was incurably wrong. He refused to let her see Ella Winter's letters, explaining that she would surely misunderstand them and be unnecessarily distressed, and each morning at the Hotel Cocumella in Sorrento he rushed downstairs alone to claim his mail so that she would not see the pang and the strangeness that he felt. With Gussie he was now privately resigned to "the natural decline of love," a formula which masked his own discontent. At the same time, if Gussie suspected that an alien force was at work, she managed to hide it from herself as well as from him.

Their defused relationship reverted to the terms of thirty-four years earlier, when they were secretly engaged and he left to study in Germany. This time Gussie went back to the States at the end of the summer reasonably sure of Steffens, even though, in Anna Louise Strong, a rival had appeared in a distant setting. "Anna Louise is in Russia and has written Len to bring her stockings, chocolate, a bottle, etc.," Gussie told his sister Laura in September. "Anna Louise fails to disturb me, however."

Steffens' quick trip to Russia that month proved to be uneventful for Gussie as well as for Anna Louise Strong. But when he came back to Paris he learned that the British were willing once again to let him have a visa. For Ella Winter October 26, 1923, her father's birthday, was to remain the day "Steffy came back to London for me." This time there was nothing deferred. They celebrated over oyster cocktails in the Strand and then she came to stay with him at the Rubens Hotel near Buckingham Palace. In February 1924 they went to Paris, took separate rooms (for the sake of a lingering sense of propriety) at a hotel near the Madeleine and, with the help of Jo Davidson's wife, set about replacing Ella's spinsterly wardrobe with something French and appropriate. Then he was ready to show her off to his friends in the newspaper offices, Gertrude Stein's apartment, Sylvia Beach's Left Bank bookshop, Shakespeare and Company. She visited the Bullitts, who had wanted Steffens to be with them in Paris when their child was born. At dinner one night at a Chinese restaurant, Hemingway and John Dos Passos assured her that she could write—she was planning a novel about her own rebellion and liberation. "You can," Hemingway said, and feinted a left to her jaw. "It's hell. It takes it all out of you; it nearly kills you; but you can do it. Anybody can. Even you can, Stef."

Soon it was time to settle down to work again, and in a quieter place than Paris. They went to Ospedaletti, a village on the Ligurian coast, where they expected to write and make plans for the future; he might go to China, he was saying—he had an invitation to lecture at the university in Peking—and the South Seas, and she would probably go with him. But after twelve years as a bachelor he was not at all sure he would ever want to be married again. He was too set in his ways to bend to another person's, too accustomed to following only his own inclination. Considering the difference in their ages he figured that they might have five or so good years together —before the worry and the jealousy set in, he told her. At that time she should have the freedom, just as she would surely have the need, to find a younger man. Steffens saw no point to putting himself at a disadvantage in an unequal competition. This was the way their plans stood until a local doctor, whom Ella visited because of some mild distress, told her that she was pregnant.

After the first shock, Steffens began to realize that something considerably more significant than a mischance had happened. He thought back to the barren years with Josephine, to his unreasoning certainty of his actual sterility and symbolic failure. During all that time, with Reed and the other protégés, with Ella as well, he had seemed to be a father in search of a child. Now, in the prospect of fatherhood, he saw the possibility of his own rebirth; in any scale this outweighed scandal, ridicule, hurt to others. "One of the deepest secret desires of my life is about to be fulfilled," he wrote to Laura. Worried about scandal and the hurt done to Gussie, she was hardly sympathetic. "You used to be a genius, and unique," she answered. "Now you are going to be a father, and there are millions of those."

For a day or two after the news, he and Ella considered going to Paris and seeking "remedies," but they dismissed this particular solution and considered some others. In sexual mores as well as politics she was yet to be radicalized by Steffens, and although he urged her to take an "anarchist" view of illegitimacy, the institution of marriage, and the disapproval of society, she balked. Her mother already hated Steffens—he was a Bolshevik and a bohemian who debauched her daughter. She would never welcome Ella's "illicit" child in her house. As for traveling in America with Steffens, Bullitt warned her, the gatekeepers of the Republic might charge her with "moral turpitude." On the other hand, if they let her through, she was likely to be hounded and practically forced to live in a cave. This, Bullitt told her, had been the fate of Maxim Gorky and his traveling companion two decades earlier when they collided with what Mark Twain called the brass, boiler iron and granite of public opinion. In the face of such practical arguments, Steffens' anti-institutional scruples did not count for much. He was willing to offer what appeared to be a distant compromise. "As soon as we're married," he told Ella, "let's turn around and get a divorce, secretly."

They were married in a Paris registry office in August, celebrated at a wedding breakfast in a café with the Bullitts and the Davidsons, and then prepared for what promised to be the last but by no means the least painful episode in a long story. Given the circumstances, there perhaps could have been no humanely adroit way of breaking off with Gussie, and when he wrote to her early in the year she became hysterical. ("I fear for my niece's sanity," a relative wrote to him. "You must be a very stupid man about women.") Soul-shriveled, he contritely promised, with Ella's consent, to see Gussie in Europe during the summer. Now, somewhat like Mary Austin (a comparison she introduced only in order to dismiss it), Gussie was eastbound on the Atlantic in pursuit of some unattainable justice and satisfaction or, at the very least, the explanation that her thirteen years and more with him entitled her to.

"He has deceived and *lied* to me, time and again," she wrote to Laura from her ship. "It sounds awful, but that is what shocks me most of all: that L., whom I have loved so completely, could stoop to such contemptible behavior. If I had a character like M. A., it would be different. How can L. write so well and stoop so low?" In her hysteria she believed that there was still "a shadow of hope" left for her and that even the child, which she now knew about, could somehow be written off as an aberration. "I told you, didn't I, that this Bullitt who fell in love with Louise Bryant was crazy for a child, and I really think L. took on some of his obsession. I have learned that so much L. does are mere gestures."

On an August evening, with Ella away in Bavaria working with Köhler, Steffens surprised Gussie at her hotel in the Rue des Pyramides, took her arm, just as he used to, and led her across the Rue de Rivoli into the Tuileries gardens. Until midnight, forgetting the speech she had rehearsed and planned to give when they met the next day, she poured out her hurt. In return she heard neither defense nor excuse but, as she had remotely hoped, the truth, or at least a form of it that answered to her needs: she heard from him self-accusation and self-incrimination which were stronger than any case she could have drawn up; she even laughed when he supported and strengthened her charges. Out of compassion he was giving her something that was clearly necessary if she was to be able to go on and make any sort of life for herself: exoneration from her belief (not altogether baseless) that some inadequacy in her—provincialism, her lack of "intellect," her distaste for radical, unconventional values—had been chiefly to blame. "She has been accusing herself," Steffens told Laura. "She didn't intend to reveal that secret, but it was good that she did. For I did defend her, and she was relieved."

By the end of a week she had drawn out of him all that she wanted to know about his old life, the new, and the link between, and she said it was time for them to stop seeing each other. For his part he believed that he had finally succeeded in muckraking himself. He had laid his shame more bare than the shame of the cities or the self-interest of the peace conference, had recounted intricate deceptions of self and of others. But, like muckraking as he had practiced it, exposure of this sort led to no structural changes, did not alter in the least the laws of his personality but merely showed how they worked. Remorseful but also relieved, he was at the same time looking forward to a child and a book, his autobiography, and he was certain that he was entering a new, creative phase of his life, even though it was partially founded on pain. "The good and the miserable of it are all out of one source," he said, and more than ever it seemed to him pointless to try to untangle them. One resolution of his years with Gussie left him baffled. Whatever self-discovery he had made he would have to keep to himself—she was to make him promise that she would not figure in his autobiography. It was her book, really, and now, in point of truthtelling, it was going to suffer by her absence. "It's too bad," he reflected. His life with Gussie had been as typical a failure as his attempt to mediate for the McNamaras, and more revealing. "What I really am is shown by that story better than any other."

II

IN SEPTEMBER STEFFENS AND ELLA MOVED TO SAN REMO and into a small villa with a garden and a sight of the Mediterranean and the foothills of the Alps. There, served by a maid, a cook and a gardener, they lived in expatriate comfort just as they would during the next three years at nearby Alassio, at St. Cergue in Switzerland, or at Saché, in Touraine, where Jo Davidson, at the peak of his fame and earnings, had bought Bêcheron, a big, remote manor house. With the birth of his son, Pete, in November 1924 Steffens in his fifty-eighth year entered what he recognized as the best and happiest part of his life. "I don't know yet why I wanted what I wanted," he wrote in an article called "Radiant Fatherhood," "but I believe that, in my bones, all my life I have wanted what I have now—a child." From time to time he joked that if it had not been for his visa troubles with the British he might have been a father years earlier. The fact remained that relatively late in life, at a time when many of his contemporaries were closing the door on new experience, Steffens had chosen openness and also had it thrust upon him. His late middle age became a time of generativity rather than self-absorption and retrospect, even though his politics hardened and he suffered increasingly from "black moods," periods of hopelessness and nightmare during which he felt that he was "at the bottom of a pit" and could not "come up to talk." But in net balance, Steffens was rewarded with a sense of the ongoing integralness of his life, with an ever-widening circle of acquaintance, and with the allegiance of the young.

In his *Autobiography* he wrote:

> I often felt like a sudden grandfather with a grown daughter and a grandson to bring up to see things as they are becoming. I had my girl to disillusion and my little boy to start off with none of our illusions and yet with interest and self-confidence.

During the early years of this marriage there was little doubt that he was the dominant partner, father and mentor to his young wife, as well as husband. It had been his decision to move away from Paris and London—which she preferred—and seek out isolation in the country, and in smaller matters he was no less firm. "If you gave me the choice between smoking in the bedroom and a divorce," he said soon after they were married, answering her objection to a longstanding habit of his, "I should take the divorce," and that was that. For a number of reasons, relating not only to his age and experience but also to his attempts at intercession in public causes, he had little faith in argument, in either direction, and sometimes he dismissed a contrary notion of hers as if he were a city editor once again and she his cub reporter.*

"Your inadequate, your 'uninspired' phrasings, may be due to your excessive quickness, to your impatience," he was to tell Ella, pointing out that when she used the word "profits" in an article on finance she really meant "dividends." "Why not try, in conversation at first, to wait a few seconds more, and hit the nail squarely on the head?" He was equally tutorial on larger issues. "The Russians have made the great turning, and when you write as you do I know that you have made the turning. You will see everything better now. You will yourself be different," he told her, recognizing a conversion,

* One reporter at the Paris Conference, Guy Hickock of the *Brooklyn Daily Eagle*, recalled with both gratitude and admiration the complete "plowing up and reseeding" he underwent at Steffens' hands during a press trip to Switzerland. Steffens could demolish an argument, Hickock said, with "one of those boomerang shots that would go around behind the idea and let the gas out with a slow hissing sound." (Guy Hickock to Ella Winter, n.d., 1936, Columbia.)

when she visited Russia in 1930. He advised her to concentrate on her "first impression of that new world," to begin with "a big, superficial survey. . . . Don't fuss with such subjects as Trotsky and his fate and Stalin and his policies. Russia is not like that. Get at the policies and ideas of the government, of the Communist Party." He was pleased with the results of five years of his tutoring. "She does not reason as she did when I first met her," he told her mother. "She looks to see. She forms theories, avoids convictions and conclusions, observes drifts or currents of conduct as experiments and can await the results. Our intellectuals can't do that."

Given their unequal relationship at the start, it should have come as no surprise to Steffens that he may have "disillusioned" Ella too fast for her own good, stripped away her liberal assumptions and, having replaced them with ideological certainties, not only made her over but, in a different set of terms, made her more royalist than the king. "Which of us do you prefer to have meet you at the station in our car?" Steffens asked his niece Jane Hollister in 1926. "Peter does not steer till she reaches the turn; she runs straight off the road and steers to get back. I foresee the turn and turn with it, but I can hardly start the car." As Steffens and Ella traveled the road that led through the 1930s he sometimes lagged behind her.

With Steffens' son, Pete, whom he idolized, he was willing, for the first time in his life, to accept a relationship in which he demanded nothing in return, no reciprocal traffic in love; he was happy simply to give, to yield to "the most violent force that ever gripped me." "Fathers are young usually, and busy downtown making a living or a career," Steffens said. "I am old enough to be through with all that silly servitude. The father's place is in the home, and there I am and there I mean to stay—on guard—to protect my child from education." Years later, the son recalled that "In a way, my father was my mother and my mother was my father. She was the one who laid down the commands. My father embraced me when I needed comforting."

Like Martin Lomasney dealing with the needs of his constituents in the wards of Boston, Steffens was going to dispense not justice and the law to his son but only help. He intended to protect his boy from "education," the schools, and all the "funny notions of the older generation that made the war and the peace." Still, even as he pursued perfect freedom for his son, funny notions from the past persisted. Steffens seemed to want to set some sort of record by toilet training his infant at eight months and even earlier. Mindful of the thrust and rules of life under capitalism, he was eager to have and make money for his son, in order to liberate him from "silly servitude" and the scramble for existence, and a few weeks after the boy was born Steffens had him registered in the admissions book of the Reverend Endicott Peabody's sternly Christian Groton School. (Two years later, following a somewhat more radical turn of mind —one of the effects of fatherhood, he claimed—he reserved a place for Pete at the notoriously heterodox school that Bertrand Russell and his wife, Dora, were running in Hampshire.)

Steffens' niece, Jane Hollister, was about to start at Bryn Mawr when she came to see him in Switzerland during the summer of 1925. She spent the following summer with him in Italy, and then, having been encouraged by him to free herself of her upbringing and look for new experience—in writing, sculpture, sociology, anything but good works—left Bryn Mawr for the London School of Economics. And as for marriage, don't worry about it now, he told her when she asked; and besides there was always divorce to keep in mind—"Nowadays we do not regard love and marriage as necessarily permanent." Eventually, following what appears to have been in their family a genetic and a nurtured predisposition toward psychology of one sort or another, Jane became a psychoanalyst, and the two men she looked back upon with gratitude for having released her to fulfill herself were Carl Jung and Steffens.

From childhood she had remembered Stef, her uncle, as a glamorously unholy person whom her parents disapproved of because of his politics and unconventional life. Once, when the express train he was riding passed through her parents' big ranch in Santa Barbara County he stood on the open platform of the last car, waved to her, and flung his hat in the air. It was such a conquering way of saying hello to a niece. Inevitably, when she grew up and rebelled against her mother's argumentativeness and her father's resistance to new ideas, Jane sought out Steffens and pinned her future on his guidance. If it was going to be jail for him, she said, it was going to be jail for her too.

For his part, Steffens flourished on her dependence in a relationship that immediately became one between equals and contemporaries—in his season of openness it was another love affair he had embarked upon, another education. "Don't suppress," he told her, recalling the Freudian gospel he heard in the Village before the war. "One of the few discoveries of our day of personal use to us is that of the danger of over-repression, over self-control; a new sort of tyranny, the mis-rule of one's self." It was not only in her own dealings with him that Jane saw that he had, in the phrase of her later profession, "a green thumb for transference," a genius (and a hunger) for encouraging trust. He was almost always "positive and generous," she remembered, "as though making the best of one, or finding the best in one; anyhow, promoting the best." She could see how as a reporter and interviewer he had exercised a magic touch that overcame suspicion and freed politicians and bankers, city bosses and crooks, reformers and revolutionaries, the guilty and the condemned to open up in the sunlight of his interest, at the same time personal and impersonal.

Living in his household in Italy, she also saw how, despite his seclusiveness, he exerted a peculiar ability—his "great attracting talent," she called it—to make the world come to him, to establish colonies. It would be like that at Carmel in his last years. In Italy, all kinds of visitors—probably incompatible in any context other than his—came to see him: diplomats, radicals, businessmen, tourists, writers; Gertrude Vanderbilt Whitney, sculptress and museum founder, and Margaret Johannsen, the wife of a suspected labor dynamiter; Sinclair Lewis, Jo Davidson and Max Eastman; Jack London's widow and the wife of the American ambassador. Jane remembered with particular vividness one Sunday lunch at which the guests were an American bank president; Jack Black, a convicted burglar who, with Steffens' backing, had written and was about to publish his unrepentant life story; and a French countess. The only person present who found this gathering out of the ordinary was the Italian girl waiting on table who suspected that the countess was a prostitute, because she wore so much lipstick.

In principle as well as longitude Steffens thought of himself as being far removed from Calvin Coolidge's America, which had just been assured on the President's authority that its business as a nation was business. Yet he had ridden with the bull market that came in with Coolidge and accumulated enough on Wall Street "to make life comfortable" and pay for the baby "several times over." And despite his sighting of a Marxist future and his lifelong antipathy to business, Steffens' *Autobiography* inevitably reflected the fact that while writing it during the 1920s he was living comfortably in Benito Mussolini's corporative state on income derived from the stock market and from the sale of Little Point to the businessman Owen D. Young, someone who was being frequently mentioned as the future President of the United States.

Young was "a big business boss," Steffens wrote in 1928, who would run the government "not for, but as, a big business." (It was a fair index of the national mood that nonetheless a number of influential people, including Young himself, believed that he was much too valuable a manager to be wasted in the White House.) Henry Ford, another hero Americans shared with the Russians, was paying his workers $5 a day to turn out Model T's, a higher wage than had ever been paid for comparable work. "Mr. Ford," Steffens was to say to him after a dinner at Nancy Astor's London house, "did you ever think of any other business outside of cars? Did you ever think of shoes?" "Yes," said Ford, who had stuck to lemonade through the evening. "You know I have a friend in Chicago who makes shoes just as I make cars—men's shoes. He makes one size, an eight and one-half shoe, but it's the best eight and one-half shoe in the world and the cheapest." "Mr. Ford," Steffens went on, "did it ever occur to you that if there were nothing but eight and one-half shoes in the world, by and by we would all have eight and one-half feet." The great rationalizer of production was delighted: "Do you see that too?"

"There is something new under the sun, new and momentous; revolutionary," Steffens was to say in 1928. "It is businessmen saying that wages must be kept up, that mass production means we must have mass prosperity." At Ponca City, Oklahoma, as Steffens heard from Jo Davidson and eventually saw for himself, Ernest W. Marland, the biggest independent oil producer in the United States, was building a Versailles in the Cherokee Strip for himself and the artists and writers he planned to surround himself with. Marland gave his workers stock in the company, a model refinery, housing, lakes, a hospital and even—in the further hope of distracting his workers from cards and liquor—a polo field and strings of ponies. Listening to other Arabian Nights stories about the wonders of "the New Capitalism" and the "big, bad captains of industry" who seemed to be more radical in their thinking than any surviving radical, Steffens came to believe that his country and Russia were embarked on experiments similarly bold and hopeful; capitalism and communism were going around the world in opposite ideological directions but they would meet on a common ground, the scientific management of production and distribution. "American business is nearer right than American ideals," Steffens said. In this rosy view, the middle class was bound to give way to a single producer-consumer class born out of what Filene was now calling "companionate prosperity." The struggle between labor and capital was another thing of the past; what remained to be settled now, according to the advanced theory of the decade, was the struggle between ownership and management. This prediction—which, as things turned out, had excluded the imminency of a crash, a depression and a second World War—could not have sounded better even if it had been accurate.

For Steffens and other Americans—intellectuals and businessmen alike, readers of *The New Republic* as well as *The Saturday Evening Post*—Benito Mussolini, miraculously purged of negative implication, also stood out as a typical hero of the times, the supreme pragmatist and achiever. "Curiously enough," the writer Emil Ludwig told Mussolini, "in the course of my travels I have found you more popular in America than anywhere else"; until Mussolini invaded Ethiopia in 1935 premature antifascism was not much of an American problem. It was all too well known that the trains ran on time in Italy, and, as far as one could judge in the absence of any opposition (an absence which visitors managed largely to ignore, together with whispered rumors of assassinations, beatings and castor oil), a once dejected people, bankrupt of initiative, had left Caporetto behind them for good and now seemed vibrant with purpose. The Italians, in terms dear to the American sensibility, were getting things done.

All about her, Ida Tarbell noted "rhythmic labor," "steady balance," and "orderly action." Although she was nearly seventy years old she was almost kittenish in her admiration for Mussolini, who put on a complete show for her, jutted his jaw, pounded the table, was stern and passionate, amusing and gallant, and bent low to kiss her hand when they said goodbye. "He had a most extraordinary smile," she said, "and when he smiled he had a dimple." In Mussolini's Italy in 1926 old Sam McClure thought he found what he had been seeking for nearly half a century, "A new and dawning civilization," the "solution of democracy," as if muckraking had been pointing in this direction all the time. In the Duce himself he found a combination of "force & charm & kindliness" which "made my heart beat hard for a long time after I left him." "He certainly has guts, that man," Jo Davidson wrote to Steffens after Mussolini had posed for him at the Palazzo Chigi. "The thing that remains with one is the way he has got them all bluffed."

"The man is as powerful as an elemental force, and he feels it," Steffens wrote about Mussolini in a magazine article in 1927. "History told him that he was historically due: he and Lenin; fascism or bolshevism. He holds that he is doing one of the two things that have to be done, as Lenin did the other. And he knows from history—including the current history of Russia—how to do what he is doing. . . . Imagine Theodore Roosevelt as aware in action of his place in the history of the United States and you will have Benito Mussolini in Italy." The "divine Dictator," as Steffens called him in his *Autobiography*, had learned what appeared to be an unanswerable counterlesson to liberalism: that in times of change, and perhaps at all other times as well, the people crave strong leaders even though they talk democracy. Hadn't this, after all, been one of the lessons of municipal reform in America? In every country there was an empty throne waiting to be seized, Mussolini said, and in the political vacuum of postwar Italy he arrived like an act of God. Caught between Italy's "thunder on the right" and Russia's thunder on the left, liberalism, beleaguered and possibly bankrupt, appeared to have no future, only an "inexorable alternative," as Max Eastman was saying, "Lenin or Mussolini." Writing in the era of the New Capitalism, Eastman, like Steffens, compared the Soviet men of power to "the big, forceful, clear-headed American captains of industry."

It would be years before "history," always invoked in the decade's mounting attack on liberalism, would say that Mussolini's capture of Italy and Stalin's capture of the revolution had been unimaginably worse than the worst failures of the old tradition. But meanwhile the issues seemed clear enough to Steffens as he watched Russia's internal struggles after the death of Lenin: the revolution had to be safeguarded at any cost, even if it meant setting the party against the people. "The fight must be fought out within the party," he argued with Max Eastman in June 1925, not in public, and meanwhile the party—the machine, as we used to call it—has to be supported, even as against Trotsky. It is liberalism to resent the injustice done to Trotsky, it is liberalism to feel as strongly as you do, I think, the crookedness of the methods of the bosses of the machine. . . . Trotsky is clearer than you are in his evident view that nothing must jar our perfect loyalty to the party and its leaders. Even as it stands, a menace not only to him and to the best of the followers of the revolution, it is the main spring of the revolution and has to be identified with it—always. Or doesn't it? That is my question. How are we to beat Paul and keep from beating Jesus?

CHAPTER SIXTEEN

"I guess I'll go down in history now"

I

FATHERHOOD BROUGHT LINCOLN STEFFENS BACK TO HIS OWN BEGIN-
nings. At first even the rudiments for autobiography were missing
from his memory. "I find that my mind is of itself brooding over the
Life and already it wants to know some things I do not remember,"
he told Laura in October 1924. "When did we move from San
Francisco to Sacramento, from Second Street to between Sixth and
Seventh, from there to K at Sixteenth? When did I get my pony,
when the colt from Col. Carter, when did I go to St. Matthew's
School? Can you answer these few starting questions?" Other questions came to him: about his father's beginnings in Illinois and the
trek westward, about his grandfather, the preacher. Steffens was
almost back in prehistory now. He spent the next six years bringing
his life up to date, and when publishers in New York expressed interest, he realized that his autobiography might turn out to be more
than a private project undertaken by a forgotten man.

At first, as he wrote the chapters of his boyhood on horseback and
re-created "the merely wondering mentality" of those years, his
narrative moved along so easily that there was little need for him to
rewrite. "If this keeps up," he said, "I shall probably enjoy death
most of all." Autobiography had become "a great joke, a sport, a
play. It is the first thing I have done for years for fun."

The writing of autobiography was also play, child's play, in another way: he relived his earliest fantasies and recast them in a highly ordered form—short stories, really, rather than conventional autobiography. And like the play and make-believe of a child, or its equivalent in the free association of an adult, autobiography generated its own stumbles and obstacles, curious disruptions that sought to tell him, by their very silence and obduracy, about the several points in his life where the accusations had begun, hatreds of self and of others. He had always been loved without being required or indeed able to give love in return; he recognized this among the childhood omens of trouble to come. (Here he was at the age of nearly sixty still assuming, out of the self-centeredness of his childhood, that his sister Laura, eight years younger than he, could recall episodes of his early years that had passed out of his own memory.)

With remarkable candor for the times—to some extent he had been liberated by a reading of *Ulysses* in Paris—he recounted the unhappy advent of sex into his life. In the "perverse, impotent, exciting, dirty" experience with an older boy in the tree house and in other experiences sequential and related he recognized the origins, or at least the first manifestations, of a crippling dissociation of love from sexuality. Eventually he became certain that he was a failure—a "dub"—as lover and husband. He was more important to his women than they were to him, and as far as his discovery of the world was concerned, he said, none of his sisters and none of his three wives (he included Gussie) had played any important part at all; they were not essential to his story. Nevertheless, he felt that he had to account for them, and it was here that autobiography began to encounter disruptions. His narrative came to a stop in June 1926, when he tried to tell the story of his student years in Europe, of the breaking of his secret engagement to Gussie, and of his secret marriage to Josephine.

He had taken Ella and his son to Paris and seen them off—"pushed them away" was more accurate, he admitted in his turmoil and depression—on the boat train for London: "It seemed to me then that if the train did not start on time I would bust or scream." He was desperate to be alone, but at the same time hungry for company, and for a while, nagged also by jealousy of his young wife, he tried to lose himself in the old Paris life. He reentered the familiar circle of visiting Americans and cronies of his bachelor days: Max and Eliena Eastman; Jo Davidson, seen in the company of Douglas Fairbanks and Mary Pickford; the Birds and Guy Hickock; Louise Bryant and Bullitt, more ebullient than ever, rejoicing in his novel and his infant daughter, who declared, to Freud's amusement, that her father was God; Ernest Gruening, the writer, future governor of Alaska, and Senator; Arthur Garfield Hays, along with Darrow one of the stars of the Scopes trial in Tennessee. As a climax to this sociability, on Saturday, June 19, Steffens attended one of the more notorious cultural events of the decade, the first performance of *Ballet Mécanique*, the American composer George Antheil's experiment in rendering the sounds of modern life.

"'Everybody,'" said Steffens, was there at the Théâtre des Champs-Élysées. "It was a sight as well as a sound. Getting there early, I stood outside and saw, I think, all the queer people in Paris, French and foreign, men and women. Wild hair, flannel shirts, no hats and big hats for both men and women." James and Nora Joyce, friends of Antheil, were there in a box. T. S. Eliot escorted an Italian countess, but the distinguished-looking lady in black, rumored to be royalty, turned out to be Sylvia Beach's concierge. Ezra Pound led the Antheil claque in the top gallery. Antheil's jagged harmonies of xylophones, electric bells, whistles, loudspeakers, nine pianos (one was a player piano), and an airplane propeller that generated hurricane gusts as well as sound set the audience to yelling and scuffling, and what went down in history as a scandal, Dadaist *chahut*, threatened for a while to become a riot. Steffens was glad when it was all over.

At the end of an evening that corresponded to his own fractured consciousness, he left Paris for the peace and order of Carlsbad, its water cure, its clientele of corpulent German businessmen, and its reassuring diet of Beethoven and Schubert. Here too he remained as stuck as ever in his book and the chapter about his first marriage. He sat down to write every day but had nothing to show for his work but crumpled pages. "I just have to tell the story," he said wearily, from the heart. "It belongs; it shows; not to me; I don't understand; but it must reveal to others what is the matter with me. I want someone with me; I want to be alone. I want to travel; I want to stay home."

Eventually he found a way out of his depression and also a way, frankly defeated, of telling his story: "It seems to me that I can see through a government or a political situation, but human relations are beyond my comprehension," he rationalized; and, in an attempt never to open up such painful areas again, he said, "Mine is not an inside but an outside story." Nevertheless, instead of plain sailing ahead he constantly ran into other blocks that frustrated his plans to write his life story as play in its simplest form, for his own entertainment. At one point he threw away two chapters by mistake and stopped writing for a year. Muckraking itself, which once made him a national hero, was now a painful subject. He no longer believed in it as a form of action and was even somewhat ashamed. Only the importunings and encouragement of Alfred Harcourt, his publisher, persuaded him to treat the subject as fully as he did. "Even Peter advised cutting the muckraking chapters, and the old muckrakers all backed her up," he told Harcourt gratefully after the book was out. "Do you realize that you are the only one that said: 'Let her run'?" It was only toward the end of what had begun to seem an interminable life and an impossibly long book that Steffens regained the hopefulness of his first chapters and also a degree of mastery. He finished his book in the fall of 1930 and, discarding the alternative titles he had been considering from the start, he decided to call it quite simply *The Autobiography of Lincoln Steffens.* "It gives a nice false impression of dignity and self-sufficiency."

II

BY 1927 STEFFENS WAS READY TO LEAVE EUROPE. "I am sick for home, sick," he said. "I wish I could come home now, next week." He wanted to see his own country again, to show it to his wife and son, and to spend the rest of his life—he was sixty-one that April—where he had started, in California. He had taken to picturing in his mind what it would be like to come back, to see the orange groves and fields of cornflowers, lupines and yellow poppies again, to step off the train at the Oakland terminal and then, the last leg of his westward return, to cross San Francisco Bay.

When they came into New York harbor in March he was as dazzled as his English wife by the thrust and boldness of the skyline. His impressions were confirmed by everything he saw in New York and Chicago, along the way home and in his later travels. As if he had been not only away but asleep as well, he was aware suddenly of "the power, the momentum of America as a going concern. The force of us had increased. There could be no stopping or turning us now. We were on the way; we might not know where we were going, but, for better or worse, we were going, going."

Like their country, two typical heroes of 1927, the golden year of the decade, were heroes of movement: Charles A. Lindbergh was "going" and went all the way, and five days after his plane touched down and a jubilant mob surged across the floodlit field at Le Bourget, another hero, Henry Ford, saw the fifteen-millionth Model T roll off his assembly line. In a business gamble comparable to Lindbergh's bold crossing, Ford shut down his factories until the first Model A's were produced. Soon the new cars were streaming along new highways and through the new Holland vehicular tunnel between Manhattan and Jersey City. The automobile had become instrument, creator and symbol of an unprecedented national prosperity and of what appeared to be the most equitable distribution of wealth ever known. In her first responses to her new country Ella Winter summed up what the 1929 crash soon showed had been only a transitory state of affairs: "This country has what the Socialists in Europe have always said they wanted, and more. You have food, shelter, and clothing for all the workers—and a car!" The seven or eight cars parked outside the house Steffens bought in Carmel that October did not signify, as an English neighbor thought, that he and Ella were having a housewarming. They belonged to the workmen who were putting the place in order.

Once again, after sixteen years, and now for the rest of his life, Steffens had a place of his own, an indigenous-looking wooden house on the corner of Ocean Avenue and San Antonio Street, about a hundred yards from the beach. It had a wild, irregular garden dominated by cypress trees and a passion vine and a broad roof-top porch facing toward the Pacific. Owning a house again gave him the sense of permanence he had been missing. He would be able to finish his book in Carmel, he was sure. He began to take an interest in the affairs of the town, in its politics and schools, tried to lure his friends into settling there, and for four years wrote a regular column for a local weekly that Ella edited, *The Carmelite*.

Steffens had known Carmel since its rustic beginnings twenty or so years earlier when a canny real-estate operator, recognizing the promotional value of bohemia, offered house lots to Jack London,

the poet George Sterling, Mary Austin, and others. In Carmel's operatic setting, Van Wyck Brooks recalled, the bohemians who
elected to spawn there like salmon lived curiously operatic lives, full
of passion and drama, before they succumbed to listlessness, beach-
combing, and a generalized postcoital tristesse. Things were more
stable when Steffens came back to Carmel. The cult of the great god
Pan had declined into gossip, artiness, and a taste for peasant
crafts, dirndl outfits, picnics, psychic phenomena, and visitations
from swamis who attempted to explain the inexplicable in a language nobody could understand. The promoter's dream had been
realized. Carmel was the nucleus of a thriving regional community
of plutocrats, socialites, sportsmen, comfortably retired persons,
and others who had "died and gone to heaven," Steffens said.

Still, there were residents and visitors who on occasion generated
some of the old excitement. Gertrude Stein and Alice B. Toklas, Jo
Davidson, George Antheil, Edna St. Vincent Millay and Lindbergh
were among the celebrities passing through. Albert Rhys Williams
arrived with reports of life in Soviet Russia. According to Williams,
Stalin's dictatorship had relaxed to a point where one no longer had
to apologize for it, and the peasants were enjoying the blessings of
both political and economic democracy. Williams was followed by
another bringer of tidings too good to be believed, Garet Garrett,
prophet and publicist of the New Capitalism. Hadley Hemingway
told the story of how her marriage to Ernest had been broken up by
a young fashion writer for *Vogue* in Paris. Sinclair Lewis, with his
new wife, Dorothy Thompson, settled for a while at Monterey.
Lewis, who was planning a labor novel, visited Tom Mooney and
J. B. McNamara at San Quentin and pumped Steffens dry on a subject which was now more painful than ever, the labor dynamiters.
One reason Steffens came back to America when he did was that
Darrow and Fremont Older begged him to intervene once again in
the cause of a pardon or parole: he shared their belief that the national mood toward labor, especially in California, which elected a
liberal governor, had softened somewhat and relinquished the old
vindictiveness. Steffens was greeted warmly enough at his father's
old house in Sacramento, and he enjoyed being taken on a tour of
the familiar ornate rooms with their Italian-marble fireplaces. Governor C. C. Young was sympathetic, encouraging, but helpless, and
Steffens' sense of accountability for the McNamaras was as heavy as

ever. Tom Mooney was another matter altogether. "I'm not interested in your case," Steffens teased him in the visitors' room at San Quentin; "you're innocent." Mooney, who reminded Sherwood Anderson of a bad actor playing Napoleon, had become something of a bore, constantly proclaiming himself the American Dreyfus. "Thank God, Jim, we are guilty," said one of the prisoners to J. B. McNamara.

At Tor House, the Celtic stone tower which he built with his own hands on a stony point of land in Monterey Bay, lived Carmel's chief lion, Robinson Jeffers, writing his austere verse to ward off evil and the society of men. But in his after-hours relations with picnic companions like Steffens and Ella, Jeffers proved to be surprisingly tolerant. Steffens' political heresies stimulated the poet but did not alter by the slightest degree his conservatism and his allegiance to the Republican party, both of which were as tenaciously rooted as the local cypresses.

There were more potent intrusions. In 1930, to the general amusement or discomfiture of the community, Mabel Dodge, writing her joyously indiscreet memoirs, arrived with her black Cadillac and her Taos Indian husband, rented a place ominously near Tor House and, still a species of head hunter, mobilized her magnetic force to "will" or "kidnap" Jeffers to New Mexico. She planned for him to fill the vacancy left in her life by D. H. Lawrence, who, Steffens remarked, had "unfeelingly died." At a party at Steffens' house she dismissed, in a manner both unanswerable and unmistakably proprietary, the bust of Jeffers Jo Davidson had modeled during several sittings on the porch overhead. "He hasn't caught the spiritual quality in the eyes," she declared with some of the old ardor, "or the poetry of the nostrils." Jeffers' work and marriage managed to survive this full-dress revival of Carmel's operatic tradition.

Steffens and Ella gratified sensation-hungry Carmel too, and not by their radicalism alone—that particular sensation was a thing of the thirties. From Salinas, the county seat, on June 6, 1929, came a grotesque but, as far as it went, substantially accurate story that became national news: Lincoln Steffens, sixty-three, was being sued for divorce by his young wife, who charged extreme cruelty. According to *The New York Times*, which gave all too literal a reading to the standard lawyer's boilerplate of the divorce complaint, Ella said that her husband "objected to her attending dances and other social events. She also asserted that he was lacking in affection and that he cared nothing for her." Their May-and-December marriage, in the newspaper stereotype, had failed out of excess of warmth or lack of it and most likely both. What made the failure especially piquant was the fact that less than a year ago, and in succeeding issues of the *American Magazine*, the aggrieved parties had published separate encomia entitled "Becoming a Father at Sixty Is a Liberal Education" and "The Advantages of Marrying an Older Man." (Reading these personal declarations Ernest Hemingway had begun to wonder when it would be their son's turn to have his say.)

There was laughter on the Carmel patios and in the little shops, and much speculation. Even Steffens' most loyal friends had to admit that there was something going on between him and Ella that Sigmund Freud, and maybe even God, couldn't begin to understand. In the ensuing turmoil, intensified by the threat of a Sunday supplement article and the arrival of photographers to take pictures of the unhappy family in their once happy home, Steffens, who was generally accustomed to being in command of his circumstances, found himself badly off balance. "The divorce business," he said bitterly to his niece Jane a few days after the story broke, "turns out to be a fine test of the intelligence and 'gentlemanliness' of one's friends. Their interpretations reflect their culture, so to speak. . . . I don't mind that so many people think it is all a matter of my age, but Peter does; and the implications as to her lightness hurt her."

Steffens had been serious, it turned out, when he told Ella in 1924 that they should divorce secretly. Jealous, he was afraid of jealousy and the shackles of a possibly outworn marriage. He wanted her to be free to leave him if she wanted, and if she chose to stay he wanted her to stay only out of love, not out of contractual obligation to an old man with a child as hostage. It was a form of self-protection against being hurt. It was also the kind of principled argument one heard from Emma Goldman in the old days and was hearing again in Judge Ben Lindsey's book *Companionate Marriage*, a sensation of the year 1927. Bewildered by what seemed Steffens' quixotic determination, Ella nevertheless had agreed to go to a lawyer in Watsonville, who assured her that the whole thing, beginning with a trumped-up complaint, could be put through the court in Salinas without any fuss at all and without anybody taking more than the barest routine notice. If it had not been for an alert local reporter who happened to scan the court calendar, Steffens and Ella might have had their secret divorce.

In the summer of 1929, after this mortifying collision of high principle, mechanic execution, and just plain bad luck, Ella saw that a "private joke" had become a "social fact." She was in England with their son, while Steffens remained in Carmel, lonely and uncharacteristically vulnerable to public opinion. He hoped that the divorce would come through, now that it had been started. But he dreaded the possibility of a real separation, not just one to satisfy the law. This odd and impossible tangle, consistent with Steffens' style of secret, half-formed or anomalous relationships, had a happy ending, even though an interlocutory decree of divorce was granted in June and a final decree in 1931.

Steffens and Ella had taken to exchanging love letters, and when she came back to America on October 29, 1929, the day of the great crash, Steffens felt that their life together, free now of shackles, could begin all over again and be better than ever. "We are running parallel again," he told her. "We are married once more." She in turn said that she planned to write a book about their long and now illicit honeymoon—"It would be a good companionpiece to our divorce." And as for the Carmelites, in answer to their fumbling speculations as to just what sort of arrangement had been worked out, Steffens was now offering whatever explanation came into his head. Was he living in sin, or merely in Carmel? Sometimes he said that he and Ella slept on opposite sides of a stone wall that ran right through the middle of their bedroom.

III

STEFFENS HAD COME BACK TO THE UNITED STATES a revenant, believing that outside the circle of his friends he might just as well have been Rip Van Winkle. A publisher's reader, reporting in 1923 on a collection of Steffens' short stories, concluded that "their whole terminology and outlook belong to an age that is more remote, psychologically, than that of Susan B. Anthony. . . . I don't personally know a human being who would derive any interest or pleasure from one of these stories." The publishing and critical career of *Moses in Red* hardly represented an improvement on this. Neither did an appraisal from a lecture manager in September 1927. "You have been out of the country so long that a number of people who ought to know who you are do not." He added, "A great number of them think unfavorably about you." Nevertheless, as lecturer and debater Steffens quickly resurfaced in the public consciousness.

Hours before he went on stage there were lines outside the doors at Ford Hall in Boston in November 1928, and the house was packed to standing room. As he had done in other cities, he talked about Stalin's Russia and Mussolini's Italy.

The next morning, at Filene's house on Otis Place, Granville Hicks, then a graduate student at Harvard, came to interview Steffens. Hicks had been doing research on the muckrakers and was familiar with their history of decline. He half expected to encounter in Steffens chiefly a vestige. Instead, after spending the morning with him, he came away with a powerful impression of the man's on-goingness. Merely throwing the rascals out or putting somebody in jail or any other variety of man-hunt associated with reform—these were all "absurd," things of the past, Steffens told him. It was time to learn from science, the experimental method, the constant challenging of axioms.

> Here, I felt at once, was a muckraker who had not grown tired and tame [Hicks recalled]. I was shocked by some of Steffens' ideas—by his willingness, for instance, to say a good word for Mussolini—but I was filled with admiration, just the same. Indeed, I felt this was a great man, and it seemed to me a pity that, after having had a tremendous following, he had fallen into relative obscurity. Everyone, it seemed to me, ought to know about Lincoln Steffens, and three years later, when the *Autobiography* appeared, everyone did.

Steffens' book became the chief instrument of his rehabilitation. By taking his own life (Henry Adams' ironic phrase for the writing of autobiography) he brought himself back from the grave. In celebration, Filene gave a dinner for him in New York on April 27, 1931, two and a half weeks after Harcourt, Brace published *The Autobiography of Lincoln Steffens* in two volumes. Even through clouds of hyperbole, cigar smoke, and obligatory tribute that hung over the banquet table at the Ritz-Carlton Hotel that evening it was possible to see clear signs that Steffens, after all was said and done, had achieved some place in recent history and that his life was far from finished. Having read his *Autobiography*, his friends were already urging him to write a sequel that would tell, in effect, what it was like to be reborn and to live in America all over again.

S. S. McClure, his memories of the palace revolution at his magazine mellowed by the passing of a quarter of a century, sent a telegram of regrets describing his willful protégé as a "Columbus" in the cause of liberty and justice. "No one in the United States gave more color and direction to the American life of our first decade than Steffens," said William Allen White, another absent veteran of muckraking's high noon. "He is one of the few honest men, thoroughly, beautifully, effectively, and courageously honest men, who were permitted to take leadership in that time."

Steffens was determined to believe no more than a minor fraction of what he heard that evening, but still it was gratifying to see a spectrum of American life in the guests who were there to honor him: politicians, businessmen, reformers, radicals, writers; Anne Morgan, the great Pierpont's daughter, and Bernard Baruch; Clarence Darrow, Ida Tarbell and Frederic Howe; defeated champions of reform, Rudolph Spreckels of San Francisco, soon to lose his fortune in the Depression and declare himself a follower of Father Coughlin's cryptofascist National Union for Social Justice, and the former mayor of Jersey City, Mark Fagan, turned out of office by his own Church, as he told Steffens, and now a funeral director; spokesmen of the left, Max Eastman, Abraham Cahan and Heywood Broun; Herbert Bayard Swope, who recalled how he had looked up to Steffens as a demigod; William G. Shepherd, Steffens' companion on the trip to Russia in 1917; Filene, chronically self-pleased; and Edward L. Bernays, the Edison of public relations, who had engineered the entire occasion as a news-generating encounter between an author and his characters.

"It was the damnedest mixed company you ever saw," Steffens exclaimed. Theodore Roosevelt, J. B. McNamara and Tom Mooney were among those who, by reason of death or detention, could not attend. Still, there to listen to him and to talk back to him if they chose were sixty of the people in his *Autobiography*, and for this occasion at any rate they were no longer figments of imagination or memory or conceivably just typographical errors. "Some of you have suggested very kindly that I might go on muckraking some more. I couldn't do it in the old way," Steffens explained at the end of his little talk. New York City was going through one of its periodic paroxysms of self-purification—this time the man-hunt was on for Mayor Jimmy Walker. "I couldn't do it without talking to Walker and understanding Walker and feeling out with imagination just what he can do and what he can't do; and I couldn't do it without pointing out what the matter is and pleading for pardon for all the crooks in town."

The *Autobiography*, published on April 9, had had an inauspicious send-off. The Harcourt, Brace salesmen grumbled because the book was expensive—two volumes at the uninflated price of $7.50 in hard times—and because many of them had never heard of Steffens or barely remembered him. Until the reviews began to come in, it seemed that Steffens' book was going to be a white elephant. "Lincoln Steffens is one of the best reporters and one of the most relentless searchers after truth that our generation has known," R. L. Duffus wrote on page one of *The New York Times Book Review*. "They are extraordinary volumes in more ways than one—in the directness, the intensity and at the same time the tolerance of the personality they reveal; in the wide range of the experiences related; in the insight they reveal into human nature; in their mingling of idealism with practicality." Carl Sandburg said, "It is one of those peculiar books which we know in our time is destined to be a classic." From Belgium came a distinctive comment:

MY DEAR STEFFENS,
        Just read your book and I like it a lot, I liked the crime wave and I liked Roosevelt and I liked me, and I may say I liked it all, I liked it in itself and I liked it because it brought back my early days, best to you always

                                                                    GTDE STEIN

Within ten days after publication Harcourt ordered a second printing and during the summer a one-volume edition at $4, which the Literary Guild took for its October selection. Soon Steffens, the forgotten man, discovered that he had written a book that was a critical triumph and a commercial success as well—60,000 copies sold by Christmastime 1931, and there was no sign of stopping. The same public that in 1931 made bestsellers of Frederick Lewis Allen's *Only Yesterday*, an informal chronicle of the 1920s, M. Ilin's *New Russia Primer*, an official Soviet account of the first Five-Year

Plan, and Drew Pearson and Robert Allen's gossipy *Washington Merry-Go-Round* was hospitable to Steffens' peculiar synthesis of backward, forward and inside views. "My amazing book keeps going—like a novel," he told Frederic Howe in February 1932. "Young people are reading it, the generation that never read our muckrakings."

He traveled about the country lecturing, being listened to "as a sort of prophet" and treated as a lion, and he learned that the *Autobiography* was assigned reading in college courses in English, journalism, government, history. Two studies published in 1932 dealt with him at length and with a full degree of historicism, C. C. Regier's *The Era of the Muckrakers* and John Chamberlain's *Farewell to Reform*—"You have no idea how significant I am or was," he told Ella about the Chamberlain book. At the Carmel Public Library thirty-six people were on the waiting list for his *Autobiography*, and he heard there were long lists in the libraries in Los Angeles and San Francisco. He was disappointed not to win a Pulitzer Prize—ironically, the 1932 biography award went to Henry F. Pringle's account of Theodore Roosevelt as a "violently adolescent" leader—but there were so many other honors and invitations and celebrations that it hardly mattered. It all seemed unbelievable to him. "I guess I am a success," he said to Ella. "I guess I'll go down in history now."

IV

THE FIELD AT ARMAGEDDON, on which a generation of warriors had done battle with the enemies of the Republic, was empty, virtually forgotten during the years Steffens spent writing his book. The crusaders against Corruption, Privilege, and the System had vanished along with their banners proclaiming that, in addition to a new broom and a square deal, what America needed to cure its ills was more democracy, not less. The progressive coalition that had swept Woodrow Wilson into office was shattered by the war and then died along with Wilson. Even by 1924 no one seemed to be quite sure any longer what "progressivism" meant or indeed whether it ever had any meaning at all. ("A progressive," said one Illinois Congressman, "is a Republican who thinks his district is going Democratic.")

The last of the crusaders, Senator Robert M. La Follette, died of exhaustion in 1925. Others had gone back to business, the law, literature, and the status quo. "Some of them are in jail," said Fremont Older, editor of Hearst's San Francisco *Call*, in 1925, "some of them, with little hope left, are still on the job, but more of them have been inoculated by the money madness that has seized America."

Of the original muckrakers—"radicals," as Theodore Roosevelt called them on special occasions—it was rumored that Lincoln Steffens spent his time "learning to be an intelligent father." Ray Stannard Baker was at work on his seven-volume biography of Wilson, a work of only mildly qualified piety. Ida Tarbell had become an apologist for big business and the old corporate scapegoats. The lieutenants who served under Golden Rule Jones and Tom Johnson were now part of the same diaspora. Newton D. Baker, Wilson's Secretary of War, practiced law in Cleveland and was president of the Chamber of Commerce. In 1925 Frederic C. Howe published his grieving account of the death of liberalism, *The Confessions of a Reformer*, and until Franklin Roosevelt revived the progressive urge and pledged himself to a New Deal for the American people, Howe renounced public life, dividing his years between Nantucket and Europe. Brand Whitlock moved into self-imposed exile at Cannes, took up novel writing again, and repudiated almost every article of the old faith. For him Franklin Roosevelt was simply a "bag of wind," "a fatuous damn fool" who had surrounded himself with "adolescent professors and a lot of intellectual snobs and parlor socialists: God save the State."

In Moscow, where John Reed lay buried, no one paid much attention to Big Bill Haywood any more. Having been dismissed by Lenin as "another American salesman," Haywood was "the loneliest soul in Asia," Steffens said. Bill Shatoff, the Chicago anarchist who made the Moscow-Petrograd express run on time, lived on as a virtual parolee in Soviet Russia and was to meet his death in one of Stalin's labor camps. Emma Goldman, the least compromised of all the Dangerous People who had frequented Mabel Dodge's Evenings, became a British subject and wrote her memoirs.

"What has become of this movement that promised so much twenty years ago? What has become of the pre-war radicals?" Howe asked in his book. "Most of the radicals of pre-war days have laid down their arms. Was the fight too hard? Did youth burn itself out?" Who was left, and how had they survived?

Steffens' *Autobiography*, written during a decade that sometimes seemed a vacuum in history and published just as the country was sliding toward the bottom of its long Depression, answered these questions out of a body of experience that had proved to be, in many respects, an accelerating series of disasters. Still, he wrote with a vividness and penetration, with a faith in the future and in the intelligence of the young, and with a gaiety and trustfulness that, in a darkening time, established his book as a controlling document and its author as one of the tutelary heroes of the 1930s. ("He knows the world and is tolerant, can explain to you the naturalness of everything" from "a philosophical point of view which few newspapermen have," Edmund Wilson said in *The New Republic*.)

At his house in Carmel until he died, Steffens served as sage for the discontented, questioning young and as mentor in their move to the left. He was, at the same time, spokesman for a future "experimental culture" and chronicler of half a century of history (he appeared to have known everybody, seen everything, been everywhere). Through his account of his frontier antecedents and his Tom Sawyer boyhood, he was also a link to a vanished America, in which problems apparently could be solved through a peculiarly democratic and pastoral combination of self-reliance, consensus and good will. He was so native to America, as he showed in his book, so deep-rooted in the Sacramento Valley, that he was able to impart to the radicals of the 1930s a historical legitimacy going back to the era of wagon trains and the country's great westward expansion. "Radical," he seemed to be reminding them, had to do with roots.

Many of Steffens' ideas dated quickly or were dishonored by events. The Depression did not support his claim that the United States was making "an experiment in hopefulness second only to Russia." His faith in the engineers and managers of the New Capitalism turned out to be just as misplaced as his faith in Stalin and the commissars, and he was compelled after a while to repudiate his enthusiastic account of Mussolini, the "divine Dictator." But the observations Steffens made about power, wealth and national purpose kept their sardonic point. In the growing economic emergency after the crash of 1929, President Herbert Hoover was summoning "big business"—precursor of the "military-industrial complex"—to come in broad daylight to a White House conference. "One can't sneer any more that Washington is the kept woman of Wall Street,"

Steffens said. "They are man and wife, and that changes everything." Versailles, he said, was the failure of a culture that persisted in remaining as indifferent to cause and effect as earliest man. "Wilson did not mean peace, not literally; nor do we Americans, nor do the British, mean peace. We do not want war; nobody in the world wants war; but some of us do want the things we can't have without war. . . . We will not give up the things that cause war."

Wilson's "typical" defeat and self-defeat were for Steffens a turning point in the career of American innocence, the shadow protagonist of the *Autobiography*. At Versailles, for all the world to see, European realism had triumphed over native idealism, intelligence had won out over character, the System had beaten reform, Tammany had routed the insurgents. Wilson was the ultimate Innocent Abroad, as innocent as Steffens said he himself had been when he first came to Europe as a student in search of the Good and the True. He suggested that he had been no less innocent when he came home after three years in the universities—"I was happily unaware that I was just a nice, original American boob, about to begin unlearning all my learning and failing even at that."

Steffens, of course, was invoking a familiar, native persona—tenderfoot, dandy, dude, bookish dupe, gullible city boy—whose usefulness for the satirist and moralist Mark Twain had established once and for all. ("By saying something with a half-boob air," Damon Runyon wrote about himself, "he gets ideas out of his system on the wrongs of this world which indicate that he must have been a great rebel at heart.") Now Steffens too was using this persona as an instrument of persuasion which allowed him to suggest that the bankruptcy of the old "moral" culture should have been evident to him even before he got off the boat if he had not been an incurable innocent who, like Henry Adams after the Civil War, heeded Emerson's advice and hitched his wagon to the star of reform.

Adams' *Education*, a popular book in 1918 and 1919 despite its knottiness, was read, if only partially understood, in the light of the war and the peace; it was not a time, in Adams' words, "that sensitive and timid natures could regard without a shudder." Steffens' book— also an "education" in Adams' ironic sense; a negative education, a process of divestment—was read in the light of the Depression and of the questions that one had to ask: How did it happen? What will we do now? The *Autobiography* said goodbye to a time safely dead and gone, but even as it established the defeat of the old order it held out hope for the future.

"Lincoln Steffens has told here the story of his own life—a part of it, at any rate," Newton Arvin said in *The Nation* when the book came out,

> but, like Mill and Tolstoy and Henry Adams, he has mainly done something else, and that a more fruitful thing than most self-portraitists succeed in doing. He has written the psychological history and, so to say the extended epitaph of a whole generation, a whole social movement, a whole class.

But the *Autobiography* was not merely an epitaph, Arvin went on: it also had "something of the stateliness of prophecy" and the utility of a handbook.

> It suggests how the transition can be made from a plastic liberalism to a resourceful and humane radicalism. It suggests how social movements can be given a personal and psychological as well as a collective aspect. It demonstrates, indirectly, the shabbiness of our fashionable cynicism. It is a source book for the critic, for the radical, for the man of action. But it is certainly not merely an "autobiography."

In other respects too—and just as much as Adams' book, with which it was frequently compared—Steffens' "life of unlearning" is less an autobiography, in the conventional sense of an attempt at a circumstantially "true" chronicle, than a form of fiction; not a strict record of things done and seen but an ironic, paradoxic fable about the process of self-regeneration that is implicit in the writing of autobiography. Consciously and unconsciously, Steffens recreated himself in his own image, recreated his experience in the light of the amused tolerance, scathing sense of reality, and mastery of event he clearly did not have as a younger man.

For nearly thirty years, as newspaper reporter, muckraker, political radical, and champion of pariah causes in general, Steffens had lived in fear of reprisal or suppression. Now, through the fictive medium of autobiography he found a way of telling things straight without losing his audience or endangering his rights. As a persuader he creates the illusion of retreat while actually advancing toward prepared radical positions.

Because he wrote as an ironic fabulist and also because he yielded to some of the coarser temptations of autobiography, Steffens, by himself and uncorroborated, is not a reliable source for his own literal history or for anyone else's, for that matter. He tells stories that are just as tall as any Mark Twain told in his autobiography. "I Make a Crime Wave," for example, Steffens' account of what happened when he and Jacob Riis competed for scoops, is basically a parable about public psychology. Another colorful episode, dealing with the disclosure of secret oil agreements which supposedly broke up the Genoa Conference, consists of about twenty percent fact and the balance propaganda. It is not likely that Steffens was single-handedly responsible for averting war with Mexico, or that he could recall with verbatim accuracy long conversations that took place decades earlier, or that he generally had the triumphant last word in his encounters with Theodore Roosevelt, a vividly caricatured case of undescended maturity.*

Steffens learned many things long after he said he had, and just as many long before. Like Henry Adams he took generous liberties with the rhythms, phases and moods of his life; at the end of his narrative he was no more a happy little boy falling out of bed than Adams was a broken man. Steffens had a messianic complex, it was said, and, if he is to be believed, he is almost always either seeing the light or showing it to others, who are all too often rendered in the allegorical flat, like characters out of *The Pilgrim's Progress*. And a sort of diffuse Augustinianism appears to guide the narrative: hardly an experience is recounted for its own sake—everything is illumination or redemption, everyone is the agent of historical process, all discoveries are didactic and newsworthy. ("And the writing!" Brand Whitlock remarked. "It's like the headlines in the Paris edition of the New York *Herald!*")

Steffens' *Autobiography* is history written not necessarily as it happened but as he chose to shape it according to the needs of retrospect and personality, the pressures of politics and the times, and the tactics of persuasion. Taken together, this is an equivalent form of the "truth" found in nakeder forms of fiction. Steffens moves freely

---

* "Throughout your book," Paul C. Smith of the San Francisco *Chronicle* said to Steffens, "you encounter the great and the near great of the world and the times, and you directly report many of your conversations. . . . Well, in these conversational duels, *you* always come out on top." Steffens answered with a smile. "Well, damn it, I'm a reporter. *I* always did!" (Paul C. Smith, *Personal File*, New York, 1964, p. 149.)

around the world, through time and a gallery of representative figures, great and small. His fable may turn out to be as useful as stricter chronicles for crystallizing the meaning of the decades that stretched between the old radicals and the new, between the great depression of the nineties and the even greater depression of the thirties, between April 1894, when Coxey's army of the unemployed was driven out of Washington, and July 1932, when General Douglas MacArthur directed the attack on the bonus army in Anacostia Flats. Steffens was squarely in the line of American autobiographers, from Benjamin Franklin on, who have been the conduit of new styles of awareness, radical responses to emergent occasions. For those who remembered the impact it had upon them in 1931, Steffens' *Autobiography*, "almost a textbook of revolution" (Max Eastman), arrived with "the force of revelation" (Granville Hicks), and it helped turn part of a generation leftward. Of Frederic Howe's "prewar radicals," one, at any rate, had made a satisfactory accounting of himself.

CHAPTER SEVENTEEN

Guru of the Left

I

"WE HAVE NOW PASSED THE WORST," President Herbert Hoover said in May 1930. The popular economist Roger Babson was almost as positive. "In 1929," he declared, "we were living in a palace with a powder mine in the cellar. In 1931 we may feel sure that we are living in a poorhouse with a gold mine in the cellar." Closer to home for Steffens, there was a new Republican governor in Sacramento, the genial and boozy James Rolph—a liberal on the issue of repeal of Prohibition—who announced that the Depression was over and that the time had come to "Smile with Sunny Jim." Steffens had not been a great deal quicker than anyone else to realize the implications of the market crash of October 1929. His income was cut by a half and more, but unlike his conservative Carmel neighbors who were hit just as hard, he now had money coming in from a new source—his radical *Autobiography*. Also, out of the knowledge that he had begun to acquire on Wall Street during the panic of 1893, he still found it possible, though he was a bear on capitalism, to be a bull in the stock market and turn an occasional profit during flurries of overselling and recovery.

"If this depression keeps up much longer," he joked in February 1931, "somebody in business will begin to think. It sometimes sounds like a mere empty threat. . . . Be sure to get a photograph of the thinker and, yes, don't forget the thought." His own residual faith in the New Capitalism took time to die. Sherwood Anderson, who came to hear him speak before some San Francisco businessmen in April 1932, was put off by Steffens' "obsession that some big businessman, a Ford or an Owen D. Young, is going to come along and save us." "Were Trotsky, Lenin, Stalin, any of them businessmen?" Anderson asked him afterward. Steffens retreated from the question in smiling confusion—"There is great vitality in the man," Anderson decided, "but a queer trickiness of thought." Even that June Steffens was hopeful enough about the possibility of a business solution through "united action" to offer his services to Young and his proposed "economic council."

Meanwhile, the testimony of the business leaders and thinkers in a series of Congressional hearings was revealing not only an almost hilarious poverty of thought and a failure of leadership but also, in instances too frequent to be dismissed as just aberrant, an abdication of probity on the most exalted levels of high finance. It was all reminiscent of the freebooting era of Jay Gould and Boss Tweed. "A holding company," Will Rogers decided after puzzling over some of the testimony, "is a thing where you hand an accomplice the goods while the policeman searches you."

Stricken in brain and heart after 1929, capitalism's behemoth crashed into the thickets of the new decade with at least the appearance of its self-hypnotic faith. But by 1933 its legs had buckled; it lay down as if dying. Thirteen million people, a quarter of the civilian labor force, were out of work. In the agricultural heartland the farmers burned their wheat and fruit, drowned their hogs, dumped their milk. Wall Street traded stocks worth a bare ten percent of their value three years earlier. Hard times had come to stay, and finally the Depression had to be acknowledged to the full extent of the nation's despair and shame. The fathers had failed, the children were betrayed, and the American system, having proved itself unable to learn anything from its own history, even from an earlier depression, seemed the captive of an unbreakable cycle of catastrophe and decline.

The "New Capitalism" was finished, Steffens said—the whole system had "gone over the top and slid down to an utter collapse. That was clear to all. I went to New York to hear the semiscientific captains of industry say in words and facial expressions that they did not know what had happened or what was to be done about it. They did not understand their experiment. Then—not till then—did I give up, and turned to see what else there was."

The Depression also came home to him in a way that seemed to be personally directed proof of the murderous nature of capitalism. "Can anybody ever own anything," he reflected, "without being possessed by it?" In happier days, when the world of his childhood had been represented to him as a perfected place, his father, among the other positions of prominence that he held, had been a vice-president and director of the California National Bank of Sacramento. In time the father's shares passed to the son. But the Sacramento bank became one of the thousands of casualties of 1932—its depositors hoped to get thirty cents on the dollar—and under existing law Steffens was liable for an amount equal to the par value of his shares. "It gets on my nerves a little, more and more, in spite of the way I take it," he told Ella in February 1933. He had just been assessed $25,000. "I understand now much better how my neighbors feel." But, although he tried to whistle away his anxiety, he was in serious trouble: the wealth of the father had been passed on to the son, now the victim of retributive justice. By the time Steffens was able to settle the bank claim two years later, with the aid of an emergency loan from Filene, he had gone through a period during which he sometimes cried and sometimes talked about suicide and murder. "The combination days on which I yearn pathetically to kill myself and others too, are a recent development," he said in September 1934. It was inconceivable to him that a man's sanity and life could be destroyed because he once owned shares in a bank and now owed money.

But there was "good news" in the Depression too, Steffens had taken to arguing; one had to throw away all the old axioms and solutions and look for new ones, and when times were hardest the searchers were happiest and most hopeful. "The Big Business era" had come to an end, Edmund Wilson was certain—"One couldn't help being exhilarated at the sudden collapse of that stupid gigantic fraud. It gave us a new sense of freedom." Malcolm Cowley recalled that, in the trough of the Depression, "everybody was trying to change the world and create the future; it was the special pride and presumption of the period." The socialism of Norman Thomas and his party seemed too mild, too late. "Becoming a Socialist now would have just about the same effect on anybody as drinking a bottle of near-beer," John Dos Passos said during the Presidential-election year of 1932. In the interests of hastening the revolution, Steffens was urging in *The Carmelite*, it was probably more effective to vote for Herbert Hoover than for William Z. Foster, the Presidential candidate of the Communist party (he ended up with 103,000 votes to Hoover's 16,000,000).

That summer Steffens and Ella put their names to a manifesto of support for the party slate. Among the fifty other writers and intellectuals who signed were Wilson, Cowley, Dos Passos, Anderson, Langston Hughes, Granville Hicks and Sidney Hook. Standing in the wreckage of capitalism—"a house rotting away," its two major political parties "hopelessly corrupt," according to the manifesto—the "brain workers," motivated by humane and patriotic concerns which for them were moral rather than economic in their immediate origins, sought an American solution to the American problem in a revolutionary alliance with "the muscle workers." And since "the muscle workers" as a whole (with the exception of small groups, among them the one known satirically as the "Workers and Peasants of Greater New York") remained largely indifferent to revolutionary solutions and the courtship of the intellectuals, American Communism seemed to be recapitulating the middle-class pattern of the muckrakers.

"I tell you," Steffens remarked to Ella in his bitterness over the bank suit, "nobody in the world *proposes* anything basic and real except the Communists." But he never joined the party. For the most part he found Communists repellent and humorless; from time to time he expressed his opinion that the party in California was a comic shambles; and he once worked up a talk on the subject of why Communists have to be such sons-of-bitches. (Ella, too, claimed that she mixed with Communists just as she mixed with the conductor or the Pullman porter—not because she liked him, but because "I need him to get me where I want to go.")

Steffens, in fact, was a figure of ridicule for party stalwarts like Mike Gold of the *New Masses*. Reviewing the *Autobiography*, Gold had derided Steffens as "Mr. Liberal himself," a man who "liked everybody" and felt at home in the role of "lettle lost cheild wandering among the social battlefields"; as the evangelist of a Christian style which had as much function in the machine age as a square wheel, he managed to radiate "a mild benevolent glow derived from frequent doses of old Dr. J. C.'s Peruna." According to Gold, Steffens had traveled among wars and revolutions like some sort of barfly in search of historical jolts and thrills. Nevertheless it was Steffens' refusal to commit himself officially to Communism—his determination to remain only an "intellectual Communist"—that made him valuable to the party. He was a persuader whom middle-class liberals and conservatives (and Rotarians, as it turned out) were willing to listen to, and this was to be his occupation during the last years of his life. "I am not a Communist," he explained to a Harvard undergraduate who had turned to him for advice. "I merely think that the next order of society will be socialist and that the Communists will bring it in and lead it."

Faced with the prospect of this "next order of society," he told a capacity audience in San Francisco in January 1933, "we behave like a cab-horse that I saw meet the first automobile in New York. The new vehicle was coming swiftly toward him. He saw it suddenly when it was close upon him. The poor beast stopped in his tracks and, from terror or amazement, collapsed. His hind legs sprawled out from under him and he actually sat down, his mouth open, his eyes and ears fixed upon that new and unknown apparition. All Europe and North America sat down on their haunches before the Russian Revolution; they haven't stood up to it yet." When the laughter subsided, he said, "So now I'm going to do with you what we used to do with a horse that shied: walk you up and down before the terrifying new object." Toward the end of the expository part of his talk he stopped suddenly and in the silence said, "Yes, I am talking Communism, Bolshevik Communism." He could hear gasps of shock. "Remember my cab-horse," he told them at the end. "Fellow Americans, I greet you. Good night." After the cheers and applause and laughter had gone on for a while he stood up again and bowed. It was no wonder that he was bombarded with invitations. "You might come home to protect me from the Communists who pester me for appearances, all fundamentally important," he told Ella. "They act as if they were glad that I'm not a Communist."

Singly and together and with varying degrees of zeal, irony and certainty, Steffens and Ella were formidable persuaders committed to the proposition that "Russia has found the way for America." To the extent that he was an old man and a broken liberal, Moses living out his life on the near side of the future, Ella had become his instructed agent, his Joshua. She had returned from Canaan bearing grapes, pomegranates, figs, and also quantities of Soviet statistics, which she accepted gratefully and without undue skepticism. As reported by Ella—and by Maurice Hindus, Louis Fischer, and other travelers—Stalin's Russia was almost too good to be true. Contrasted with such glowing accounts, the prominent night-school philosopher Will Durant's anti-Soviet *The Tragedy of Russia* reminded Steffens of the peasant fable about a pig who entered a great castle, looked around for a while, and concluded, "All I saw was some garbage, and not enough of that."

Ella Winter's book *Red Virtue*, published in 1933 with the subtitle *Human Relationships in the New Russia*, extolled the quality of individual and collective life under Communism, the changes (all for the better) in customs and behavior, the high morale in family, factory and farmhouse. Even before her book came out, Ella was a conspicuous figure in her own right, much in demand as lecturer and Soviet expert and energetically involved in activist and propaganda causes all the way from a New York-based Committee for the Victims of Fascist Oppression to the migrant lettuce pickers in the Salinas Valley. In Carmel—where, Steffens said proudly, she was now "the bane of the town's existence" as "Red Ella"—she formed and ran the local John Reed Club. "A near Communist organization for near-writers and near-artists" was the way Steffens described it in June 1932. "They have nine members, with many sympathizers who would like [to] but dare not join." Aside from his mild ridicule, he found himself in the curious position of being caught between the John Reed clubs and John Reed's mother. Having threatened, while Reed was still alive, to kill herself because of the disgrace he brought on the family, she was now nearly insane with rage to see his name being used in the service of the party. She demanded that Steffens intervene. Reed

> became a hero in Russia; he will be for ages a Soviet Russian hero [he told her]. And, Mrs. Reed, I'm afraid that you are wrong about his not standing for the use of his name by the clubs. My impression is that Jack would approve of that, or if he objected, he would have complained only that the John Reed clubs do not go far enough. He might say to them what he said to me that night on a street corner in New York: "Go on—the limit."

When Hitler achieved absolute power at the beginning of 1933 a dominant social and political myth of the decade finally crystallized. "The choice is between Fascism and Communism, between Russia and Germany," said Steffens, one of the makers of that terrible simplifier (it was to be succeeded after World War II by a later "choice" between Communism and Freedom). If one accepted the characteristic rhetoric as well as the logic of the argument, it seemed that Trotsky's dung-heap of history was waiting for the Western democracies, for all "good fellows and liberal compromisers who want to get together," as Steffens said, for men of "hopeful, democratic instincts and principles." "There is a time for thinking and planning; there comes a time to close our open minds, shut up our talking, and go to it," Steffens wrote—"lest Hitler do his things his way." Over and over again during that darkening time Steffens responded to the double urgency of Fascism and the Depression and sounded the same note. "I am introduced to you as a tired liberal," he told a Tom Mooney rally at the Civic Auditorium in San Francisco. "I am not a liberal, but I am tired—tired of a lot of things and I am going to tell you some of them. I am tired of liberalism. I mean that I am tired of this open-mindedness, this willingness to consider the facts of history and of the present and the next thousand years. We haven't got a thousand years. I think as a liberal that we have come to the time when we must stop thinking and decide and do it." After what now seemed to him a long life in limbo he had finally come around to urging John Reed's imperative—"Go on, the limit." He was doing this from what he called "the second line," but nonetheless, at the age of sixty-seven he was willing to do it at whatever cost.

By Labor Day 1933 Steffens was ill with stomach trouble, high blood pressure, and what proved to have been a warning stage of coronary artery disease. Apparently restored in vitality after a few weeks in bed, he was soon busier than ever. Within a period of a few days in October he debated with Wisconsin's Governor Philip La Follette in Los Angeles and with Norman Thomas in San Francisco, lectured to the university students at Berkeley and the same afternoon flew to Sacramento to talk to Governor Rolph, urge the interests of the labor prisoners and the agricultural workers, endure the usual questions about what it had been like to live in the official mansion in the old days, and in general probe for humor and compassion in high places.

In November he was in Boston having been driven by his bank troubles to take on the job of supervising Filene's biography and finding a writer for it; he tried Whittaker Chambers but eventually recruited Robert Cantwell of *The New Republic*. With Filene—"the man is a bore," Steffens admitted, "but not his life"—he was at the Harvard-Yale game on the twenty-fifth and the following night at a Nazi meeting in Ford Hall, ringed with police and angry, silent crowds. At Harvard the next day Steffens was introduced by Professor Arthur Holcombe, who had assigned the *Autobiography* in his government course and now warned his students that if they were not careful they might get some new ideas from the visiting lecturer. There was a time for the open mind, Steffens told them, following a practiced line of argument; there was also a time for the closed mind and for action. After the lecture the discussion went on for over an hour. "He was unmercifully brilliant to questioners," one of the students recalled. "I never witnessed such slaughter."

In New York the pace quickened. There were so many people to see—Bullitt; the *New Masses* editors; the writers Kyle Crichton, Max Lerner and W. E. Woodward; Alfred Harcourt, who was now pressing him for a sequel to the *Autobiography*. Steffens had lunch with an English counterpart, John Strachey, author of the pro-Communist analysis *The Coming Struggle for Power* and another persuader in the move to the left. He had lunch, too, with Whittaker Chambers, whose short stories in the *New Masses* he praised for demonstrating that "proletarian literature" could be both proletarian and literary. What troubled Steffens about the party, he confessed to Chambers, was its coldness, its suspension of generosity and civility in favor of "discipline" and "self-criticism." How did this square with Strachey's image of the Communist as "the champion of civilization against all and every form of barbarism"? As they parted at the Hotel Commodore, Steffens, still and ever a child of the old order, called softly down the carpeted corridor, "Keep a warm spot in your heart, Whittaker." A few days later he went off to Boston again to introduce Strachey at a public meeting and to settle, he hoped, the matter of Cantwell's biography of Filene.

On December 11 Steffens was in Chicago to address a group of eight hundred members of Rotary at a lunch at the Hotel Sherman.

His talk was "a whirl of a success"; he had discarded the microphone, he felt so confident of himself; Clarence Darrow said it was the best speech he ever gave. The businessmen and bankers had been willing to listen, were enthusiastic about what they heard, and he was planning a more radical presentation for the next day. "What I seem to have done here (beside earn $200)," he wrote to Ella immediately after, "is to make the Rotarians feel that radicals have something to say and can get you to hear it, face it, without being an offense."

But, at what appeared to be a turning point in his career as public persuader, something grave and hurtful had been happening to him, a physical betrayal of purpose. For two days before his talk his left leg had shown an alarming tendency to buckle under him; he had to hold on to someone else to get around; and it was getting worse. He collapsed on December 13. The diagnosis of the Chicago doctors, as wired to Ella, was "hardening of the arteries localized in brain. Possible progressive incapacity or paralysis." He refused to enter a hospital. The next day, on his insistence, he was carried on a stretcher aboard the Union Pacific's Overland Limited at the Union Station and for the last time traveled homeward to California.

II

STEFFENS DREADED MOST OF ALL A SECOND "STROKE" that would not kill him but instead would render him totally helpless and dependent. He had it from his doctors that arteriosclerosis was incurable, but still he had fantasies of recovery and a fresh start. What he knew and what he hoped were in collision and intensified the depressions he associated with the terminal years of his father and grandfather. Now he associated these depressions with his sister Laura as well. She had become psychotic and remained immune to psychiatric treatment in Zurich and New York. When Steffens thought of Laura he became frightened for himself.

The bank business, too, hung heavy over his head, making him "intolerant and bitter," Ella told Alfred Harcourt. In March 1935, suit was brought against him in the United States District Court in San Francisco. He was charged with attempting to escape his liability by transferring to Ella title in several parcels of land in Carmel, his book royalties, the mortgage note from Owen D. Young in payment for Little Point, and various stocks and bonds, something of a fortune in depression times. "Steffens, Radical Writer, Is Wealthy, Suit Reveals," *The New York Times* reported; he and Ella, "noted writers and champions of radical political beliefs," had been "dragged into a decidedly capitalistic limelight." To compound his misery, he was now compelled to give testimony and answer questions from his sickbed. The case was settled at the end of June with Steffens paying $14,000, $8,000 of which was supplied by Filene in response to a desperate cable to him in Paris. "He saved me my home here. My health too," Steffens wrote to Robert Cantwell about Filene's last-minute intervention. "You don't got to be grateful, but I am."

Cantwell had little reason to be grateful to either of them. He had given up his job at *The New Republic* and moved to Boston only to be told, immediately upon his arrival on a day so arctic that the world seemed to have come to a stop, that because of Steffens' illness Filene was no longer sure he wanted to go ahead with the biography. Nevertheless, Cantwell, already depressed, was asked to immerse himself in the thirty bound volumes of Filene's public speeches that occupied a prominent place on the book shelves at Otis Place. "Most of them were dull," Cantwell concluded after a day or two of horror, "and all were familiar; and many were hollow and hypocritical with that strained baccalaureate optimism that can only be attained, in times of crisis, by the amputation of great areas of experience." He had also been struck by Filene's maniacal egotism and by the spirit of dissimulation and sharp trading that appeared to hover over the entire withered personality, and he conceived at that moment an aversion to his subject so powerful that it was literally murderous; he was determined to write that biography—to "take" Filene's life—out of the most disinterested of motives, pure hatred. The book from which Steffens hoped to recoup some of his losses by serving as its editor or senior author or impresario had turned into a battlefield. Caught between Cantwell's savagery and Filene's mercurial interventions, Steffens derived what humor he could from the situation.

In 1934 Upton Sinclair was running for governor on an E.P.I.C. (End Poverty in California) platform that appeared to be so radical

—he proposed to turn over some farms and factories to the workers —that his Republican opponents accused him of trying to Sovietize the state and nationalize the children. (In the implacable days before the Seventh Communist International declared a United Front of peace-loving antifascists and defenders of democracy, Sinclair was anathema to the Communists as well—Robert Minor, a party hatchet-man, described him as a social fascist who was advancing "the most cold-bloodedly pro-capitalist and reactionary proposals that were offered by any candidate in any election in the United States in a decade.")

That July a general strike was called in San Francisco, and the workers walked off their jobs in sympathy with the striking members of the International Longshoremen's Association. To the degree that in the course of Steffens' long career he had become an institution of dissent, his dissent had in turn become institutionalized and tolerated.* For the most part he was left alone to pursue his gadfly activities in columns for various local journals, *The Carmelite*, *Controversy* and *Pacific Weekly*. But when panic in California became epidemic, having been fed by massive administrations of the vigilante spirit and a white terror, the world immediately outside his garden gate, once merely skeptical or derisive, turned enemy.

Steffens and Ella were both prominently listed in Mrs. Elizabeth Dilling's guide to the Stalinist penetration of America, *The Red Network*—so, for that matter, were Mahatma Gandhi, Albert Einstein, Eleanor Roosevelt and Secretary of Labor Frances Perkins—and, as far as the town was concerned, Ella was a conduit by which Moscow gold flowed to the San Francisco waterfront, the California Communist party, and the strike-torn agricultural fields. It was in addition falsely rumored that Ella's reason for marrying Steffens had been to exploit his respectable left background in the service of international Communism.

In the eyes of Carmel, "we are almost as dangerous as the Party,"

---

* In his novel about the coming of fascism to the United States, *It Can't Happen Here* (1935), Sinclair Lewis acknowledged the tolerated nature of Steffens' role. "All over the country, books that might threaten the Pax Romana of the Corporate state were gleefully being burned by the more scholarly Minute Men. . . . It was not such obvious anarchists and soreheads as Darrow, Steffens, Norman Thomas, who were the real danger; like rattlesnakes, their noisiness betrayed their venom." "Lewis puts me by name in a group not worth killing," Steffens wrote in a *Pacific Weekly* column.

Steffens said in September 1934. American Legionnaires were observed writing down the license numbers of cars parked outside his house; friends and visitors were ostracized; there was a telephoned threat to burn down his house; he had a well-founded suspicion that the police were intercepting private letters; and some time after the general strike the shipowners sent a spy to live in the town and become friendly with the dangerous people. It was possible for Steffens to be stoical about all this. "People will forgive you for anything else," he told Leslie White, a frequent visitor, who now found himself one of the pariahs of Carmel because of his association with Steffens and Ella. "You can commit a crime, break any rule of etiquette, violate any custom, but they will never, never forgive you for using your head, for thinking."

At times he was amused by the vigilantes. "The only way I can keep them from lynching me is to ask them to," he said, and when a local newspaper credited Ella with having slept with twenty-nine black men, he asked, "Why not thirty?" "Dear Governor," he wrote to Rolph in February 1934,

> Pursuant of my unpromising probing for humor in high places, I am going to ask you to contribute personally a dollar or so toward a fund to buy a typewriter for Caroline Decker, the tiny little labor agitator who is doing what no big A.F. of L. leader has ever dared undertake; to organize the migratory workers of the lovely orchards and vegetable ranches of California. You remember her! She is the so-called amazon who led the workers in their well-led strikes for a living wage in the valleys last year. . . . If the fund should exceed the price of one cheap typewriter I'll keep the difference for the purchase of another if the first one should be wrecked in some righteous raid.

The Governor refused the bait, but other people "on the wrong side of the class war," including Louis Oneal, the political boss of San Jose, were won over, and Steffens' "Caroline Decker Typewriter Fund" even showed a small surplus after the machine was bought. When her Sacramento headquarters were raided in July by the police "Red Squad" and she and other organizers were arrested and charged with vagrancy, Steffens turned to the same constituency as before and appealed for flowers and a legal defense fund. "I wish

I could call on you some day in your office, close the door and not say a word," he wrote to Oneal, "just laugh and laugh."

In time the vigilante spirit focused on Steffens' nine-year-old son, Pete, the conspicuous beneficiary of a laissez-faire upbringing. The boy was described in local newspapers as an undoubted Communist and a savage who, among his other offenses, had publicly urinated in the school playground and was capable of things much worse. "Not the kid, if you please," Steffens protested. "Let's leave out the children till they're old enough to understand; and can take it." "Violations of good taste are traditional and too common to inspire protest," the novelist Martin Flavin, a family friend, wrote. "Still, I do not recall that I have hitherto encountered an attack on an adversary which undertook to score—by slapping a child."

The person to whom Steffens had made the deepest and purest commitment of his life had been menaced. "Every man has his price," he told Ella. "I learned that years ago, and they're reaching mine. My price is Pete." The veils of play and irony dropped away, and he was revealed to himself in his heart-hurt and bafflement. At such times, despite the quizzical style of his mind, Steffens looked for comfort to Soviet Russia and a preeminent dogma of the period.

"What do you mean by getting knocked out just as I was expecting you as my May Day guest in Moscow?" Bullitt wrote to him in January 1934. It was a season of triumph for Bullitt, who two years earlier had brought a wreath to John Reed's grave in the Kremlin and stood there in tribute to the faith and passion of the revolution. Now it seemed that the long failure of Bullitt's mission in 1919 was about to be undone. At the White House, Franklin Roosevelt received the Soviet Commissar for Foreign Affairs, Maxim Litvinov, and after twenty-five years of pretending that the revolution would go away, the United States reopened diplomatic relations with the Russians and sent Bullitt to them as ambassador. "You must get well at once," Bullitt now told Steffens, "and see how beautifully things are working out in the U.S.S.R. You have been so right about everything that has happened in the United States and the rest of the world for so many years that it is just time for you to blossom as a prophet in your own country and many others." But by 1936, when he resigned his post in bitterness, Bullitt had seen Reed's ideals and his own expectations betrayed at every turn by Stalin and the commissars. A second mission, a second failure: the envoy who was given a hero's welcome when he came back to Moscow spent his last months there virtually a prisoner in the embassy at Spasso House.

In the prison of his own invalidism Steffens was guarded from such direct collisions with reality. "Poetry, romance—all roads in our day lead to Moscow," he said in April 1936, believing—this time under the influence of Granville Hicks's undeviatingly "official" biography of Reed (dedicated to Steffens)—that Reed's revolution was still being fulfilled. Sometimes, when he felt that his life had become unbearable, he thought that he would go to Russia again and, with his sister Laura and her husband, settle in some resort city in the Crimea or the Caucasus. He had been told that the Russians would be glad to have him back as a sympathetic interpreter and might even make special arrangements that would permit him to live first-class in the workers' paradise.

Steffens talked with his doctor about the best way for him to make the long trip when he should be well enough to travel—by ship all the way, through the Panama Canal into the Atlantic and then past Gibraltar and Athens into the Strait of Bosporus and the healing climate of the Black Sea. He told Jo Davidson, "My ideas would be to write there the new end of my book and write it as the end of my life-journey, of my search for a way out." It was all "a lovely dream to dream," he admitted, and probably impossible. The prospect of a great journey and a new life was as illusory as the restoration of his health or his sister's return from the dark continent of psychosis or, for Old Bolsheviks and other visionaries of 1917, the equable terms of survival in Stalin's Russia.

Still, Steffens managed to stay clear of any formal connection with the party and also of a pathetic scheme, surfacing in the spring of 1934, to run him from his sickbed as the Communist candidate for United States Senator from California. Sam Darcy, a district organizer of the party, wrote to Comrade Steffens on behalf of the central committee. "Since you are to run on a Communist ticket and platform, and since you want to issue a statement saying that it is the conclusion of your many years of activity, they think you might as well join the party, because you will appear as a Communist in everybody's eyes anyway." Darcy wanted him to fill out an application for membership and send it in along with sixty cents and a public statement. What Darcy received was a letter which followed a distinctively antiliberal line of argument in order to say no.

> We liberals must not have power, not ever; we must not be leaders, we must not be allowed to be parties in the leadership. Too much to lose, besides our chains, which we are too used to.
>
> The liberals, all privileged persons, and all the associates of the privileged, belong in the second line,—when their eyes are opened. And this goes for me. See? I am not doubting others; I am doubting me. I think that I am not to be trusted in the party or in the front rank of the struggle that is on. I know it, and that's what I'd like to say conspicuously at this critical stage of our common history; that it's true: we, who have fitted successfully into the old culture, are to the very degree of our education and adjustment,—we are corrupted and unfit for—the kingdom of heaven.
>
> You Communists say it. I also say it, see it, believe it and—I am clear—I must act upon it.

He was willing to serve the kingdom of heaven from the second line only. "Swatting Flies in Russia" was the derisive title of Steffens' review (in the June 20, 1934, *New Republic*) of Max Eastman's *Artists in Uniform*, a report on the suppression of cultural freedom under Stalin. Steffens depicted Eastman, "our Max," as a "mad pilgrim" standing helplessly on the station platform waiting for a local train as the revolutionary express rockets by and covers him with dust. It was no matter of routine that Steffens reviewed the book in the first place. Eastman "is turning definitely into an enemy now," Ella had written to Steffens about *Artists in Uniform*. "It is unbelievable that anyone could turn so bad." It was Ella, according to Steffens, who proposed him as reviewer to *The New Republic* editors. Rejecting as liberal stereotypes what Eastman had described as "a sad story of the regimentation of the creative spirit," Steffens argued that according to the laws of revolution, the first obligation of "Justice," for the present, at any rate, was to "the prosaic, anonymous mob"—to the revolution itself—and not to Trotsky or the intellectuals or the artists. "They really act, that immense mass of people, upon the scientific perception that whether it's with Stalin or Trotsky, they must all follow one leader, one party, one plan."

Even before Eastman was willing to acknowledge it to himself, Steffens saw that *Artists in Uniform*, ostensibly a critique of Soviet

Communism, was in effect a total rejection. Consequently his review, together with the rejoinders it provoked, was marked by the rancorous *ad hominem* arguing of the literary-ideological wars of the thirties. And Steffens, who had become accustomed to a certain amount of derision from the party, was now being praised for his hard-line attack on Eastman by Joseph Freeman, editor of the *New Masses* and leader of the Stalinist literati. "Your extraordinary approval of my review of Max Eastman was gratifying to me, of course, and surprising," Steffens wrote to Freeman on July 5. "I never expect to get such things right in the eyes of the party."

Soon after, Eastman charged that Steffens, having been "trotted out" by the Stalinists to do their work, had fallen back on the standard maneuvers of Stalinism in his review—historical distortion, "the literary frame-up," "excommunication" and "personal slander." And all this, Eastman went on, had come from a man who two years ago "brought to my door a copy of his autobiography with an inscription which I should be proud to have graven on my tombstone." (Somewhat later, and with little basis in fact, Eastman blamed Ella —"unmellowed by experience" and "born to be a zealot"—for having effected this transformation of Steffens "from a sentimental rebel preaching Jesus on both sides of the class struggle to a hard-cut propagandist of the party line." In Eastman's mind, Steffens' face had merged with that of Felix Dzerzhinski, head of the Cheka and "the revolution's Lord High Executioner.")

For the unaffiliated Marxist Sidney Hook, an associate professor of philosophy at New York University, the entire episode carried more than a taint of sellout on Steffens' part. There was also the possibility that failing judgment and illness might have to be taken into account. "My dear Lincoln Steffens," Hook wrote in an open letter published in *The Modern Monthly*, the radical journal that served as an ideological battleground:

> I have just read your review of Max Eastman's *Artists in Uniform* in the *New Republic* and it has left me puzzled and disappointed. My reason for writing you is in part to repay a debt incurred in reading your *Autobiography*, that fascinating history of liberal disillusion, and in part, to discover what the hidden premises and arguments are for a position which is neither liberal nor communist, and what is much worse, is so foreign to everything for which Lincoln Steffens ever stood. . . .

Can you really believe that the Communist Party is the one true church whose infallible dogmas and actions cannot be criticized without falling into counter-revolutionary sin? Can you, after a brave life of forthright struggle against oppression and indecency make yourself a party—even by silence—to a campaign of brutal repressions, slander and character assassination against people who have been guilty of nothing more than attempting to examine the actions of the Communist Party here and abroad from the point of view of Communist principles? I cannot believe it because I cannot understand it. It does not fit into the pattern of the life whose auto-biography you wrote.*

The boy who regarded his stern, capricious father as a "household god" had grown up with a conflicted regard for authority and for figures of authority—Theodore Roosevelt and Tom Johnson were precursors of Stalin in the line of Steffens' allegiances just as much as Mussolini was. There were other consistencies within "the pattern of the life whose autobiography you wrote." In the debate with Eastman over revolutionary justice Steffens had yielded to the same

* Lillian Symes, a caustic observer of events on the left, took issue with this conclusion. "I should like to express my amazement at the naïveté of Sidney Hook," she wrote in a letter published in *The Modern Monthly* for October 1934. "There should be nothing in Mr. Steffen's espousal of the Correct Party Line to surprise anyone who has watched him in action over the years or who has read his autobiography. In the light of his enthusiasm for Mussolini would one expect him to choke over the 'liquidation' of a few novelists, philosophers, and scientists? Mr. Steffens is our American G.B.S. without that revolutionary playboy's one-time creative brilliance. He can crack a paradox on almost any side of any question and while he has not followed his Irish contemporary into the ranks of Der Führer's meistersingers, the rise of an American Mosley or any other sufficiently 'daring' and romantic leader would undoubtedly find him cheering from the side-lines. He simply cannot resist the Man on Horseback.
"The trouble with Lincoln Steffens is that he doesn't know what it is all about and never has. He is thrilled by the spectacular—War, Riot, Revolution—and the Revolution would be the biggest spectacle of all, great Copy for the Special Correspondent. That is why, in his speeches, while carefully denying that he is a Communist, he consistently urges the proletarians present to go out and 'do something.' (The more heads cracked by police clubs, the bigger the story.) At a San Francisco meeting a year ago, he stated that the Russian Revolution was the work of less than 15,000 people. Then, pausing for dramatic effect, added: 'Well, there are nearly 15,000 people in this hall.'
"Seasoned radicals have a word—in fact, two—for this sort of thing. They don't apply to Mr. Steffens. But official Communism has more to lose than to gain by such romantic verbal exhibitionism. Their enemies might well greet the con-version of Mr. Steffens to the One True Faith with grim satisfaction. A few of the more realistic Party members realise this."

disastrous understanding of events that had guided his intrusion into
the McNamara settlement. Beguiled by abstractions both times,
Steffens "minimized the savagery of the struggle he otherwise saw
so clearly," Robert Cantwell was to say of him.

Now despair and illness bred intermittent gullibility and desperate
faith; and further, morally disarmed by Lenin's own sanctioned use
of terror, Steffens even became an apologist for the purges that followed the murder of Sergei Kirov in December 1934. He explained
it this way in the *Pacific Weekly*:

> A colleague of Stalin in the government was killed and Stalin's
> government, jerked thus suddenly to a realization that the job was
> not yet done, that security was not yet secured, ran back to the
> Terror and put sixty or more men to death. Of course. Liberty is
> not a fact yet in Russia and that very wise man, Lenin, did not ex-
> pect to have established it in less than "two or three generations."

He himself welcomed, he said, the "new ethics" of accountability
that the trials and the executions demonstrated, and he was not above
trotting out the familiar *tu quoque* argument that Stalinists were in
the habit of using to answer criticism of the promised land.

> Liberals in this country enjoyed the new Soviet Teror and making
> comparisons. But they did not see quite straight or even all around
> their theme. They think we have liberty "under the law" over
> here. Lots of workers know by painful experience that we haven't.
> I have seen with my own eyes, if not with a bruised head, that
> there's a whole class that haven't liberty and that we cannot . . .
> have Liberty, Democracy, Justice, etc., till these good things have
> been founded, not in the law, but in a fearless, unprivileged eco-
> nomic system.

Nevertheless, there were times when he suspected that he was no
longer up to debating such issues responsibly. He wrote to Hook:

> Your long, thoughtful letter deserves a thorough answer, but I can't
> send you one. Laid up here in bed, I lack the energy even to con-
> template such a job; my doctor says I must not do it. And my spec-
> tator's interest in the world, I can see from here, is in history; not in
> the wrong or the right of, but in the play which I find I cannot
> direct or act in.

III

"A PILLAR OF THE STALINIST CHURCH IN AMERICA"—this was Max Eastman's description in 1936 of Steffens in his final role; but it was more a reflection of the sectarian ferocity of the period than of Eastman's personal feeling for an old friend. "I went away with a choking heart," he remembered of his last visit to Steffens in Carmel. "He was sweet and true." Others too tended to dismiss Steffens' public orthodoxy in favor of altogether opposed qualities and values. "He was growing wiser all the time, and more worth listening to," said the reviewer R. L. Duffus, who had known him for twenty-five years. To the countless visitors who came to pass an hour or two with him and feed his "spectator's interest in the world," Steffens, despite his repeated denials of liberalism, had come to stand for the deep-struck foundations of that dishonored tradition: free inquiry, good hope, the rejection of dogma.

An old man, and bedridden, Steffens nevertheless seemed to represent some vital principle of self-renewal, for it was now well known that, with his first fame as a muckraker long behind him, at the age of fifty and beyond he had gone on to great adventures—Russia, fatherhood, his *Autobiography*. Even in 1936, at seventy, he had no intention of closing down. "Too many Americans die with their boots on," he told Leslie White, "and leave nothing behind from which others can learn." He was determined to take his time over "this business of dying" and perhaps come up with a few leads for his friends and readers.

Meanwhile Steffens lived chiefly in his bedroom. He had asked to have his white iron bedstead placed by the window so that he could lie on his side and look out at the garden for the sake of looking out and also to see who was coming to visit him. On a table next to his bed was his Corona portable—even after a setback late in 1934, which left him weaker than ever and made it difficult for him to use his hands or write anything more sustained than a paragraph, he continued to do a regular column for the *Pacific Weekly*. On days when he felt strong enough to get up, he put on a red silk dressing gown and walked with his son in the garden, had lunch in the redwood living room, sunned himself on the porch upstairs, or, reduced by his illness to a simplicity of exercise that he recognized as being in the style of Diogenes, he lay on the tiny lawn in front of his house and pulled weeds. Occasionally he went visiting or on outings by car along the coast to Big Sur or to Monterey.

Always there were the visitors who came to see him—a frail, small man who in his little gray beard and metal-rimmed glasses had a certain resemblance to King George V of England and Leon Trotsky as well as to Don Quixote. No one in Carmel seemed to care anything about knocking; there was too little privacy, his friends felt, too much exhausting talk, and yet how could he possibly give it up? He stayed alive, in part, through the exercise of his talent for making the world come to him and, as in his days as an interviewer, yield up its confidences. In turn he became the center of a web of association and also something rare in his country, a dissenter sage. His house in Carmel, like Walt Whitman's in Camden, was a shrine for the faithful. He was to be seen in the newsreels on January 1, 1936; in April, when he turned seventy, he received messages and greetings from all over the world; the fluctuations of his health were reported in the papers. "I'm not dead yet," he announced, challenging a rumor that proved to have originated in Walter Winchell's gossip column. "I changed my mind last week without a creak, pain, or rage. Anybody will recognize that this is not a sign of death, but that I am still living."

Jo Davidson and Max Eastman came to visit him. So did Filene, bearing gifts for the sickroom, Gertrude Stein, the veteran muckraker Samuel Hopkins Adams, and other writers and journalists—Jeffers, Carl Sandburg, Langston Hughes, Carey McWilliams, Cantwell, Anna Louise Strong, Witter Bynner, Rhys Williams, Frazier Hunt, George West of the San Francisco *News*, Liam O'Flaherty, the young John Steinbeck. There were visiting intellectuals: the philosopher Alexander Meiklejohn, the refugee economist Dr. Emil Lederer, Professor George S. Counts of Columbia, on his way to Russia. There were Hollywood people: Sam and Bella Spewack, James Cagney, Kyle Crichton and his wife, the Dutch director Joris Ivens. Ella's circle of propagandists, labor organizers and activists filled the room with "constructive" conversation about strikes, boycotts, and the prospect of liquidating the bourgeoisie and activating the masses.

Various Russians came to the house at Carmel—students, the

consul general in San Francisco, and the touring Soviet humorists Ilf and Petrov, who provided readers in America and back home with a highly colored account of Steffens as a party Communist who wept with despair over his wasted life. "I had been bribed by bourgeois society," they represented him as saying after Ella gave him a handkerchief to dry his tears. "I did not understand that the fame and respect with which I was rewarded were only a bribe for the support I gave to this iniquitous organization of life."

Leslie White, former detective, cultural troglodyte, and Redbaiter, frequently drove down from his ranch near Santa Cruz to spend the day with Steffens. White underwent a complete transformation, found himself radicalized and considerably heightened in awareness, perception and self-confidence. "So he rebuilt you to his specifications, eh?" Filene said to him. Paul C. Smith of the conservative, antilabor San Francisco *Chronicle* came to Carmel wary of what he called "people of the left." He soon found, however, that he worshiped Steffens altogether as much as he did his original mentor, Herbert Hoover, and he listened to Steffens by the hour. "It's a tragedy for you," Steffens told him (presciently, as it turned out), when Smith, still in his twenties, was put in charge of the *Chronicle*, "because, having become an editor so young, you will never again have the chance to learn anything."

But Steffens' principal visitors—in their number, in his interest in them, and in the impress which they took from him—were students and the young. Mostly unannounced or uninvited, they came to see a guru of the left and to give him news of the outside. The writer and scholar Lawrence Clark Powell had just repeated Steffens' pattern of three years of European study and travel when he became a regular visitor in the fall of 1933. Powell felt, he said, "what young Athenians experienced when they were questioned by Socrates." It was all "something rather classical and far away," Martin Flavin, Jr., remembered in 1938 when he was a freshman at Harvard. "It was like a school, with people coming from far away to hear and see him." In the end the people took away with them not solutions or knowledge or even the party line but instead a dilation of faith and inquiry. "What he gave the people, all of them, who came and talked to him, was self-confidence," Flavin wrote in gratitude for his own enlargement as an adolescent. "He made people believe not in ideas but in themselves, and that is why they came to him."

Throughout his life Steffens had been occupied with the shame
and promise of the cities, with mass movements, with the thrust of
history; he came to argue that individualism was dead, and he wrote
an autobiography that many of a restive generation read as a call to
revolution and collective action. But toward the end he remembered
from his youth in the Sacramento Valley how he had felt about the
herd and about herding habits of mind. The familiar orchards and
plains were again heavy with summer in July 1936, the month before Steffens died. "A boy who can swim and ride a horse," he told
his young son, "can always escape in the night. Or in broad daylight."

Afterword

When Lincoln Steffens died on August 9, 1936, four months after his seventieth birthday, his country's newspapers memorialized him as the last, most fearlessly independent of the great reporters. "No other journalist of our time has exerted so great an influence upon the public mind," said the San Francisco *Chronicle*. "No other journalist of our time has used his power with more consistent devotion to the principles of human justice."

His friends spoke tributes to him in Carmel and at Cypress Lawn Cemetery in San Francisco. At the funeral Ella Winter read a paragraph Steffens had written only a few days earlier. "When I finished my life, I did not die as I might gracefully have done," he recalled and he told what he had been doing or trying to do in the years since 1931:

> The collapse of our economic system, for instance, had to be explained, and only a known fool could do that and be allowed to live. I did it gingerly and—well, I lived. I did it locally and nationally; in magazines and weeklies better read than mine. But I did it with all my heart to the perplexed students, teachers, statesmen, businessmen, crooks, and artists who all my life have needed to know the keys to their, our, and my business. I had some keys; I handed them some keys which fitted some of the locks they brought me unopened. Some day I am going to narrate the story of how I finally found my way to a solution of the typical problems that fretted all my life and theirs. I think now that I can really end my autobiography, but later, not just now.

On this quizzical note Steffens entered upon a posthumous life which was already betraying him at several turns.

Mussolini had conquered Ethiopia, Hitler had blood-purged his party and reoccupied the Rhineland. During the summer of 1936 Franco was driving on Madrid, but it seemed, nevertheless, that in Spain the democracies, side by side with Russia, might finally make their stand at Armageddon against fascism. "Spain's is the first, the opening battle of man for man," Steffens had written in a paragraph that Ella found in his typewriter after he died; "perhaps it is the most decisive battle."

Events scarcely bore him out; and after Russia and Germany concluded a nonaggression pact in 1939, Steffens' reputation as sage and hero of a popular front against fascism underwent a series of erosions. His *Autobiography*, for years required reading in colleges and also published in several editions and abridgments as a book for children and a high-school text, was either neglected or stigmatized. *The Shame of the Cities*, with which both Steffens and muckraking made their name, had already been out of print for years, and for all practical purposes the *Autobiography* eventually joined it. Altogether, Steffens barely survived the surgical resectioning of American history (in particular the recent history of American radicalism) that took place when the hot war ended in 1945 and the Cold War began. Forgotten were the boldness and sophistication, the personal courage and artistic flair that set Steffens apart from the other reformers, muckrakers and radicals of his generation. He had consistently asked the right questions, and his work and career as a whole were so powerfully marked by ethical fervor, compassion and good hope tempered with shrewd realism that he deserved to remain a considerable personage. But soon the very impulses that had guided him —reformism, exposure, dissent, structural criticism—went underground in the national style.

The critic Oscar Cargill, writing in 1951, claimed that Steffens had been neither more nor less than the "Pied Piper of the Kremlin." (In the political climate of the early 1950s it was convenient to ignore the fact that Steffens represented a thoroughly native tradition of grass-roots, home-grown, pragmatic radicalism that owed a great deal to personality, experience and accident, and hardly anything to ideology or systems of any sort.) Other commentators, including former admirers of Steffens, relieved themselves of embarrassment by accusing him of dogmatism, intellectual dishonesty, naïveté, deception of self and others, and so on. During the 1960s, fortunately, two important books, Daniel Aaron's *Writers on the Left* and Christopher Lasch's *The New Radicalism in America*, served as correctives to this line of denial. Rejecting the rhetoric and tactics of anathema, these writers showed that political heterodoxy could once again be examined, equably, as a subject for history and biography. Aided, too, by the reprinting of *The Shame of the Cities*, Steffens began to return from oblivion.

He had, of course, made an earlier return in 1931, with the publication of his *Autobiography*. But a man's life is one thing and his autobiography something else altogether, and the blurring of this distinction had ironic results. The man who had such a remarkable career as a muckraker during the first half of his life became, through the autobiographer's own, deliberate doing, hopelessly confused with the hero of a remarkable autobiography; and this hero, in order to support new positions taken late in life, repudiated muckraking along with the liberal impulse historically associated with it. But after leading a sort of cryptobiotic existence for about twenty years, the muckraking spirit, repudiated by Steffens and in general scorned and scarcely even missed, came to life again during the period of Steffens' return to popularity, the first two administrations of Franklin D. Roosevelt. "The whole apparatus of municipal improvement came to Washington in 1933," said a member of Roosevelt's Brain Trust, the economist Rexford Guy Tugwell. "And it would have enormous effect there before the New Deal had run its course. The Muckrakers had not lived in vain." Few men, Tugwell said, had done as much as Steffens "to reveal America to itself in all its contradictions, all its humbugs, its vices, its hypocritical acceptances of necessary corruptions so long as they were hidden from the light."

Steffens had predicted the arrival of a time when the acknowledged "political government" of the United States would give way to a government representing a consortium of special interests. He described this change as "the very process of corruption which we reformers and liberals opposed." From the nature of the forces that increasingly play a part in determining public policy it can be argued that Steffens' prediction is coming true. But as a muckraker he had also demonstrated once and for all the aptness of the adversary mode for dealing with actualities in America. At no other time since the high noon of S. S. McClure and his crusaders has muck-

raking—in its full range of investigation, exposure and advocacy—
had the force and effectiveness it has achieved in the era of Ralph
Nader, My Lai and Watergate. Never before, perhaps, has there
been quite so much to expose or so strong a resistance to exposure.
Never before has muckraking had to contend with such elaborate
safeguards and such an advanced state of moral numbness on the
one side and, on the other, so high a threshold of moral outrage in
the public sensibility. Never before has muckraking—"the letting
in of light and air"—been so nakedly recriminated and menaced by
men in power. Lincoln Steffens' bold thrust and Theodore Roosevelt's seemingly operatic parry prefigured a conflict of as yet un-
settled dimension and outcome.

ACKNOWLEDGMENTS

Lincoln Steffens' niece, Jane Hollister Wheelwright, of Kentfield, California, and her husband, Dr. Joseph B. Wheelwright, have generously provided me with materials and information. I thank them and others who have helped, including Edward L. Bernays, Robert E. Brownell, Robert Cantwell, Josephine Young Case, Linda Collins, Max Eastman, John Evans, Martin Flavin, Dr. Martin Flavin, Jr., Ronald Gottesman, Philip Hamburger, Leon Harris, James D. Hart, Burnet Hershey, J. R. K. Kantor, Isaac Don Levine, Carey McWilliams, Daniel P. Moynihan, Rabbi Louis I. Newman, Charles A. Pearce, Moses Rischin, Robert Rosenstone, Muriel Rukeyser, Maurice Sagoff, Herbert Shapiro, Everett M. Sims, Sam Spewack, Ronald Steel, Robert E. Treuhaft, Dr. Alfred Vagts, Marie West, Helen White.

Walter Lippmann kindly permitted me to quote from his letters to Steffens. I am indebted to libraries holding manuscript materials by Steffens and his circle: Columbia University Libraries, New York; Bancroft Library, University of California, Berkeley; Boston University Libraries, Boston; Harvard University Library, Cambridge; Labadie Collection, University of Michigan Library, Ann Arbor; Library of Congress, Washington; Lilly Library, Indiana University, Bloomington; University of Oregon Library, Eugene; Van Pelt Library, University of Pennsylvania, Philadelphia; Yale University Library, New Haven. I am grateful also for access to archival materials held by the Oral History Research Office at Columbia University and by Harcourt Brace Jovanovich, Inc., New York.

I owe special thanks to Professor Daniel Aaron of Harvard University, Michael V. Korda of Simon and Schuster, and my wife Anne Bernays.

Notes

These notes are keyed to the text by page number and catch phrase. Since for the most part the notes identify primary sources only, I make grateful acknowledgment here of my debt to Louis Filler's history of muckraking, *Crusaders for American Liberalism* (Yellow Springs, Ohio, 1964) and to two unpublished doctoral dissertations: Irving G. Cheslaw, "An Intellectual Biography of Lincoln Steffens" (Columbia University, 1952) and Herbert Shapiro, "Lincoln Steffens: The Evolution of an American Radical" (The University of Rochester, 1964). Place of publication is New York unless otherwise cited.

Abbreviations:

A	*The Autobiography of Lincoln Steffens*, 2 vols., 1931.
ANTY	Ella Winter, *And Not to Yield*, 1963.
Bancroft	Bancroft Library, University of California, Berkeley.
Col	Lincoln Steffens Papers, Columbia University Libraries.
EW	Ella Winter
HB	Steffens file, Harcourt, Brace, Jovanovich, Inc.
JBS	Josephine Bontecou Steffens
JSP	John S. Phillips
L	Ella Winter and Granville Hicks, eds., *The Letters of Lincoln Steffens*, 2 vols., 1938.
LS	Lincoln Steffens
LTR	Elting E. Morison, ed., *The Letters of Theodore Roosevelt*, 8 vols., Cambridge, Mass., 1951–1954.
Speaking	*Lincoln Steffens Speaking*, 1936.
SSM	S. S. McClure
World	Ella Winter and Herbert Shapiro, eds., *The World of Lincoln Steffens*, 1962.

Chapter One (pages 13–33)

14. . . . "my pony carried me": *A*, 25.
14. . . . a letter of reference: G. Clayton & Bro. "to whom it may concern," April 28, 1862 (Col).
15. ". . . waiting for an opportunity": Joseph Steffens to Hattie Steffens, April 10, 1866 (Bancroft).
15. ". . . an organization man": Address to citizens of Sacramento, around 1900 (Col).
16. ". . . always talking about school": *A*, 17.
16. "I wish I had had an education": *L*, 621.
17. . . . a "palatial residence": *An Illustrated History of Sacramento County, California*. Chicago, 1890, 447–48.
18. "All I want is a pony": *A*, 19.
19. ". . . to catch the 'suckers' ": *World*, 210.
20. . . . practical jokes: *World*, 203–4.
20. . . . "not as a girl": *A*, 8.
20. . . . "the influence was not explicit": *L*, 744.
20. "We must get away": *L*, 60.
20. "One of the wrongs": *A*, 77.
21. "As I grew up": *L*, 733–34.
23. "I suppose I was selfish": *L*, 142.
24. . . . "soft disturbance": *A*, 104–5.
25. Evelyn Nixon: *A*, 112–15; *L*, 920; Elizabeth A. N. Winstanley to EW, Nov. 24, 1936 (Col).
27. Norris: quoted in Franklin Walker, "Frank Norris at the University of California." *University of California Chronicle*, July 1931, 331.
27. "I led my class": *A*, 121.
29. Theta Nu Epsilon: Faculty Recorder's Report to University of California Academic Senate, November 24, 1886 (Bancroft).
30. . . . "a significant uniformity": *A*, 117.
30. . . . a running dispute with the authorities: transcript, petitions, and other papers relating to LS as a student at Berkeley (Bancroft).
31. . . . "the relation of knowledge": *A*, 119.
31. "It might have saved me years of fumbling": *L*, 963.
31. "They did not understand me very well": *A*, 120.
32. "I hunted far enough": *A*, 125.
32. "Whatever may be the sentiments": "The Relation of Political Theory to Political Practice in England," June 1, 1889 (Col).
32. In a short story: "Hon. Frank Ditson," around 1890 (Col).

Chapter Two (pages 34–52)

34. James Morgan Hart's standard account: *German Universities: A Narrative of Personal Experience*, 1878, 35, 264.

35. "The people of Hamburg": *L*, 14.

35. George Santayana: *The Middle Span*, 1945, 2–5.

36. Butler still held: Nicholas Murray Butler. *Across the Busy Years*, 1935, Vol. I, 126.

38. "I have got to work": *L*, 41.

38. "Classical music is a bore": *L*, 25.

38. "They say New Yorkers": *L*, 44.

38. ". . . nastiest and vilest on *earth*": *L*, 60.

39. "Italy is the worst-governed country": *L*, 73–74.

39. . . . his first Thanksgiving abroad: *L*, 26–27.

39. "I am a conundrum": *L*, 39.

40. "It never occurred to me": *L*, 932.

40. Friedrich Paulsen: *L*, 34.

41. . . . two articles that he wrote: "American Artists in Europe" and "A Visit to Toby Rosenthal's Studio," unpublished MSS., 1890 (Col).

42. . . . a philosophic paper: "Ethics and Evolution," unpublished MS., 1890 (Col).

42. "My private impression": quoted in Ralph Barton Perry, *The Thought and Character of William James*. Boston, 1935, Vol. II, 116.

42. . . . "repelled by the method": *L*, 30.

43. . . . "where we sought the facts": *A*, 149.

43. "Wundt's philosophy": *L*, 53.

43. . . . "is only laying a scientific foundation": *L*, 56.

43. "Out of my life here": *L*, 61–62.

44. "The account Steffens gave": *A*, 150–51.

44. "I hope she will succeed": LS to F. Willis, April 19, 1890 (Col.)

45. "She is a strong character": *L*, 65.

46. . . . a bouquet of flowers to General Lafayette: Walter Lippmann, unpublished memoir, Oral History Collection (Columbia University).

46. "I know that you would like my choice": *L*, 64–65.

46. "I shall use the time well": *L*, 69.

47. . . . a triumphant lecture demonstration: *A*, 161–62; Josephine Bontecou Steffens, *Letitia Berkeley, A.M.*, 1889, 144–45.

48. . . . "the paradise of students": "Women at the University of Paris," *The Nation*, March 1, 1894, 151.

48. "We found ourselves drawing apart": *L*, 113–14.

49. Dot has been saying: LS to Mrs. Joseph Steffens, May 26, 1892 (Col).
50. "I was a beautiful thing": *A*, 166.
50. "Do you think a short course": LS to Joseph Steffens, June 28, 1892 (Col).
50. "It would be a bitter thought": LS to Joseph Steffens, May 4, 1892 (Col).
50. "I am both eager for": LS to Joseph Steffens, May 26, 1892 (Col).
50. "I have never been able": LS to Max Eastman, January 7, 1927 (the late Max Eastman, Chilmark, Mass.).
51. "I look to that coming century": *L*, 79.
51. Lorimer's book: *Letters from a Self-Made Merchant to His Son.* Boston, 1902; reprinted 1970, 7, 29, 48, 51. Marcus Cunliffe pointed out the parallel between Steffens and Lorimer in *Encounter*, Sept. 1966, 77.
52. "My dear son": *A*, 169.

Chapter Three (pages 53–65)

53. "Here I was": *A*, 170.
53. . . . short story: "Sweet Punch: A Monologue," *Harper's New Monthly Magazine*, December 1893, 126–29.
54. . . . conventional weddings: Hutchins Hapgood, *A Victorian in the Modern World*, 1939, 161.
54. . . . . "on account of my political leanings": *L*, 86.
55. "To my generation": William James, *Letters*. Boston, 1920, Vol. II, 182.
55. Godkin's aim: Rollo Ogden, ed., *Life and Letters of Edwin Lawrence Godkin*, 1907, Vol. II, 127.
56. "What I did not like": Allan Nevins. *The Evening Post: A Century of Journalism*, 1922, 530.
56. . . . "perhaps the finest journal": LS to Frederick Willis, Feb. 5, 1893 (Col).
57. "With fresh and present outrages": *The Shame of the Cities*, 1904, 281.
58. . . . ablest reporter on the staff: Norman Hapgood. *The Changing Years*, 1930, 107–10; Nevins, 550–51.
58. "What reporters know": *A*, 223.
58. . . . short story: "A Dismal Holiday," unpublished (Col).
58. ". . . so-called psychological drama": New York *Evening Post*, October 2, 1894, Steffens scrapbooks (Col).
59. "I think the same": *L*, 88.
60. "The daily newspaper": Isaac F. Marcosson. *David Graham Phillips and His Times*, 1932, 219.

62. "When a man seeks his stuff": Hutchins Hapgood. *Types from City Streets*, 1910, 24.
63. "... the right of might": *L*, 88.
63. "The successful businessman": Theodore Roosevelt. *An Autobiography*, 1914, 79.
64. James B. Dill: *A*, 194, 220.
64. Richard Croker: *A*, 237–38; M. R. Werner, *Tammany Hall*, 1928, 335, 345.
64. ... "honest graft": William L. Riordon, *Plunkitt of Tammany Hall*, 1905; reprinted 1963, 3, 32.
65. The challenge to the reporter: *A*, 235.

Chapter Four (pages 66–81)

67. Parkhurst: Charles H. Parkhurst, *Our Fight with Tammany*, 1895, and *My Forty Years in New York*, 1923; M. R. Werner, *It Happened in New York*, 1957, 36–116 ("Dr. Parkhurst's Crusade").
69. "They sounded alike": *A*, 250.
70. "The day of scientific method": Jacob Riis to LS, August 8, 1906 (Col).
70. "Now I can go into a strange city": "An Exposer of Municipal Corruption" (interview), *Bookman*, Nov. 1903, 247–50.
70. "The word 'corruption' ": *L*, 873.
71. ... "me and my doings": *A*, 292.
72. "I feel pretty well started": *L*, 106.
72. ... "not to leave off": LS to Joseph Steffens. Nov. 4, 1894 (Col).
72. "I believed in the police force": Riis is quoted in the *Bookman* interview cited above.
72. "The Tenderloin": for the Williams attribution see *American Notes and Queries*, August 1945, 72–74, and October 1945, 107–8.
73. "In view of your report": New York *Evening Post*, October 18, 1894, Steffens scrapbooks (Col).
73. "Machine rule": *L*, 102.
73. "... some moral stomach": *L*, 107.
74. "What is being done in the police": *L*, 108.
74. "... Taken me in as his advisor": *L*, 109.
75. ... "afford to be identified with": *LTR*, Vol. I, 439.
76. "... a man's work": *LTR*, Vol. I, 548.
76. "The clamor of the peace faction": *LTR*, Vol. I, 504.
76. "We will have this war": quoted in Mark Sullivan, *Our Times*, 1927–1935. Vol. I, 74.
76. "I always told you": Theodore Roosevelt to LS, August 8, 1901 (Col).

76. "His life has been so sudden": "The Real Roosevelt," *Ainslee's*, December 1898, 478–84.
76. ". . . Tom Sawyer of the political world": Bernard DeVoto, ed., *Mark Twain in Eruption*, 1940, 49.
77. "We have no plans yet": New York *Evening Post*, May 6, 1895, Steffens scrapbooks (Col).
77. "It was just as if we three": *A*, 258.
77. . . . "knew nothing": *L*, 795–96.
77. "Roosevelt is all there is": Alfred Connable and Edward Silberfarb. *Tigers of Tammany*, 1967, 215.
77. "He is a personal friend of mine": Theodore Roosevelt to H. E. Scudder, August 6, 1895 (Col).
78. . . . an editorial writer: quoted in Henry F. Pringle, *Theodore Roosevelt*, 1931, 136.
79. . . . "a mixture of hope and fear"; Sacramento *Record-Union*, April 12, 1895, Steffens scrapbooks (Col).
80. "The end of the reign": New York *Evening Post*, n.d., 1897, Steffens scrapbooks (Col).
80. "They tried to stand so straight": Connable and Silberfarb, *Tigers of Tammany*, 218.
80. "I have seen my last mayoral election": Rollo Ogden, ed., *Life and Letters of Edwin Lawrence Godkin*, 1907, Vol. II, 143.
80. "A man that'd expect": Finley Peter Dunne, *Mr. Dooley's Opinions*. Boston, 1900, 186.
81. . . . "new perfected system": "The Real Roosevelt," *Ainslee's*, December 1898, 483.

Chapter Five (pages 82–100)

82. ". . . the good old grandmother of journalism": column by Roy L. M'Cardell in unidentified trade paper, no date, Steffens scrapbooks (Col).
83. "I have the beginnings": *L*, 130.
83. "Hurry up": H. J. Case, *Guy Hamilton Scull*, 1922, 63.
83. Abraham Cahan: Moses Rischin. "Abraham Cahan and the New York Commercial-Advertiser," *Publications of the American-Jewish Historical Society*, September 1953, 10–36.
84. "Cahan took us": *A*, 317–18.
85. . . . opposed currents of philo-semitism: Oscar Handlin. "American Views of the Jew at the Opening of the Twentieth Century," *Publications of the American-Jewish Historical Society*, June 1951, 323–44.

85. "As to the restrictions": JBS to Robert Wellstood & Son. February 17, 1909 (Col).

85. "The uptown Jews": *A*, 243.

86. "All the fellows": *L*, 267.

86. "Anyone can make money": Robert Dunn, *World Alive*, 1956, 9–10.

86. "He was almost incredibly 'fresh'": Hutchins Hapgood, *Types from City Streets*, 1910, 107–8.

87. . . . the "revolutionary instinct": Hutchins Hapgood, *A Victorian in the Modern World*, 1939, 138.

89. "I feel like a bull moose": "Theodore Roosevelt, Governor," *Mc-Clure's*, May 1899, 57–64.

90. "A jim-dandy": SSM to LS. March 14, 1899 (Col).

90. Fresh out of Knox College: the chief source for McClure here and in the chapters following is Peter Lyon, *Success Story: The Life and Times of S. S. McClure*, 1963.

91. "Go over to the East Side": "Leisure of the Poor," *Commercial-Advertiser*, April n.d., 1898, Steffens scrapbooks (Col).

92. "Our cyclometers": *L*, 118.

92. . . . Steffens talked: John D. Barry, Steffens obituary, San Francisco *News*, August 11, 1936.

93. "We are getting up in the world": *L*, 128–29.

94. . . . "she collapsed": *L*, 119.

94. "She is discontented": *L*, 122.

95. ". . . perfectly conventional, dull and commonplace": Hutchins Hapgood, *Types from City Streets*, 1910, 110–12.

95. "We've got out of that man": *A*, 353.

95. "I have not been well": *L*, 137.

95. "Because I know and trust you": JSP to LS. May 3, 1901 (Col).

96. ". . . the question to be decided": *L*, 138.

96. ". . . he is too artistic": JBS to Joseph Steffens. May 8, 1901 (Col).

96. "Then for the novel": *L*, 140.

96. "Nothing but dreamless nights": *A*, 359.

97. "It had better not circulate": *L*, 145.

97. "Politics is a business": "Great Types of Modern Business—Politics," *Ainslee's*, October 1901, 213–20. Steffens incorporated this article, written before he started his muckraking career, in his preface to *The Shame of the Cities* (1904).

98. "McKinley is better": *L*, 146.

99. "My dear sir": LS to Theodore Dreiser. October 29, 1901 (Van Pelt Library, University of Pennsylvania, Philadelphia).

99. "I feel ready": *L*, 156.

99. "Each editor is to regard himself": *L*, 228.

100. . . . "incredibly outspoken": Ida M. Tarbell, *All in the Day's Work,* 1939, 198–202.

100. "Get out of the office": *L,* 154–55.

100. ". . . most powerful constitutional ruler": "The Overworked President," *McClure's,* April 1902.

100. "If I should be entrusted": Tarbell, *All in the Day's Work,* 200–201.

Chapter Six (pages 103–122)

103. Folk: the chief source is Louis S. Geiger, "Joseph W. Folk of Missouri," in *University of Missouri Studies,* Vol. 25, No. 2, 1953.

103. ". . . really was an accident": "The Shamelessness of St. Louis," *McClure's,* March 1903, 553.

104. . . . "the prince who broke": William Allen White, "Folk," *McClure's,* December 1905, 111.

106. "When I set out": *The Shame of the Cities,* 1904, 14.

106. "It is too early to judge": LS to JSP, May 24, 1902 (Lilly Library, Indiana University).

108. . . . "a sound, conservative manager": "Labor Leader of Today: John Mitchell," *McClure's,* August 1902.

109. distressed and even angered: S. S. McClure, *My Autobiography,* 1914, 256–59.

109. "I have been thinking seriously": SSM to JSP, March 20, 1903 (Lilly Library, Indiana University).

110. "We had a pretty hot fight": *A,* 375.

110. "Nearly all of the daily papers": Joseph W. Folk to LS, March 28, 1903 (Col).

111. "Whenever anything extraordinary": "The Shame of Minneapolis," *McClure's,* January 1903, 227.

111. "Even lawlessness": *McClure's,* January 1903, 227.

112. "Can a city be governed": *McClure's,* January 1903, 239.

112. "I ought to write to you": SSM to LS, November 10, 1902 (Col).

113. "How many of those": "Concerning Three Articles in this Number of McClure's, and a Coincidence that May Set Us Thinking," *McClure's,* January 1903, 336.

114. "I doubt whether any other magazine": Ray Stannard Baker, *American Chronicle,* 1945, 169.

114. . . . "a new method": McClure, *My Autobiography,* 240–45.

115. . . . the circulation of *McClure's*: Peter Lyon, *Success Story,* 1963, 251.

115. . . . nearly two thousand articles: David Mark Chalmers, *The Social and Political Ideas of the Muckrakers,* 1964, 15. Other guides to the literature of muckraking are: Louis Filler, *Crusaders for American*

Liberalism, Yellow Springs, Ohio, 1964 (the standard history); Arthur and Lila Weinberg, eds., *The Muckrakers,* 1961 (a reader).

115. . . . Mr. Dooley: quoted in Mark Sullivan, *Our Times,* 1927–1935, Vol. 3, 87.

116. . . . new range of characters: Robert Cantwell, "Journalism—The Magazines," in Harold E. Stearns, ed., *America Now,* 1938, 345–49.

117. "He did not know": Baker, *American Chronicle,* 130.

118. "Physical escape": Frederic C. Howe, *The Confessions of a Reformer,* 1925, 16–17.

119. ". . . the result of merely taking up": S. S. McClure, *My Autobiography,* 246.

120. "It seems to me": McClure is quoted in Lyon, *Success Story,* 76.

121. ". . . the dissatisfaction I sometimes felt": Ray Stannard Baker, *American Chronicle,* 173.

122. ". . . a series of articles": Brand Whitlock, *Forty Years of It,* 1914, 158.

Chapter Seven (pages 123–143)

123. "Do we Americans": "New York: Good Government in Danger," *McClure's,* November 1903, 85.

124. . . . "this man will stick us": SSM to JSP, March 20, 1903 (Lilly Library, Indiana University).

124. "Steffens' articles": SSM to JSP, October 15, 1904 (Lilly Library, Indiana University).

124. "You must always remember": SSM to LS, November 7, 1902 (Col).

124. "Your narrative lacks force": SSM to LS, January 20, 1903 (Col).

124. "We are paring it down": JSP to LS, March 24, 1903 (Col).

125. "In regard to the point": SSM to LS, June 11, 1903 (Col).

125. . . . "a serious disaster": SSM to LS, June 11, 1903 (Col).

125. "I must tell you": SSM to LS, June 17, 1903 (Col).

126. ". . . resented my impersonal attitude": *L,* 158.

127. "A course of lectures": Benjamin I. Wheeler to LS, November 9, 1903 (Col).

127. . . . permission to name a cigar: *L,* 161; American Lithographic Company to LS, December 7, 1903 and February 3, 1904 (Col); Dixon Wecter, *The Hero in America.* Ann Arbor, Michigan, 1963, 387.

128. Religious crisis: *A,* 522–24; Christopher Lasch discusses this episode in *The New Radicalism in America,* 1965, 268.

128. "When I got home": *A,* 521–22.

129. ". . . a hard day's work": *A,* 523.

129. "I was having troubles": *L,* 159.

129. "Steffens means well": William L. Riordon, *Plunkitt of Tammany Hall*, 1905; reprinted 1963, 29–32.

130. . . . "mingled feelings": James Bryce to unidentified recipient. January 3, 1905 (Col).

130. William Allen White: "Editorial," *McClure's*, June 1904, 220–21.

131. "I got corruption from corruptionists": "An Exposer of Municipal Corruption" (interview), *Bookman*, November 1903, 251.

131. "The corruption that shocks us": *The Shame of the Cities*, 1904, 10.

132. . . . "head of state": "Wisconsin," *McClure's*, October 1904, 563.

133. "I never was a reformer": Allan Nevins, ed., *The Letters and Journal of Brand Whitlock*, 1936, Vol. I, 537; Brand Whitlock, *Forty Years of It*, 1914, 221, 239.

133. ". . . practicing what they preached": *A*, 470.

134. . . . walked along St. Clair Street: Whitlock, *Forty Years of It*, 164–65.

135. . . . "set the precedent": *Speaking*, 110–11.

135. "When the history of America": Allan Nevins, ed., *The Letters and Journal of Brand Whitlock*, Vol. I, 120.

135. ". . . dangerous theorist": "Ohio: A Tale of Two Cities," *McClure's*, June 1905, 302.

137. "The best evidence": as above, 305.

138. "He cleared my head": *A*, 478–79.

139. "The article settled things": Robert M. La Follette to LS, November 14, 1904 (Col).

141. "The political leaders": *McClure's*, April 1904, 587.

141. "Aldrich article": SSM to JSP, October 15, 1904 (Lilly).

141. "I know nothing": *LTR*, Vol. IV, 1255.

142. "Poor Payne": *LTR*, Vol. IV, 965.

142. ". . . to follow such a line": *LTR*, Vol. V, 35–39.

142. ". . . Steffens ought to put more sky": Theodore Roosevelt to SSM, October 4, 1905 (Baker Papers, Library of Congress).

142. "If a public, non-profit": *A*, 530.

143. "We, the American people": *L*, 171.

143. ". . . more than any other one man": Harlan Fiske Stone to LS, November 9, 1905 (Col).

143. "It must make you feel good": Joseph W. Folk to LS, November 9, 1905 (Col).

Chapter Eight (pages 144–162)

145. ". . . the terminology of Continental politics": quoted in G. Wallace Chessman, *Theodore Roosevelt and the Politics of Power*. Boston, 1969, 130.

145. "To any officer": Theodore Roosevelt to LS, January 9, 1906 (Col).

145. "As a matter of fact": *LTR*, Vol. V, 148.

146. "You ought to put someone on the rack": Charles H. Taylor, Jr. to LS, February 10, 1906 (Col).

146. . . . "The Sudden School": *New York Times*, February 15, 1906, 6:2.

147. "I aimed at the public's heart": Upton Sinclair, "What Life Means to Me," *Cosmopolitan*, October 1906.

147. . . . Mr. Dooley: *Collier's*, June 23, 1906.

147. "The things you tell": Upton Sinclair, *The Brass Check*, 1919, 32.

148. ". . . a chamber of traitors": *A*, 503–4; San Francisco *Bulletin*, March 17, 1906, clipping (Col).

149. "Treason is a strong word": David Graham Phillips, *The Treason of the Senate*. Chicago, 1964, 59.

149. . . . an item in *Collier's*: this source is identified in Theodore P. Greene, *America's Heroes*, 1970, 172n.

150. ". . . he didn't mean me": *New York Times*, April 17, 1906.

150. . . . "the letting in of light and air": the Baker-Roosevelt exchange is in Ray Stannard Baker, *American Chronicle*, 1945, 202–4.

150. Roosevelt's speech: as reported in New York *Tribune*, April 15, 1906.

152. "It was a great day": the *Sun* is quoted in Mark Sullivan, *Our Times*, Vol. III, 97. As a Western paper: Portland *Oregonian*, June 28, 1908. *Life*: May 24, 1906. *American Magazine*: May 1906, 111–12.

152. Shun "hysteria": clippings in Theodore Roosevelt Collection (Harvard College Library).

152. Baker: *American Chronicle*, 204.

153. "The longer I live": *New York Times*, April 17, 1906, 1:4.

153. "If muck were mere muck": "Graft," lecture notes, 1906 (Col).

153. "He had built up": Willa Cather, "Ardessa," *Century Magazine*, May 1918.

154. ". . . a big fool scheme": *L*, 173–74.

154. "No man": *L*, 174.

155. "I own a majority": *New York Times*, May 5, 1906, 7:4.

156. "He had discovered": *A*, 540.

157. ". . . part of the fault": "Hearst, The Man of Mystery," *American Magazine*, November 1906, 3–22.

158. . . . full of praise: Newton D. Baker and others to LS, October 28, 1906 (Col).

159. . . . Phillips told him: JSP to LS, April 24, 1907 and May 11, 1907 (Col).

159. . . . the People's Lobby: *New York Times*, September 18, 1906, 6:3.

160. . . . "an intellectual aristocrat": E. W. Scripps to LS, March 23, 1907 (Col).

160. "You haven't confidence": JSP to LS, February 28, 1907 (Col).

160. "My husband": JBS to W. Lorenz, December 17, 1907 (Col).

161. . . . biographical sketch: dated March 25, 1908 (Col).

161. "Fighting dishonesty": *L*, 184.

161. Friday, August 23, 1907: *L*, 186–88; LS to Francis Heney, August 27, 1907 (Col); Chessman, *Theodore Roosevelt*, 120–21; Sullivan, *Our Times*, Vol. III, 146–62.

Chapter Nine (pages 163–179)

164. "Before I die": *L*, 202.

165. . . . "Contaminated Constantinople": Samuel G. Blythe, "The Complete Muckraker," *Saturday Evening Post*, November 14, 1908, Steffens scrapbooks (Col).

165. ". . . new and broader base": *L*, 250.

165. ". . . old parties offer no choice": LS to New York *Evening Post*, October 28, 1908, Steffens scrapbooks (Col).

165. "You have written": *L*, 202.

166. Edward A. Filene: this account draws on Robert Cantwell's manuscript biography of Filene (University of Oregon Library, Eugene)

166. "Maybe your life shows": *L*, 860.

167. ". . . the practice of hypocrisy": *A*, 607.

167. "It will take time": *The Shame of the Cities*, 199.

168. ". . . biggest piece of work": *L*, 218.

168. "I know of no instance": statement to the Boston press, October 6, 1908, Steffens scrapbooks (Col).

168. . . . dinner at the City Club: Allan Nevins, ed., *The Letters and Journal of Brand Whitlock*, Vol. I, 107–9.

169. Eliot: *A*, 608.

169. "More than any one man": John Reed, "Almost Thirty," *New Republic*, April 29, 1936, 333.

170. . . . "powerful conservatives": Walter Lippmann, *A Preface to Politics*, 1914, 314.

170. "The college political clubs": John Reed, "Almost Thirty," *New Republic*, April 29, 1936, 333.

170. ". . . not enough intellectual curiosity": *L*, 227–230.

170. "We are seeking out": *L*, 215–16.

171. *The Survey*: Paul U. Kellogg, "Boston's Level Best," June 5, 1909, Steffens scrapbooks (Col).

171. New York *Sun*: April 10, 1909, Steffens scrapbooks (Col).

171. ". . . a cause for every effect": *L*, 232.

172. ... urgent appeal: E. A. Filene to LS, November 19, 1909 (Col).
172. ... "may have made you sick": *L*, 223.
173. "... should not be grateful": *L*, 239.
173. "... leave the man alone": LS to Francis Heney, December 14, 1909 (Bancroft).
174. "... crystallize all the sentiment": *L*, 225.
174. "... a depressing effect": E. W. Scripps to LS, September 6, 1909 (Col).
174. "My dear Lincoln": JBS to LS, November 12, 1909 (Col).
175. "What my committee expected": *L*, 858.
175. ... "something happened to me": *L*, 347.
176. ... was "like dying": *A*, 586.
176. "What I have dreamed of doing": Walter Lippmann to LS, May 18, 1910 (Col).
176. "Lippmann, the student": LS to unidentified, August 22, 1911 (Col).
177. ... "bold and brilliant guess": Walter Lippmann, *A Preface to Politics*, 1913, 19–20.
177. "The invisible government": Lippmann, *A Preface to Politics*, 21.
178. ... "too whimsical": Walter Lippmann, unpublished memoir, Oral History Collection (Columbia University).
178. "... blind leading the blind": LS to Francis Heney, December 23, 1910 (Bancroft).
178. "... willful, able mind": *L* 256.
179. "... deepens and grows": LS to Francis Heney, February 27, 1911 (Bancroft).
179. "I, a muckraker": *Out of the Muck*. Riverside, Conn., 1911, unpaged.

Chapter Ten (pages 183–195)

183. "Before I left": Walter Lippmann to LS, April 17, 1911 (Col).
184. "... large generous room": Hutchins Hapgood, *A Victorian in the Modern World*, 1939, 352.
184. "I said I didn't know": John Reed, "Almost Thirty," *New Republic*, April 29, 1936, 333.
185. "... so near to pure joy": "John Reed: Under the Kremlin," *Freeman*, Vol. II, November 3, 1920.
185. "I couldn't help but observe": John Reed, "Almost Thirty," *New Republic*, April 29, 1936, 334–35.
186. "The Crime of the Century": Graham Adams, Jr. *Age of Industrial Violence, 1910–1915*, 1966, 1–24.
186. "Murder is murder": Theodore Roosevelt, "Murder is Murder," *The Outlook*, May 6, 1911, 12–13.

187. . . . "insidious indictment": Samuel Gompers. *Seventy Years of Life and Labor*, 1925, Vol. II, 182–93.

187. . . . a hundred similar dynamitings: William F. Burns. *The Masked War*, 1913, 33–39.

187. "I don't have to wait": *L*, 279.

188. . . . "the situation back of the McNamara trial": *L*, 278.

189. According to Scripps: E. W. Scripps, "Belligerent Rights in Class Warfare," in Oliver Knight, ed., *I Protest: Selected Disquisitions of E. W. Scripps*, Madison, Wis., 1966, 396–403.

189. ". . . intelligence and tact": Clarence Darrow. *The Story of My Life*, 1932, 186.

190. "I negotiated": *L*, 1049.

190. "I'm famous again": *L*, 281.

191. "The sermons of that black Sunday": *A*, 688.

191. . . . "repellent to just men": *New York Times*, December 6, 1911.

192. ". . . challenging the modern ideals": *L*, 282.

192. "I will show him": the encounter is described in *A*, 690–91 and in Anton Johannsen to EW, October 16, 1937 (Col).

192. "The Larger Bearings of the McNamara Case": *The Survey*, December 30, 1911, 1412–34.

192. . . . "sickening timidity": Emma Goldman, *Living My Life*, 1931, 486–88.

193. ". . . an utter fool of himself": *LTR*, Vol. VII, 453.

193. "Jack Reed, 'my own boy' ": *A*, 690.

193. "Have you seen this?": Max Eastman, "John Reed and the Old Masses," *The Modern Monthly*, October 1936, 22.

194. . . . Steffens took him to dinner: *L*, 284–85.

195. ". . . Machiavellian, itinerant preacher": Mabel Dodge Luhan, *Movers and Shakers*, 1936, 69.

Chapter Eleven (pages 196–213)

196. "Portrait of Mabel Dodge": Carl Van Vechten, ed., *Selected Writings of Gertrude Stein*, 1946.

197. ". . . the Heads of things": Mabel Dodge Luhan, *Movers and Shakers*, 1936, 83–84.

197. "All sorts of guests": *A*, 654–55.

198. "You attract": *Movers and Shakers*, 80–81.

198. . . . "something going on": Max Eastman, *Enjoyment of Living*, 1948, 523.

198. "Why not organize": *Movers and Shakers*, 80–81.

199. . . . "a revolutionary and not a reform magazine": "Editorial Note," January 1913, reprinted in William L. O'Neill, ed., *Echoes of Revolt: "The Masses," 1911–1917*, Chicago, 1966, 29.

199. ". . . most important public event": quoted in John Malcolm Brinnin, *The Third Rose*, 1959, 177.

199. . . . "a naked man going down stairs": Theodore Roosevelt, "A Layman's View of an Art Exhibition," *Outlook*, March 29, 1913, 718–20.

199. . . . "barriers went down": *Movers and Shakers*, 39.

200. "The most to be hoped": *L*, 313.

200. "Freud has a way": Walter Lippmann, "Freud and the Layman," *New Republic*, April 17, 1915; reprinted in Lippmann *Early Writings*, 1970, 297–301.

201. "I remember thinking": *A*, 655.

201. "Don't suppress": *L*, 753.

201. "The speech of your body": *Movers and Shakers*, 231.

202. "Let the women destroy": *New York Times*, January 13, 1914, 2:5.

202. "Women are in error": *L*, 728.

202. "Sex Antagonism": *Movers and Shakers*, 234–41.

203. . . . "the delicious shudder": Tom Wolfe, *Radical Chic and Mau-Mauing the Flak Catchers*, 1970, 11.

204. "It affects your nerves": quoted in Edmund Wilson, *To the Finland Station*, Garden City, New York, 1953, 384.

205. "When I go": *L*, 335–36.

205. "I was sick at heart": *L*, 337.

205. "All the editors": *L*, 334–35.

206. ". . . neither pretty, nor very young": *L*, 290.

207. "Social position": *L*, 303.

207. . . . Mary Austin: the chief source here is *Movers and Shakers*, 66–69, supplemented by the considerably more explicit account in the unedited manuscript of the book (Yale University Library).

208. "I killed a man": quoted by Mabel Dodge Luhan, in *Mary Austin, A Memorial*, Santa Fe, 1944, 21.

208. . . . "almost any kind of change": Mary Austin, *No. 26 Jayne Street*, Boston, 1920, 56–57, 347.

208. "My theory": *A*, 712.

209. "The same system": *World*, 78.

209. "There was a moment": Walter Lippmann, *Public Opinion*, 1922, 4.

209. . . . "astonished and rather annoyed": Walter Lippmann, *U.S. Foreign Policy*. Boston, 1943, xi–xii.

210. . . . "the State becomes": Randolph S. Bourne, *War and the Intellectuals*, 1964, 69.

210. "I did not therefore go": *World*, 78.

210. "They didn't mix": *World*, 11.

211. ". . . you can't commit rape a little": *A*, 716.

211. "Toward evening": John Reed. *Insurgent Mexico*, 1969, 39.

212. ". . . not according to Marx": *World*, 79.

212. . . . "a mere indignant gentleman": *World*, 18-19.
212. "I'd do almost anything": LS to Lou Suggett, April 16, 1916 (Col).
212. "It was like a trip": "Into Mexico and Out," *Everybody's*, May 1916, 539.
213. ". . . heard American money talking": *A*, 732.
213. ". . . had not run its course": *A*, 732.
213. "What you don't understand": *World*, 18.

Chapter Twelve (pages 214–238)

214. "If the world wants to know": William G. Shepherd, "The Road to Red Russia," *Everybody's*, July 1917, 11. A controlling source for this chapter is Adam B. Ulam, *The Bolsheviks*, 1968.
214. . . . "high and dry": *A*, 753.
215. "We can no longer distinguish": Cahan is quoted in Peter G. Filene, *Americans and the Soviet Experiment*, Cambridge, Mass., 1967, 15–16.
215. "The autocracy that crowned": Wilson's war message is discussed in George F. Kennan, *Russia and the West*. Boston, 1961, 19.
216. "It's my story": *L*, 395.
217. "He knows everybody": *L*, 396.
218. "It seems to me": *L*, 397.
218. "The Millennium first": "The Rumor in Russia," *The Nation*, December 21, 1918, 766–67.
219. "I suddenly realized": John Reed, *Ten Days that Shook the World*, 1960, 341.
219. ". . . these unfinished lives": *L*, 394.
220. "It is a wound": *L*, 397.
220. "What we knew": "What Free Russia Asks of Her Allies," *Everybody's*, August 1917, 132.
221. . . . liberty, "a right": *A*, 756.
221. "Comrades": *A*, 760–61.
222. "Now that the dam is broken": Bessie Beatty. *The Red Heart of Russia*, 1918, 8.
222. "The first time I went": *A*, 759.
222. "A great, strong, young people": "What Free Russia Asks of Her Allies," *Everybody's*, August 1917, 132, 133.
223. "The Russians can be made to fight": *L*, 399–400.
224. . . . "a *great* friend of President Wilson": Boris A. Bakhmeteff, unpublished reminiscences, Oral History Collection (Columbia University).
225. "But the way he said it": *A*, 770.
225. "Another chapter is done": *L*, 400.

225. "Every unpopular cause": *L*, 401.

225. "Rage is developing": *L*, 401–2.

226. "When a nation is at war": Mr. Justice Holmes in *Schenck v. U.S.* (1919).

226. ". . . no preparation for peace": L, 435.

227. . . . "a plain publicity proposition": George Creel, *How We Advertised America*, 1920, 4–5.

227. "No use": *L*, 412.

227. "In America the month just past": John Reed, "One Solid Month of Liberty," *The Masses*, September 1917.

227. ". . . the health of the state": Randolph S. Bourne, *War and the Intellectuals*, 1964, 71.

228. . . . "the cardinal fact": Bourne, 20.

228. "I hated the new state": Frederic C. Howe, *Confessions of a Reformer*, 1925; reprinted Chicago, 1967, 279–82.

229. "Only in a world": Bourne, 5, 7.

230. "Be it on our heads": Robert Dunn, New York *Post*, February 27, 1915.

230. "It would have been 'discreet' ": *L*, 353–54.

230. . . . "the slightest tendency": *L*, 425; "Catching the Kaiser," unpublished manuscript (Col).

231. "This morning": Reed's cable is quoted in Max Eastman, *Love and Revolution*, 1964, 70.

232. . . . "the rumor says": *L*, 414.

233. ". . . Socialist compromisers": Trotsky is quoted in Reed, *Ten Days that Shook the World*, 131.

233. ". . . impact of the Bolshevik revolution": Theodore Draper, *The Roots of American Communism*, 1957, 101.

233. . . . "acid test": *World*, 258.

233. ". . . complete change of mind": *L*, 724.

234. ". . . perpendicular lines": *L*, 430.

234. ". . . not pro-German": Leon Trotsky, *The Bolsheviki and World Peace*, 1918, 15–16.

234. ". . . jars all hearers": *L*, 415–16.

235. . . . "glorifying the bolsheviki": clipping in Steffens scrapbook (Col).

235. "Rumor here": telegram in Steffens scrapbook (Col).

235. "Rumors absurd": *L*, 405.

236. . . . "no man who criticized": *New York Times*, April 27, 1918, 3:2.

236. ". . . criticizing the United States Government": *L*, 427.

236. "One clog": *L*, 419.

236. Karl Radek: quoted in Charles Seymour, ed., *Intimate Papers of Colonel House*. Boston, 1926–1928, Vol. III, 89.

236. "Trotsky making epochal blunder": John Reed manuscripts, Houghton Library (Harvard).

237. ". . . you must have been suffering": John Reed to LS, June 9, 1918 (Col).

237. "I wouldn't ask Walter L.": John Reed to LS, June 29, 1918 (Col).

237. "Go on—the limit": *L*, 921–22.

237. "Jack, you do wrong": *L*, 428–29.

Chapter Thirteen (pages 239–255)

239. ". . . not been forgotten": *A*, 776–77.

239. ". . . sympathize with revolutionists": *L*, 438–40.

239. ". . . anonymous stuff": *L*, 481.

239. "Not yet": *L*, 440.

240. . . . "too radical": *L*, 433–34.

241. "If you ever do that again": Jo Davidson, *Between Sittings*, 1951, 132–37.

241. ". . . emphatically repudiated": Roosevelt is quoted in Alexander L. George and Juliette L. George, *Woodrow Wilson and Colonel House*, 1964, 205.

242. "I really believe": Lloyd George is quoted in the work cited above, 230.

243. ". . . Notes from Sinai": John Maynard Keynes, *The Economic Consequences of the Peace*, 1920, 38.

243. ". . . A demi-god": Transcript of Dinner to Lincoln Steffens, April 27, 1931 (Col).

244. . . . Steffens innocently assured the reporter: *L*, 453–55.

244. "What an ignoramus": Ray Stannard Baker, *American Chronicle*, 1945, 489.

245. . . . a characteristic scheme: among the sources for my account of the Bullitt mission are: Beatrice Farnsworth, *William C. Bullitt and the Soviet Union*, Bloomington, Indiana, 1967; John M. Thompson, *Russia, Bolshevism, and the Versailles Peace*, Princeton, N. J., 1966; "Reports of the Bullitt Mission on Russia," *The Nation*, October 4, 1919, 475–82 (issued as *The Bullitt Mission to Russia*, 1919).

245. "You are fighting them": *A*, 790.

245. . . . "You are hereby directed": Orville H. Bullitt, ed., *For the President: Personal and Secret*. Boston, 1972, 4.

245. . . . newspaperman in Paris: Burnett Hershey (interview with author, March 3, 1967).

246. "As to Bill Bullitt": Ezra Pound to LS, November 21, 1934 (Col).

246. "I am full of our project": *L*, 460.

246. . . . "skylarked": *A*, 792.

247. ". . . in the long run of history": *L*, 398.
247. "Do you mean to tell me": *World*, 86.
248. . . . "well to the right": *The Bullitt Mission to Russia*, 63–64.
248. "Yes, Mr. Chicherin": *Speaking*, 301.
249. ". . . most favorable opportunity": George F. Kennan, *Memoirs: 1925–1950*. Boston, 1967, 80.
250. Swope: his dispatch is quoted in E. J. Kahn, Jr., *The World of Swope*, 1965, 222.
250. "So you've been over into Russia": *A*, 799.
250. "According to Bullitt": Thompson, 175–76.
250. "A trip into the future": *L*, 463.
250. ". . . Extreme nationalists": James T. Shotwell, *The Paris Peace Conference*, 1930, 230.
251. ". . . abolished prostitution": William Allen White, *Autobiography*, 1946, 562–63.
251. ". . . the blooming philanthropy": *L*, 464–65.
252. *New York Times*: April 8, 1919, 6:1; *New York Tribune*: March 24, 1919; *New York Sun*: March 25, 1919; *Collier's*: April 19, 1919.
252. . . . "there was some suggestion": *New York Times*, April 20, 1919, 3:2.
253. ". . . a League of Nations": *L*, 465–66.
253. . . . possibly melodramatic recollection: Berle is cited in Arthur Schlesinger, Jr., *The Crisis of the Old Order*. Boston, 1957, 14. Admiral Morison characterizes the Berle account as "very imaginative" (to author, December 2, 1971).
254. ". . . in the old muckraking days": *A*, 802.
254. "It is my conviction": *The Nation*, May 31, 1919, 859.
254. "lie on the sand": *New York Times*, September 23, 1919.
254. "To bed": Harold Nicolson, *Peacemaking: 1919*, 1933, 371.
254. ". . . passeth understanding": White, *Autobiography*, 553.
254. ". . . the dead season": Keynes, *The Economic Consequences of the Peace*, 297.
254. ". . . evening of my life": *L*, 554.

Chapter Fourteen (pages 259–271)

259. *Good Morning*: October 8, 1919.
259. "We Americans": *L*, 519.
260. . . . "man put to the test": *L*, 600–605.
261. . . . "speak more of peace": *L*, 609.
261. Ernest Hemingway: William White, ed., *By-line: Ernest Hemingway*, 1967, 61–65.

261. ". . . the old game of politics": Los Angeles *Examiner*, December 23, 1922.
262. ". . . I might stay here forever": *L*, 467.
262. Owen D. Young: LS to Owen D. Young, June 1920; Owen D. Young to LS, November 29, 1920 (Mrs. Josephine Young Case).
262. ". . . a charming enigma": George Slocombe, *The Tumult and the Shouting*, 1936, 170.
263. Mary Colum: *Life and the Dream*, 1947, 307–8.
264. "thru the barbed wire": Ezra Pound, *The Cantos*, New Directions, 1965, 118.
265. ". . . all become atheists": William C. Bullitt, *It's Not Done*, 1926, 274.
265. ". . . capering virgin heifer": Bullitt, *It's Not Done*, 340.
266. . . . "suburban bacchanalia": Sinclair Lewis, *Babbitt*, 1922, 289.
266. "It all looks to me": LS to Marie Howe, December 28, 1919 (Col).
266. . . . "a radical and a Red": *L*, 617n.
267. Anna Louise Strong: *I Change Worlds*, 1935, 86–88.
267. . . . "the big points": *L*, 622.
267. . . . "disgusted with me": *L*, 744.
268. ". . . a Presbyterian heaven": *A*, 844.
268. ". . . promised land": Bertrand Russell, *Autobiography: 1914–1944*. Boston, 1968, 141–143.
268. "He met me on the street": LS to Granville Hicks, November 7, 1934 (Col).
268. "You see, in Moscow": "John Reed: Under the Kremlin," *Freeman*, II, November 3, 1920.
269. "You know how it is": Reed is quoted in Max Eastman, *Love and Revolution*, 1964, 260.
270. "To those who are prepared": *A*, 799.
270. ". . . Revolutionists who do not go through": *L*, 543.

Chapter Fifteen (pages 272–287)

272. ". . . never heard anyone": *ANTY*, 54.
273. "I was certain": *ANTY*, 11.
274. "What is to *become*": *L*, 518.
275. "She knows about Us": *L*, 528–29.
275. . . . "she is used to me": *L*, 559–60.
276. . . . "Steffy came back": EW to Charles A. Pearce, October 26, 1936 (HB).
276. . . . Hemingway said: *A*, 835.
277. ". . . deepest secret desires": *L*, 641.

277. . . . "remedies": LS to Laura Suggett, April 20, 1924 (Col).

277. "As soon as we're married": *ANTY*, 104.

278. "He has deceived": Gussie B. Nobbes to Laura Suggett, July 10, 1924 (Col).

278. ". . . accusing herself": *L*, 654.

279. "What I really am": *L*, 744.

279. "I don't know yet": *Speaking*, 4.

280. "I often felt": *A*, 821.

280. ". . . 'uninspired' phrasings": *L*, 859; *L*, 878; *L*, 880–81; *L*, 851.

281. ". . . meet you at the station": LS to Jane Hollister, December 10, 1926 (Bancroft).

281. "Fathers are young": *Speaking*, 18.

281. ". . . my father was my mother": Dusty Sklar, "Radiant Fathers, Alienated Sons," *The Nation*, October 2, 1972, 279–81.

282. "Nowadays": LS to Jane Hollister, December 16, 1925 (Bancroft).

283. "Don't suppress": *L*, 753.

283. . . . "a green thumb for transference": Jane Hollister Wheelwright to author, June 6, 1967.

284. . . . dinner at Nancy Astor's: Jo Davidson, *Between Sittings*, 1951, 254–55.

284. ". . . something new under the sun": *Speaking*, 71–75.

285. "Curiously enough": John P. Diggins, *Mussolini and Fascism: The View from America*. Princeton, N. J., 1972, 17.

285. Tarbell: *All in the Day's Work*, 1939, 377–84; McClure: Peter Lyon, *Success Story*, 1963, 400–01; Davidson: *Between Sittings*, 230.

286. ". . . as powerful as an elemental force": "Stop, Look, Listen!" *Survey-Graphic*, March 1, 1925, 735–36.

286. ". . . American captains of industry": Eastman is quoted in Daniel Aaron, *Writers on the Left*, 1961, 316.

286. "The fight must be fought out": Max Eastman, *Love and Revolution*, 1964, 475–76.

Chapter Sixteen (pages 288–306)

288. "I find that my mind": *L*, 661.

289. "It seemed to me": *L*, 756.

290. " 'Everybody' ": *L*, 749.

290. ". . . tell the story": *L*, 755–56.

291. "Even Peter": LS to Alfred Harcourt, March 10, 1932 (HB).

291. ". . . nice false impression": *L*, 884.

291. ". . . sick for home": *L*, 776.

292. . . . "the power, the momentum": *A*, 850.

292. "This country": *A*, 855.

294. "I'm not interested": *ANTY*, 123.

294. "He hasn't caught": *ANTY*, 134–35.

294. *New York Times*: June 7, 1929, 25:4.

295. "The divorce business": LS to Jane Hollister Wheelwright, June 10, 1929 (Bancroft).

296. "We are running parallel": *L*, 855–56.

296. . . . "their whole terminology": B. W. Huebsch to LS, March 24, 1923, Huebsch Papers (Library of Congress).

297. ". . . out of the country so long": W. B. Feakins to LS, September 2, 1927 (Col).

297. The next morning: Granville Hicks, *Part of the Truth*, 1965, 76–77.

297. Filene gave a dinner: Transcript, Dinner to Lincoln Steffens, April 27, 1931 (Col).

298. ". . . damnedest mixed company": *L*, 891.

299. "Some of you": Transcript, Dinner to Lincoln Steffens (Col).

299. ". . . one of the best reporters": *New York Times Book Review*, April 12, 1931.

299. ". . . extraordinary volumes": Chicago *Daily News*, April 14, 1931.

299. "Just read your book": Stein's letter quoted in LS to Alfred Harcourt, September 17, 1931 (HB).

300. "My amazing book": *L*, 917.

300. "You have no idea": *L*, 938.

300. "I guess I am a success": *ANTY*, 154.

300. . . . one Illinois Congressman: Henry T. Rainey, *The Nation*, February 13, 1924, 161.

301. "Some of them are in jail": Fremont Older, *Survey*, February 1, 1926, 560.

301. . . . "bag of wind": Robert M. Crunden, *A Hero in Spite of Himself*, 1969, 426.

301. ". . . this movement that promised so much": Frederic C. Howe, *Confessions of a Reformer*, Chicago, 1967, 195–96.

302. "He knows the world": Edmund Wilson, *New Republic*, September 28, 1932, 173–75.

302. "One can't sneer": *A*, 863–64.

303. "Wilson did not mean peace": *A*, 783.

303. ". . . happily unaware": *A*, 166.

303. Damon Runyon: Edwin P. Hoyt, *A Gentleman of Broadway*, 1964, 71.

304. Newton Arvin: *The Nation*, April 15, 1931, 415–16.

305. "And the writing!": Allan Nevins, ed., *The Letters and Journal of Brand Whitlock*, 1936, Vol. I, 499.

NOTES

Chapter Seventeen (pages 307–328)

307. "If this depression": *World*, 214.
308. Sherwood Anderson: Howard Mumford Jones, ed., *Letters of Sherwood Anderson*. Boston, 1952, 257–58.
308. "A holding company": quoted in Robert Bendiner, *Just Around the Corner*, 1967, 55.
308. . . . "gone over the top": *L*, 894.
309. "Can anybody": *Speaking*, 169.
309. "It gets on my nerves": *L*, 949.
309. "The combination days": *L*, 999.
309. Edmund Wilson: *The Shores of Light*, 1952, 498; Malcolm Cowley: *Exile's Return*, 1951, 11; John Dos Passos: quoted in Irving Howe and Lewis Coser, *The American Communist Party*, 1962, 280.
310. . . . a manifesto: Daniel Aaron, *Writers on the Left*, 1961, 196–97, 423 n. 73.
310. "I tell you": *L*, 949.
310. . . . mixed with Communists: EW to LS, July n.d., 1933 (Col).
310. "Mr. Liberal": "Mr. Steffens Liked Everybody," *New Masses*, June, 1931, 5–6.
311. "I am not a Communist": *L*, 934.
311. ". . . a cab-horse": *World*, 81.
311. "Yes, I am talking Communism": *L*, 947–49.
312. ". . . some garbage": *L*, 943.
312. . . . local John Reed Club: *L*, 923, 927.
312. Having threatened: John Reed to LS, June 9, 1918 (Col).
312. "became a hero in Russia": *L*, 921.
313. "The choice": *L*, 955.
313. ". . . a time for thinking": *World*, 259.
313. ". . . tired liberal": Manuscript speech, March 19, 1933 (Col).
314. At Harvard: *L*, 969–70; Beverley M. Bowie to EW, n. d. (Col).
314. Lunch with Whittaker Chambers: *L*, 961, 971; Chambers, *Witness*, 1952, 601.
315. "What I seem to have done": *L*, 973–74.
315. The diagnosis: George L. Treadwell to EW. December 14, 1933 (Col).
316. *New York Times*: March 22, 1935, 7:3.
316. "He saved me my home": *L*, 1005.
316. Cantwell concluded: Robert Cantwell, manuscript biography of E. A. Filene (University of Oregon Library, Eugene).
317. Robert Minor: quoted in Eugene Lyons, *The Red Decade*, 1941, 170.
318. "People will forgive": Leslie T. White, "Two Years of Steffens," *Pacific Weekly*, n. d. (White Papers, Boston University Libraries).

357

318. "The only way": *L*, 1016.

318. "Dear Governor": *L*, 974–75.

319. "Not the kid": LS to editor, Pacific Rural Press, August 4, 1934 (Col): Martin Flavin is quoted in *ANTY*, 207.

319. ". . . May Day guest": William C. Bullitt to LS, January 27, 1934 (Col).

320. "Poetry, romance": "Letter about John Reed," *New Republic*, May 20, 1936.

320. . . . the long trip: LS to Alfred Harcourt, June 19, 1935 (HB): *L*, 996, 1018.

320. "Since you are to run": Sam Darcy to LS, April 28, 1934 (Col).

321. "We liberals": *L*, 983.

321. ". . . turning definitely into an enemy": EW to LS, July n. d., 1933 (Col).

322. "Your extraordinary approval": *L*, 986.

322. . . . "Eastman charged": *New Republic*, August 1, 1934; *Love and Revolution*, 1964, 474.

322. "My dear Lincoln Steffens": Sidney Hook, "An Open Letter to Lincoln Steffens," *Modern Monthly*, September 1934, 486–92.

324. . . . "minimized the savagery": Robert Cantwell, "Lincoln Steffens' Voice," *New Republic*, November 18, 1936, 81.

324. "A colleague of Stalin": *Speaking*, 176–77.

324. "Your long, thoughtful letter": *L*, 991.

325. "Too many Americans": Leslie T. White Papers (Boston University Libraries).

326. "I'm not dead yet": quoted in San Francisco *Chronicle*, August 10, 1936.

327. . . . touring Soviet humorists: Ilya Ilf and Eugene Petrov, *Little Golden America*, 1937, 284–88.

327. Paul C. Smith: *Personal File*, 1964, 151.

327. ". . . young Athenians": Lawrence Clark Powell, "Lincoln Steffens' Boy on Horseback." *Westways*, August 1970, 55.

327. . . . "something rather classical": Martin Flavin, Jr., "Conversations with Lincoln Steffens." *Harvard Advocate*, June 1938, 13–16, 37–39.

Afterword (pages 614–19)

329. "No other journalist": San Francisco *Chronicle*, August 10, 1936.

329. "When I finished my life": *Speaking*, ix–x.

330. "Spain's is the first": *Speaking*, 303.

330. "Pied Piper": Oscar Cargill, "Lincoln Steffens: Pied Piper of the Kremlin," *Georgia Review*, Winter 1951.

331. "The whole apparatus": Rexford Guy Tugwell, "The Sources of New Deal Reformism," *Ethics*, July 1954, 257, 275.

Index

Austin, Mary, 207–8, 277–78, 293
*Autobiography of Lincoln Steffens,
   The*, 302–7, 331
   financial relationship with
      father described in, 53–54
   first sexual encounter described
      in, 21
   Hearst described in, 156
   Leipzig described in, 44
   McNamara case described in, 193
   marriage to Ella Winter
      described in, 280
   Munich art colony described in,
      41
   Mussolini described in, 286
   New Masses review of, 310–11
   New York Jews described in,
      85–86
   publication of, 297–300, 307
   as required reading in schools,
      331
   student life at Berkeley
      described in, 27
   Theodore Roosevelt described
      in, 77
   Wilson described in, 225
   writing of, 284, 288–91

Babson, Roger, 307
Baer, George, 108
Baker, George Pierce, 83
Baker, Newton D., 136, 158, 177,
   215, 301
Baker, Ray Stannard, 121, 301
   childhood of, 117
      religious upbringing, 118
   on *McClure's* staff, 96, 99,
      115–16, 146, 150, 152–53
   on anthracite miners' strike,
      109, 113, 114
   on labor-management
      collusion, 128–29
   resignation, 155
   in Wilson administration
      on Committee for Public
         Information, 229
      at Versailles peace conference,
         243–44, 246
Bakhmetieff, Boris, 224
Bakunin, Mikhail, 47, 84, 204
Ballet Mécanique (Antheil), 290

Barnum, P. T., 199
Barry, John, 92, 93
Baruch, Bernard, 250, 298
Beach, Sylvia, 276, 290
Beard, Charles A., 32
Beethoven, Ludwig von, 36, 204
Bellamy, Edward, 61, 132
"Belligerent Rights in Class
      Warfare" (Scripps), 189
Berkeley, Bishop George, 30
Berkeley, University of California
      at, 26–32, 127, 170
Berkeleyan (magazine), 34
Berkman, Alexander, 203–5, 234,
      266
Berle, Adolph, Jr., 253
Berlin, University of, 34–37
Bernays, Edward L., 298
Beveridge, Albert, 149
Bierce, Ambrose, 211
Big business, 16, 97–98, 283–85
   power of, 97–98
      anatomy of, 177
      in Ohio, 132, 136, 139
      in Rhode Island, 139, 141
      in Wisconsin, 139–40, 142
   regulation of, 146, 148
Binet, Alfred, 47
Bird, William, 264, 290
Birth control, 201
Bitter Cry of the Children, The
      (Spargo), 132
Black, Jack, 283
Blaine, James, 55
Bolsheviki and World Peace, The
      (Trotsky), 234
Bolsheviks, 221–22, 224, 225,
      230–37, 244–52
Bontecou, Susan, 45, 54
"Bonus army," 306
Bordwell, Walter, 191
Bosses
   political, *see* Tammany Hall;
      specific names
   of Wall Street, 63–65
Boston, Massachusetts, 94
   corruption in, 125, 167–72
   political bosses in, 65
   speeches in, 297–98, 314
Boston Associated Board of
      Trade, 171

Free speech, 204
Freeman, Joseph, 322
Freeport, Illinois, 14
"Frenzied Finance" (Lawson), 140
Freud, Sigmund, 18, 47, 200, 265, 290
  study of Woodrow Wilson by, 265n
Freudianism, 198–201
Frick, Henry Clay, 203
Futurism, 199

Gallatin, Albert, 16, 17
Gandhi, Mohandas K., 317
Garland, Hamlin, 91
Garrett, Garet, 293
General Intelligence Division, U.S., 266
Genoa, Italy, 275
Germany, 29, 33–43
  culture of, 38
  popularity of American culture in, 36
  postwar, 262
  in World War I, 36
    Bolshevik revolution and, 224, 232
    closing of frontiers, 209
    offers of military support to Mexico, 213
    spring offensive of 1918, 230
    U.S. declaration of war, 226
George, Henry, 14, 120, 134–35
George Washington (ship), 242, 243
Gestalt psychology, 275
Glaspell, Susan, 201, 269
Glyn, Elinor, 264
Goddard, Morrill, 56
Godkin, Edwin Lawrence, 54–57, 85, 125
  Parkhurst and, 67, 74
  retirement of, 80
Goff, John W., 69
Gold, Mike, 310
Golden Rule
  as Christian solution to social problems, 118
  class warfare and, 165
  factory run by, 133
  practical applications of, 173

Golden Rule (Continued)
  self-interest liberalism and, 190, 193
Goldman, Emma, 173, 203–5, 270, 295, 301
  deported from United States, 266
  disillusioned with Russian revolution, 267–68
  draft-obstruction trial of, 234
  on McNamara case, 192
Gompers, Samuel, 186–87
Good Government Association, 167–68, 171, 172
Good Government Clubs, 74
Good Morning (newspaper), 259
Gorky, Maxim, 152n, 204, 277
Gospel Christianity, 173
Göttingen, University of, 16, 34, 35
Gould, Jay, 64, 74
Graft, see Corruption
Grant, Ulysses Simpson, 115, 121
Greece, 209
  1922 war between Turkey and, 259
Greenwich, Connecticut, 99, 163, 177
Gridiron Club, 149
Groton School, 282
Gruening, Ernest, 290

Hall, G. Stanley, 36, 42
Hall, Oakley, 62
Hamburg, Germany, 35, 37
Hamilton, Alexander, 55
Hanna, Mark, 76, 98, 108, 132–135, 139, 141
Hapgood, Hutchins, 62–63, 65n, 86, 184
  on Commercial Advertiser staff, 83, 93, 96
  Mabel Dodge and, 198, 202
Hapgood, Norman, 58, 93
Harcourt, Alfred, 291, 314, 315
Hardie, Keir, 187
Harding, Warren G., 262, 266
Harper's Monthly (magazine), 53, 117
Harper's Weekly (magazine), 92
Harriman, Job, 187, 190